Springer Studies in the History of Economic Thought

This series offers an outlet for research in the history of economic thought. It features scholarly studies on important theoretical developments and great economic thinkers that have contributed to the evolution of the economic discipline.

Springer Studies in the History of Economic Thought (SSHET) welcomes proposals for research monographs, edited volumes, textbooks and handbooks from a variety of disciplines that seek to study the history of economic thinking and help to arrive at a better understanding of modern economics. Relevant topics include, but are not limited to, various schools of thought, important pioneers and thinkers, ancient and medieval economic thought, mercantilism, cameralism and physiocracy, classical and neoclassical economics, historical, institutional and evolutionary economics, socialism and Marxism, Keynesian, Sraffian and Austrian economics, econometrics and mathematical studies as well as economic methodology and the link between economic history and history of economic thought.

All titles in this series are peer-reviewed.

For further information on the series and to submit a proposal for consideration, please contact Johannes Glaeser (Senior Editor Economics) Johannes.glaeser@springer.com.

Manuela Mosca
Editor

Women at Work in Italy (1750–1950)

Their Economic Thought and Actions

Springer

Editor
Manuela Mosca
University of Salento
Lecce, Italy

ISSN 2662-6098 ISSN 2662-6101 (electronic)
Springer Studies in the History of Economic Thought
ISBN 978-3-031-64280-7 ISBN 978-3-031-64281-4 (eBook)
https://doi.org/10.1007/978-3-031-64281-4

This Springer imprint is published by the registered company Springer Nature Switzerland AG
The registered company address is: Gewerbestrasse 11, 6330 Cham, Switzerland

Contents

Women in Education

Women in Politics

Italian Women of the Past: Their Economic Culture and Actions

Manuela Mosca

This book reconstructs the economic thought and actions of many Italian women of the past in relation to the subject of work: their work as businesswomen, as employed, in the educational system, as well as their reflections as politicians on female labour are at the centre of the analysis.

In the history of economics there is a huge gap of knowledge and analysis about their presence, as is clearly shown in Faucci's (2014) history of Italian economic thought, which does not mention a single contribution by women. Very few studies have dealt with this theme, for instance, Fornengo (1997), Del Boca and Di Tommaso (1997), Corsi and Zacchia (2019) and Zacchia (2019), which mainly focus on the second part of the 1900s. Dimand (2000) mentions the presence of women in Sweden, Austria, France, Denmark, German, Poland and other non-Anglo-Saxon countries, but only one in Italy: Costanza Costantino (1913–1992). The latter is also included, together with Vera Cao Pinna (1909–1986), in *A Biographical Dictionary of Women Economists*, edited by Dimand, Dimand and Forget (2004). No other studies have

This book is part of the research project The Economic Thought of Italian Women (1750–1999): Methodological Issues, Ideas, Impact, International Links, a Census and an Online Database (financed by the European Union—Next Generation EU—PRIN 2022—code 2022KKWTTK_001). It is also in collaboration with the research project Mujeres a la vanguardia del activismo entre siglos (XIX y XX): influencias en la filosofía femenina (PID2020-113980GA-I00 financiado por MCIN/AEI. https://doi.org/10.13039/501100011033). I thank the participants in the AISPE session of the STOREP conference (Bari, 16 June 2023), in the kickoff meeting of PRIN 2022 (2 October 2023, online), in the 2023 Luigi De Rosa Lecture on Global History (Rome, 14 December 2023) and in the 2024 ASSA Conference (San Antonio, TX, 6 January 2024) for their useful comments and suggestions. I also thank the many referees who read and commented on previous versions of the book's chapters. The usual disclaimers apply.

M. Mosca (✉)
Università del Salento, Lecce, Italy
e-mail: manuela.mosca@unisalento.it

M. Mosca (ed.), *Women at Work in Italy (1750–1950)*, Springer Studies in the History of Economic Thought, https://doi.org/10.1007/978-3-031-64281-4_1

gone further back than 1930, except for the work on Jenny Griziotti Kretschmann (Parisi 2007) and for the case of American women based in Italy analysed in Laurenzi and Mosca (2021). Women are absent not only as creators of economic thought, but also as topics of study, and economic history as well needs more research on the economic position and role of women in Italy.[1]

This book fills this gap by examining the economic thought and impact of the overlooked or forgotten Italian female "economists", and by studying women's economic activities from a gender perspective. Given the difficulties encountered in bringing out the ways in which women from the distant past contributed to economic facts and thinking, it covers a very wide time span. To focus especially on the period when women suffered most from invisibility, the volume does not deal with modern times,[2] where there is a greater presence of women in the academic world and in economic activities: it starts from the Enlightenment and goes up to the end of the 1940s. The economic dualism that has characterized Italian development since its unification[3] is also reflected in this book: the reader will find some chapters specifically devoted both to the North and to the South of the country.

As it is well known, the lack of conventional sources for reconstructing the intellectual history of women, like academic books and scientific articles, is due to the fact that female access to university positions was limited or precluded. This is also the main cause of their invisibility in the history of economic thought: there is no volume of herstory of economics that fails to mention the problem of women's scarce visibility (Chassonnery-Zaïgouche et al. 2022; Kuiper 2022; Mosca et al. 2022; Reeves 2023; Rostek 2021). Economic historians too face similar problems, due to scarcity of sources, misinterpretations and statistical biases.

The methodology adopted in this book[4] helps reconstruct the economic thought and actions of many neglected Italian women. Some of its chapters deal with single individuals (in particular, Isabella De Mari Doria, Aurelia Josz, Anna Kuliscioff and Margherita Grassini Sarfatti), others with groups of women (entrepreneurs, politicians and researchers in economics), so that the number of names discovered and analysed in this book are multiplied. Other chapters employ new sources, new data and new perspectives to study women's ordinary economic activities (in the labour force and in schools as teachers).

Women often didn't sign their written works (as in the case of Mary Shelley), or used pen names pretending to be men (like the Brontë sisters), or signed their writings with just their initial, so it is hard to find them, and the attribution cannot be certain, unless the name they used is already known. An example from this book is that of Margherita Grassini Sarfatti, who used the initial S. to sign her journal articles

---

[1] See the literature cited by Licini, in this book, Chapter "Women and Business: Fresh Evidence from the Probate Records of Milan (1862–1900)", footnote 3.

[2] For a book in English on the transformation of the lives of Italian women over the course of the twentieth century see Willson (2010).

[3] The Italian political unification took place in 1861. On the history of its economic dualism see, among others, Fratianni (2012).

[4] For a wider exposition of this proposed methodology see Mosca (2024).

(Chapter "Margherita Grassini Sarfatti,the Economic Thought of the Jewish Woman Who Popularized Fascism"). In some cases, they worked in economic institutions in which reports were published unsigned. If this is the situation, how can we find their names and their ideas? One effective way is to search in writings by relatives, friends and colleagues: these sources are crucial testimonies for the reconstruction of the intellectual history of women, starting from the attribution of writings. Very good results have also been obtained by looking in various, non-academic genres, like novels, pamphlets, travel reports, political speeches, poetry or women's magazines. A similar case dealt with in this book (Chapter "In the Name of Equality. Women's Action to Shape the Right to Work in the Italian Constituent Assembly") is that of the twenty-one women, out of 556 members, who in 1946 were elected to the Constituent Assembly, and whose ideas are recorded in official documents.

A well-known method of finding the women of the past is by looking in unprinted sources, like diaries, letters, memoirs, family archives and private papers, as in the case of Isabella De Mari Doria (Chapter "Isabella De Mari Doria, a Female Investor and Gambler in the Genoese Aristocracy"), who left only account books and financial instructions to her agents. It's also helpful to reconstruct their networks. For example, the life of the already mentioned women who participated in the Constituent Assembly are reconstructed thanks of experience they gained in their areas of commitment: the Italian resistance movement, women's organizations and trade unions.

What is the "economic thought" that one must look for in research on women in history? In a few cases women's economic ideas can be reconstructed within the traditional canon of the discipline, as in the case of Joan Robinson, one of the very few cases of female names mentioned in traditional textbooks. Examples here are the women students and graduates in business and economics in Turin (Chapter "Female Students and Graduates in Business and Economics in Turin (1906–1940)"), or those who embarked on university careers in economics during the fascist regime (Chapter "Academic Research and University Careers of Women Economists During the Fascist Regime"). All of them can be considered women economists in the strict sense, as they wrote theoretical essays on economics.

In other cases, the historical research of women's economic ideas requires an expansion of the conventional perimeter of the discipline, to encompass the themes that made women reflect and the issues related to the activities they performed. There are two possible ways to expand this perimeter: the first is by adopting an internalist approach, related to economic theory, in which however research must go well beyond the confines of market analysis, to include economic reflections on other spheres, such as the home, business, politics, solidarity, etc.[5] For example, the topics dealt with by the politician Anna Kuliscioff (Chapter "Anna Kuliscioff's Labour Economics") are theoretical and concern the importance of work for women emancipation.

---

[5] We are referring here in particular to gender and feminist economics, on their history see Becchio (2020).

But the internalist approach, limiting its research only to theory, and focusing exclusively on the originality of the contributions, underestimates women's presence in intellectual history. To overcome these problems, in looking for the economic thought of the women of the past, the present book proposes an externalist approach based on the concept of "economic culture".[6] Following this approach, it examines the ideas of women who, based on their economic culture, challenged the existing reality. Examples are those of Aurelia Josz, who founded an agricultural school for girls (Chapter "Aurelia Josz, Educational Entrepreneur, and Her School of Agriculture for Girls"), and the already mentioned professional journalist and expert in art Margherita Grassini Sarfatti. In both cases, from their writings we can glean their economic culture, their opinions on the economic situation of their time and on the motivations for the pioneering solutions they aimed to propose. In the cases of Anna Kuliscioff and of the women who took part in the Constituent Assembly, who were not strictly economists, the concept of economic culture helps in restoring their visibility as proponents of economic reforms as well.

So far, we have talked about the difficulties for the historian of economic thought to find women of the past who produced written sources, published or unpublished. But many other women are even more invisible, as the only sources available to reconstruct their ideas are the activities they promoted. The methodological challenge of this book is to demonstrate that it is possible to find economic culture not only in what women wrote, but also in what they did. In this respect, a fundamental contribution is made by economic historians, who reconstruct economic facts and describe economic activities using alternative sources, much more suited to discovering the women's presence in history. The chapters in the first section of this book (*Women in business*) are an example. By illustrating the economic thought and actions of women entrepreneurs, they disprove the stereotypes that see women as risk adverse, and in general interested more in social or charitable activities than in financial investments. This is the case of the already met investor and gambler Isabella De Mari Doria, or of the 25 Italian millionaire heiresses who lent, invested or managed firms in the industrialized sectors, which were invisible for conventional sources, but discovered thanks to their probate records (Chapter "Women and Business: Fresh Evidence from the Probate Records of Milan (1862–1900)"), or of the three generations of female entrepreneurs with a remarkable talent in business who worked in the textile and fashion industries (Chapter "Female Entrepreneurs and Economic Development in Capri (1900–1960). A Case Study:*La Parisienne*"). These women were all innovative, and by reconstructing their figures through their actions, it is possible to reconstruct also their economic culture, their values, their convictions and motivations.

As we said, women are neglected not only as creators of thought, but also because their economic activities lacked visibility. Economic history plays a pivotal role also in the research on women's everyday life, as it collects data in a gender perspective to supply unbiased statistics on issues related to their activities. This is

[6] The concept of economic culture was introduced by Barucci (2012) as the link between economic theory and economic policy. It was also employed by Phelps (2011) as a tool to explain differences in economic performance of different countries.

the case of the second section of this book (*Women in the labour market*) which tackles one of the most debated economic issues in the history of women: female employment and wage discrimination based on gender. Chapter "From the Edge to the Heart: Female Employment in Nineteenth-Century Italy" deals with the limitations of conventional measures, such as female labour force participation, and the historiographical debates surrounding the portrayal of women's work in traditional sources. Chapter "Labour Market Segregation: Female Teachers in Southern Italy (1861–1937)" reconstructs the work of female teachers in the South of Italy from 1861 to 1937, while Chapter "Incomes and Employment of Italian Women (1900–1950)" investigates the measures adopted (mostly unsuccessfully) by the fascist regime (1925–1943) to reduce female employment. These studies are based on more inclusive economic categories (like a wider definition of labour) and gender disaggregated data.

The authors of the third section (*Women in economics*) deal with women economists in the first half of the twentieth century: Chapter "Aurelia Josz, Educational Entrepreneur,and Her School of Agriculture for Girls" is devoted to the already mentioned educational entrepreneur Aurelia Josz, while the two following chapters focus, as said, on the presence of women in universities, both as students and graduates in economics from 1906 to 1940 (Chapter "Female Students and Graduates in Business and Economics in Turin (1906–1940)"), and as researchers during the fascist regime (Chapter "Academic Research and University Careers of Women Economists During the Fascist Regime"). In the last section (*Women in politics*) the intellectual contributions of names that we have already met are examined: the socialist Anna Kuliscioff (Chapter "Anna Kuliscioff's Labour Economics"), the fascist Margherita Grassini Sarfatti (Chapter "Margherita Grassini Sarfatti,the Economic Thought of the Jewish Woman Who Popularized Fascism") and the few women who took part in the Italian Constituent Assembly in 1946 (Chapter "In the Name of Equality. Women's Action to Shape the Right to Work in the Italian Constituent Assembly").

As well as taking up a methodological challenge, this book seeks to remedy the fact that at present most of the literature on women economists of the past focuses on the Anglo-Saxon world.[7] This leads to a situation where also the history of women's economic thought sees a repetition of what has already happened with male economists, that is, the canon that is established and then consolidated is predominantly Anglo-Saxon. To combine the Anglo-Saxon tradition with other female traditions, no less rich in economic culture, this research responds to the need to delve into the history of different geographical and cultural areas, and to produce reconstructions that go beyond those on Anglo-Saxon women. Recently, work has been done on reconstructing women's economic thought on a European scale.[8] In this book the conceptual tools of both history of economic thought and economic history are used together to show how rich the presence of Italian women in economic history and

[7] Among the many examples, see the most recent Rostek (2021), Kuiper (2022), May (2022) and Reeves (2023).

[8] See for example Mosca et al. (2022).

thought actually is. This is just an initial research study to be extended and deepened with future studies, as there is still a great deal to discover about the Italian women who have tackled economic issues and about their economic activities.[9] It represents one more step in the adoption of a global and pluralist perspective on the topic of women in the history of economic facts and ideas.

References

Barucci, P. (2012). *L'economia politica e la sua storia*. Polistampa.

Becchio, G. (2020). *A History of Feminist and Gender Economics*. Routledge.

Chassonnery-Zaïgouche, C., Forget, E. L., & Singleton, J. D. (2022). Women and Economics: New Historical Perspectives. *History of Political Economy, 24*, 1–15.

Corsi, M., & Giulia, Z. (2019). The Two Faces of Economic Forecasting in Italy: Vera Cao Pinna and Almerina Ipsevich. In K. K. Madden & R. W. Dimand (Eds.), *The Routledge Handbook of the History of Women's Economic Thought* (pp. 358–372). Routledge.

Del Boca, D., & Di Tommaso M. L. (1997). Nora Federici e l'economia della famiglia. *Storia del pensiero economico, 33–34*, 183–191.

Dimand, R. W. (2000). Women in the Canon of Economics. In E. L. Forget & S. Peart (Eds.), *Reflections on the Classical Canon in Economics*. Routledge.

Dimand, R. W., Dimand, M. A., & Forget, E. L. (Eds.). (2004). *A Biographical Dictionary of Women Economists*. Edward Elgar.

Faucci, R. (2014). *A History of Italian Economic Thought*. Routledge.

Fornengo, G. (1997). Vera Cao Pinna (1909–1986): un'antesignana dell'econometria in Italia. *Storia del pensiero economico, 33–34*, 159–182.

Fratianni, M. (2012, December). 150 Years of Italian Political Unity and Economic Dualism: An Introduction. *Rivista italiana degli economisti, XVII*(3).

Kuiper, E. (2022). *A Herstory of Economics*. Polity.

Laurenzi, E., & Manuela, M. (Eds.). (2021). *A Female Activist Elite in Italy: Its International Network and Legacy*. Palgrave Macmillan.

May, A. M. (2022). *Gender and the Dismal Science: Women in the Early Years of the Economics Profession*. Columbia University Press.

Mosca, M. (2024). Women in Economics: Their Thought and Actions in the Past. *The Journal of European Economic History*, forthcoming.

Mosca, M., Małecka, M., & Calderòn, A. A. (2022). Women, Economics and History: Diversity within Europe. *Oeconomia, 12*(3), 371–378.

Parisi, D. (2007). Una lunga vita da economista. L'itinerario biografico e scientifico di Jenny Kretschmann Griziotti (1884–1980). *Il Politico, 72*, n. 2(215), 145–165.

Phelps, E. S. (2011). Economic Culture and Economic Performance: What Light Is Shed on the Continent's Problem? In E. S. Phelps & H.-W. Sinn (Eds.), *Perspectives on the Performance of the Continental Economies*. The MIT Press.

Reeves, R. (2023). *The Women Who Made Modern Economics*. Basic Books.

Rostek, J. (2021). *Women's Economic Thought in the Romantic Age: Towards a Transdisciplinary Herstory of Economic Thought*. Routledge.

Willson, P. (2010). *Women in Italy in the Twentieth Century Italy*. Palgrave Macmillan.

Zacchia, G. (2019). Alla ricerca del contributo perduto: (in)visibilità delle economiste nelle riviste italiane dal 1930 al 1970. *Moneta e credito, 72*(286), 89–104.

[9] One of the aims of the already mentioned research project *The Economic Thought of Italian Women (1750–1999)* is to carry out the first ever census of these figures in order to set up an online database, now available at www.echiw.it.

Women in Business

Isabella De Mari Doria, a Female Investor and Gambler in the Genoese Aristocracy

Antonio Iodice

1 Introduction

This chapter focuses on the life of Isabella De Mari Doria, a Genoese noblewoman who lived from 1708 to 1785. Although she did not write pamphlets or treatises, she was a prominent figure in the world of finance of her time, with extensive connections in the Genoese patriciate and involvement in various European financial markets. Additionally, she was involved in gambling and card games on almost a daily basis. The emphasis of this chapter is on her experiences and the role of women in finance during the early modern period in Italy. It presents her 'economic culture', a key concept of this volume as explained in the first chapter, through the documents she produced.

Currently, the business world has an underrepresentation of women, both as business owners and managers. In the past decades, this led to the assumption that independent businesswomen were almost non-existent in the pre-feminist past, specifically before the nineteenth century. If women were doing business, it was assumed they did it through their husband or an immediate male relative (Fontaine & Borrello, 2011). The spread of the 'separate sphere ideology' during the nineteenth century further complicated the conception about their involvement in the economic sphere (Becchio, 2024).[1]

[1] According to this theory, men and women are profoundly different and are meant for different activities. Men are physically strong and independent, while women are weak. Men are meant to belong to the public sphere and to participate in politics, while women are meant to run households and raise families. See Victorian Era. In *Britannica*. Retrieved June 6, 2023, from https://www.britannica.com/event/Victorian-era#ref1274694. Unless stated otherwise, the translations of the quoted texts are our own.

A. Iodice (✉)
University of Exeter, Exeter, UK
e-mail: ai290@exeter.ac.uk

University of Roma Tre, Rome, Italy

M. Mosca (ed.), *Women at Work in Italy (1750–1950)*, Springer Studies in the History of Economic Thought, https://doi.org/10.1007/978-3-031-64281-4_2

On the contrary, the narrative behind recent research on eighteenth- and early nineteenth-century British women started challenging this assumption and uncovered evidence of a robust female presence among high-end and mid-level retailers, some crafts and even large-scale business owners (Aston, 2016; Barker, 2006; Burnette, 2008; Kay, 2009; Phillips, 2006). The majority of self-employed women operated in a small number of sectors typically associated with female responsibilities such as food, textiles and clothing. They were not restricted to these sectors, and were thinly spread across a wider range of occupations. According to the traditional literature—albeit this assumption is currently under re-evaluation—widows were more likely to be found in non-traditionally feminine sectors when they stepped in to take care of their deceased partners' businesses (Moring & Wall, 2017).[2]

At present most of the literature on women involved in economic activities in medieval and early modern Europe focuses on the English-speaking countries (Kuiper, 2022; Rostek, 2021). Such countries were not at all exceptional in such regard. Research studies published in English on the Netherlands (Van den Heuvel, 2007), Denmark (Gold, 2018), Germany (Beachy, 2002; Rabuzzi, 1995), Russia (Ulianova, 2009) and northern France (Craig, 2017) describe similar situations and the strong involvement of women in economic activities. However, the literature on businesswomen in English is still limited and Anglo-centric, ignoring large parts of the European continent, especially regarding Southern Europe where local studies have provided useful insights into similar dynamics. A clear example are the works of Guglielmotti (2020) or Guglielmotti and Petti Balbi (2012) about medieval Genoa.

This marginalization is even stronger when we try to investigate the participation of women in high finance. There is a wealth of knowledge available regarding men's financial affairs including their attitudes towards risk, market participation and the professionalization of banking, stockbroking and accounting. Due to the assumption that men significantly outnumber women in this field, women's financial behaviour is often considered insignificant or supplementary to men's. When women are considered per se, they are typically regarded as conservative in their choice of investments and management. Female business decision-makers are also typically considered as non-risk-takers (Laurence et al., 2009). Assumptions about women's incapacity influenced both historians and present-day commentators to treat women's financial management as conservative and averse to undue risk, directed at providing income rather than trading gains or capital growth.

Historically, women have played a small role in the emergence of financial professions, with also institutionalized limitations such as the exclusion from the London Stock Exchange until 1973 (Laurence et al., 2009, 3). As several scholars have recently shown, at least for the eighteenth century with a particular focus on Northern Europe and the Atlantic, women were present and active in financial markets (Froide, 2017). While many of them did require an income, they were also active traders (Carlos & Neal, 2004; Rutterford & Maltby, 2006). Their role is well-known in the South Sea Bubble of 1720, for example (Carlos et al., 2006). Italy and particularly

[2] According to recent studies by Guglielmotti Petti Balbi (2012, 23), unmarried and married women seem to have had similar margins of freedom, at least in the Italian context.

the small Republic of Genoa, an understudied cradle of early modern financial capitalism, can further contribute to rebalance these biases, as it will be shown in the pages that follow.

This chapter is organized as follows. The second section introduces the Italian and Genoese context, with specific emphasis on the role of women in economic activities and the cultural process that led them to master accounting techniques in the domestic sphere. This sets the stage for the subsequent section, which outlines the key events in the life of Isabella De Mari. Family donations and inheritances played a crucial role in establishing her initial capital, which she managed independently. The fourth section is divided into thematic sub-sections dedicated to reconstructing Isabella's activities and investment strategies. This section also draws parallels between her investment activities and gambling, an endeavour in which Isabella regularly engaged alongside the leading figures—both men and women—of the Genoese nobility. The conclusions underscore the profoundly pragmatic nature of Isabella's writings, which are evidence of her economic acumen.

2 Women in Italy and Genoa in the Eighteenth Century

The alphabetization process slowly extended to women, the gradual access to non-religious education spreading in the cities to the detriment of the old religious-moral teaching imparted by the clergy since the thirteenth century, and the minimal notions of accountancy and law proper to mercantile knowledge, led some women in Italy to learn how to navigate between records and money, contracts and profits, almost always in front of a notary. They developed a familiarity with the written document and the possession of a minimal commercial culture aimed at keeping up with their business, as Enea Silvio Piccolomini—the future Pope Pius II—asserted for the Genoese (Petti Balbi, 2009, 129). In Genoa or Venice, already from the Medieval period, are examples of education given by female teachers to pupils of both sexes: in Genoa during 1339 school teacher Marietta Spagnola (*magistra scholarum*), for example, received a life annuity from Sorleone de Castro probably for her role as teachers to his children (Petti Balbi, 1979).

In the medieval period there do not seem to be many female entrepreneurs, but businesswomen occasionally intervened in the commercial sector and made a profit on money. In Genoa they underwrote and became owners of stock or shares in public debt as in the case of the 'compera mutui vecchi'. In 1393 women outnumbered men, albeit slightly: out of 1462 owners or companies, there were 639 women compared to 597 men, with 508,000 *lire* invested compared to 526,000 *lire* invested by men (Guglielmotti & Petti Balbi, 2012, 18). This situation was not unique to Genoa but concerned at least all Italian states. The disproportionate growth of the financial sector in Genoa between the seventeenth and eighteenth centuries further allowed the emergence of women financiers such as Isabella De Mari.

The Republic of Genoa in the early modern period was a small state, roughly coinciding with today's Liguria region, surrounded by powerful monarchies. It was a financial centre with its own merchant marine, ruled by an élite of powerful patricians engaged in all sorts of businesses with networks extending on a global scale (Bitossi, 1990; Felloni, 1998). Family groups made up this patriciate monopolistically holding public, often inherited offices. The possibility of enjoying political power was transmitted by inheritance to legitimate male children who had been enrolled in the register of nobility upon reaching the legal age of majority, twenty-five years old. Economic power was instead not limited to men also because of demographic reasons. Throughout the early modern period, the count of Genoese nobility experienced an inexorable decline, with several family branches either becoming extinct or comprising solely of female heirs. Ensuring women the ability to manage familial estates became an imperative practical need.

The Genoese established an informal 'merchant empire' between the second half of the sixteenth century and the second half of the seventeenth century, which expanded within the Spanish Empire in a simultaneous and symbiotic manner. Genoa funded Spain's expansionist policies and in return its patricians obtained formal or informal privileges that allowed them to set up operational bases from which they profitably carried out their businesses. Widespread Genoese presence in all major European cities and their ability to diversify into multi-sectoral businesses such as trade, finance and land ownership allowed the Genoese to accumulate considerable capitals and points to the existence of a common model defined as the 'Genoa system' (Doria, 1995). This system was based on the ability of a compact and relatively small group of patricians to develop different business strategies to seize market opportunities: it was a 'discreet and sophisticated rule', according to Fernand Braudel who even referred to an Age of the Genoese (Braudel, 1984, 187).

Frequent Spanish bankruptcies and growing French influence between the seventeenth and the eighteenth centuries led to a readjustment of the Genoese patriciate's interests towards the financial sphere and neutrality policies, exploiting the networks and capitals built in the previous period. Genoese capitals were growingly employed in the financial sector, with Spain's financial market conspicuously receding from the forefront of attention. According to Giuseppe Felloni, in the late eighteenth century:

> An entire city, […], discovered [...] an unstoppable financial vocation, which invested ever larger groups not only of the aristocracy, the centuries-old protagonist of local financial life, but also of the artisan and mercantile bourgeoisie. And an ever more conspicuous flow of foreign income poured into Genoa, breaking the traditional balance between the various economic activities. (Felloni, 1971, 13)

There was no specialization of the Genoese aristocracy in finance: most noblemen were involved at the same time also in real estate, trade, manufacturing and so on. As proved by the wealth of primary sources in the city archives, women participated in financial and economic activities. For no other regional context in Italy is there such a wealth in terms of earliness, quantity and quality of the sources (Guglielmotti, 2020).

To manage their finances women needed knowledge. As mentioned, women from the medieval period onwards were accustomed to keep records of household expenditure, guided by advice books (Mitchell, 2011). Already in the fifteenth century the

Italian-born French poet and court writer Christine de Pisan wrote about the need for women to carefully supervise their revenues and expenses. Advice books, manuals of husbandry and housekeeping all preached the virtues of thrift and keeping accounts. Even Rousseau in his *Émile* (1762)—while describing Émile's bride Sophie—specified that she could manage a household and its budget and that her serious reading was confined to François Barrême's *Teach-yourself Arithmetique*(!) and Fénelon's didactic novel *Télémaque* (Lukowski, 2003, 167). Similar to the logic behind the need for accounting of religious orders, accounting allowed the shielding of the woman's wealth through the visibility provided to flows of goods, services and money, allowing her at the same time to maintain her virtue and make a profit.[3] Women had to be active as managers that could keep extensive written records about purchases, stores and wages: 'Like novels, diaries and autobiographies trace their genealogy to the account book, and share that genre's preoccupation with calculations of the individual's fluctuating balance of personal debits and credits' (Vickery, 1998, 127).

This practical need clashed blatantly with regulations and pamphlets in which the women were relegated to the role of mothers and/or courtesans with no economic interests. In 1631, Vincenzo Nolfi, a writer from the Marche region, wrote a well-known treatise for the education of the future wife entitled *Ginipedia* (Nolfi, 1646). The book is full of advice on how to behave in public and at home, but there is no reference to economic activities. In notarial deeds, it seems that women did not have much freedom in managing their own affairs because they generally acted before the notary with the assistance of two advisors. In reality, it can be assumed that this was only a formal procedure and that the woman, if not dependent on her husband, acted with a certain freedom (Bezzina, 2020).

The same attitude can be found in Genoa in the main publications by nobles or members of the local upper middle class. In the seventeenth century, the Genoese nobleman Andrea Spinola, doge of the Republic from 1629 to 1631, proposed to the aristocracy of his city, in one of his many pedagogical writings that were still reprinted in the following century, a return to sober customs by recalling the importance of women in the management of the household economy:

> Those who wish to have regulated their house and introduce good discipline of economy, it is necessary that they get up in time: because, with their example, laziness will be banished from their children and servants. [...] Prudent women must be so busy that they have no time to read. But if they wish to do so, let them read only spiritual books, or even that of the perfect wife. [...] Those women who take a vow not to wear silk and not to go to parties deserve to be called wise. (Bitossi, 1981, 231–238)

A very different model, as will be seen, from that of Isabella De Mari Doria. In the same period, Pietro Paolo Tiscornia wrote a biography of his brother, Francesco Maria, a Genoese physician. The manuscript, rich in illustrations, offers direct testimony of what a virtuous woman was through the description of the author's mother, Baneta Drago, and her sister, Maria Gerolama (Benvenuto, 2002).

[3] For a comparison with accounting in religious order, specifically in the Jesuit religious order, see Quattrone (2004).

Tiscornia described his mother as 'a woman cloaked in pious virtues: wise, humble, honest, modest; a respectful and submissive wife; a perfect mother in educating by word and example; a kind but strict lady of the house with her subordinates, modest and courteous with strangers'.[4] She spent the day at home praying or doing the housework with the servants: this housework probably included keeping the household accounts.

One of the most important figures in the training of the married woman was the husband, who had to train his bride in domestic economy, enabling her to administer the home and property 'by diligently multiplying them, conserving them with caution and dispensing them with prudence' (Duby & Perrot, 2005, 144). An example was the Genoese nobleman Marcello Doria who married Barbara Spinola in 1612 and declared that he wanted her 'to leave out reading Tasso and other similar books, offering her books for her pleasure to give her both entertainment and learning' (Grendi, 1975, VIII–XIX). In this case the young bride rebelled, threatened divorce and probably obtained it considering that, four years later, her father Battista Spinola had her back at home and started a quarrel with his son-in-law over the dowry.

Finally, the Civil Statutes of the Republic of Genoa also placed serious limitations on women's freedom of action in the economic sphere. Book IV, Chapter XX stated how women could not sign any contract without the authorization of their father or, if married, of their husband. In case of widows, they needed to seek the authorization of the husband's fathers or close relatives (Statuti Civili, 1613, 146). The Civil Statutes were republished without modifications until the fall of the Republic in 1797 but we know that most of its content was by then out of date in the ordinary practice.

3 The Life and Capital of Isabella De Mari

The ample documentary evidence preserved in the Genoese archives on various powerful women active in the seventeenth and eighteenth centuries allows us to readdress their presence in the financial sphere through significant case studies, and to have some glimpses of their economic thought based on practical experience. Isabella's life and investment strategies are a splendid example that we can use to extrapolate typical relevant indicators, not just an exceptional story. This analysis is based on her three account books from 1748 to 1786, one letter book from 1760 to 1773, and a small journal account book only related to her gambling activities in card games from 1762 to 1771. It is unusual to have such a large amount of documentation about an early modern European female investor, but this does not mean that Isabella's case was unique. Her experience reflects 'the exceptional normal', an aphorism of the Genoese microhistorian Edoardo Grendi (1994, 544). According to a sample made up of thirteen Genoese noble firms studied by Felloni (1971), which he judged to be representative of the financial activities of the aristocracy in the eighteenth century,

[4] Biblioteca Civica Berio m.r.II.1.36, Vita Francisci Marie Tiscornie, 1680.

as many as three were managed by noblewomen: Maria Teresa Gropallo Pallavicino, Maria Ignazia Durazzo Brignole Sale and Isabella De Mari Doria.[5]

Isabella was born on 12 June 1708 to Stefano Maria De Mari and Maria Durazzo. The De Mari family was traditionally involved in the ship-owning business. Until the end of the seventeenth century they had many commercial interests in Southern Italy and Spain.[6] Several of the De Mari family obtained Neapolitan citizenship and signed loans to the Spanish crown. The Spanish bankruptcies hit the De Mari family hard but still between 1624 and 1626, for example, Stefano De Mari was an *asentista* of Spain with his brother Giovanni Battista. Like most Genoese patricians, he was also involved in politics. He was the consul of the Genoese 'nation' in Naples and became *doge* of the Genoese republic from 1663 to 1665.

One of his numerous sons, Domenico Maria, was Isabella's grandfather. Domenico was born in Genoa in 1653. He probably resided for some time in Spain and held various political offices in Genoa: he was *doge* in 1707, during the War of the Spanish Succession. The date of his death is not certain, but he was certainly still alive in 1720 in Spain. In total four De Mari members, including Domenico Maria, held the highest charge in the republic, that of *doge*. The last one was Lorenzo De Mari, Isabella's cousin, in 1744–1746. This made the De Mari one of the most prominent Genoese noble families in the eighteenth century.

The De Mari family tree (Saginati, 2004, CVI).

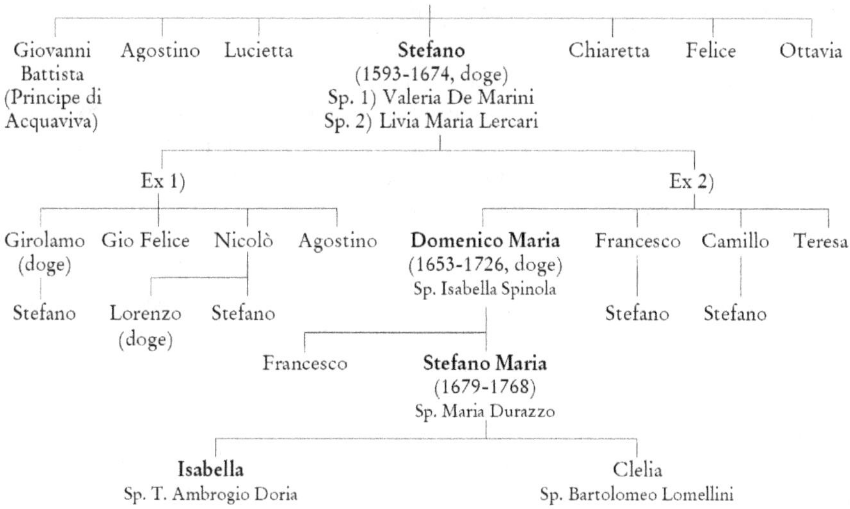

Legend: Sp. = 'married to'.

[5] Unfortunately, known sources related to Maria Teresa Gropallo Pallavicino and Maria Ignazia Durazzo Brignole Sale do not contain the same wealth of information as those on Isabella De Mari Doria. Additional research is essential to facilitate a more thorough comparison of the economic undertakings of these three women or to uncover more case studies.

[6] There are no complete reconstructions on the economic activities of the members of the De Mari family, except for a generic description in Saginati (2004, XXIV–XXXII).

Fig. 1 Anonymous, *Villa de Mari*, postcard, Genoa, 1899. This image is part of a series of postcards on Genoese patrician villas printed in Genoa in 1899. The villa De Mari, in Sestri Ponente and now abandoned, was one of the residences of Isabella De Mari Doria

Stefano Maria De Mari, Domenico Maria's eldest son and Isabella's father, was born in 1679 and inherited the family businesses, while his brother Francesco became a clergyman. Stefano had a long political career that is hard to trace back since at least five of his contemporary cousins of the same name are mentioned without further details in official documents. He was certainly Commissioner in Corsica in 1747, a Genoese possession until 1755.

He was a wealthy merchant thanks to the import of high-quality fabrics and textiles, particularly from France. He mainly dealt in 'French goods' and he also imported and exported spirits, eels, pastries, chocolates and so on, on commission. His financial activities were marginal, but he invested part of his money in various Italian and European countries.

Stefano had two daughters: Isabella, the eldest, born in 1708, and Clelia. We do not have information on Isabella's infancy. In 1728, Stefano arranged Isabella's wedding to Tommaso Ambrogio, son of Giorgio Doria of the Montaldeo branch. The Doria were another one of the best known Genoese noble families throughout the Republic's history and it was a sumptuous wedding mostly paid for by the Doria family.[7] Following her wedding with Tommaso, Isabella had four daughters—Teresa, Vittoria, Marina and Gleba—and one son, Giorgio. The family lived between their palace in Genoa, the De Mari villa in Sestri Ponente (Fig. 1), the Doria fief of Montaldeo and the holiday residence of Novi, in the inland.

[7] ADG 641, Giorgio Doria di Ambrogio, 1728.

In 1739, after eleven years of marriage, Tommaso Ambrogio died at the age of forty-eight, while Isabella was thirty-one. There are some account books with Tommaso's name, but as he died before his father, he was never the owner of the family estate. He simply held some annuities assigned to him by his father and his uncle Clemente at the time of his marriage.[8]

Following Tommaso's death, it was Giorgio Doria who formally took over the financial management of the family and administered Isabella's dowry, contrary to the local custom that stated that the widow should have her dowry back immediately. Probably because of the lack of money, in 1746 Isabella for the first time faced serious financial issues, which were partly solved thanks to loans from her father Stefano.

Two years later, in 1748, Maria Durazzo died, and Isabella came into possession of half of her mother's dowry, equal to 107,967 Genoese *lire*, 13 *soldi* and 1 *denaro* (1/240 of a *lira*).[9] Her mother's inheritance consisted of a series of public bonds from a number of Italian cities in Isabella's account books reported as: *Monte di San Pietro* in Rome, *Monte Ristoro Primo* in Rome, *Monti Diversi* in Bologna, *Depositi Capitali* in Venice at the mint. The management of these bonds was entrusted to agents, one for each city: the Rome bonds to Francesco Maria Arieti, who later took care of Isabella's other Roman investments; Ignazio Testori took care of the Venetian bonds, while Sebastiano Negri took care of the Bolognese ones. Her mother's inheritance gave Isabella her first opportunity to put her skills as an investor to the test. Previously, the few entries in her first double-entry bookkeeping register starting in 1748 concerned the purchase of and interest accrued on the French royal lottery bond that we will see later.[10]

It is the tradition of Genoese patricians, as far as possible, not to disinvest money already committed. It was probably because of this choice and in order to obtain the necessary capital for new investments that Isabella, despite her mother's inheritance, preferred to ask her father for loans again between 1761 and 1765. This element reveals her faith in the familial 'safety net' and her priority for lucrative investments. In total, her father lent her around 16,680 *lire*, which Isabella repaid in full.

Over these same years Stefano De Mari, who had only Isabella and Clelia as heirs, began to entrust Isabella some of his financial investments and probably to train her in financial management: his financial assets, too, mainly focused on the public debt of Italian pre-unification states and on institutions (Venice and Bologna) or on France. The 12 August 1761, for example, he entrusted Isabella with his investments in several Venetian magistracies—around 28,694 Genoese *lire* on the *Magistrato della Zecca, Depositi, Bastioni, Generale delle Entrate*—and asked in exchange for 54% of the interest on those sums.[11] In this period she bought silver ornaments on

[8] ADG 811–812, Tommaso Ambrogio Doria di Giorgio, 1728–1739.

[9] For comparison, keep in mind that the purchasing power of one Genoese *lira* in 1770 was equivalent to four litres of wheat. An average apartment was worth less than 3000 *lire* (Felloni, 1971, 31).

[10] ADG 821, IDMD, c.1, 28 December 1748. The note refers to lottery tickets bought until 1739 that provided an annual revenue of 240 *lire*. On the *Loterie Royale* see Carlos (2020).

[11] ADG 821, IDMD, c. 68, 12 August 1761.

commission for other Genoese noblewomen.[12] Stefano also donated some assets to Isabella and Clelia. In those cases, the investments' interest was shared by the two sisters (54% to Isabella, 46% to Clelia) but it was only Isabella who managed them, transferring Clelia's share to her. Clelia did not show any interest in handling money and investments and always delegated it to her father, her sister or her husband Bartolomeo Lomellini.

Other counsellors (*fidecommissari*) to Isabella were Stefano Doria, her brother-in-law who lived in the same palace as she did, with his wife, and Agostino Airoli. As stated in the Statutes, counsellors were mandatory for women when signing contracts, loans or other documents in the Republic of Genoa, but Isabella remarked to her agents that she had ample authority to dispose of her assets by herself. In a letter to her agent in Paris in 1760, Nicolò Verzura, she explicitly required him to send directly to her every information regarding her assets.

Isabella's wealth was definitively consolidated as a result of two other inheritances: that of her father and, a few years later, that of her uncle Francesco. Stefano De Mari died on 14 June 1768, leaving his two daughters Isabella and Clelia as universal heirs. Stefano's legacy consisted of public bonds in the Kingdom of Sweden, Ferrara, Bologna, Paris, Wien, Genoa and La Spezia, besides private loans—usually to noblemen from different European countries—and other bonds.[13] Around 271,918 Genoese *lire* belonged to Isabella. Isabella immediately wrote to her father's agents, handling the transfer of funds also on behalf of her sister Clelia, whose share she later liquidated. In 1769, one year after her father's death and thirty years after Tommaso's death, the Doria family finally returned Isabella her dowry, equal to ninety-five thousand Genoese *lire*.[14]

As mentioned, Isabella received another inheritance in 1770 from Francesco De Mari, Stefano's brother and Isabella's uncle. He had made a career as a clergyman and accumulated enormous wealth: according to the eighteenth-century French writer Charles Dupaty, in Genoese society 'among many noble and wealthy families, the priest is the treasurer' (Dupaty, 1788, 113). The legacy consisted, for the most part, of investments in both Italian and foreign public bonds, furniture and furnishings, paintings, copper and silver, as well as books and wine. Public bonds alone were worth 215,382 Genoese *lire*, plus 11,242 *lire* of other assets. In 1770, therefore, the value of Isabella's assets accumulated through donations and inheritances, excluding the loans she repaid to her father, amounted to approximately 613,938 Genoese *lire*.

[12] ADG 819, IDMD, 1 December 1760.

[13] ADG 824, IDMD, c.15, 1 August 1768.

[14] ADG 824, IDMD, c. 75, 25 August 1769.

4 Isabella's Investment Strategies

Isabella inherited a large sum from her family, largely consisting of investments throughout Europe. The bonds that she inherited were largely preserved but there are instructions from Isabella to her agents to cancel some investments and use her money in new ones. For example, her account of 31 December 1779 records the acquisition of shares in the French East India Company and the participation in loans to the Austrian Empress Maria Theresa.[15] Let us now examine how she divided her investments and how remunerative they were, in comparison with the other noble firms examined by Felloni (1979). Her investment choices reflect a risk-oriented strategy and her economic culture.

4.1 *Non-Interest-Bearing Financial Assets*

Around 22.6% of Isabella's investments by 1778 were in non-interest-bearing financial assets. Such assets were made up of cash, 'bank' deposits, dowry for her daughters and non-interest-bearing loans. As was the case with Genoese aristocracy, there was a very high inclination to liquidity, which can be explained partly by a marked tendency to cash in, partly by the desire to build up a cash reserve to profit from unexpected lucrative investments as soon as the opportunity arose. The investments preferred by investors were not always available.

Isabella had a marked tendency to cash in compared to the other firms analysed by Felloni, which invested in this sector on average around 6% of their assets (Felloni, 1971, 32). This difference is even stronger when looking at the investment strategies of other firms managed by noblewomen who cashed in only between 4 and 2.5% of their assets. The ready availability of money was necessary to operate the numerous loans in which Isabella was involved (see Sect. 4.4).

4.2 *Movable Assets*

It seems that Isabella followed strategies different from the average investors even in the movable assets sector. She invested only 3.6% of her capital here, compared to the 13.2 and 5.4% of the two other female firms (Felloni, 1971, 35). Movable assets could be paintings, furniture, books or even the bottles of wine that she received from her uncle Francesco. Movable and immovable assets were safe but usually non remunerative investments and Isabella did not seem to care too much about them. Other Genoese male patricians also invested proportionally small shares of their money in this sector.

---

[15] ADG 826, IDMD, 31 December 1779.

4.3 Immovable Assets

Immovable assets, mainly constituted by real estate properties, in Genoa as elsewhere in Europe, were irreplaceable cornerstones of domestic wealth according to the customs of the time. The search for a material and lasting property could prevail over that for a conspicuous but more uncertain income. Plus, Genoese patricians competed for the prestige connected to buying and embellishing their palaces. The entire city of Genoa had gone through an urban renovation and exponential growth of high-value buildings since the sixteenth century as a way to 'petrify' the significant fluxes of money that arrived, thanks to the financial investments (Doria, 1986). Isabella spared no expense for the Doria palace, but in total only 0.2% of her investments went into real estate, the lowest share compared to the aristocratic Genoese firms studied so far, which invested between 10 and 40% in this sector (Felloni, 1971, 54). This choice by Isabella reflects her attitude to risk that strongly emerges in the following sectors.

4.4 Bonds

Another primary area of investment for the Genoese nobility was bonds. Bonds usually consisted of holdings in non-redeemable, redeemable and life-long loans requested by public or private institutions. They conferred a variable annual income based on the agreed interest. The portfolio of bonds held by Isabella was significant: she invested as much as 49% of her assets in this activity, a lower percentage sum only in comparison to the investment strategies of Marcello Durazzo and Maria Ignazia Durazzo with respect to the sample analysed in Felloni (1971, 38). Another example of the exceptional normal: 49% was an exceptional value, but she was not the only woman who invested such a high percentage of her assets in this sector.

Sixty per cent of the bonds held by Isabella were non-life-long bonds, most of them inherited from her father Stefano and her uncle Francesco. They were mainly concentrated in France and the regional states of Northern Italy. In addition to preserving the family investments, Isabella had her agents purchase new bonds or other shares in institutions in which she already had bonds, thus showing her will to actively carry on business: for example, she ordered Nicolò Verzura, her agent in Paris, to buy in local currency a further 7000 *lire tornesi* of shares in the French East India Company, in addition to the 12,250 inherited from her uncle, at an annual rate of 4%; she also acquired further shares in the 'Terme Generali' and the 'Lotteria Quarta' in France and, in 1768, she invested 6191.10.7 Genoese *lire* in shares of the 'Monte San Pietro' in Rome.[16] New investments included the purchase of 22,387.10.9 Genoese *lire* of shares in the 'Clero di Francia', showing a circumstantial and non-systemic interest

[16] Genoese *lire* were subdivided into *soldi* (of which there were twenty to a *lira*) and *denari* (of which there were twelve to a *soldo*). Prices are expressed in the paper using a point to separate each unit of value.

in investment in religious institutions, at an annual rate of 4%; of 26,208.3 Genoese *lire* in the 'Hotel de Ville', the City of Paris, at a rate of 6%; finally, 10,000 Genoese *lire* were invested in the 'Ospedale della Carità di Lione' at a rate of 4.5% for fifteen years, in 1776. These investments are mentioned in her balance of 1778 but not all of them proved to be remunerative as expected. The shares in the Ospedale della Carità, for example, were recorded as of 'little hope' (*poca speranza*) in her balance of 1780.[17] As much as Isabella's strategy was aimed at achieving maximum profit even through risky investments, there was no lack of spending on charitable deeds and alms, as was perhaps the case with the Ospedale della Carità. In 1778, fulfilling a vow, she went on a pilgrimage to the shrine of Nostra Signora della Misericordia in Savona. Between 1778 and 1784, she spent a yearly average of 4,000 *lire* on alms. These were negligible sums compared to the capital she invested and traded on the major European financial and credit markets but are evidence of the religious faith of this female investor with a passion for risk-taking investments.

Isabella's life-long bonds were a minority, but they shed light on her love for gambling and her contacts with the Genoese nobility, for whom she could act as a sort of 'financial broker'. In Paris, Isabella's agent bought three tickets for the 'Lotteria regia seconda' for a value of 1,875 Genoese *lire* at an 8% interest rate on the life of her daughter Teresa Maddalena. This contract, which I also mentioned earlier, was the equivalent of a lottery bond: while in the ordinary bond the number of issue facilitates the redemption of the amount loaned following the numerical order, in the lottery bond the number of issue was extracted among all numbers and could be associated with lottery prizes consisting of huge sums of money (Lévy-Ullmann, 1896). She also invested 3754.4.9 *lire* in the 'Tontina decima' of 1760. *Tontine* enables subscribers to share the risk of living a long life by combining features of a group annuity with a kind of mortality lottery. Each subscriber pays a sum into a trust and thereafter receives a periodical payout. As members die, their payout entitlements devolve to the other participants, and so the value of each continuing payout increases. On the death of the final member, the trust scheme is usually wound up (Weir, 1989). 62.5% of this investment was on Isabella's own life and the remaining 37.5% on the lives of six other people—women included—mostly belonging to the Genoese nobility: Giuseppe Maria Torre, Giovanni Battista Enrile, Andrea Francesco Maria Granara, Maria Giovanna Groppallo Ferretta, Maria Francesca Saveria Brignole Spinola and Giovanni Antonio Ragno.

4.5 *Loans*

Finally, 24.6% of Isabella's investments were dedicated to non-life-long loans, a percentage in line with other investors in the Republic. Unlike loans related to trade and navigation, which were widespread in Genoa, Isabella's loans were exclusively

[17] ADG 826, IDMD, 31 December 1780.

loans or loan subscriptions to both Genoese and European citizens, for which the repayment of the capital was expected within a certain period.

Most of the international loans of the Genoese nobility in this period were granted through contracts drawn up in Genoa by city notaries. Since 1760 such contracts were known in Europe as 'mutui fruttiferi all'uso di Genova' (Felloni, 1998, 675–676). They were usually granted by Genoese financiers, united in private partnerships, to foreign borrowers. The contract provided for the protection of creditors, stating that subscription, repayment and payment of interest should take place in Genoa, in stable currency, in full measure, without deductions and at agreed-upon deadlines. It specified the guarantees owed by the debtor (pledge of precious objects or public securities, mortgage on property and income, guarantees from third parties, etc.) and established the debtor's obligation to have the contract approved in their country of residence, in order to give it legal validity, including the exemption of creditors from any foreign tax or withholding. These loans had an average duration of 8–12 years and typically yielded a real interest of 4–5%. Subscribers could freely resell their shares. Loan requests came from all parts of Europe, which Genoese capitalists competed to fulfil. Some bourgeois, welfare or religious organizations and even private foundations also joined in these profitable business ventures.

Loans presented a higher risk compared to bonds because the only guarantee was the personal wealth of the contracting party, although they were often protected by mortgages on real estate and other revenues considered 'safe'. Isabella's debtors included nobles and prominent figures of the European period who paid relatively reliable interest. For example, Austrian Empress Maria Theresa received loans from Genoese capitalists, including Isabella, in 1767, 1771, 1778 and 1779, which were guaranteed by her 'sovereign treasury' and deposits in notes of the Bank of Wien that covered the entire amount.[18] This was not always the case. Maximilian Joseph, Duke of Bavaria, only offered a partial guarantee for a loan of 500,000 *fiorini*: allodial properties, the lordship of Suezburg and Birbaum with their respective adjoining land and a brewery located in Muklhausen, a total value of 37,000 *fiorini*. Among the loans directly made by Isabella—not as participation in loans negotiated by Genoese capitalists—are the 10,000 Genoese *lire* loan to the Duke of Anjou and additional loans to Empress Maria Theresa. The remaining active loans owned by Isabella were almost all contracted in the Republic of Genoa and in Germany, and often derived from inheritances left by Stefano and Francesco Maria De Mari.

[18] Nevertheless, the loans to Maria Theresa were not secure either. In Isabella's balance sheet of 1780 there is a transfer of the 1779 loan to Maria Theresa to the section of the account book of loans 'of little hope' and the alienation of interest on the 1767 loan.

Table 1 Isabella De Mari's wealth, 1768–1785

Year	Net wealth
1768	117,822.1292
1770	613,938.3042
1778	654,450.0125
1779	861,738.5083
1780	834,083.5958
1785	915,728.7583

4.6 A Life-Time Balance?

Thanks to her account books and her will, it is possible to trace a balance sheet of Isabella's economic activities over a period of about two decades, from 1768 to 1785. The result is visible in Table 1.

By 1770, Isabella had already received the dowries of her mother, father and uncle. Therefore, the increase of approximately 33% in her fortune observed between 1770 and 1785 was the result of both the accumulated interests on the inherited sums and her investment strategies.

5 The Gaming Balance Book

In addition to her balance books, Isabella left an account book entitled 'Gaming Balance Book' in which she reported on a monthly base the positive or negative balances of the days she spent at the gaming tables of the leading members of the Genoese nobility between 1762 and 1771 (Fig. 2). Despite the brilliant conduct of her investments and speculative activities, Isabella closed her gaming balance with 4169 *lire* in winnings against 6284 *lire* in losses. The resulting net loss was of 2115 *lire*. What is even more revealing from her gaming book is the network of Genoese noblemen and noblewomen with whom she regularly met to play. Isabella played in the houses of the Centurione, Durazzo, Fieschi, Grillo, Grimaldi, Lercari, Sauli and Spinola, among the wealthiest and more powerful Genoese noble families. She hosted a few gaming gatherings herself, and a few more were hosted by noblewomen such as Giovannetta Centurione, Giovannetta Mari, Antonietta Sauli or Marina Spinola. Gambling tables played the role that in other parts of Europe was played by cafes or clubs (Clark, 2000; Kümin, 2007). Traditionally, noblewomen since the Renaissance used games of chance to demonstrate their honour, character and virtue in a manner identical to their male peers. What mattered was neither victory nor defeat, but the way the games were played, unconcerned by material gain (Scott Baker, 2021, 29–31). The situation was more blurred in the eighteenth century with gaming tables being a place of equal relationships between male and female players. Plus, even if an event ended in a small monetary loss, the interaction with fellow investors could lead

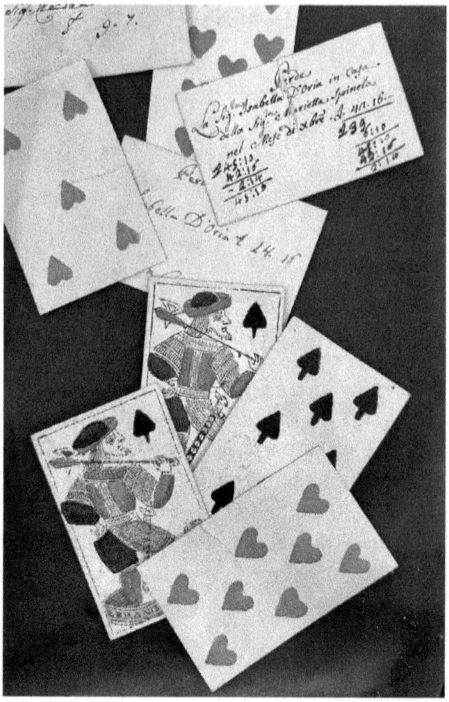

Fig. 2 Centro di Studi e Documentazione di Storia Economica «Archivio Doria» 818, Isabella De Mari Doria, game cards (c.1778–1786). These game cards were those used by Isabella De Mari. They were kept together with the 'Gaming Balance Book'. Isabella De Mari kept track of where she played and the total gains or losses on the back of her cards

to far greater benefits in terms of information gathering and investment strategies. According to Ingrassia, the early stock market was presented as an extension of gaming for upper-class women (Ingrassia, 2005, 35).

6 Conclusion

Unlike other Genoese businesswomen and female investors studied so far, Isabella showed a strong inclination towards 'risky' investments, and this inclination paid off well over the years. At her death on 30 March 1785, Isabella's net wealth amounted to more than 900,000 Genoese *lire*. The universal heir was her son Giorgio, who was married to Aurelia Grimaldi in 1759 (Saginati, 2004, XCV). Isabella also left her only surviving daughter, Teresa Maddalena, who had become a nun, 500 *lire* and a life annuity of 200 *lire* a year. This is not a large sum compared to that left to the son who would carry on the household, indicative of a traditional family choice compared to Isabella's own experience. The question remains whether she passed on some of her knowledge and interests to Teresa Maddalena or to any of her other daughters, who unfortunately died prematurely.

Isabella's writings were mostly created for practical purposes, but they reveal her economic culture and the determination with which she operated in the financial sphere. Isabella's practical experience is closely related to the economic thought and culture of the European investors of her time in terms of financial tools used, without being relegated in a gender role. As mentioned, her activities fit perfectly into the broader trend of investments by the Genoese nobility of the time, and her status as a woman in charge does not seem to have influenced her investment choices: she was probably educated in finance by her father Stefano. Social circles across Europe showed how women could be intellectual and social companions, not merely agents of procreation and property transmission (Lukowski, 2003, 166). In this sense, Isabella seems to have been an example of well-integrated noble female investor whose wealth and status allowed her to successfully express her economic aptitude in a field traditionally dominated by men.

References

Aston, J. (2016). *Female Entrepreneurship in Nineteenth Century England: Engagement in the Urban Economy*. Palgrave McMillan.

Barker, H. (2006). *The Business of Women, Female Enterprise and Urban Development in Northern England, 1760–1830*. Oxford University Press.

Beachy, R. (2002). Business Was a Family Affair: Women of Commerce in Central Europe, 1680–1870. *Histoire Sociale—Social History, 34*, 307–330.

Becchio, G. (2024). *The Doctrine of the Separate Spheres*. Palgrave Macmillan.

Benvenuto, G. (2002). *"Una vita esemplare". Storia di un medico nella Genova barocca*. Clueb.

Bezzina, D. (2020). Gestione di beni e patrimonio: spazi di iniziativa delle donne a Genova nei secoli XII e XIII. In P. Guglielmotti (Ed.), *Donne, famiglie e patrimoni a Genova e in Liguria nei secoli XII e XIII* (pp. 207–242). Società Ligure di Storia Patria.

Bitossi, C. (1981). *Andrea Spinola. Scritti scelti*. SAGEP.

Bitossi, C. (1990). *Il Governo dei Magnifici. Patriziato e Politica a Genova fra Cinque e Seicento*. ECIG.

Braudel, F. (1984). *Civilization and Capitalism, 15th–18th Century*, vol. III, *The perspective of the world* (S. Reynolds, Trans.). William Collins & Sons. (Original work published 1979).

Burnette, J. (2008). *Gender, Work and Wages in Industrial Revolution Britain*. Cambridge University Press.

Carlos, A., Maguire, K., & Neal, L. (2006). Financial Acumen, Women Speculators, and the Royal African Company During the South Sea Bubble. *Accounting History Review, 16*(2), 219–243.

Carlos, A., & Neal, L. (2004). Women Investors in Early Capital Markets 1720–1725. *Financial History Review, 11*, 197–224.

Carlos, P. (2020). Le pari des Lumières. Loterie royale et projets de pouvoir du XVIIIe siècle. In L. Brunori, S. Dauchy, O. Descamps, & X. Prévost (Eds.), *Le Droit face à l'économie sans travail*, vol. II, *L'approche international* (pp. 223–238). Garnier.

Clark, P. (2000). *British Clubs and Societies 1580–1800: The Origins of an Associational World*. Cambridge University Press.

Craig, B. (2017). *Female Enterprise Behind the Discursive Veil in Nineteenth Century Northern France*. Palgrave Macmillan.

Doria, G. (1986). Investimenti della nobiltà genovese nell'edilizia di prestigio (1530–1630). *Studi Storici, 27*(1), 5–55.

Doria, G. (1995). *Nobiltà e investimenti a Genova in età moderna*. Istituto di Storia Economica.

Duby G., & Perrot, M. (2005). *Storia delle donne in Occidente*, vol. II, *Il Medioevo*. Laterza.
Dupaty, C. (1788). *Lettres sur l'Italie en 1785*, vol. I. s.e.
Felloni, G. (1971). *Gli investimenti finanziari genovesi in Europa tra il Seicento e la Restaurazione*. Giuffré.
Felloni, G. (1998). Il Ceto Dirigente a Genova nel Secolo XVII: Governanti o Uomini d'Affari? *Atti della Società Ligure di Storia Patria, 38*, 1323–1340.
Fontaine, L., & Borrello, B. (2011). Il posto delle donne nella piccola economia finanziaria in Europa, in età moderna. *Quaderni Storici, 46*(137), 513–532.
Froide, A. M. (2017). *Silent Partners: Women as Public Investors during Britain's Financial Revolution, 1690–1750*. Oxford University Press.
Gold, C. (2018). *Women in Business in Early Modern Copenhagen 1740–1835*. Museum Tusculanum Press.
Grendi, E. (1994). Ripensare la microstoria? *Quaderni Storici, 29*(86), 539–549.
Grendi, E. (Ed.). (1975). *Inventione di Giulio Pallavicino di scriver tutte le cose accadute alli tempi suoi (1584–1589)*. SAGEP.
Guglielmotti, P. (Ed.). (2020). *Donne, famiglie e patrimoni a Genova e in Liguria nei secoli XII e XIII*. Società Ligure di Storia Patria.
Guglielmotti, P., & Petti Balbi, G. (Eds.). (2012). *Dare credito alle donne. Presenze femminili nell'economia tra medioevo ed età moderna*. Cassa di Risparmio di Asti.
Ingrassia, C. (2005). *Authorship, Commerce, and Gender in Early Eighteenth-Century England: A Culture of Paper Credit*. Cambridge University Press.
Kay, A. C. (2009). *The Foundations of Female Entrepreneurship: Enterprise, Home and Household in London c.1800–1870*. Routledge.
Kuiper, E. (2022). *A Herstory of Economics*. Polity Press.
Kümin, B. (2007). *Drinking Matters: Public Houses and Social Exchange in Early Modern Central Europe*. Palgrave Macmillan.
Laurence, A., Maltby, J., & Rutterford, J. (Eds.). (2009). *Women and Their Money 1700–1950: Essays on Women and Finance*. Routledge.
Lévy-Ullmann, H. (1896). Lottery Bonds in France and in the Principal Countries of Europe. *Harvard Law Review, 9*(6), 386–405.
Lukowski, J. (2003). *The European Nobility in the Eighteenth Century*. Palgrave Macmillan.
Mitchell, L. E. (Ed.). (2011). *Women in Medieval Western European Culture*. Routledge.
Moring, B., & Wall, R. (2017). *Widows in European Economy and Society, 1600–1920*. Boydell Press.
n.a. (1613). *Degli Statuti Civili della Serenissima Repubblica di Genova*. Giuseppe Pavoni. (Original work published 1589).
Nolfi, V. (1646). *Ginipedia, ovvero avvertimenti civili per donna nobile*. Gio. Pietro Pinelli. (Original work published 1631).
Petti Balbi, G. (1979). *L'insegnamento nella Liguria medievale. Scuole, maestri, libri*. Tilgher.
Petti Balbi, G. (2009). *Genova medievale vista dai contemporanei*. Compagnia dei Librai.
Phillips, N. (2006). *Women in Business 1700–1850*. Boydell Press.
Quattrone, P. (2004). Accounting for God: Accounting and Accountability Practices in the Society of Jesus (Italy, XVI–XVII Centuries). *Accounting, Organizations and Society, 29*, 647–684.
Rabuzzi, D. (1995). Women as Merchants in Eighteenth Century Northern Germany: The Case of Stralsund, 1750–1830. *Central European History, 28*, 435–456.
Rostek, J. (2021). *Women's Economic Thought in the Romantic Age: Toward a Transdisciplinary Herstory of Economic Thought*. Routledge.
Rutterford, J., & Maltby, J. (2006). "The Widow, the Clergyman and the Reckless": Women Investors in England 1830–1914. *Feminist Economics, 12*, 111–138.
Saginati, L. (2004). *L'Archivio dei Doria di Montaldeo. Registri contabili, manoscritti genealogici e pergamene*. Centro di Studi e Documentazione di Storia Economica «Archivio Doria».
Scott Baker, N. (2021). *In Fortune's Theater: Financial Risk and the Future in Renaissance Italy*. Cambridge University Press.

Ulianova, G. (2009). *Female Entrepreneurs in 19th Century Russia.* Pickering & Chatto.
Van den Heuvel, D. (2007). *Women Entrepreneurship: Female Traders in the Northern Netherlands 1580–1815.* Aksant.
Vickery, A. (1998). *The Gentleman's Daughter*. Yale University Press.
Victorian Era. *Britannica.* https://www.britannica.com/event/Victorian-era#ref1274694
Weir, D. R. (1989). Tontines, Public Finance, and Revolution in France and England, 1688–1789. *Journal of Economic History, 49*(1), 95–124.

Women and Business: Fresh Evidence from the Probate Records of Milan (1862–1900)

Stefania Licini

> *I strongly advise my son, when married, neither to involve directly his wife in his business nor to allow her to assume a partnership in the firm. Women's natural inclination and disposition are absolutely inappropriate to commercial activities and my son has to find at home only restful tranquillity, not further business concerns. He must consider the family and the firm as two separate spheres and then he will be able to do well in his life.* Edoardo Haas, Last will, 1888 (ASM-RS, *ad nomen*)

The advice given by the prominent silk entrepreneur Edoardo Haas to his son does not come as a surprise to scholars interested in women's role and position in the nineteenth century. Societal expectations placed on women at the time confined them within the boundaries of domesticity. They were expected to fulfil roles as wise, patient wives, besides loving mothers, while keeping themselves away from the public domain of politics, economics, and business (Mitchell & Sanson, 2013; Musiani, 2016). These prescriptions have long been considered descriptions by historians, as recently emphasized in the literature (Baijot & Le Chapelain, 2022), primarily due to the scarcity of sources that provide insights into women's real lives and activities in the past (Aston & Bishop, 2020b; Spence, 2018). Middle/high-class women in particular have been overlooked (Khan, 2015). As no, or few, female names appear in coeval official documents such as trade directories, registers of public representatives, or rolls of professions, it has been assumed that rules and norms were generally accepted and respected, reinforcing the perception that entrepreneurship and business were exclusively male domains. However, by exploring alternative sources and re-examining existing ones, a different picture begins to emerge.

The analysis of subscribers' lists of consols, stocks, and bonds, along with the examination of mortgage, insurance, and bankruptcy accounts, as well as fiscal

S. Licini (✉)
Università degli studi di Bergamo, Bergamo, Italy
e-mail: stefania.licini@unibg.it

M. Mosca (ed.), *Women at Work in Italy (1750–1950)*, Springer Studies in the History of Economic Thought, https://doi.org/10.1007/978-3-031-64281-4_3

rolls and documents, has provided scholars with valuable insights into the extensive involvement of women in various economic activities. These sources have revealed numerous instances of women who financed companies and the state, owned shops and craftworks, provided loans, subscribed to partnership shares, and, in some cases, even managed large enterprises.[1] While France and the English-speaking countries have received considerable attention in the existing literature,[2] there remains a significant gap in comprehensive research on the economic role of women within the Mediterranean area, particularly in Italy.[3] This chapter aims to address this gap by examining the assets and the economic behaviour of a specific group of 25 affluent women who were residents in Milan and passed away between 1862 and 1900.

These ladies have been identified by utilizing an archive source that has proven to be particularly suitable for shedding light on women's economic roles and positions in the past: the acts of successions or declarations after death, and probate records in English-speaking countries.[4] All the female estates probated in Milan during the second half of the nineteenth century have been considered (ARSM-DB), and bourgeois women owning at least one million lire have been selected (Table 1). According to the literature, the sum of one million lire was a significant watershed in the echelon of wealth (Cardoza, 1995; Rubinstein, 1981, 1980, 2011). Moreover, only bourgeois women have been taken into account, scholars having ascertained that landed, aristocratic fortunes were much less likely to be divested to pursue other financial employments (Bengtsson, 2018; Rothery, 2007).

The first part of this work is dedicated to the critical examination of the source, with a comparative perspective in mind. The legal context with particular attention to the family and property regime is outlined as well. The section also provides detailed

---

[1] See, for example, Allen and Truman (2016), Antheaume and Paulette (2012), Aston (2012, 2016), Aston and Bishop (2020a), Barker (2006), Baskerville (1999), Beachy (2001), Beachy et al. (2006), Cleary (1995), Colvin (2012), Craig (2001a, 2001b, 2015, 2020a, 2020b), Doe (2010), Erickson (2022), Freeman et al. (2006), Green (2011, 2000), Green and Owens (2003), Guy (1997), Haggerty (2010), Heinonen and Vainio-Korhonen (2018), Henry (2018), Henry and Schmitt (2008), Honeyman (1996, 2007), Khan (2016), Laurence (2006), Laurence et al. (2009), Igersheim and Le Chapelain (2022), Leanne (2006), Newton and Cotrell (2006), Petterson (2006), Rabuzzi (2001), J. Rutterford (2006, 2021), J. Rutterford et al. (2011), Rutterford and Maltby, (2007), Van Remoortel (2017), Wiskin (2006), and Yeager (1999).

[2] Such as Aston (2016), Aston and Bishop (2020a), Baskerville (1999), Beachy et al. (2006), Bishop (2020), Craig (2015, 2020a, 2020b), Davidoff and Hall (1987), Gordon and Nair (2000), Green (2011), Honeyman (2007), Hunt (1996), Inwood (2004), Khan (1996), Laurence et al. (2009); Lemire et al. (2001), Moring and Wall (2017); Morris (2005), Newton and Cotrell (2006), Petterson (2006), Rutterford (2021), Rutterford et al. (2011), Rutterford and Maltby (2007), Sharpe (2001), Shepard (2015), Spicksley (2007), Vickery (1993), Wilson (2013), Wiskin (2006), Yeager (1999), and Yohn (2016).

[3] See Castagnoli (2007), Castelluci (2005), Curli (2002, 2005), Licini (2011, 2020a), Martinez-Rodriguez (2019, 2021), Minoglou (2007), Picciaia (2017), Rinaldi and Tagliazucchi (2019), and Rubio-Mondejar and Garrues-Irurzun (2022).

[4] For example, Baskerville (2008), Davidoff and Hall (1987), Erickson (2022), Escobar (2017), Green (2011), Green et al. (2011), Inwood and Van Sligtenhorst (2004), Lane (2000), Laurence et al. (2009), Licini (2011, 2020a), Morris (2005), Nazer and Llorca-Jaña (2020), Pompermaier (2022), Rutterford (2006), and Wyse (2006).

Table 1 Bourgeois female millionaires probated in Milan, 1862–1900

Date of death	Civil status	Surname	Name	Estate	Ancestors	Sector
06/03/80	Widow	Angiolini	Carolina	3,350,683.99	Landowners	Agriculture
17/06/74	Married	Antonelli	Adele	1,331,653.99	Entrepreneurs	Textiles
26/10/79	Widow	Berra	Teresa	1,918,127.34	Entrepreneurs	Cotton
20/05/69	Widow	Besana	Teresa	1,059,523.70	Entrepreneurs	Silk
05/06/80	Spinster	Brambilla	Giovannina	1,550,484.64	entrepreneurs	textiles
05/08/89	Widow	Carones	Anna Maria	1,355,117.76	Entrepreneurs	various Trade
11/12/94	Widow	Crivelli	Emilia	1,090,456.32	Entrepreneurs	Buildings
25/01/00	Married	Ebers	Emilia	1,574,176.32	Entrepreneurs	Bank
27/10/93	Widow	Erba	Carolina	1,701,302.39	Entrepreneurs	Liquor
08/06/89	Married	Gambarini	Rosa	2,640,120.64	Landowners	Agriculture
28/06/94	Widow	Levi	Clementina	1,492,820.51	Entrepreneurs	Bank
07/03/97	Spinster	Manzoni	Teresa	1,437,559.08	Entrepreneurs	Trade
14/12/74	Widow	Mennet	Sofia	1,386,631.83	Entrepreneurs	Silk
19/06/82	Widow	Pollastri	Enrichetta	1,473,453.64	Entrepreneurs	Bank
09/08/80	Spinster	Ponti	Angelica	2,488,957.86	Entrepreneurs	Cotton
04/12/91	Widow	Rossari	Rachele	3,848,082.50	Entrepreneurs	Trade
09/03/91	Married	Rovelli	Giuseppina	1,487,224.97	Entrepreneurs	Buildings
02/01/94	Widow	Sala	Rosa	1,695,868.57	Landowners	Agriculture
10/02/82	Married	Taccioli	Margerita	1,790,916.43	Entrepreneurs	Silk
18/07/99	Widow	Turati	Giuseppina	2,412,994.95	Entrepreneurs	Cotton

(continued)

Table 1 (continued)

Date of death	Civil status	Surname	Name	Estate	Ancestors	Sector
22/11/94	Widow	Valle	Maria	1,697,402.93	Landowners	Agriculture
20/03/88	Widow	Vigoni	Teresa	1,970,722.74	Landowners	Agriculture
16/10/78	Widow	Vonwiller	Elisa	2,119,258.05	Entrepreneurs	Silk
06/08/95	Widow	Vonwiller	Sofia	1,005,873.28	Entrepreneurs	Silk
21/01/97	Married	Weill Schott	Sofia	1,538,766.30	Entrepreneurs	Bank

Sources Author's elaboration based on Archivio di stato di Milano, Ufficio del registro successioni—Data base (ARSM-DB); Archivio di stato di Milano, Ufficio del registro successioni, Successioni milionarie-Database (ARSM-MIL-DB); Archivio di stato di Milano, Registro Successioni (ASM-RS), *ad nomen;* Archivio storico Camera di commercio di Milano, Registro Ditte (ASCM-RD, *ad nomen*

insights into the research methodology employed. Then, the study capitalizes on the inherent characteristic as "serial source" of the act of successions (Chaunu, 1970; Daumard, 1958). By leveraging the availability of records associated with individuals from the same family or kinship, the estate of nine millionaire bourgeois women is meticulously scrutinized to determine whether their inheritance remained unchanged or they personally acquired additional assets. Subsequently, an overall glance at the composition of the fortunes held by all the 25 rich women is provided, thus assessing their contribution to local and national financial and economic activities. Further details from the succession papers provide insights into their investment choices and reveal how they engaged in the world of business. Concluding remarks follow.

1 Source, Methodology, and Data

In the aftermath of the Unification of Italy, which occurred in 1861, on 21 April 1862 a Registry law, following the French example, was enacted. Under this law, a Registrar's tax was imposed on every deed relating to property transfer. In the case of *mortis causa* transmission, successors, executors, or administrators were required to submit a complete inventory list of the assets included in the succession along with an estimate of their value, to the Registrar's office nearest to the deceased's last residence (Ministero, 1862). Property had to be categorized into real property (land and buildings), credits (loans), equities and securities (stocks, bonds, government securities, partnerships, personal and family business), interest arrears, furniture and clothing, jewellery and cash. Although documents, such as last wills, prenuptial agreements, cadastral certificates, stock listings, or other papers useful for proving the declaration were legally required to be enclosed, they were not always included. Moreover, it is important to note that the rate of tax evasion and avoidance in Italy was high, ranging between 30 and 80 per cent (Gini, 1914; Nitti, 1904). In anglophone countries scholars consider the gross valuation entered in the probate records absolutely reliable (Green & Owens, 1997; Piketty & Zucman, 2015), while avoidance and undervaluation need to be accounted for when analysing the Italian documentation.

Personal property, especially cash, bills, bearer bonds and securities, besides "credits", were entries more likely to be omitted and underestimated (Licini, 2011, 2020a). Yet, according to available data, movables accounted for nearly half of women's overall property. Unsecured loans to friend, family member, and other individuals constituted 53 per cent of female financial assets (Licini, 2009, 2011, 2020a). Thus, it can be assumed that there were many more rich women in reality than those captured by the fiscal records and that their fortunes were higher than declared. Although perfectly aware of this limitation of the source, this study takes the sum of 1 million lire as benchmark to distinguish between wealthy and very wealthy individuals, and it specifically focuses on all the bourgeois female millionaires whose declaration was recorded in Milan in the period 1862–1900. They were a total of 25 women, with 20 belonging to entrepreneurial dynasties and 5 to great landowning families (Table 1), engaged also in silkworm growing and trade. This study does not consider very rich noblewomen (22) who are known to own mostly, if not exclusively, large estates located in the fertile plain of Lombardy (Licini, 2006, 2020a, 2021), whose mobilization was difficult and likely not even advantageous. Given the cultural and legal constraints in force in Italy at that time, which allowed women to become rich only through gifts or inheritance, and considering that female investment behaviour is the main interest of this study, it has been deemed more appropriate to focus solely on bourgeois millionaires. In fact, when a fortune included both real and personal property, by custom, following the ancient and deeply rooted dowry tradition, daughters were left cash, stocks, bonds, securities, and loans, while sons were bequeathed land and business that they would be appointed to manage in the family's name (Macry, 1988; Palazzi, 2002).

As succession records provide information about civil status and genealogy of the deceased, besides the list of all the individuals who received inheritance or bequests, it has been possible to identify the male relatives of each female millionaire and search for their names through trade and industrial directories, fiscal rolls, coeval yearbooks, registers of exhibitors, and members of various associations as well.[5] The investigation reveals that among the 25 fortunes held by millionaire women, 7 had been accumulated by ancestors or other relatives in the decades preceding the Restoration (1815), 16 during the first half of the nineteenth century, and 3 in the years immediately following the Unification of Italy (Licini, 2021). These data confirm the profitability of agriculture and silk trade in the era prior to the Napoleonic wars, as

[5] Such as Almanacco (1811–1821, 1836), Canetta (1888), Interprete (1823–26, 1827–28), Metrà (1793), Ministero (1873), Sabbatini (1893), Guida (1824–89), and Vitali (1880).

well as the opportunities for profit in private banking, silk and cotton manufacturing, textiles and colonial goods trade between the Vienna Congress and the 1848 Milan insurrection. Moreover, the findings highlight the relevance of non-traditional and overlooked sectors, such as the liquor industry and building constructions, in the first decades following the foundation of the new Kingdom in Italy (Della Peruta, 1987; Hunecke, 1982). The overall picture provided by linking the millionaire women's estates to the activity of the men from whom they inherited, points out that banking and commerce were still dominant sectors, while agriculture showed signs of gradual decline (Table 1). On the other hand, the manufacturing sector grew, particularly driven by the prominence of "king cotton", and the building speculation connected with the urban expansion of the time likely opened the doors to new, profitable entrepreneurial experiences (Table 1).

Before delving into the composition of women's wealth and inferring their investment behaviour, it is important to focus on the pattern of inheritance that channelled the whole or a portion of the family fortune into their hands. Such an analysis also provides insights into the succession strategies of the bourgeois milieu of Milan and offers the opportunity to highlight both the legal and cultural constraints of the time.

Nearly half (12) of the bourgeois millionaires inherited their wealth from their fathers, while 3 received it from their uncles, 2 from their brothers, 2 from their predeceased sons, and 6 from their husbands (Table 2). These data can be fully understood by considering the forced heir regime that existed in Italy, whereby only 50 per cent of the fortune was at the disposal of the testator. Under the so-called *legittima*, which was the legally mandated share of the estate, children had the first right of inheritance, regardless of age or sex, and parents were in the second line. The spouse had only the right to a share of usufruct on the estate (Codice, 1865). Therefore, demographic circumstances played a crucial role. Out of the 12 women who inherited from their fathers, 5 were only children and the family fortune necessarily had to pass to them (Table 2). For the 2 women who had brothers and the 3 who had both brothers and sisters, it is likely that the inheritance amount was substantial enough to secure a large fortune for the daughters as well. It is widely acknowledged that in nineteenth-century Milan, wealthy parents typically favoured male offspring in their wills, which was true for both mothers and fathers with very few exceptions (Licini, 2020a). Despite this prevailing custom, some women acquired significant inherited fortunes, and this is precisely the case of the 25 bourgeois millionaires who died in Milan between 1862 and 1900.

They left to their heirs a total of over 45 million lire (Table 1). The average value of the estates was close to 2 million lire (1,816,727.229), with a median value of 1,574,176.32 lire. More than one third (37%) of the overall wealth belonged to 6 women whose fortunes exceeded 2 million lire (Table 1). The data first confirm the high level of wealth concentration that characterized many industrializing towns in the nineteenth century (Atkinson, 2006; Atkinson & Bourguignon, 2000; Piketty et al., 2006), including Milan (Licini, 2020a). Secondly, they highlight the significance of female fortunes. Holding more than one million at the time, not only signified great affluence, but also provided the opportunity to play a substantial role in the local economic development. It is worth noticing that the largest company based in Milan

Table 2 Bourgeois millionaire female fortunes: patterns of inheritance, by family situation

Inheritance from	Total	Only child	Only brothers	Only sisters	Mixed siblings	n.a.
Father	12	5	2		3	2
Other ancestors	3	2		1		
Brother(s)	2	1			1	
Son(s)	2					
Husband	6					

Sources Author's elaboration based on Archivio di stato di Milano, Ufficio del registro successioni, Successioni milionarie-Database (ARSM-MIL-DB); Archivio di stato di Milano, Registro Successioni, *ad nomen*

at the time, the Linificio e canapificio nazionale (linen and hemp manufacturing), had a social capital of 3 million lire (Licini, 1994). Additionally, according to the information revealed by the succession papers, well-established individual businesses in silk and cotton manufacturing were valued at a few hundred thousand lire, and even famous private banks operated with assets ranging from 500,000 to 1 million lire (Licini, 2020a).

Succession papers provide a snapshot of individuals' estate at the time of their death. They are documents not intended to trace the previous management of wealth: nevertheless, some insights into the topic can be gained by thoroughly analysing them. In fact, like all other fiscal papers, they have the inherent characteristic of "seriality", as they are regularly generated and available throughout the duration of administrative obligations. This means that by knowing the personal information, surnames, and kinship relations of deceased persons, one can search for records registered under their name as well as their relatives' names. In the case of Milan, the research undertaken identified 9 women who inherited from one or more millionaires who had their estates probated between 1862 and 1900 (ARSM-DB; ARSM-MIL-DB). By comparing the assets these women received through inheritance with the assets they left behind, it is possible to gain insights into their investment behaviour. Therefore, the following section assesses in detail the findings of this comparison.

2 Inheritance and Investments

Unsurprisingly, the analysis shows a very nuanced and scattered picture. While 4 women bequeathed nearly the same assets they had received to their heirs, and 3 likely made minor changes, the remaining 2 individuals unequivocally operated in a more dynamic way. The first group included Sofia Weil Schott, who belonged to a well-known Jewish dynasty of bankers that was still in activity at the time. Sofia had inherited the joint ownership of a share of the limited partnership F.lli Weill Schott which was founded in 1850 by her father and uncle and run by her brothers up to 1898 (ASM-RS, *ad nomen*; ASCM-RD, *ad nomen*) (Maifreda, 2000). In order to ensure the continuity of the business, the assets in Sofia's name had to be made available to the firm. It was common for many entrepreneurs' successions to involve the bequest of undivided property to all the children. Such an arrangement aimed to safeguard the legal rights of the daughters and ensure the survival of the enterprise, in male hands (Licini, 2020a). Of the remaining 3 "inactive" heiresses, one, Teresa Manzoni, died less than one month after her brother, who, lacking other relatives, had named her as his universal heir (ASM-RS, *ad nomen*). Among the other two, one woman, Emilia Crivelli, as the only child, inherited the entire fortune of her father, a retired building entrepreneur (ASM-RS, *ad nomen*). The other woman, Margherita Taccioli, shared the estate left by their father and their uncle with her sister (ASM-RS, *ad nomen*). Both the father and uncle were previously involved in silk manufacturing and trade and decided to close the activity as they had no (male) heirs (Levati, 1992). Whether these heiresses were satisfied with the rents provided by their estate or chose not to engage in more profitable yet riskier activities is difficult to ascertain. The analysis of their papers indicates that they just preserved and maintained their inherited wealth without significant alterations and do not provide further information. However, inaction does not seem to have been the predominant behaviour among bourgeois female millionaires.

For example, comparing Maria Valle's succession act with the papers associated with her predeceased son, Carlo Bonomi, it becomes evident that she possessed a certain amount of financial acumen. At the time of her death, her estate amounted to 1.7 million lire, representing an increase from the 1 million lire inheritance she received from Carlo (ASM-RS, *ad nomen*; ARSM-MIL-DB). In his last will, Carlo not only acknowledged his mother's affluent background, but also recognized her aptitude for handling her wealth (ASM-RS, *ad nomen*). Clementina Levi and Enrichetta Pollastri can be classified, as well, as part of the group of millionaires who made slight modifications to the size and structure of their inherited fortune. They were both childless widows and heirs to Jewish bankers. In the case of Clementina Levi, her husband David Leon Levi stipulated in his will that she should preserve and maintain the bequest to be eventually transferred to his nephews. As a result, she likely sold some of her own personal financial assets to invest 100,000 lire in shares of Richard & C., a newly established and innovative ceramics manufacturer operating as a joint stock company (ASM-RS, *ad nomen)*. Enrichetta Pollastri, who was a successful but poor dancer, received all what she possessed from her husband, Sebastiano Mondolfo, a well-known and very affluent private banker (ASM-RS, *ad nomen*; ASCM-RD, *ad nomen*). Without any limitations prescribed by her husband, their papers reveal that she chose to divest from government securities and invest in purchasing buildings in Milan (ASM-RS, *ad nomen*), which presented a highly attractive earnings opportunity at the time.

In the first decades after the Unification, Milan witnessed a rapid urban development. The town centre underwent a complete redesign and renovation, and the construction of the first central railway station took place (1864), which was interconnected with all the existing lines. Numerous residential blocks were erected in the increasingly populated suburbs. This period of extensive building construction was accompanied by financial speculation. Alongside the Società Fondiaria Italiana, the first property development company established in Milan by Banco di Credito Italiano in 1881, many private investors engaged in the risky yet profitable activity of buying and selling land and buildings (Rossari, 2016; Tiepolo, 1987). Besides Enrichetta Pollastri, for instance, another woman among the 9 whose papers are now under our scrutiny engaged in real estate operations. She was Giuseppina Turati, daughter and heiress of a very rich cotton industrialist (Conca Messina 2020; Romano 1992).

Giuseppina's father, Francesco Turati, died in 1873 leaving behind more than 7 million lire to his four heirs: two sons and two daughters (ASM-RS, *ad nomen*). The sons, Ernesto and Ercole, were named universal heirs, while the daughters, Giuseppina and Erminia, were entitled to the *legittima*, likely amounting to around 700,000 lire each. Both the succession papers of Giuseppina and Ercole, who died respectively in 1899 and 1881, are available, providing an opportunity for a cross-comparison of their assets, as well as their father's. First and foremost, it is noteworthy that Giuseppina's estate appears to have experienced a much more significant increase compared to Ercole's. Moreover, the assets that Ercole owned at the time of his death were nearly the same as what he had received from his father, whereas Giuseppina's reveal significant differences in their composition (ASM-RS, *ad nomen*).

Considering the detailed items listed in Francesco and Giuseppina's acts of succession, as well as the annotations made by the Registrar's officers, it becomes evident that Giuseppina's investment behaviour was more dynamic. She probably divested a portion of the securities portfolio she received from her father to acquire a significant block of property in the rapidly expanding area of Milan in 1885. Additionally, she purchased a prestigious ancient mansion in the town centre in 1881 and entrusted the renowned architect Bagatti Valsecchi with its renovation. The total valuation of her urban properties at the time of her death amounted to nearly 1 million lire, none of which had been inherited. Moreover, she autonomously invested 225,000 lire in a company that manufactured silk waste. This sector of activity may have been linked to her husband's business, but the commitment was made in her own name with her own money (ASM-RS, *ad nomen*). In contrast, her brother appears to have simply preserved untouched the stocks, bonds, partnership shares, and the family firm that he had inherited (ASM-RS, *ad nomen*). While Giuseppina actively engaged in stock trading and building speculation, her brother did not demonstrate the same level of involvement in investment activities. These findings not only challenge the assumption that women of that era were uninterested in economic affairs, but also contradict the hypothesis of their presumed risk aversion (Maltby & Rutterford, 2006). In this regard, further evidence is provided by the examination of Carolina Erba's papers, the last woman among the nine whose relatives were probated in the period 1862–1900.

Carolina was the widow of Bernardino Branca, the founder of the very well-known Fratelli Branca distillery, even then famous for the production of the globally known herbal liqueur Fernet Branca (Sabbatini, 1893) (Fig. 1). Carolina died in 1893 after outliving all her three sons Luigi, Giuseppe, and Stefano. The succession documents for each of her sons are available for examination (ASM-RS, *ad nomen*; ARSM-MIL-DB). Luigi Branca, who died in 1886, had already withdrawn from the family business a few months before his death. Since he died intestate, his fortune was inherited by his daughter. Giuseppe, who had no children, passed away in 1888 and in his last will he named his wife Giulia Villa as his universal heir. However, according to the law, Carolina inherited one third of his assets, including a portion of the family business. At that time, the value of the distillery was assessed at 4 million lire, which belonged entirely to Giuseppe (ASM-RS, *ad nomen*). After Giuseppe's death, Carolina, along with her daughter-in-law, assumed control of the firm (ASCM-RD, *ad nomen*). She made the decision to donate a portion of her ownership stake in the company to her other son, Stefano, and also provided him with significant loans (ASM-RS, *ad nomen*). It is worth noting that Stefano did not own any shares of the company, but he had patented the Fernet Branca liquor in his own name. As a result, an agreement was signed allowing the firm to produce the liquor and use the well-known trademark, with Stefano receiving a share of the profits in return (ASM-RS, *ad nomen*). In 1891 Stefano died leaving behind three minor children: Carolina, Dolores and Bernardino (ASM-RS, *ad nomen*). As the only male heir in the Branca dynasty, Bernardino was appointed by his grandmother Carolina Erba as the entrepreneurial successor. In her last will, the latter not only forgave all of his son's significant debts, but also advised Stefano's wife to purchase the company shares from the other legitimate heirs (ASM-RS, *ad nomen*). This strategic move ensured the seamless transition to the third generation, securing the future of the family business under the leadership of Bernardino.

Besides sustaining, managing, and financing the firm established by her husband, Carolina Erba demonstrated astute financial acumen by diversifying the company's large revenues she received. She invested a portion of the funds in secure government securities but also engaged in profitable real estate speculation. Furthermore, she lent money to her sister for the purchase of shares in the aforementioned Società Fondiaria Milanese (ASM-RS, *ad nomen*).

Although Carolina's active involvement in the business world and her proactive management of resources would in itself be sufficient to confirm the repeated blurring of boundaries between the private and public domains, widely underlined in the literature, further evidence is provided by examining the succession papers recorded under the name of the remaining (16) bourgeois millionaire women.

3 Wealth Composition and Female Agency

In addition to listing and valuing each asset, Italian registrar's officers sometimes included annotations in the succession papers. For instance, they specified the date of purchase of land and buildings when necessary for tax purposes, as the "market value" that was used for assessing the fiscal charge. Moreover, they often recorded the identity of the borrower in the case of loans. As a result, it is sometimes possible to move beyond a purely quantitative approach and delve into the investment choices made by the deceased individuals. Before discussing the possible additional insights provided by the source, however, an overall glance at female fortunes is required to fully grasp the significance of individual instances.

Fig. 1 Fernet Branca advertising poster 1904

By entering the value of each item listed in the succession documents into a database and grouping them according to the categories provided by the registrar's office, a comprehensive picture of the composition of the wealth of very rich bourgeois women can be drawn (Table 3). First, it emerges that personal property constituted more than half of the bourgeois female estates (57%), with government securities having the lion share (20%). The data, on one hand, confirm the widespread custom of bequeathing safe public certificates to daughters in order both to grant them a safe return and to secure their inheritance rights. On the other hand, they highlight the opportunity for women of the middle class to possess highly liquid assets that can be readily invested elsewhere.

Secondly, the overview of the estates belonging to millionaire bourgeois women points out the importance of landowning (21%) (Table 3). Unsurprisingly, women from landed dynasties had a larger share of land compared to women from entrepreneurial dynasties, both in terms of their individual fortunes and when considering the total amount of land included in the probated estates (Table 4). Conversely, heiresses from entrepreneurial backgrounds held a larger portion of financial assets. They owned 93% of public certificates, 95% of stocks, 85% of bonds, and 100% of

Table 3 Bourgeois millionaire female fortunes: composition

Land	9,328,228.07	21%
Buildings	7,801,549.08	17%
Family Business	4,086,160.24	9%
Limited partnerships	252,700.00	1%
Stocks	2,274,062.25	5%
Bonds	2,595,096.73	6%
Government securities	9,023,213.83	20%
Personal loans	2,146,416.68	5%
Mortgage loans	3,362,536.63	7%
Other loans	1,889,249.38	4%
Bank deposits	374,028.96	1%
Rent and interest arrears	313,734.33	1%
Cash, jewellery, furniture	1,467,571.50	3%
Not specified	503,633.05	1%
Total	45,418,180.73	100%

Sources Author's elaboration based on Archivio di stato di Milano, Ufficio del registro successioni, Successioni milionarie-Database (ARSM-MIL-DB); Archivio di stato di Milano, Registro Successioni (ASM-RS), *ad nomen*; Archivio storico della Camera di commercio di Milano, Registro Ditte (ASCM-RD), *ad nomen*

partnership shares (Table 5). Moreover, they possessed a capital of 4 million in what is labelled in Table 3 as "family business". It is important to clarify that the administrative officials rarely classified a business as a specific unit, and in only a few cases did they assess a trade or manufacturing activity as a whole. Therefore, all the items connected with the firm, such as industrial buildings, equipment, land dedicated to silkworm breeding, commercial loans, stocks, and raw materials, in addition to shares of partnerships held under the names of relatives, have been grouped together, and their value has been included in the category of "family business".

Besides Carolina Erba and Sofia Weill Schott, three other women had a direct significant financial interest in the family firm. Elisa Vonwiller, the daughter of a

Table 4 Bourgeois female millionaires: landownership (%)

Women belonging to	Share of land on the estate (%)	Share of total land (%)	Share of total probated estates (%)
Landed family	39	39	21
Entrepreneurial family	16	61	79

Sources Author's elaboration on Archivio di stato di Milano, Ufficio del registro successioni, Successioni milionarie-Database (ARSM-MIL-DB); Archivio di stato di Milano, Registro Successioni (ASM-RS), *ad nomen*; Archivio storico della Camera di commercio di Milano, Registro Ditte (ASCM-RD), *ad nomen*

Table 5 Bourgeois female millionaires: financial assets (%)

Women belonging to	Share of government securities (%)	Share of bonds (%)	Share of stocks (%)	Share of partnership (%)	Share of family business (%)	Share of total probated estates (%)
Landed family	8	12	5	0	0	21
Entrepreneurial family	93	85	95	100	100	79
Total	100	100	100	100	100	100

Sources Author's elaboration based on Archivio di stato di Milano, Ufficio del registro successioni, Successioni milionarie-Database (ARSM-MIL-DB); Archivio di stato di Milano, Registro Successioni (ASM-RS), *ad nomen*; Archivio storico della Camera di commercio di Milano, Registro Ditte (ASCM-RD), *ad nomen*

prominent Austrian businessman, not only had a share of 200,000 lire in the silk manufacturing and trade partnership company under her son's name Scheibler and C., but also purchased land allotments in the silkworm area valued at nearly 150.000 lire (ASM-RS, *ad nomen*). These lands were probably used to provide raw materials for the enterprise. Elisa's sister, Sofia Vonwiller, had a bank deposit with her brother's firm in Wien worth almost one million lire, and Sofia Mennet provided a loan of the same value to her son Herich Mylius to set up a private bank in Genova (ASM-RS, *ad nomen*). If it were not for the availability of the succession papers, such a level of female involvement in the economic arena would have remained completely unknown. Similarly, scholars would never have imagined the substantial sum of money women provided through private lending. As Spicksley pointed out "inventories and probate documents remain the best source of evidence for credit provision, even if they tend to underplay the amount of credit extended" (Spicksley, 2007, p. 189).

Whether secured by mortgage, a simple IOU, or without any guarantees, bourgeois female millionaires in Milan lent a total of more than 7 million lire (Table 3). Female lending activity was particularly valuable at the time, due to the relative backwardness of the local banking system. During the Restoration period, Lombardy, being on the periphery of the Austrian empire, did not have a branch of the Austrian Central Bank established in Milan, despite the town's vibrant commercial activity, mostly focused on exports. Following the Italian Unification, Milan finally received a local branch of the National Bank, but the main offices of the new Italian corporate banks modelled after the French Credit Mobilier, namely Credito Italiano (1863) and Banca Generale (1872), were located in Turin and Rome, respectively. In 1871, a commercial joint stock bank, Banca Lombarda di Depositi e Conti Correnti, was established in Milan, which strengthened the banking structure that had until then relied solely on the ancient Savings Bank, Cassa di Risparmio delle Provincie Lombarde (1823), and the "new" Cooperative Bank, Banca Popolare (1866). However, it was not until the end of the nineteenth century, with the establishment of Banca Commerciale Italiana in

1894, that Milan and the surrounding region acquired a modern and effective credit organization (Cafaro, 1990; Polsi, 1993).

In such a context, money provision was predominantly carried out by individual lenders, and women played a significant role in this regard. This is further supported by another fiscal source known as the *ricchezza mobile*, a tax imposed on "capital revenues" (Frascani, 1988). According to the rolls available, on provincial basis, for the year 1873 (Ministero, 1873), in Milan, women accounted for 37% of the taxpayers and owned 33% of the overall declared income, totalling 1,752,744.77 lire. With an interest rate of approximately 5%, women's yearly return amounted to 1.7 million lire. This indicates that they lent out approximately 35 million lire in 1872 alone (Licini, 2007, 2020b). Comparatively, the agricultural branch of the Milanese Savings Bank (Cassa di Risparmio delle Provincie Lombarde) had a chargeable income of 439,467.50 lire, and the private/merchant bankers listed in the roll declared an overall revenue of 23,392.80 lire (Ministero, 1873). While these figures highlight that also in Milan, women "were frequent participants" in the local capital market (Khan,, 2016, p. 19), further evidence from the succession papers provides insight into the specific directions of this substantial flow of money. As a coeval economist observed, the analysis of a loan must consider first of all the use the borrower makes of it (Allievi, 1857).

Keeping in mind that in the 7 million lire classified in Table 3 as "loans" the capital directly invested in "family business" is not included and classifying all the "credits" recorded by the Registrar's officers according to their recipient, it emerges that nearly one third (2,146,416.68) of the sum lent by bourgeois female millionaires went into the hands of relatives, mostly for personal purposes, such as credit on undivided inheritance or advance on dowry. Once confirmed that rich women were the "rescue agency" for the family network (Davidoff & Hall, 1987, p. 274), it is worth underlining that they also were professional lenders, as testified by the substantial sum (3,362,536.63) they gave against mortgage (Table 3). This was a very widespread, safe, and profitable investment at the time, with the revenue assessed at around 5 per cent. Often daughters were left a loan portfolio by their fathers, and sometimes women autonomously decided to participate in the financial market as providers of liquidity for aristocrats, landowners, professionals, and businessmen as well. This was the case, for example, of Carolina Angiolini, who hailed from a landed dynasty and was the widow of the well-known painter and art collector Pietro Bagatti Valsecchi. She granted credits against mortgage for more than 1 million lire and held a prominent position on the tax roll of *ricchezza mobile*. With an annual revenue of 44,750 lire, she ranked fifth among taxpayers, preceded only by the land credit branch of the Cassa di Risparmio, two joint stock companies (Società anonima strada ferrata Vigevano Milano, Società del pubblico macello), and the wealthy cotton manufacturer Francesco Turati (Table 6).

Three other bourgeois female millionaires also featured among the top twenty taxpayers. These included the aforementioned Sofia Vonwiller and Sofia Mennet, with annual revenues of 35,525 and 23,622 lire, respectively (Table 6). Additionally, there was Adele Antonelli, the sole daughter and heiress of a prosperous tradesman (Table 6). The first two primarily lent money to their families, whereas Adele

Table 6 Taxpayers *Ricchezza Mobile*-A: yearly revenue > 20.000 lire, Milan 1872

Company/Surname	Name	Yearly revenue
Istituto di Credito Fondiario		439,467.50
Società anonima Strada Ferrata Vigevano Milano		120,000.00
Società del pubblico macello		80,045.00
Turati	Francesco	56,040.00
Angiolini	Carolina	44,750.55
Robecchi	Pietro	40,591.02
Vonviller	Sofia	35,525.00
Ponti	Gio. Battista	33,458.57
Antonelli	Adele	32,393.75
Besana	Angela e Giovannina	29,035.00
Mylius	Hermann	27,300.00
Pezzoli	Innocente	26,667.34
Brioschi	Francesco	25,951.54
Fumagalli	Saverio	25,500.00
Borromeo Arese	Giberto	24,110.00
Mennet	Sofia	23,622.26
Trotti	Lodovico	21,432.83

Source Author's elaboration based on Ministero (1873). *Ministero, della Finanze. Direzione generale delle imposte dirette. Elenco dei contribuenti all'imposta sulla ricchezza mobile aventi un reddito imponibile complessivo superiore alle 1000 lire, desunti dai ruoli principali del 1872, Vol. 1*. Firenze: Stamperia reale

Antonelli's borrowers were mostly prominent members of the aristocracy (ASM-RS, *ad nomen*). She died at a young age, so it is likely that the loan portfolio she left behind was exactly the same as the one she had inherited. In contrast, Carolina Angiolini appears to have independently decided where and to whom to direct the substantial liquidity she possessed. While her list of mortgagors also includes a couple of noblemen, nearly half her extensive loan portfolio (1.6 million lire) consisted of building contractors (ASM-RS, *ad nomen*). What is noteworthy is that lending to entrepreneurs involved in the renewal constructions of the time was not her only way of participating in the speculative business of the era. In fact, she also purchased, restructured, and sold a number of blocks in the town's expansion, likely generating uncertain but substantial profits. The significant proceeds from such a risky activity were partially reinvested in the building sector, while another portion was allocated to government securities, bonds, and additional private loans (ASM-RS, *ad nomen*). In summary, Carolina Angiolini, both ventured herself into very profitable activity and wisely diversified her investments: she acted as a true financier, a "capitalist", and made a substantial contribution to the economic development of the time. However, despite her significant achievements, her name is primarily known for being the wife of Pietro Bagatti Valsecchi and the mother of Fausto and Giuseppe Bagatti Valsecchi, the two brothers famous for promoting and directing building works in the Italian Renaissance style and collecting art masterpieces. These artworks are now exhibited in the museum named after them in Milan.

Not all the bourgeois millionaire women were so proactive as Carolina Angiolini or as deeply involved in their family firms as Carolina Erba. Some rich women simply lived off their inherited fortunes, while others independently managed only a small portion of their inheritances. Unsurprisingly, widows seem to have exhibited a more dynamic behaviour, perhaps due to the fact that they were not required to seek their husband's marital authorization to engage in market activities, such as buying and selling land and buildings, lending money, or investing in shares and securities. Regardless of their civil status and level of involvement, the analysis of their wealth composition reveals that all of these women played a significant role in financing the local manufacturing sector and supporting the public expenditures of the newly established Kingdom.

4 Concluding Remarks

The analysis of the succession papers under the name of 25 bourgeois millionaires registered in Milan in the period 1862–1900 have added a fresh perspective of the female role in society in the nineteenth century. In Milan, as in Paris, in London, and in many other cities in Europe, the hidden nature of women's economic activity has been, at least partially, unveiled. Some rich heiresses were semi-professional lenders, others consistently participated in risky building speculation and in the foundation of family business as well, even managing the difficult entrepreneurial succession process.

Women in Italy, until the end of the nineteenth century, were prevented by law from accessing high school and university. They were subjected to the marital authorization regime and confined to the private, domestic domain by a common consent etiquette. Conduct books, traditional costumes and social attitudes, possibly boosted, as in Spain, by the Catholic religion, emphasized marriage and motherhood. Middle-class girls attending female schools were primarily taught to excel as perfect housewives. Moreover, they were discouraged from showing any interest in money or economic affairs, as discussions about dowries, for example, were handled by their fathers in negotiations with prospective husbands without their knowledge. The only public role they were allowed was participation in the governance and activities of charitable organizations (Licini, 2011). However, as this study has demonstrated, not all women conformed to these restrictions and some managed to engage in business ventures, achieving notable success and greatly contributing to the local and national economic development.

It is impossible to determine what would have happened and how much faster the industrialization process, along with economic growth, would have advanced if more women had been involved in finance and business. What is evident is that, notwithstanding the many legal and cultural devices preventing them, moneyed women occasionally managed to participate in the market economy. Their activities, however, often went unnoticed. Due to their forced seclusion from public eyes, official and traditional sources tend to overlook their contributions. Yet, it is not simply "a matter of records" (Simonton, 2018, p. 4). As Craig pointed out, business and economic historians have long embraced the male concept of the Schumpeterian entrepreneur, while also assuming a clear separation between the private and public spheres and treating "prescriptions" as "descriptions" (Craig, 2015; Vickery, 1993). Consequently, they did not actively seek archive papers that could shed light on female involvement in the economic arena. Although scholars have begun to address this issue in recent years, there is still much progress to be made. This study, based on succession papers registered in Milan in the second half of the nineteenth century, is expected to contribute to the ongoing exploration of women's economic roles in the past.

Archive Sources and Data Base

Archivio di stato di Milano, Ufficio del registro successioni (ASM-RS), *ad nomen*

Archivio di stato di Milano, Ufficio del registro successioni—Data base (ARSM-DB) https://www.researchgate.net/publication/371470693_ARSM_DBzip

Archivio di stato di Milano, Ufficio del registro successioni, Successioni milionarie-Database (ARSM-MIL-DB) https://www.researchgate.net/publication/371470761_successioni_milionariepdf

Archivio storico della Camera di commercio di Milano, Registro Ditte (ASCM-RD), *ad nomen.*

Bibliography

Allen, S., & Truman, C. (2016). *Women in Business: Perspectives on Women Entrepreneurs.* Routledge.

Allievi, A. (1857). *La Cassa di risparmio di Lombardia*: Fondazione Cassa di risparmio delle provincie lombarde.

Almanacco. (1811–1821). Almanacco e Guida di Milano. Per l'anno 1811, 1812, 1813, 1814, 1815, 1816, 1817, 1818,1819, 1820, 1821. In. Milano: Sonzogno.

Almanacco. (1836). Almanacco del commercio di Milano. Guida per l'anno bisestile 1836. In. Milano: Placido Maria Visaj.

Antheaume, N., & Paulette, R. (2012). From Wife to Widow Entrepreneur in French Family Businesses An Invisible-Visible Role in Passing on the Business to the Next Generation. hal-00694367v2. https://hal.science/hal-00694367v2

Aston, J. (2012). *Female Business Owners in England, 1849–1901.* University of Birmingham.

Aston, J. (2016). *Female Entrepreneurship in Nineteenth-Century England: Engagement in the Urban Economy.* Palgrave Macmillan.

Aston, J., & Bishop, C. (2020a). *Female Entrepreneurs in the Long Nineteenth Century: A Global Perspective.* Springer.

Aston, J., & Bishop, C. (Eds.). (2020b). *Female Entrepreneurs in the Long Nineteenth Century: A Global Perspective.* Springer.

Atkinson, A. B. (2006). *Concentration Among the Rich* (Unu wider Research Paper No. 2006/151).

Atkinson, A. B., & Bourguignon, F. (Eds.). (2000). *Handbook of Income Distribution* (Vol. 1). Elsevier.

Baijot, S., & Le Chapelain, C. (2022). Reassessing Women's Participation in Entrepreneurial Activities in the Nineteenth Century: A Review of the Literature. *Œconomia. History, Methodology, Philosophy* (12–3), 405–442.

Barker, H. (2006). *The Business of Women: Female Enterprise and Urban Development in Northern England, 1760–1830.* Oxford University Press.

Baskerville, P. (1999). Women and Investment in Late-Nineteenth-Century Urban Canada: Victoria and Hamilton, 1880–1901. *Canadian Historical Review, 80*(2), 191–218.

Baskerville, P. (2008). *A Silent Revolution? Gender and Wealth in English Canada, 1860–1930 375 p.* McGill-Queen's University Press.

Beachy, R. (2001). Business Was a Family Affair: Women of Commerce in Central Europe, 1650–1880. *Histoire Sociale-Social History, 34*(68), 307–330.

Beachy, R., Craig, B., & Owens, A. (Eds.). (2006). *Women, Business and Finance in XIXth-Century Europe.* Berg.

Bengtsson, E., Missiaia, A., Olsson, M., & Svensson, P. (2018). Aristocratic Wealth and Inequality in a Changing Society: Sweden, 1750–1900. *Scandinavian Journal of History.* https://doi.org/10.1080/03468755.2018.1480538

Bishop, C. (2020). On Their Own in a 'Man's World': Widows in Business in Colonial Australia and New Zealand. In *Female Entrepreneurs in the Long Nineteenth Century* (pp. 169–193). Springer.

Cafaro, P. (1990). Finanziamento e ruolo della banca. In S. Zaninelli (Ed.), *Dall'unità politica alla Grande guerra* (Vol. II). Il Polifilo.

Canetta, P. (1888). *Cenni sull'ospedale maggiore di Milano e sulla beneficenza con notizie storico-biografiche sui suoi maggiori benefattori.* Cogliati.

Cardoza, A. (1995). La ricchezza e i ricchi a Torino, 1862–1912. *Società e storia, 68*, 297–340.

Castagnoli, A. (2007). The Female Entrepreneur's Point of View and the Italian Economy. *Business and Economic History Online, 5*, 1–17. Business History Conference, 2007. All rights reserved. http://www.thebhc.org/publications/BEHonline/2007/castagnoli.pdf

Castelluci, L. (2005). L'imprenditorialità feminile in Umbria nel '900. Uno studio sui censimenti tra sviluppo eocnomico e rappresentazione statistica. 1911–1981. In B. Curli (Ed.), *Donne imprenditrici nella storia dell'Umbria. Ipotesi e percorsi di ricerca* (p. 50). Franco Angeli.

Chaunu, P. (1970). L'histoire sérielle. Bilan et perspectives. *Revue historique, 243*(Fasc. 2)(494), 297–320.

Cleary, P. (1995). She-Will-Be-in-the-Shop, Womens Sphere of Trade in 18th-Century Philadelphia and New-York. *Pennsylvania Magazine of History and Biography, 119*(3), 181–202.

Codice. (1865). *Codice civile del Regno d'Italia.* Firenze.

Colvin, C. L. (2012). Men, Women, and Money: Perspectives on Gender, Wealth, and Investment 1850–1930. *Business History, 54*(4), 642–643. https://doi.org/10.1080/00076791.2011.637707

Conca Messina, S. A. (2020). Turati, Francesco Antonio. In *Dizionario Biografico degli Italiani* (Vol. 97). Treccani.

Craig, B. (2001a). Patrons mauvais genre: femmes et entreprises à Tourcoing au XIXe siècle. *Histoire sociale/Social History.*

Craig, B. (2001b). Women and Business in Eighteenth-Century Northwestern Europe—Introduction, Is Business Women's Business? *Histoire Sociale-Social History, 34*(68), 277–281.

Craig, B. (2015). *Women and Business Since 1500: Invisible Presences in Europe and North America?* Palgrave Macmillan.

Craig, B. (2020a). A Constant Presence: The Businesswomen of Paris, 1810–1880. In *Female Entrepreneurs in the Long Nineteenth Century* (pp. 113–136). Springer.

Craig, B. (2020b). Lending Women, Borrowing Women: Middle-Class Women, Investments and Credit in Northern France in the Nineteenth Century. In *Women and Credit* (pp. 51–69). Routledge.

Curli, B. (2002). Women Entrepreneurs and Italian Industrialization, Conjectures and Avenues for Research. *Enterprise and Society, 3*, 634–650.

Curli, B. (Ed.). (2005). *Donne imprenditrici nella storia dell'Umbria. Ipotesi e percorsi di ricerca.* Franco Angeli.

Daumard, A. (1958). Sur l'histoire sociale du XIX e siècle: Paris et les archives de l'Enregistrement. *Annales. Histoire, Sciences Sociales, 13*(2), 289–303.

Davidoff, L., & Hall, C. (1987). *Family Fortunes: Men and Women of the English Middle Class, 1780–1850.* London.

Della Peruta, F. (1987). *Milano. Lavoro e fabbrica, 1814–1915.* Franco Angeli.

Doe, H. (2010). Waiting for Her Ship to Come In? The Female Investor in Nineteenth-Century Sailing Vessels. *Economic History Review, 63*(1), 85–106.

Erickson, A. L. (2022). Wealthy Businesswomen, Marriage and Succession in Eighteenth-Century London. *Business History*, 1–30.

Escobar Andrae, B. (2017). Women in Business in Late Nineteenth-Century Chile: Class, Marital Status, and Economic Autonomy. *Feminist Economics, 23*(2), 33–67.

Frascani, P. (1988). *Finanza, economia ed intervento pubblico dall'unificazione agli anni Trenta.* Guerini.

Freeman Mark, P. R., & James, T. (2006). A Doe in the City": Women Shareholders in Eighteenth- and Early Nineteenth-Century Britain. *Accounting Business Financial History, 16*(2), 265–291.

Gini, C. (1914). *L'ammontare e la composizione della ricchezza delle nazioni.* F.lli Bocca.

Gordon, E., & Nair, G. (2000). The Economic Role of Middle-Class Women in Victorian Glasgow. *Womens History Review, 9*(4), 791–814.

Green, D. R., Owens, A., Maltby, J., & Rutterford, J. (Eds.). (2011). *Men, Women, and Money: Perspectives on Gender, Wealth, and Investment, 1850-1930.* Oxford University Press.

Green, D. R. (2000). Indipendent Women, Wealth and Wills in Nineteenth-Century London. In J. Stobart & A. Owens (Eds.), *Urban Fortunes: Property and Inheritance in the Town, 1700–1900.* Ashgate.

Green, D. R., & Owens, A. (2003). Gentlewomanly Capitalism? Spinsters, Widows, and Wealth Holding in England and Wales, c 1800–1860. *Economic History Review, 56*(3), 510–527.

Green, D. R., Owens, A., Swan, C., & van Lieshout, C. (2011). Assets of the Dead: Wealth, Investment, and Modernity in Nineteenth and Early Twentieth-Century England and Wales. *Men, Women, and Money: Perspectives on Gender, Wealth, and Investment, 1850–1930*, 54–80.

Green, D. R., & Owens, A. (1997). Metropolitan Estates of the Middle-Class, 1800–50: Probates and Death Duties Revisited. *Historical Research, 70*(173), 294–311.

Guida. (1824–89). *Utile giornale, ossia Guida di Milano per l'anno 1824...1889.* Milano: Giovanni Bernardoni poi Giuseppe Bernardoni di Giovanni poi Tip. Bernardoni di C. Rebeschini e C. Milano, Giovanni Bernardoni poi Giuseppe Bernardoni di Giovanni poi Tip. Bernardoni di C.

Guy, K. M. (1997). Drowning Her Sorrows: Widowhood and Entrepreneurship in the Champagne Industry. *Business and Economic History*, 505–514.

Haggerty, S. (2010). Enterprising Women and Shipping in the Nineteenth Century. *Business History, 52*(2), 342–343. https://doi.org/10.1080/00076791003612275

Heinonen, J., & Vainio-Korhonen, K. (2018). *Women in Business Families: From Past to Present.* Routledge.

Heinonen, J., & Vainio-Korhonen, K. (Eds.). (2018). *Women in Business Families: From Past to Present.* Taylor & Francis.

Henry, N. (2018). Women Investors in Fact. In N. Henry (Ed.), *Women, Literature and Finance in Victorian Britain: Cultures of Investment* (pp. 29–51). Springer International Publishing.

Henry, N., & Schmitt, C. (2008). *Victorian Investments: New Perspectives on Finance and Culture.* Indiana University Press.

Honeyman, K. (1996). The First Industrial Woman. *Business History, 38*(3), 131–131.

Honeyman, K. (2007). Doing Business with Gender: Service Industries and British Business History. *Business History Review, 81*(3), 471–493.

Hunecke, V. (1982). *Classe operaia e rivoluzione industriale a Milano, 1859–1892.* Il Mulino.

Hunt, M. R. (1996). *The Middling Sort: Commerce, Gender and the Family in England, 1680–1870.* University press of California.

Igersheim, H., & Le Chapelain, C. (2022). Women Leaders in Industry in Nineteenth-Century France: The Case of Amélie de Dietrich. *Business History*, 1–24. https://doi.org/10.1080/00076791.2022.2098951

Interprete. (1823–26). *L'interprete milanese ossia Guida per l'anno...1823–1826.* Visaj Placido Maria.

Interprete. (1827–28). *L'interprete milanese o sia Guida generale del commercio e dei recapiti di Milano per l'anno 1827, 1828.* Visaj Placido Maria

Inwood, K. (2004). Introduction: Women, Property and Legal change. *Continuity and Change, 19*(1), 9–11.

Inwood, K., & Van Sligtenhorst, S. (2004). The Social Consequences of Legal Reform: Women and Property in a Canadian Community. *Continuity and Change, 19*, 165–197.

Khan, B. (2016). Invisible Women: Entrepreneurship, Innovation, and Family Firms in Nineteenth-Century France. *The Journal of Economic History, 76*(1), 163–195. https://doi.org/10.1017/S0022050716000449

Khan, B. Z. (1996). Married Women's Property Laws and Female Commercial. *The Journal of Economic History, 56*(2), 356–388.

Khan, B. Z. (2015). *Invisible Women: Entrepreneurship, Innovation and Family Firms in France During Early Industrialization* (NBER Working Paper 20854). http://www.nber.org/papers/w20854

Lane, P. (2000). Women, Property and Inheritance: Wealth Creation and Income Generation in Small English Towns, 1750–1835. In J. Stobart & A. Owens (Eds.), *Urban Fortunes: Property and Inheritance in the Town, 1700–1900.* Ashgate.

Laurence, A. (2006). Women Investors, "That Nasty South Sea Affair" and the Rage to Speculate in Early Eighteenth Century England. *Accounting Business Financial History, 16*(2), 245–264.

Laurence, A., Maltby, J., & Rutterford, J. (Eds.). (2009). *Women and Their Money, 1700–1950: Essays on Women and Finance.* Routledge.

Leanne, J. (2006). The First Female Shareholders of the Bank of New South Wales: Examination of Shareholdings in Australia's First Bank, 1817–24. *Accounting Business Financial History, 16*(2), 293–314.

Lemire, B., Pearson, R., & Campbell, G. (2001). *Women and Credit: Researching the Past, Refiguring the Future.* Berg.

Levati, S. (1992). *Da "tencin" a banchieri. I Taccioli: l'ascesa economica e sociale di una famiglia di negozianti tra Ghiffa e Milano.* Intra.

Licini, S. (1994). Finanza e industria a Milano nel triennio 1870–73: azionisti e nuove imprese. *Rivista di storia economica, 11*(2), 213–252.

Licini, S. (2006). Women's Wealth in the 19th Century Italy: Some Evidences from the Probate Records of Milan (Italy, 1862–1900). *Women's History Magazine* (53/), 13–21.

Licini, S. (2007). Donne e affari, a Milano nell'800. *Annali di storia dell'impresA* (18), 53–73.

Licini, S. (2009). Women's Wealth and Finance in Nineteenth-Century Milan. In Laurence, A., Maltby, J., & Rutterford, J. (Eds.), *Women and Their Money, 1700–1950: Essays on Women and Finance.* Routledge.

Licini, S. (2011). Assessing Female Wealth in Nineteenth Century Milan, Italy. *Accounting History, 16*(1), 35–54.

Licini, S. (2020a). *Ricchi e ricchezza a Milano nell'Ottocento.* Tabed.

Licini, S. (2020b). Women, Business, and Finance in 19th Century Milan. *Journal of Modern Accounting and Auditing, 16*(3), 117–129.

Licini, S. (2021). Sketching the Very Wealthy: Men and Women of Property (1861–1900). In *Leading the Economic Risorgimento* (pp. 242–258). Routledge.

Macry, P. (1988). *Ottocento. Famiglia, élites e patrimoni a Napoli.* Einaudi.

Maifreda, G. (2000). *Gli ebrei e l'economia milanese: l'Ottocento* (Vol. 261). Franco Angeli.

Maltby, J., & Rutterford, J. (2006). 'She Possessed Her Own Fortune': Women Investors from the Late Nineteenth Century to the Early Twentieth Century. *Business History, 48*(2), 220–253.

Martinez-Rodriguez, S. (2021). Female Shareholders of Private Spanish Banks (1920–1948): A First Approach. *Quaderni storici, 56*(1), 37–60.

Martínez-Rodríguez, S. (2019). Mistresses of Company Capital: Female Partners in Multi-Owner Firms, Spain (1886–1936). *Business History*, 1–22. https://doi.org/10.1080/00076791.2018.1551364

Metrà, A. (1793). *Il mentore perfetto de negozianti, ovvero guida sicura de' medesimi, ed istruzione, per rendere ad essi più agevoli, e meno incerte le loro speculazioni.* Stamperia di G.T. Hoechenberger.

Ministero. (1873). *Ministero, della Finanze. Direzione generale delle imposte dirette. Elenco dei contribuenti all'imposta sulla ricchezza mobile aventi un reddito imponibile complessivo superiore alle 1000 lire, desunti dai ruoli principali del 1872, Vol. 1.* Stamperia reale.

Ministero. (1862). *Ministero, della Finanze.* Legge delle tasse di registro, n. 585 del 21 aprile 1862.

Minoglou, I. P. (2007). Women and Family Capitalism in Greece, c. 17801940. *Business History Review, 81*(3), 517–538.

Mitchell, K., & Sanson, H. (2013). *Women and Gender in Post-Unification Italy.* Peter Lang AG.

Moring, B., & Wall, R. (2017). *Widows in European Economy and Society, 1600–1920* (NED—New ed.). Boydell & Brewer.

Morris, R. J. (2005). *Men, Women and Property in England, 1780–1870.* Cambridge University Press.

Musiani, E. (2016). "La giovane nella famiglia. Consigli di una vecchia nonna"-Women's Writings and Writings for Women in Nineteenth-Century Italy. *Women and Gender in Italy (1500–1900)/ Donne e gender in Italia (1500–1900)*, 185–203.

Nazer, J. R., & Llorca-Jaña, M. (2020). Succession in Large Nineteenth-Century Chilean Family Businesses. *Business History*, 1–26. https://doi.org/10.1080/00076791.2020.1717471

Newton, L., & Cotrell, P. L. (2006). Female Investors in the First English and Welsh Commercial Joint-Stock Banks. *Accounting Business Financial History, 16*(2), 315–340.

Nitti, F. S. (1904). *La ricchezza dell'Italia.* Societa Cooperativa Tipografica.

Palazzi, M. (2002). Economic Autonomy and Male Authority: Female Merchants in Modern Italy. *Journal of Modern Italian Studies, 7*(1), 17–36.

Petterson, T. (2006). The Silent Partners: Women, Capital and the Development of the Financial System in 19th Century Sweden. In R. Beachy, B. Craig, & A. Owens (Eds.), *Women, Business and Finance in XIXth-Century Europe* (pp. 34–50). Berg.

Picciaia, F. (2017). "In Spite of Everything?" Female Entrepreneurship from a Historical Perspective: The Italian Businesswoman Luisa Spagnoli (1877–1935). *Journal of Management History, 23.* https://doi.org/10.1108/JMH-02-2017-0004

Piketty, T., Postel Vinay, G., & Rosenthal, J.-L. (2006). Wealth Concentration in a Developing Economy: Paris and France, 1807–1994. *American Economic Review, 96*(1), 236–256.

Piketty, T., & Zucman, G. (2015). Wealth and Inheritance in the Long Run. In A. Atkinson & T. Pikkety (Eds.), *Handbook of Income Distribution* (Vol. 2, pp. 1303–1368). Elsevier.

Polsi, A. (1993). *Alle origini del capitalismo italiano.* Il Mulino.

Pompermaier, M. (2022). Women and Wealth in Sweden: The Case of Uppsala, 1850–1910. *Scandinavian Economic History Review*, 1–18.

Rabuzzi, D. (2001). Fading Images, Fading Realities? Female Merchants in Scandinavia and the Baltic. *Histoire Sociale—Social History, 34*(68), 355–370.

Rinaldi, A., & Tagliazucchi, G. (2019). Women entrepreneurs in Italy: A prosopographic study. *Business History*, 1–23. https://doi.org/10.1080/00076791.2019.1642325

Romano, R. (1992). *L' industria cotoniera lombarda dall'unità al 1914.* Banca Commerciale Italiana.

Rossari, A. (2016). Milano che si costruisce: i piani regolatorI. *Istituto Lombardo-Accademia di Scienze e Lettere-Incontri di Studio.*

Rothery, M. (2007). The Wealth of the English Landed Gentry, 1870–1935. *Agricoltural History Review, 55*(2), 251–268.
Rubinstein, W. D. (1981). *Men of Property: The Very Wealthy in Britain Since the Industrial Revolution.* Taylor & Francis.
Rubinstein, W. D. (2011). The Wealth Structure of Britain in 1809–39, 1860–1, and 1906. In D. Green, A. Owens, J. Matby, & J. Rtterford (Eds.), *Men, Women and Money* (pp. 31–52). Oxford University Press.
Rubinstein, W. D. (Ed.). (1980). *Wealth and the Wealthy in the Modern World.* St. Martin's Press.
Rubio-Mondejar, J. A., & Garrues-Irurzun, J. (2022). Women Entrepreneurs and Family Networks in Andalusia (Spain) During the Second Industrial Revolution. *Business History*, 1–22.
Rutterford, J. (2021). The Forgotten Investors: Women Investors in England and Wales 1870 to 1935. *Quaderni Storici, 56*(1), 13–35.
Rutterford, J., Green, D. R., Maltby, J., & Owens, A. (2011). Who Comprised the Nation of Shareholders? Gender and Investment in Great Britain c. 1870–1935. *Economic History Review, 64*(1), 157–187.
Rutterford, J., & Maltby, J. (2007). The Nesting Instinct: Women and Investment Risk in a Historical Context. *Accounting History, 12*, 305–327.
Rutterford, J. M. J. (2006). She Posessed Her Own Fortune: Women Investors from the Nineteenth Century to the Early Twentieth Century. *Business History.*
Sabbatini, L. (1893). *Notizie sulle condizioni industriali della provincia di Milano.* U. Hoepli.
Sanson, H., & Lucioli, F. (Eds.). (2016). *Conduct Literature for and about Women in Italy, 1470–1900: Prescribing and Describing Life.* Classiques Garnier Paris.
Sharpe, P. (2001). Gender in the Economy: Female Merchants and Family Businesses in the British Isles, 1600–1850. *Histoire Sociale/Social History, 34*(68), 287–306.
Shepard, A. (2015). Minding Their Own Business: Married Women and Credit in Early Eighteenth-Century London. *Transactions of the Royal Historical Society, 25*, 53–74.
Simonton, D. (2018). 'All the Days of Their Lives': Women, Business, and Family. In *Women in Business Families* (pp. 111–133). Routledge.
Spence, C. R. (2018). Merchant Trade: A Family Affair. In *Women in Business Families* (pp. 67–81). Routledge.
Spicksley, J. M. (2007). 'Fly with a Duck in thy Mouth': Single Women as Sources of Credit in Seventeenth-Century England. *Social History, 32*(2), 187–207. https://doi.org/10.1080/03071020701265809
Tiepolo, M. (1987). La proprietà immobiliare nel quartiere dell'ex Lazzaretto a Milano dal 1882 al 1892. *Storia Urbana, 39*, 163–184.
Van Remoortel, M. (2017). Women Editors and the Rise of the Illustrated Fashion Press in the Nineteenth Century. *Nineteenth-Century Contexts, 39*(4), 269–295.
Vickery, A. (1993). Golden-Age to Separate Spheres—A Review of the Categories and Chronology of English Womens History. *Historical Journal, 36*(2), 383–414.
Vitali, l. (1880). *La beneficenza in Milano. Notizie storiche, economiche e statistiche.* Pirola.
Wilson, D. (2013). *Women, Marriage and Property in Wealthy Landed Families in Ireland, 1750–1850.*
Wiskin, C. (2006). Businesswomen and Financial Management: Three Eighteenth-Century Case Studies. *Accounting Business Financial History, 16*(2), 143–161.
Wyse, S. (2006). *Gender, Wealth and Margins of Empire: Urban New Zeland Women and Theri Investments, c.1890–1950.* Paper Presented at the 6th European Social Sciences History Conference, Amsterdam.
Yeager, M. A. (Ed.). (1999). *Women in Business.* Edward Elgar.
Yohn, S. M. (2016). Crippled Capitalists: The Inscription of Economic Dependence and the Challenge of Female Entrepreneurship in Nineteenth-Century America. *Feminist Economics, 12*(1–2), 85–109.

Female Entrepreneurs and Economic Development in Capri (1900–1960). A Case Study: *La Parisienne*

Rossella Del Prete

1 Introduction

Studying female entrepreneurship requires a multi-disciplinary approach that, starting from studies of business and work history, considers the transformation of markets, technologies, products and job markets. The investigative approach towards entrepreneurial and productive realities promoted and managed by women started recently, and it is still too timid and sporadic. The figure of the entrepreneur has come down to us as that of an isolated economic animal, brilliant and inventive according to the Schumpeterian view, but also traditionally a "masculine" figure, modelled on the opposition between the affective and relationship sphere and the economic and rational sphere (Franchi, 1994, p. 134).[1]

Today it has been redefined by situating its economic action in social and interpersonal networks, institutional frameworks and cultural and value systems, which, in addition to the market, help explain the historical evolution of business types and territorial performance, shaped in turn by historical forces (Colli & Rose, 1999, p. 27). Women would have much to tell in this perspective but, although they have always participated in business, they have remained absent from the dominant narratives of history. The most recent research and studies carried out in the field of business history on entrepreneurship, insisting on new elements of knowledge related to the importance of social culture, value systems, economic and institutional relations, technological and sociological changes, have shifted the focus from large managerial enterprises to a renewed prominence of small and medium-sized enterprises and so-called family firms (Amatori, 2011; Chandler, 1977; Colli & Rose, 2003) that represent a constant in the entrepreneurial affairs of southern Italy.

[1] Unless stated otherwise, the translations of quoted texts are our own.

R. Del Prete (✉)
Università degli Studi del Sannio, Benevento, Italy
e-mail: delprete@unisannio.it

M. Mosca (ed.), *Women at Work in Italy (1750–1950)*, Springer Studies in the History of Economic Thought, https://doi.org/10.1007/978-3-031-64281-4_4

To the recent interest in women's enterprises in Italy (Castagnoli, 2007; Curli, 2002) should be added the many valuable studies on women's work that have restored visibility to the decisive, active and productive role of women in the job market (Pescarolo, 2019). Slightly preceding the American historiography on the subject, business history began to analyse women's engagement in business only in the 1990s (Gamber, 1994; Kwolek-Folland, 1998). These works were then followed by some special issues on gender and business history in major journals.[2] However scarce, the existing literature has broken down the topic of female entrepreneurship into at least three points of interest: (1) Gender phenomenon, (2) Family claim and social motherhood, (3) Similarities and differences between male and female entrepreneurs.

Gender is a cultural construction through which men and women define their identities, understand their economic affairs, make decisions and allocate resources (Scott, 1998). As a result, deeply rooted notions about "women's work", as "appropriate" work for women, usually conceived as an extension of the traditional domestic role, have defined the supply, wages and type of work for women, granting them access to a few niche markets and, at the same time, "segregating" their entrepreneurial environment, limiting it to an exclusively female clientele, calibrating it to small-scale and labour-intensive forms of business organisation: food trade and domestic services, restaurant, catering, laundry, tailoring, clothing, luxury goods retail and lodging (Kwolek Folland, 1998).

The idea of the "family claim" sees the advent of capitalism in the Western world as coinciding with a dualistic gender system that, while granting women a status associated with the privacy of family life, granted men a status characterised by public involvement. Therefore, women's relationship with the family became an integral part of their economic role. It is enough to recall that in many countries the law excluded married women from business ownership and property rights for centuries, justifying their involvement in any business exclusively for family requirements (e.g. as widows or mothers) (Kwolek-Folland, 1998). The family business can thus become an opportunity for women to engage in typically male-dominated industries, such as metalworking or shipbuilding, or in non-traditional activities in which they introduce innovations, take risks and manage large enterprises (Berg, 1993). This is still the case today, and many women entrepreneurs see their businesses embedded in family relationships and responsibilities (Jennings & Brush, 2013).

The third point invites reflection on the different entrepreneurial styles of women and men. Working women, particularly female entrepreneurs, perhaps precisely because of the extension of their traditional domestic role, are inclined to pursue goals that often go far beyond financial gain. In this perspective, Holden (2010) introduced the concept of "social motherhood" in which women's traditional maternal role has been extended to philanthropic work in society as a whole. In this view, women entrepreneurs are expected to be maternal and thus inclined to an entrepreneurial style that educates the children of others, with a greater propensity for social engagement, promotion of education, philanthropy and respect for the environment. In contrast,

[2] Such as *Business History Review* (1998, 2007), *Enterprise & Society* (2001), and *Management & Organizational History* (2010).

Aston & Di Martino (2017) argued that women entrepreneurs not only operated in traditionally male sectors, but also did business similarly to their male counterparts in terms of business size, risk-taking and ultimately success. However, their conclusion is limited to the world of sole proprietorships and partnerships and does not extend to corporations, where the presence of women was probably much less frequent.

Similarities and differences between male and female entrepreneurship remain hotly debated topics in need of further investigation. This paper aims to contribute to the debate by focusing on an exemplary case of female entrepreneurship, from a particular area of southern Italy—Capri—, analysing the evolution and emancipation of a typical domestic occupation—that of the seamstress—into a creator of fashion and of commercial and tourist events in the international fashion industry.

2 Tailors, Milliners, Designers and Artists: The Origins of *Mare Moda Capri*

Capri is an internationally renowned Italian seaside tourist island in the Campania region, in the metropolitan city of Naples. The nineteenth century produced significant economic and social transformations in Capri, which moved from primary production to an exuberant tertiary economy. By the end of the nineteenth century, it was already a resort with a strong tourist vocation (Lembo, 1994). Before the spread of mass tourism, the island welcomed intellectuals, *flâneurs*, painters, sculptors, poets and revolutionaries fleeing from censorship all over Europe. The year 1906 was a particularly important year for the island's affirmation as an international *en plein air* laboratory of art, culture and politics, when a series of extraordinary personalities began to congregate on the island: from the Russian writer Maksim Gor'kij who landed there in November of that year and remained until 1913 with his court of painters, writers and revolutionaries, to the Bohemian-German poet Rainer Maria Rilke who, between 1906 and 1907, wrote beautiful poems during his island sojourn in the secluded annexe of Villa Discepoli along Via Tragara; from Baron Jacques Fersen, who had completed his famous Villa Lysis, to Norman Douglas who, in those years, was drafting and writing his masterpieces on the island (Esposito, 2009). These years, masterfully described by Compton Mackenzie in his novel *Vestal Fire* (1993), were characterised by the explosion of a Capri in which elegance, glamour and *joie de vivre* were accompanied by recklessness and intrigue. The astonishing peculiarity of those years, which would be repeated in the post-World War II period in different ways, was a sort of "island madness" that pervaded an island in which very different characters coexist (Esposito, 2009). In such a context, while holiday makers from the most diverse parts of the world enjoyed all the comforts and luxuries of the refined carriages that awaited them on their arrival, the inhabitants were forced to juggle a thousand difficulties in adapting to such a heterogeneous society. However, their standard of living grew greatly in the first decade of the twentieth century, also thanks to major foreign investments on the island.

In this social and geographical context, we describe profiles and cultures of some industrious and enterprising women who took on a fundamental role in late nineteenth century. Our research is centred on, but not limited to, the exemplary story of a female enterprise in the fashion industry which is now 117 years old and is in its third generation of women entrepreneurs. The sources and the data used in this study come mostly from the private archive of the tailoring boutique *La Parisienne*, partly from the Historical Archives of the Naples Chamber of Commerce and partly from the Documentation Centre of Capri.[3] The printed sources consist of the existing literature on female entrepreneurship and the specific literature on the history of Capri and fashion "Made in Italy". The descriptive approach of the paper is enriched by the results of the cluster analysis that helped us outline the main characteristics of the female entrepreneurship in the Campania region, and its differences from typically male entrepreneurship.

Looking at the trend in businesses, sole proprietorships and companies registered with the Chamber of Commerce of Naples between 1870 and 1929,[4] the situation was exactly the one described above: plenty of small or medium-sized businesses which mostly belonged to the sphere of handicrafts, retail or wholesale trade. The tourism and service sectors (restaurants, hoteliers, room rentals, theatrical enterprises, cinemas, transport, car rental, etc.) were equally present with a precise gender connotation of certain activities. The range of activities in which women were involved saw many of them engaged in the hotel sector, from the most modest room-rental activities to inn-keepers to hotel owners.[5] In the tourism sector there was still a significant percentage of women working in bathing establishments, restaurants, inns, car rental, bars and cafes. An equally significant number of female owners has been detected in the jewellery and goldsmiths' sectors, as well as in trinkets and fine arts. One of the most misused genres was certainly that of groceries: from pasta makers, bakers and confectioners, to brewers. Many were owners of purely buying and selling businesses, many others were producers and sellers. The long list of commercial, production or service activities named after women also includes several who owned pawnshops, typing or printing offices, agencies for representation and mediation, brothels, theatrical and film companies, piano and musical instrument tuning companies, some generically involved in the tourism sector and some who even registered with the Chamber of Commerce as "curator of her husband's property".[6]

Certainly, the highest percentage of female business owners is found in the textile and fashion industry. Tailors, milliners and embroiderers were distributed

[3] The gap for historical-economic research of this kind is the scarcity of documentary sources at our disposal: the culture of business archives is still too little rooted in the various economic institutions, both public and private, especially in southern Italy (Del Prete 2015).

[4] Historical archive, chamber of commerce of Naples, Economic registry, Registers of business reports and terminations, nn. 1–80, years 1870–1920.

[5] Ibidem. The percentage is significant: out of a total of 10,000 businesses surveyed so far in the province of Naples, the total number of hotel or accommodation businesses reported by women and men is over 3,000, half of which are owned by women.

[6] *Ibidem.*

in an intense production activity of tailoring for ladies: linens, ribbons, trimmings, furnishing fabrics and upholstery, hats (for women, men and children), hosiery, women's corsets and gowns, women's dresses, furs, boutiques and ateliers. In Capri, particularly, one of the productive sectors in which women's skills traditionally found great space was weaving, needlework and fashion, alongside services, including tourism. The knowledge of some cases of sartorial excellence, combined with the natural beauty and landscape of some famous seaside resorts and the social life that has characterised them since the beginning of the twentieth century, evokes the sartorial and stylistic skills of some haute couture boutiques that, even today, more than a century after their opening, are still resisting the market, while operating in the wake of tradition.

In Italy, especially in Capri, fashion and tourism have always been two complementary worlds. An example was *Mare Moda Capri*, a decade-long event, from 1967 to 1977, which jointly promoted fashion and tourism. The concept of *mare moda* (beach fashion) was based on a few key elements: luxury, elite tourism, prestigious resorts and five-star holidays. The clothing required had to be sporty, elegant, casual, but also very trendy and, above all, it had to fit in with leisure time. In this chapter we show that *Mare Moda Capri* has distant origins, rooted in a community of women who wove fabrics for household linen or made the robes of the monks residing in the *Certosa* of Capri since the Middle Ages.

To date, Italian business history has mainly provided us with biographies of businessmen who, by their "visibility", personified the company they headed. Here, we profile three of Capri's most enterprising women who, certainly favoured by a local context spontaneously oriented towards international tourism, during the course of the twentieth century demonstrated creativity, innovation and refined managerial skills in their tailoring boutiques: Maria Della Monica (called Mariuccia), Maria Chiara Gallotti (called Claretta) and Adriana Di Fiore.

3 Capri 1906: *Donna Mariuccia* Founds *La Parisienne*

The story of the resourcefulness of a very young seamstress began in a symbolic place of this fascinating international island: the *Piazzetta* of Capri.[7] Following an urban reorganisation of the entire area, in 1905 a funicular railway was built, and its first ride marked a real turning point, not only for the movement of the inhabitants themselves, but above all for the development of entrepreneurial and tourist activity on the island. That little train became a symbol of the island, with its panoramic cabins transporting everyday hundreds of tourists who, as soon as they disembarked at the small port of Capri, reached the *Piazzetta* in a few minutes.

It was in the *Piazzetta* that in 1906 an enterprising islander founded Capri's oldest and most famous boutique, *La Parisienne*, still operating today (Spinelli, 2010). At that time Italian fashion did not exist and anything new came from the *maisons*

[7] The original name of the square is Piazza Umberto I, but it is internationally known as *Piazzetta*.

of Paris. Maria Della Monica, known as Donna Mariuccia, was born in Capri in 1884. Her father, Vincenzo Della Monica, arrived in the island to repair the clock on the historic bell tower that still dominates the *Piazzetta* today. He fell in love with Maddalena Persico and decided to settle there, opening the island's only tobacco shop. Their daughter Mariuccia was an intelligent and proactive young woman, a skilled seamstress. On 20 October 1904 she married Michele Di Fiore, who opened an antique and handicraft shop in the *Piazzetta,* where he cultivated his passion for archaeological trouvaille. Before he married, Michele had travelled extensively on cruise ships, spoke perfect English and French, and soon made his shop a pleasant stop-off point for all those foreign dignitaries who resided on Capri at the time, who were happy to stop by and chat in their own language. In 1906 Michele, happy to encourage his wife Mariuccia in her passion for sewing, had her open a small tailor's shop (the first on the island) on the upper floor of his antique shop, called *Seterie a mano à la Parisienne.*[8]Donna Mariuccia, together with three or four seamstresses, at the age of 22 decided to try her hand at dressing the Russian aristocrats who, having fled the first Russian revolution, had formed a veritable colony on Capri. In time, following the echo of the extraordinary success of the Parisian fashion houses (Worth, Ducet, Lanvin and Chanel), that first tiny Capri atelier became synonymous with elegance and refinement. In the tailor's shop, they sewed and embroidered silk shirts, with lace and embroideries as the fashion of the time dictated. Mariuccia had all the fashion magazines and patterns flown in from Paris in order to better serve her excellent clientele. So it was that, a few years later, given the success of the tailor's shop, the Di Fiore couple decided to transform Michele's shop into a larger clothing, embroidery, silk, fabric and shawl shop dedicated to women. Mariuccia had always been fascinated by the elegance and fashion that came from Paris and probably, without even knowing it, was greatly influenced by the changes brought about by the birth of Parisian Haute Couture.[9] This is why her shop could only be called *La Parisienne.*

A woman of great commercial talent, creative and clever, she distinguished herself for her ability to organise the work of her atelier by delivering it to homes and coordinating a dozen seamstresses, taking care of a system of relations based on a trusting, cordial and often friendly relationship with her upper crust clientele. Won over by Mariuccia's charm, in the first decades of its life *La Parisienne* was frequented by the most famous jet-setters living on the island. In her atelier, Mariuccia received ladies with high-sounding names: from Maksim Gor'kij's companion, Marija Andrejeva, to the sought-after countess Ephy Lovatelli; from Faith Mackenzie, wife of the writer Compton, to Princess Helene Soldatenkov, who had fled revolutionary Russia. Poetess Ada Negri was also a customer of hers, who loved to browse and dress up in

---

[8] *La Parisienne* Private Archive.

[9] On the initiative of an Englishman, Charles Frederick Worth, a new organisational form of European fashion was born in Paris in the nineteenth century: until then, the tailor had been a mere material executor, who was required to have technical skills but no creativity. Worth's success was as *tailor* and dressmaker, overturning the relationship with the clientele, redeveloping the function of the tailor from an anonymous *tailleur* to a recognised couturier, *i.e.* a craftsman who put his creative genius at the service of feminine elegance (Gnoli, 2020).

that well of wonders where she breathed the smell of fabrics and work and from which she drew inspiration for her lyrics. Donna Mariuccia recounted that the Duchess of Camastra, lady-in-waiting to the Savoys, often lingered in the salon shop to chat and learn about the latest news from the island and that it was the Walcott-Perry ladies who had suggested that she name her newborn daughter Adriana: opera enthusiasts, they wanted her to celebrate the beautiful edition of their beloved *Adriana Lecouvreur*, at that time performed at the San Carlo Theatre in Naples.[10] The early decades of the twentieth century were the era of the great island residents. Lady Lennox planted immense gardens on Monte San Michele; American portrait painter Romaine Brooks lived at Villa Cercola; Swedish physician Axel Munthe built his home in Anacapri.[11] This is how a simple young woman with a marked talent for business, was able to transform a small and often home-based activity into a creative economic enterprise projected onto the international market. Donna Mariuccia became Capri's first milliner to represent what in the 1950s, as we shall see later, was to be consecrated in so-called "boutique fashion":

> *Boutiques* are those delightful workshops that are generally headed by just one person, who is, at the same time, the inventor of each creation; they have much lower overheads; they have, however, exclusive fabrics as they either make them themselves or have them made, in very limited quantities, by special textile houses'. (Foschini, 1953)

The early twentieth century was eventful and laborious for her, not only in the choice of fabrics but also in stylistic research: having abolished busts and splints, dresses began to have a soft, supple line that followed the natural contours of the body. Lace and embroidery embellished bodices and vaporous jabots adorned blouses.

In a climate that could be described as one of productive tranquillity, the news of Italy's declaration of war on Austria arrived unexpectedly on the island, resulting in departures of young islanders for the front and a veritable collapse of the Capri economy, which, being based mainly on the tourist sector, suffered a sudden interruption in the flow of visitors, with very serious repercussions on hotels and other accommodation facilities. This phenomenon was also accompanied by a worrying drop in incomes, as many of the men who worked in this sector were called up for military service. A report on the activities carried out after thirty months of war shows the social, economic and tourist conditions on the island before and after Italy's entry into the war (Di Tucci, n.d.). When the war broke out, while the foreign residents immediately realised the gravity of the situation and quickly left Capri, local people was under the illusion that the conflict would be of brief duration. The social and economic structure of the whole country found itself unprepared to face events of such great magnitude. To aggravate the country's already precarious situation, as

[10] Mariuccia had seven children: Marta (1909), Ersilia (1910), Mario Michele (1912), Lidia (1914), Maddalena (1916), Flora (1921) and Adriana (1926). With the first four children, after the Second World War, relations were not good and years of lawsuits over inheritance issues followed, even against the mother herself, Donna Mariuccia. Family relations were therefore completely and irreparably compromised. Donna Mariuccia's relationship with her last three daughters, Maddalena, Flora and Adriana, was different: a perfect partnership, in work as in affection.

[11] Anacapri is a town in the island of Capri.

in the rest of the world, in 1918 the so-called "Spanish flu" pandemic broke out, which lasted until 1920 and caused millions of deaths. Donna Mariuccia's tailoring business was severely affected by all the difficulties of those years, but managed to survive the Great War, even though they were years of heavy losses. There is a treasured memory of Princess Mafalda of Savoy who, confidentially and in a gentle spirit, stopped at *La Parisienne* to enquire about the needs of the island's destitute families (Settanni & Ciuni, 2006, p. 16).

The recovery was slow and gradual and had to adapt to the changes in Capri's inhabitants. With the First World War, the Capri of Fritz Krupp, of Oscar Wilde, of Christian Allers, was over. The new personalities who frequented the island were now men of letters like the father of Futurism, Filippo Tommaso Marinetti and painters like Fortunato Depero. The latter, during his stay on the island between 1917 and 1918, had turned his attention to the island's traditional and very characteristic textile economy, kept alive by local craftsmen including many women. Depero, a protagonist of early Futurism, experienced an initial fruitful contact between the collective craft creativity of those women weavers and individual artistic inventiveness, creating his first Futurist tapestries, mosaics of coloured fabrics on which he reproduced automata and fantastic figures that would become the leitmotif of his work, not only on the fabrics but also in his paintings (Camillini, 2021).

After the war, it would be Edwin Cerio who relaunched the local textile business. Cerio was a naval engineer, originally from Capri, who returned to the island at the end of the 1910s after a long period spent travelling the world, representing and working for the Krupp war industry. He triggered an irrepressible explosion of creativity, civic passion and organisational hyperactivity that led him to be elected Mayor of the Municipality of Capri in 1920. He was a tireless organiser of conventions and initiatives aimed at the recovery and protection of Capri's natural landscape and monuments and at the valorisation of a number of local crafts, including weaving. In this decade the island's economy was on the upswing, thanks to the return of Italian and foreign tourists, who were also attracted by a number of initiatives prompted by Mayor Cerio. An important turning point came with the fascist government, which invested heavily in the island, making it a symbol of the regime's efficient tourism policy in the eyes of the world. Capri thus obtained a series of facilities and services designed to better welcome guests and various public works were carried out. Among these, the most important was the construction of the harbour, which allowed the docking of the steamers that shuttled to Naples, Sorrento and the Amalfi Coast. During the so-called roaring 1920s, fashion changed: necks were bare, necklaces were long and skirts were shortened, opening up into corolla shapes while necklines opened deep at the back: it was Charleston time.

Capri was preparing to face, like the whole of Italy, the sad pre-war period. Five years of economic sanctions and autarchy[12] gave *La Parisienne* atelier a new rhythm and a new way of life. The shop stayed alive, once again, thanks to Donna Mariuccia's resourcefulness and adaptability. Among other difficulties, the fascist regime did not

[12] The Italian government adopted autarky in 1936 as a response to the sanctions decided by the League of Nations following the Italian invasion of Abyssinia in 1935.

agree with the French name of *La Parisienne*, as foreign words were not allowed by the government, and, above all, did not tolerate the female ownership of the business.[13] It was later to be Adriana Di Fiore, Donna Mariuccia's last daughter who, in one of her many interviews, recalled the episode of how the original name was changed, and then finally restored after the end of fascism in 1945:

> Because *La Parisienne* was a foreign word, during the twenty years of fascism the fascists covered the shop sign with black sheets and changed the name of the shop. It became "Seterie M. Di Fiore". After 25 April, I climbed up a ladder with a sponge and peeled off the black sheets. When the old *La Parisienne* sign reappeared, people applauded in the *Piazzetta.* (Della Regione, 2014)

In those same 1930s, also in response to local demand for yarns and fabrics, the visionary Edwin Cerio purchased several hand looms that were to be propaedeutic and served as the driving force behind a renewed textile economy. The project, called *The Island Weaver* (Cerio, 1930), which was not ratified by any commercial company or association, intended to involve a number of local craftsmen in the creation of a network, also and above all a domestic one, through which to launch, or rather re-launch, the art of hand-weaving garments and furnishings created by the skilled and knowledgeable professionals of Capri. Certainly, Cerio's initiative, while linked to a local tradition, was part of the fascist regime's policy aimed at the recovery, or rather the exaltation, of Italian traditions. *The Weaver* project, in fact, beyond its declared and worthy objectives, did not have the chance to fully materialise, because of a form of utopian and outdated vision that characterised many of Cerio's initiatives. The dream of reactivating and enhancing a group workshop in which women would hand-weave fabrics to create cushions, tablecloths, towels, shawls, beach outfits and dresses, giving free rein to their imagination, received the support of the fascist government in 1935, and the processing of broom and agave also took root, for the production of typical fabrics intended for clothing and home furnishings (Caputi, 1938): a "household" industry that satisfied the many tourists, who even then "wished to bring typical products, mainly fabrics, to their countries".[14]

Among Capri's most assiduous characters between the two world wars, alongside rich Americans, aristocrats of the oldest European nobility, maharajas, ousted kings, millionaires and men of letters from all over the world, some notable Italian frequenters stand out: Prince Umberto di Savoia, heir to the throne of Italy, with his wife Maria Josè, his sister Mafalda, wife of the German Prince Philipp of Hesse, who was very close to the Nazis, and the whole entourage of nobles and aristocrats revolving around the royal court. In those years, another well-known family made the island its favourite place: the family formed by Edda Ciano, daughter of Mussolini and the most influential woman in the regime, and her husband Galeazzo Ciano, a young foreign minister and Mussolini's *protégé.* Around them gathered the elite of the fascist party, including the powerful party officials Roberto Farinacci, a jazz

[13] Historical archive, chamber of commerce of Naples, Economic registry, Registers of business reports and terminations, the fascist period (46.104 archival units produced in the years 1925–1945).

[14] *Ginestre e agavi di Capri*, L'artigianato (6 dicembre 1936) (dai Fondi del Centro Caprense Ignazio Cerio, Capri.

enthusiast, Italo Balbo, who always arrived flying a seaplane, and ambassador Bruno Bottai, surrounded by a court of journalists and writers: the already mentioned Filippo Tommaso Marinetti—who wanted to put a lift on the Faraglioni—with his extravagant brigade of painters and poets; the writer and journalist Curzio Malaparte; a little more secluded, but not too much, Alberto Moravia, a young and already famous writer, with his wife and writer Elsa Morante. The anti-fascist Alberto Albertini, co-founder and co-director, with his brother Luigi, of the *Corriere della Sera*, the prestigious daily newspaper that the regime forced them to sell off, obviously stayed in the background in his villa (+2018).

4 A Different Example of Female Entrepreneurship in Capri: Claretta Gallotti

That of 1939 was the last summer of peace. With the first roars of the cannon that on 1 September would mark the outbreak of the Second World War, the great international worldliness that had decreed Capri's success as a tourist destination was hastily abandoned. During the years of adaptation to the difficulties imposed by the war, Donna Mariuccia could count on the increasingly active collaboration of her last three daughters, Maddalena, Flora and above all Adriana, who, living the reality of tailoring to the full, brought a touch of youth and freshness to the activity started by their mother and gradually took over the reins of the business. "During the war years», Adriana recalls, «we sold clothes to the ladies of Naples, but we had to go

Fig. 1 The first two generations of *La Parisienne*: Donna Mariuccia and her daughters

to Sorrento because our customers were afraid to cross the Gulf: the sea was full of mines" (Locatelli, 2009)[15] (Fig. 1).

Immediately after the Second World War, in 1946, Edwin Cerio gave the looms of *the Weaver* to a woman who at the time certainly did not have the means to buy them, but in whom he glimpsed the competence and mastery necessary to realise his small insular utopia: the baroness Claretta Gallotti. His intuition turned out to be right. Claretta developed the workshop and continued to call it *The Island Weaver*, giving effective, as well as valuable, continuity to the knowledge of the islanders (Verbena, 2005). The uniqueness of her work, considered exemplary in the entire Italian textile manufacturing panorama, lay in the combination of raffia and natural fibres with others of an artificial type, with which she produced fabrics for furnishings and clothing. The post-World War II period, marked by severe economic straits, suggested the use of alternative materials. By integrating the weaving techniques she had learnt in Ethiopia and local customs with the chromatic suggestions "distilled from the nature of Capri itself" (Ciuni, 2001; Robiola, 1953), Gallotti created an unusual form of craftsmanship that brought her sudden international prestige, to the point of being recognised by critics as one of the ambassadors of Italian fashion in the 1950s. Her "art applied to fashion" carried the name of Capri to America and even Japan, conveying an "unmistakable way of dressing created on the spot" (Robiola, 1953), acting everywhere as a testimony of Italian taste and as a sensitive, indirect instrument for promoting tourism (Cirillo & Rupe, 2018). Claretta Gallotti became, between the late 1940s and 1960, one of the most significant interpreters of Italian fashion, a protagonist of the Florentine catwalks from the first fashion show in 1951, as we shall see. She made clothes inspired by the colours of Capri, popular costumes and the Neapolitan artistic repertoire in an unusual creative form.

The experience of *The Island Weaver* complemented the creative force of *La Parisienne*, whose growth had been progressive, tenacious and experimental. *The Weaver*, although also based on the originality of Capri's tailoring craftsmanship and the resourcefulness and creative and managerial skills of Claretta Gallotti, was an intense phenomenon that made hand-woven fabrics from Capri famous throughout the world, but it lasted little more than a decade. In the 1960s, for reasons not entirely known, Gallotti interrupted her activity and left Capri (Morini, 2010).[16] Two very different types of women, Claretta Gallotti and Donna Mariuccia: the first had noble origins, experience of life in an unusual system of traditions such as Ethiopia, a solid education and an elevated entourage; the second had a marked sense for business and was accustomed to the practice of a matronage that was widespread in the southern regions of Italy. In those years *La Parisienne*, as well as all the other businesses on the island, was once again marked by particular economic straits that Donna Mariuccia faced with her pragmatism: once again she adapted to the times, co-opted a fair number of homeworkers and, coordinating them with her own strength, also

[15] Sorrento was easily accessible from Naples and Capri by sea.

[16] Her boutique, changing management, later became "Fausta di Capri". She created fabrics, patterns, scarves and bags painted by her. One of the most famous creations were the Capri-style trousers, model Liz, expressly created for Liz Taylor (Spinelli, 2010, p. 39).

adapted to the use of alternative materials as she had already done after the First World War. The first inventory from the 1940s dates back to 1942 and includes a quantity and variety of goods in the warehouse of great value: cotton fabrics, linen cloths, Roman silk, *fiochin*, Panama cloth, *piqué* silk, Venus *crepe*, Bemberg linen, coloured percale, opaline, cotton flannels, wool and wool-blend fabrics.[17] In September 1946, at the end of the war, from a new inventory of the material available in the *Piazzetta* warehouse[18] there clearly emerges, alongside the "blouses in lace, jersey, voile, pearl cotton or cretonne", the presence of garments (blouses, women's or children's dresses) in parachute silk, which in those years was mainly used for making wedding dresses.[19]

5 Adriana Di Fiore, the Queen of the *Piazzetta*

Having overcome the crisis, the Italian economic miracle of the 1950s was waiting in the wings. The lust for life returned overwhelmingly and clothes, especially women's clothes, strongly expressed this desire with lively colours, styles and designs. That inexhaustible burst of gaiety, followed by peace, spread the Capri fashion of broad-cloth cotton tunics and trousers. It was as if everyone, tired of deprivation, shared a desire for fresh, unexpected, irreverent garments. Donna Mariuccia's boutique became a source of ideas and extravagance where the customers themselves imagined and created new models with the aim of refreshing demoralised spirits. Her three daughters, by now her most active collaborators, gave new impetus to the business in creation and fashion. Of the three, it was Adriana who proved to be the true talent of the family: she took the name of *La Parisienne* even higher and become, until her death in 2015, the "Queen of the *Piazzetta*". Adriana Di Fiore was born in 1926, twenty years after the opening of the shop, at a time when the atelier was prosperous. She studied at grammar school and reviewed Latin declensions in the tailor's shop, so as not to be left alone at home.

> When I was 13, I used to deliver dresses to the ladies of the noble class of Capri. … I studied, I went to high school, but I never left *La Parisienne*. I cannot forget the afternoons spent repeating Latin versions in the company of Delia, the workshop seamstress. (Locatelli, 2009)

She enrolled at the magistral school, and only a few months away from graduating the events of life, the war and the death of her father in 1942 induced her to interrupt her studies, much to her mother's chagrin. After losing her husband, the man who had encouraged and supported her so much in her business, Mariuccia knew how to guide her daughters and dressmakers. Adriana was ready to take over the family business

[17] "Ditta Michele Di Fiore, Ricami e seterie *La Parisienne*, Capri, Merchandise included in the 1st Inventory 1942", *La Parisienne* Private Archive.

[18] At that time, it was still in the name imposed by the regime, although the inventory register clearly shows the use of the name, in fact never abandoned, *La Parisienne*.

[19] *La Parisienne* Private Archive, "Ditta Michele di Fiore. Inventory of material in stock carried out on 2 September 1946, Warehouse located in Piazza Umberto I *La Parisienne*".

full-time and was entrusted with one of the most responsible tasks: the purchase of raw materials and the relationship with the boutique's numerous suppliers. In order to be able to travel to Naples, to negotiate batches of fabrics to take to Capri, Adriana, not yet of age, had to ask the court for emancipation.[20] In this way she guaranteed the continuity of the family business, now run by women only. At only 20 years old, Adriana was already the new reference point of *La Parisienne*. In those years of recovery, the whole island was experiencing a ferment of production, in every house people sewed with skill and dexterity and often groups of girls gathered under the expert guidance of a more enterprising and capable veteran seamstress. Work was done on a piecework basis and it was Adriana, now, who had to look after all the units scattered around the island. *La Parisienne* has always been the centre of fashion on Capri, even when cheap aviation fabric was all that could be salvaged.

> Suddenly abundance returned: with fabric from American parachutes, we made blouses. Then we had the idea of silk scarves from embroidered military coats of arms. They were a great success, the Americans loved this kind of work. (Locatelli, 2009)

The 1950s were for Adriana what the 1920s had been for her mother Mariuccia: years of great transformation for life and fashion on Capri, as it was throughout Europe. Coinciding with the implementation of the Marshall Plan, the recovery throughout Italy of craftsmanship and manufacturing districts gave life to fashion "Made in Italy", while the *dolce vita* was exploding in Capri. Adriana found herself managing *La Parisienne* with passion and great dedication, accompanying it through the transformation of Capri's golden years, the 1950s and 1960s, when the entire jet-set arrived on the island. The clientele stood out for being very wealthy and international, especially the Americans. Adriana favoured bright colours, reminiscent of those on the island, and, by managing a team of tailors, she was able to meet the demands of her clientele quickly and with excellent results in terms of wearability (Anonymous, 1954, pp. 175–176). The famous *Piazzetta* became the setting for history in the making: the Germans left the island and the Americans arrived. In the 1950s Capri was the *buen retiro* for those who left the city and their daily commitments behind. Princes walked barefoot on the pavement of the *Piazzetta*, the Neapolitan musician Roberto Murolo sang and played in the street, Mussolini's daughter Edda Ciano created a small colony on the island. Adriana recounts what was a real ritual in the 1960s:

> The *Piazzetta* was the stage for these people who used to meet in the bars. The ritual was simple: you would sit at Bar Tiberio, then cross the square and enter *La Parisienne*. There were people who would carefully choose the moment to pick up their clothes, or they would enter for no reason. Just to say hello. They were actually parading from one bar to another. But only after five o'clock: before that, the appointment was on the beach. (Esposito, 2015b)

Adriana immediately proved her unquestionable talent and opened up great possibilities for the future. She took over the reins of the house and the company long

[20] Article 84 of the Italian Civil Code states, inter alia, that an emancipated minor acquires full capacity to act, performing acts that do not exceed ordinary administration. In particular, the emancipated minor may, with the assistance of the curator, collect capital on condition of suitable employment and may stand trial both as plaintiff and defendant.

before her mother's death in 1967. In the 1950s, a series of important encounters marked the entrepreneurial turning point of *La Parisienne*. In 1951, fashion designer and nobleman Emilio Pucci, after a long frequentation of the island, during which he had met both Clarette Gallotti and Adriana Di Fiore, having become aware of the original and qualified craftsmanship of Capri, opened his own shop on the island, undertaking a series of promotional activities aimed at making Capri the "Centre of European fashion" (Villari, 1950). Revolutionary media actions were taken, such as fashion shows as early as 1951 (Pistolese, 1972), photo campaigns, interviews and articles in the main international magazines in the sector. A convinced proponent of fashion as a useful sector for the growth of the country, for the economic and occupational spin-off it triggers, and also "as a testimony in the world of Italian taste [...] and, lastly, of tourist propaganda" (Ascanio, 1954), Emilio Pucci was able to exploit the media potential of the island and its stock of fabrics to give life to an ambitious project. The tailor-marquis, who opened his boutique in Capri, designed trousers and shirts in bright colours, scarves with the island's themes, launched the fortunate "tagliatelle" hats, organised fashion shows, relying as much on a captivating narrative form as on appropriate clothing.

These were the very early years of the 1950s when Capri became a "metropolis that dictated the laws of elegance and fashion to the world, as much as and more than Paris" (Esposito, 2015b). At first, the native craftswomen and artisans saw this new fashion system as a threat and soon organised themselves in defence of the authenticity of local manufactures. First and foremost, in February 1954, they set up the Capri Fashion Centre, the institutional framework through which they could "defend original Capri production from the countless counterfeits and endless products of women's clothing made to appear to be from Capri while they are made in Florence and the cities of northern Italy".[21] At the same time, a group of producers, merchants and public and private entities established the Voluntary Consortium for the Defence of Capri Products. This operation responded to the marked desire to watch over the genuineness of local handicrafts and to defend from imitations produced elsewhere what was "conceived, designed and made on Capri by the people of Capri" (Foschini, 1954, p. 55). Among the many tailors, merchants, master shoemakers, jewellers and many others, *La Parisienne* also joined the Consortium.

The first fashion show in Italy was organised in Florence in 1951, and it was attended by both Claretta Gallotti and Adriana Di Fiore. There they met Livio De Simone, an eclectic Neapolitan who directed his initial artistic flair towards textiles, with the advantage of finding a winning field of application in clothing for holiday living. It was Adriana who launched De Simone into fame. She called him to Capri to her boutique and proposed that he collaborate on her fashion line.[22] This was the beginning of a very long and fruitful collaboration, a phase of great creative and commercial intensity, as witnessed by one of the main documents in the historical

[21] Il Centro di Moda Capri, *Il Mezzogiorno*, 3 February 1954.

[22] Livio de Simone, a lawyer, was born in Naples in 1920. He discovered his artistic vocation in the 1950s and, contravening the expectations of his parents who wanted him to study law, began to pour his creativity into fabric printing.

archive, an album in which the many famous people who frequented the boutique left their signatures, often jotting down thoughts and offering themselves for a photo shoot.[23] Livio De Simone also created for Emilio Pucci and in 1957 showed his garments at the prestigious fashion show in *Palazzo Pitti*, in Florence. Adriana also participated in that show with her "boutique fashion".

Meanwhile, the year before, in the winter of 1956, Adriana left for America to visit her sister Flora. She stayed with her for six months, during which she also attended a regular school where she perfected her English. On her first trip to the United States, Adriana travelled on the Cristoforo Colombo transatlantic, the first luxury liner on which a big fashion show was held on 20 February 1956 (Pervinca, 2019). Adriana soon realised that her personal wardrobe, made in Capri with her own designs, carefully prepared for that trip, was a huge success among the ladies in the American salons to which she was introduced by her sister. Having to stay in California for the entire winter, she had brought with her a large wardrobe to wear during her long stay but ended up selling almost all of it to the "clients" she met in the various salons she frequented. In particular, she was pleasantly surprised when Lola Dunkelman, owner of a boutique on Madison Avenue, placed an order with her for fifty skirts, in all colours, to be made up as soon as possible. This was how Adriana began her first export to the United States.

One of the most famous creations of the 1950s was the *Margherita* (daisy) skirt "with overlapping petals outlined by borders in contrasting colours" (Settanni & Ciuni, 2006, p. 21). *La Parisienne* knew how to follow fashion trends, catering to

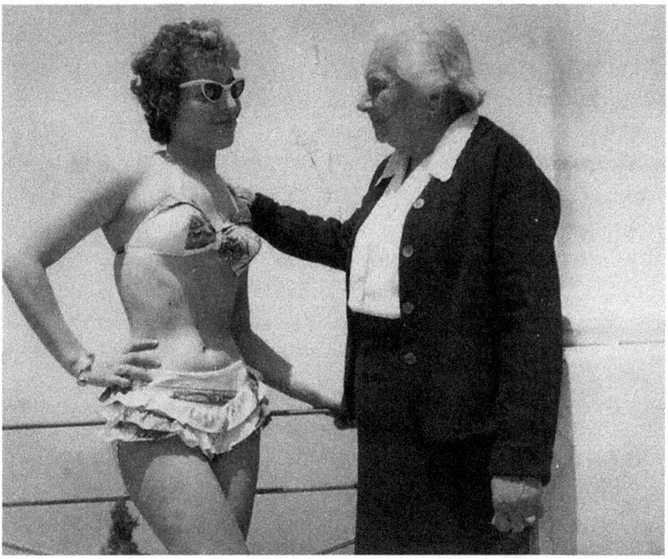

Fig. 2 Donna Mariuccia and the first bikini

[23] *La Parisienne* Private Archive.

the tastes of its increasingly sophisticated and international clientele. The boutique became an icon of Capri's *dolce vita* and was frequented by famous and charming women: among them, Jacqueline Kennedy, Liz Taylor, Audrey Hepburn, Farah Diba, Ingrid Bergman and Oona O'Neil, Charlie Chaplin's wife. But it is also the epic of the bikini. One of Adriana's faithful collaborators, Anna Mosca, and her pupil Gilda Mulieri were its main creators. The 1950s closed with the triumph of Italian high fashion and the debut of Capri style; the emerging designers were flanked by a series of boutique-fashion names, and Adriana Di Fiore was among them. The fashion magazines of the time were unanimous in their praise: "The famous Capri trousers in gabardine enhance a thousand models of blouses" (Consiglio, 1933), and "Precious sheer wools enrich the wide skirts to be worn in the evening over the jersey bodice at aperitif time in the cafés of the famous *Piazzetta*".[24] Adriana started to produce her own design lines by supplying the patterns to tailors and seamstresses who cut and sewed at home on a piecework basis. She called together everyone who was producing for her, hired them directly and opened a garment company (Fig. 2).

In 1967, when their mother died, Adriana and her sister Lena continued the business, with two workshops, second-hand machinery and a dozen seamstresses. Then in 1968, on the occasion of the second edition of *Mare Moda Capri*, the *Linea Capri* brand appeared, bringing together 14 boutiques on the island.[25] In 1969 Adriana opened a second workshop and invested all profits in more modern tailoring machinery. She realised that expensive machinery had become necessary, and it was impossible to supply them to every pieceworker. It was necessary to assemble the workforce, organise them, guide them personally and constantly. In addition, the cutting had to be done differently than before» (Settanni & Ciuni, 2006, p. 50).

She travelled a lot, always searching for fabrics and colours, catching ideas and images of the changing feminine firmament on the fly. By investing in machinery and technology, Adriana began to avail herself of the valuable collaboration of talented tailors.[26] In the same year Adriana launched the brands *Adriana's Originals* and *Adriana's Capri*. The latter was essentially born to cope with requests from abroad, especially from New York and Florida. The initial silk and handicraft shop, already transformed into a boutique, also became the showcase for her brands.

As we have seen, between the 1950s and 1960s, thanks to the enterprise of local craftsmen or foreign visitors, tailor's shops, boutiques and workshops sprang up in response to patrons' demands for garments and accessories in tune with the style of the place. In that period, Capri had a great identity and was targeted by the jet-set.

[24] To the flourishing activity of Capri, the fashion magazine *Arbiter* dedicated a special column, *Vita di Capri* (Capri's life), in which both the social life and the sartorial novelties of the island were described (Anonymous 1954, pp. 51–55).

[25] Among the documents in the Historical Archive of the Naples Chamber of Commerce is a list of the garments presented at the 1968 edition of *Mare Moda*. The list, which is very precise, shows the cost of the clothes and objects exhibited, both in lire and in dollars, and is signed by Ms. Adriana (Historical archive, chamber of commerce of Naples, MareModa Capri fund, b. C, MareModa Accessory and Craftsmanship Exhibition, 1968).

[26] Luciano Ferrigno, Anna Coppola, Rita Amitrano, Umberto Arcucci, among many others who over the years have worked in the two facilities on Capri.

The film *The Bay of Naples*, with Clark Gable and Sophia Loren, was shot. Gods and demigods sailed between the Faraglioni with their yachts. Reza Pahlavi Shah of Persia, King Constantine of Greece, Paul Newman, Cristina Onassis and many of them set foot in *La Parisienne*. We have already mentioned Jacqueline Kennedy, who was an expert in fashion, and had twelve pairs of white trousers made and who enjoyed choosing tastefully printed cotton fabrics for sarongs to give to her friends. This whole epic experienced first by Donna Mariuccia, then with greater intensity by Adriana Di Fiore, is encapsulated in two large albums, jealously guarded in the Historical Archive of *La Parisienne*, with newspaper cuttings from all over the world and an impressive number of autographs from VIP clients.

In 1973 there was the fashion show in *Palazzo Pitti* in Florence, where the holiday fashion collection was presented. Through the *Pitti Donna* fashion presentations, from 1976 to 1985, Adriana's two brands spread throughout the world. High-end boutiques such as Veneziano on Madison Avenue and Haas Kassel in New York, Bettina di Capri in Palm Beach, Miller-White in Hartford, Buffy in London, "Gretel Schultz" in Germany and Takashimaia in Japan, together with many others, are just some of the names that offered her holiday line. Fundamental to the brand is the sartorial relationship with "Ognibene - Zendmann" in Rome who, with their know-how, perfected the working of jersey to the point of incredible virtuosity. Writers Graham Greene and Roger Peyrefitte now frequented the piazza. *La Parisienne* at this point, under the creative verve of architect Mario Settanni, Adriana's husband, renewed its look: on the outside, the stucco frames of the large shop windows echo the typical architecture of the vaults, mirroring the play of the domes of the former cathedral that dominates the front.

6 Conclusion

The first two generations of entrepreneurs who gave life and a future to *La Parisienne* (Maria Della Monica and Adriana Di Fiore) based all their commitment on very innovative economic ideas, on organisational and therefore managerial skills. Animated by a strong motivation to cultivate a passion for their work, but also by a strong sense of duty and responsibility, they were resilient, strong-willed women, forced to overcome the difficulties of the great war and, in Mariuccia's case, a state of widowhood which reinforced her resourcefulness. Moreover, she and her daughter Adriana were married to open-minded, understanding men, always ready to guarantee their support (including entrepreneurial) to their wives. Over the years, more than once, billion-dollar offers have come in to sell the prestigious boutique, but Adriana Di Fiore's response has always been the same: "there is no amount of money that can repay the pleasure of so many decades of work and success" (Locatelli, 2009).

Francesca and Luciana, two of Adriana's three daughters, lead *La Parisienne* into the Third Millennium. Francesca graduated from the Academy of Fashion and Costume in Rome, completed her fashion master's degree in the USA, at the FIDM in San Francisco in 1985; Luciana, a graduate in architecture (like her father), dedicates herself to the administrative part of the company. The heirs of Adriana Di Fiore are women of our time and adapt the rhythms and creative line of the historic boutique to the changes in fashion, consumption and tourism on Capri. Their motivations are certainly different from those of their mothers: they most likely experience a different, but equally strong, feeling towards the boutique and feel all the responsibility of those who, in times very different from Capri's *dolce vita*, feel the need to keep the name of their atelier high, protecting everything important that was created by the great women who preceded them. Their economic culture and their entrepreneurial behaviour have adapted to the present, which poses them perhaps more complex economic choices, but which they are able to handle with the appropriate tools: a greater awareness of the market logic and a fresher knowledge of the imaginative world of fashion, in a situation where there is less worry from having to affirm their entrepreneurial role in a world already more accustomed to relating to women entrepreneurs and women managers.

With them, the workshop became increasingly equipped to meet the daily orders of a clientele that was still rich and well-to-do, but very different from that which had animated the salon boutique founded by Mariuccia for much of the first century. In the 1980s Capri began to succumb to the lure of the "designer labels" that, within a few years, had gained the upper hand on the island. In the 1980s, Capri began to give in to the flattery of the designers and for Adriana's daughters, Francesca and Luciana, the need arose to combine the *Adriana's Capri* label with other Italian and foreign brands which, however, shared the "resort" spirit of the *maison*. Thanks to them, *La Parisienne* remains one of the last bastions of a great ancient tradition of Capri fashion and the boutique way of doing things, with the constant search for special garments that can interpret holiday tastes. Even today the historic shop, overlooking Capri's famous picturesque *Piazzetta*, is still active and run by women, entrusted as it is to the third generation. Above all, there remains the charm of an extraordinary experience of female emancipation, of great management and creative skills, of great resourcefulness and extraordinary beauty.

References

Alisio, G. (1994). *Capri nell'Ottocento. Da meta dell'anima a mito turistico*, Electa Napoli Edizioni La Conchiglia.

Amatori, F. (2011). Entrepreneurial typologies in the history of industrial Italy: Reconsiderations. *Business History Review, 85*, 151–180.

Anonymous. (1954) Arbiter, XXVII, no. 172.

Ascanio, E. (1954). Arbiter. Rivista di eleganza e di vita moderna, 175–176, sett.-ott., 41.

Aston, J., & Di Martino, P. (2017, August). Risk, success, and failure: Female entrepreneurship in Late-Victorian and Edwardian England. *The Economic History Review, 70*(3), 837–858.

Berg, C. (1993). Perspectives for viewing intellectual development throughout life. In R. Sternberg & C. Berg, (Eds.), *Intellectual development*. Cambridge University Press.

Business History Review. (1998/2007).

Camillini, G. (2021). *Fortunato Depero and Depero futurista 1913–1927*, Rubbettino, Soveria Mannelli.

Caputi, G. (1938). *Ginestre e agavi di Capri nella battaglia per l'autarchia*, Il Mattino.
Castagnoli, A. (2007). The female entrepreneur's point of view and the Italian economy. *Business and Economic History, 5*, 1–17.
Cerio, E. (1930). *La tessitura a mano.* Le pagine dell'Isola, Capri.
Chandler, A. D., Jr. (1977). *The visible hand. The managerial revolution in American business.* Harvard University Press.
Cione, E. (1957, giugno). Capri salotto del mondo. In *Napoli e le riviere del sole.* Annuario turistico con il patrocinio del Comune e della Giunta Provinciale di Napoli, f.s.n.
Cirillo, O., & Rupe, M. (1957). *"La Tessitrice dell'isola", un'interprete della moda italiana alla metà del Novecento tra artigianato e ricerca artistica*, in *Diseño al Revés*, CIMODE 4° International Fashion and Design Congress, a cura di Broega A. C., Cunha J., Carvalho H., Blanco M., Garcìa-Bardell G., Goméz-Chacòn L. D., 48–59, Guimarães: Centro de Ciência e Tecnologia Têxtil Universidade do Minho, 2018.
Cirillo, O. (2018). Fashion and tourism in Campania in the middle of the twentieth century: A story with many protagonists. *Almatourism, Journal of Tourism, Culture and Territorial Development, 9*(9), 23–46.
Ciuni, R. (2001). *La piazzetta di Capri. Storia, protagonisti, stravaganze.* La Conchiglia, Capri.
Colli, A., & Rose, M. B. (2003). Family firms in comparative perspective. In F. Amatori & G. Jones (Eds.), *Business history around the world* (pp. 339–352). Cambridge University Press.
Colli, A., & Rose, M. B. (1999). Families and firms: The culture and evolution of family firmsin, in Britain and Italy in the nineteenth and twentieth centuries. *Scandinavian Economic History Review, 47*(1), 24–47.
Consiglio, A. (1933, Maggio 21). Corriere della Sera.
Curli, B. (2002). Women entrepreneurs and Italian industrialization. Conjectures and avenues for research. *Enterprise and Society, III*(4), 634–656.
Del Prete, R. (2015). L'imprenditoria femminile nel Mezzogiorno industriale: il caso della Campania. In S. Chemotti & M.C. La Rocca (Eds.), *Il genere nella ricerca storica* (pp. 606–642). Il Poligrafo.
Della Regione, A. (2014, Gennaio 19). *La signora della piazzetta di Capri.* http://achillecontedilavian.blogspot.com/2014/01/la-signora-della-piazzetta-di-capri.html
Di Tucci, E. (n.d.) .*Capri nella grande Guerra.* Centro Documentale dell'Isola di Capri
Enterprise & Society. (2001).
Esposito, R. (2015a). *Caprimoda. Protagonisti, imprese, eventi.* La Conchiglia.
Esposito, R. (2015b). *La signora de La Parisienne.* Capri Review. https://www.caprireview.it/news/la-signora-della-parisienne/
Esposito, R. (2009). *L'isola del dio nascosto. Improbabile passe-partout per introdursi a Capri.* La Conchiglia.
Foschini, V. (1953, Agosto 2). *Partirà dalle "boutiques" capresi la riscossa della Moda meridionale*, "Roma".
Foschini, V. (1954). Vita di Capri. "Arbiter". *Rivista di eleganza e di vita moderna, 172*, 51–55.
Franchi, M. (1994). Api o tartarughe? In P. David & G. Vicarelli (Eds.), *Donne nelle professioni degli uomini* (pp. 133–171). FrancoAngeli.
Gamber, W. (1994). Gendered concerns: Thoughts on the history of business and the history of women. *Business and Economic History, 23*(1), 129–140.
Gender and Business, fascicolo monografico di. Business History Review, 1998, 72–2.
Gender and Business, fascicolo monografico di. Enterprise & Society, 2001, 2–1.
Gnoli, S. (2020). *Moda. Dalla nascita della haute couture a oggi.* Carocci.
Holden, G. (2010). Childrearing and developmental trajectories: positive pathways, off-ramps, and dynamic processes. *Child Development Perspectives, 4*(3), 197–204.
Il Centro di Moda Capri, "Il Mezzogiorno", 3 febbraio 1954.
Jennings, J. E., & Brush, C. (2013). Research on women entrepreneurs: Challenges to (and from) the broader entrepreneurship literature? *The Academy of Management Annals, 7*(1).

Kwolek, F. A. (1998). *Incorporating women: A history of women and business in the United States.* Twayne.

Lembo, A. (1994). *Capri nel 1800—Popolazione e toponomastica*, La Conchiglia, Capri.

Leone De Andreis, M. (2018). *Capri 1939. L'isola in bianco e nero. Nobili e stravaganti, imprenditori e artisti, camicie nere e antifascisti alla vigilia della Guerra.* La Conchiglia, Capri.

Locatelli, G. (2009). *In piazzetta c'è un'ape regina.* https://it.readkong.com/page/capri-in-piazzetta-c-e-un-ape-regina-9752308

Mackenzie, C. (1993). *Vestal Fire*, ristampa Ed. La Conchiglia, Capri.

Management & Organizational History. (2010).

Mannucci, E. (1996). *Il marchese rampante. Emilio Pucci: avventure, illusioni, successi di un inventore della moda italiana.* Baldini&Castoldi.

Morini, E. (2010). *Storia della moda XVIII-XXI secolo*, Skira.

Pervinca Bellini, E. (2019, Giugno 20). *Fashion tales. Il Transatlantico della Moda*, podcast, Vogue.it.

Pescarolo, A. (2019). *Il lavoro delle donne nell'Italia contemporanea.* Viella.

Pistolese, R. (1972). *A Capri la moda come costume, in MareModa Capri 1972.* Artigianelli.

Robiola, E. (1953). *"Bellezza" mensile dell'alta moda e della vita italiana* (pp. 12–18).

Scott, J. W. (1998). *Gender. A useful cathegory of historical analysis.* In J. W. Scott (Ed.), *Gender and the politics of history.* Columbia University Press.

Settanni, M., & Ciuni, R. (2006). *La Parisienne. 1906–2006 racconta il suo secolo di vita nel panorama del mito di Capri.* Nappa, Capri.

Spinelli, A. (2010). *La moda mare a Capri e Positano, un crescendo di successi tra jet-set e nuove tendenze.* In M. A. Taglialatela, a cura di, *La creatività sartoriale campana. Abbigliamento maschile e moda balneare* (pp. 36–40). Arte'm.

Verbena, G. (2005). *Anacapri la rinascita dopo il 1945.* Ciammurre.

Villari, C. (1950). *Siren Land vuol battere Parigi. Capri centro della moda europea*, Corriere lombardo, 24 luglio 1950, in Archivio del Centro Documentale dell'isola di Capri, Emeroteca. D 52.

Women in the Labour Market

From the Edge to the Heart: Female Employment in Nineteenth-Century Italy

Giuliana Freschi

Women have long been at the edge of economic history. According to Humphries (1991) and Sharpe (1995), shifting them from there "to the heart" goes into stages. The first stage involves recognising the extent to which the role of women has been neglected. The second stage aims to integrate women into the mainstream of economic history, with potentially revolutionary results. As stated in the first chapter of the present book, the methodological challenge lies in proving that it is possible to uncover the economic culture not only in women's writings, as many did not leave behind written records, but also in their actions. Therefore, this book goes beyond the scope of Humphries and Sharpe by placing women not only at the core of economic history but also at the centre of the economic culture of their times.

The first part of the book focuses on women who have left traces of their economic thought, not through their writings, but through their experiences. It explores the stories of women in business, female investors, and their untold or forgotten narratives. The following two parts of the book will delve into the role of women in education, politics, and economics. They rely on sources that have not been traditionally used to study women's work, such as correspondence or unprinted material, to reconstruct the intellectual history of women who contributed to the history of economics and the economy. This second part of the book delves into debates and patterns regarding women in the labour market, utilising often overlooked sources.

I thank all the participants of the two AISPE workshops "Le donne e l'economia in Italia (1750–1950)", for their comments which helped me shaping this work. Earlier drafts, or rather research ideas, have been presented at the Oxford Labour and Precariety Workshop, CAMPOP Occupations Workshop, Sant'Anna Gender and Labour Seminar Series. I am indebted to Eloisa Betti, Giacomo Gabbuti, Manuela Mosca, Alessandro Nuvolari, Leigh Shaw-Taylor, Claudia Sunna, Maria Enrica Virgillito, and Giulia Zacchia for their feedback. In particular, the present chapter is based on a joint work with Marco Martinez (Freschi & Martinez, 2024) and would not have been possible without his invaluable and constant help. The usual disclaimer applies.

G. Freschi (✉)
Scuola Superiore Sant'Anna, Pisa, Italy
e-mail: giuliana.freschi@santannapisa.it

M. Mosca (ed.), *Women at Work in Italy (1750–1950)*, Springer Studies in the History of Economic Thought, https://doi.org/10.1007/978-3-031-64281-4_5

The present chapter reflects on the significance of re-evaluating the role of ordinary, "everyday" women's work in the economic development of countries (Bateman, 2019). It contributes to the ongoing discussion on female labour force participation in the past and concludes that when work was available, women worked. In the applications for poor relief in the city of Florence between 1810 and 1812, families had to describe the occupational status of all their members. Hence, the applications represent a valuable source to explore female work. For instance, Maddalena and Elisabetta worked with silk when they "had it" or when they "could". The 26-year-old daughter of one of the households requesting the poor relief, bleached "when she found it", while her younger sister was engaged in a "little job" (*il lavorino*).[1]

Thus, it aligns with a strand of the debate that emphasises the importance of demand factors, rather than supply factors, in determining women's employment from historical perspective.[2] However, providing new estimates of female employment in the past is outside the scope of this chapter. The main contribution is that, alongside demand factors, also cultural ideology had a pivotal role. Thus, I focus on the tendency of women to *report* their occupation, and how the reporting patterns varied over time, across locations, and social classes.

In line with the book's objectives, this chapter conceptualises, on the one hand, the importance of using new, previously not used, sources to study women's work (Humphries & Sarasúa, 2012) and, on the other hand, the drawbacks of conventional measures, such as labour force participation (Burnette, 2021). It attempts to combine insights from women's history and feminist economics, which advocates for a comprehensive social reproduction framework to study female employment. The chapter proceeds as follows: Section 1 provides a concise description of the concept of work and underscores the importance of including "invisible women" in the mainstream of economic history. It sheds light on the long-standing historiographical debates within Italian economic history literature. Section 2 addresses measurement issues, including sources, methods, and theoretical methodologies and proposes alternative approaches. Section 3 presents an empirical application that investigates the determinants of non-reporting of female labour and its relationship with social class. Was women's invisibility influenced by social class? And has it remained consistent over time? Sect. 4 concludes.

---

[1] Archivio di Stato di Firenze (ASF), Congregazione di San Giovanni.

[2] Humphries and Sarasúa (2012, 43–44) argue that "supply-side factors, such as marital status and number and age of children, which are conventional determinants of women's decision to enter the labor force, appear to have been less prominent in historical contexts. Instead, women responded to opportunities; the demand for labor was decisive".

1 Invisible Women, Visible Sources

1.1 What is Work?

When examining female employment in the past, several questions arise. Have women always worked outside the home? How do we measure women's employment in the past, and are the available measures suitable? Do historical sources provide an accurate depiction of female employment in the past, and if so, which sources should be relied upon?

However, before addressing these questions, there is a fundamental query that serves as a foundation for these investigations: What was work, particularly female work, in the past, and how did it evolve over time? The latter question has recently been extensively explored in the book *What is Work?* edited by Sarti et al. (2018). In modern times, when we refer to work, we generally mean activities that can be accounted for and contribute to GDP calculations. The development of modern statistical measures, pioneered by the work of Simon Kuznets and the establishment of the System of National Accounts after World War II, conceptualises work as a market-oriented measure (Folbre, 2018). These methodological advancements coincided with the "invention" of the standard employment model, which portrays a stable and continuous work relationship as the universal employment model in the Western world (Betti, 2018). However, as highlighted by Sarti et al. (2018) in their introduction, since the 1970s, activists, female and feminist scholars have emphasised the need for a broader concept of labour. The work of Boris (Boris, 2018; Boris et al., 2018) investigating the International Labour Organisation's engagement with female employment and the progressive feminisation of the concept of work exemplifies this shift. Current gender statistics recognise the statistical bias inherent in the traditional concept of labour and advocate for a more inclusive and less stereotyped data collection mechanism (Corsi & Zacchia, 2021). Recent research on precariousness has also aimed to broaden the conceptualisation of work beyond stability and full-time employment. Consequently, the standard model of employment has been questioned and deconstructed both in the present and in the past (Betti, 2016).

Historical research has provided essential tools to understand the evolution of female and male work over time, considering that its definition is fluid, and shaped by historical and cultural contexts. In ancient times and in the Ancien Régime, the ability to live without working was a requirement for the aristocracy and elites to belong to their social class. Artisans in mediaeval and early modern times held a positive perception of work, considering it a crucial element of collective identity (Bellavitis, 2002). In the nineteenth century, male work gradually became associated with rights and dignity, but tensions persisted between work as alienation and self-realisation (Sarti et al., 2018). These definitions of work are inherently gender-biased, as highlighted by the authors. Pescarolo (2019) examines the historical evolution of women's work through the lens of social class. In higher strata of society, female work outside the home was viewed as deplorable and only acceptable in cases of economic necessity. In lower social strata, traditional work ethics prevailed, as exemplified by the willingness of women to work in the fields, which contradicted the maternalistic policies of the elite aimed at demeaning working women. Whereas (male) urban identity was rooted in the "complementarity between the citizens' body and trades" (Bellavitis, 2002),[3] women in the cities juggle disparate jobs on the margins of society, making it challenging to develop a strong sense of work identity.

Pescarolo (2019) demonstrates that the distinction between different spheres to emphasise women's domestic role has existed since antiquity. However, the differentiation between productive and unproductive work by Adam Smith further confined female work to the realm of the household, rendering women more invisible in the economy.[4] Humphries and Sarasúa (2012) emphasise that the word "worker" historically carried strong implications in terms of political and property rights, and as a result, it was predominantly associated with men. Work experiences differed between women and men. The distinction between market and domestic, paid and in-kind, regular and unstable work was much more nuanced for women. However, many women did engage in regular paid work outside the house, while simultaneously many men were not employed in stable activities. Consequently, the estimation of male labour force participation rates at around 100% is as much a historical ideological construct as the low female participation rates (Zucca Micheletto, 2013).

When discussing work in the past, particularly in pre-industrial societies, it is crucial to understand that most workers did not identify with a single occupational title over time. Artisans, especially those affiliated with guilds and corporations, as well as urban manufacturers, were not the norm. As early as 1990, Groppi underlined the necessity of exploring female employment beyond predefined categories to better capture the economic activities both of men and women (1990).[5] Analysing work in the past using a verb-oriented method (Ågren, 2017) or focusing on tasks rather than single occupational titles (Whittle & Hailwood, 2020) allows us to unveil the complexity of work activities that was concealed by the use of a single occupational title (Carus & Ogilvie, 2009). These approaches reveal a significant discrepancy between self-reported occupational titles and the qualitative sources describing the daily activities in which individuals engaged.

---

[3] The distinction of gender roles was not so clearcut also among corporations. Groppi (1996) has extensively researched women's role in guilds and corporations in Italy, underlining women's awareness of the existence of gender roles and their capacity to subvert them, on the one hand, and to wisely exploit them, on the other.

[4] Although this contribution does not focus specifically on the role of care-work, a note on its definition is necessary. Pescarolo (2018) outlines the evolution of the reproductive-productive work dichotomy, shedding light on its origins, limitations, and the abuses perpetrated. In conclusion, she adopts a very broad definition of work, originally proposed by Tilly and Tilly (1998), which embraces its multiple dimensions. Work is conceived as any human effort, with variable intensity featuring different technical conditions, which gives use value to goods and services. For other seminal contributions on productive and reproductive work see: Chisté, Del Re, and Forti (1979); Picchio (1992).

[5] Angela Groppi has been a pioneer in women's history studies in Italy, combining the study of economic activities and of women's rights. Her contributions and legacy have recently been discussed in the monographic volume *Angela Groppi e la storia sociale* (2021).

Two projects, one focusing on Sweden and the other on England, arrive at similar conclusions. Both male and female work typically involved multiple tasks. However, female work was notably more multifaceted, with an average of around 5–7 tasks compared to 2–3 tasks characterising male work. Women, not only single and widows but also married women, participated in almost every sector of the economy, with female and male activities overlapping rather than being strictly segregated.

Bellavitis (2016) argues that there was no direct correlation between female occupational activity and marital status or the number of children. Also, supply-side factors worked differently historically than in modern times, certainly when it comes to age-participation profiles (Humphries & Sarasúa, 2012). The presence of children below the age of two in the household did not decrease female participation in the labour market, but, on the contrary, had a positive effect on the probability of the woman working. Women dropped out of the labour force as their children grew older, that is, when they could substitute them in the labour market (Horrell & Humphries, 1997). However, women mostly responded to opportunities presented by the market. The shift from a supply-side, worker-driven narrative to a demand-side employer-driven perspective has been supported by the influential works of Humphries and Sarasúa (2021). According to their findings, the hypothesis that women would choose not to work for pay if given the option is untenable. If work was available, women engaged in various market activities, paid domestic work, and unpaid care work. When considering both paid and unpaid work, studies demonstrate that women have historically shouldered most of the workload. This trend persists in developing and industrialised countries today, as it did in the past.

1.2 Female Work in Italian History

The statistical biases in recording female occupations in official sources mirror the differing attitudes towards female work. Social and cultural factors led to the perception of men as workers and women, particularly married women, as non-workers. The idea that women who did not report an occupation in official documents did not actually work is often unrealistic. For instance, it is implausible to assume that women from shopkeepers' households did not engage in any work, considering recent research on paid and unpaid work within family-run economic activities.[6] The understanding that women from shopkeepers' and business owners' households performed a diverse range of activities was already evident to statisticians during the first Italian censuses. Sarti (2018) presents an excerpt from the general report of the 1881 census, which outlines the various activities carried out by daughters of innkeepers, tailors, hatmakers, and shopkeepers. Some of these activities pertain to the domestic sphere, while others clearly fall under market-oriented endeavours. Similar patterns have been observed in other parts of Italy and Europe, such as among glassmaker

[6] The project was led by the editors of the book *What is work?* (Sarti et al., 2018).

families in the Liguria region from the sixteenth to the eighteenth century, families involved in small textile manufacturing between the eighteenth and nineteenth century (Maitte, 2016), and mid-nineteenth-century Barcelona family workshops, where women played significant roles in various activities bridging the domestic and market realms (Romero-Martín, 2016). Zucca Micheletto (2014) attempts to unravel the intricate dynamics of female labour within family businesses, emphasising the inadequacy of downplaying the significance of unpaid labour. The author highlights that women not only contributed to the workforce of family businesses but also frequently invested their own financial resources, particularly through dowries.

This gendered view of work became increasingly prominent by the late nineteenth century with the widespread adoption of the male breadwinner model. Pescarolo (2019) describes the cultural diffusion of this model among the bourgeoisie during the nineteenth century. In contrast to the aristocracy of earlier times, the bourgeoisie sought to establish the male breadwinner model as a universal norm. This shift is evident in the legislative efforts of the early twentieth century, which aimed to protect women in their biological reproductive role in society. The ultimate objective was to construct a female identity aligned with her maternal vocation (Pescarolo, 2019).

Hudson (2008) talks about a "historical construction" arguing that gender ideology, rather than biology, has been the determining factor in shaping the distribution of work and gender segregation. She traces the definition of specific gender roles and the separation of home and work to the advent of industrial society. Prügl (1999) explores this debate from a transnational perspective and adds the term "global" to the notion of "construction". She acknowledges the existence of a process that led to the creation of distinct gender identities: the working mother, who faced social challenges, contrasted with the home-based mothers engaged in various activities but excluded from the realm of recognised work, and the wage-earning worker, namely the male breadwinner. This perspective became pervasive in the second half of the nineteenth century and was internalised by male enumerators, whose assumptions influenced how they reported data. It also affected women, who increasingly felt ashamed to disclose their involvement in paid activities (Humphries & Sarasúa, 2012). This pattern has been identified in the Italian case. Betti (2012) provides a succinct but effective *excursus* of the historiography on the intricate relationship between the concept of female work and statistics. Curli and Pescarolo (2003) investigate this relationship in the Italian censuses focusing on the use of statistical labels and the consequences of the diffusion of the male breadwinner model on reporting occupations. Alberti (2015) digs deeper into the representation of female unemployment through censuses. Borderías (2018) finds a similar pattern in the Spanish context, confirming that the decline in female labour force participation at the turn of the nineteenth century and its link to ideological assumptions was a global phenomenon.

1.3 *The Story and the Historiography of Female Work in the Italian Censuses*

The first Italian censuses (1861, 1871, 1881, 1901) provide valuable insights into how the male breadwinner model gained prominence in Italy, shaping ideologies and stereotypes. Two interconnected aspects require analysis. First, there is the underreporting of working women, particularly in agriculture, which is a common characteristic of historical sources (Humphries & Sarasúa, 2012). Second, there is the increase in the number of women identifying as housewives across these four censuses, accompanied by a decline in women employed in the textile industry. Sarti (2018) traces the origin of the term *casalinga* (housewife) in the first censuses. In 1861, they were defined as *donne di casa* (women of the home) totalling nearly 3 million and were included among those without a profession. However, in the subsequent census ten years later, this distinction was not made. In the 1881 census, a new category was introduced, namely *persone attendenti alle cure domestiche* (those attending domestic tasks), which was included in the broader category of people without an occupation.

The general report attached to the census highlights the difficulty in classifying women's activities because the taxonomy was designed for workers with a single occupation, which was inadequate for those, especially women, engaged in multiple activities. In 1881, women involved in multiple activities were classified as workers (Sarti, 2018). Following these criteria, the census recorded a significant number of women employed in the textile industry, particularly in Southern Italy. The 1901 census marked a shift in this trend, since these working women were instead categorised as people carrying out domestic activities. The question posed by enumerators during these twenty years also changed. In 1881, workers were asked to report their occupation, while in 1901, they were asked to specify the occupation that provided their primary source of income. In this census, the number of women defining themselves as employed in the textile industry decreased dramatically, while the number of women "attending domestic tasks" increased.

Pescarolo (1990) argues that the decline in female labour force from 1881 to 1901 was a consequence of the increasingly rigid distinction between "employed" and "non-employed", which devalued the model of the family economy. Ortaggi Cammarosano (1991) acknowledges that the decrease in the number of women registered as working from the 1881 census onwards was a result of Italian statisticians' attempt to define a "modern" industrial sector that differed from the putting-out system. Patriarca (1998) suggests that the decline in female labour force observed in the early unitary censuses has been overestimated. This was due to a gendered conception of labour that aligned with the spread of a more domestic view of women. According to Patriarca, the often-criticised 1861 census should be re-evaluated as it provides a more comprehensive definition of industry and offers a nuanced understanding of women's employment. Sarti argues that the "criteria adopted then represent an excellent demonstration of how ideas on the proper roles of men and women and their changes over time affect the representation of socioeconomic reality provided by the censuses" (2018, p. 192). While men in the 1901 census were categorised based on their occupation rather than their condition, the opposite criteria were applied to women. If a woman reported being in charge of domestic tasks (condition), but also engaged in other activities (occupation), the former took precedence.

Alongside the historians' critique of the progressive masculinisation of the concept of work in the censuses, an economic perspective has offered various adjustments to the figures of female textile employment. Vitali (1968) was among the first to recognise the issue of "overcounting" women in the textile industry. Zamagni (1987) proposed an adjustment to the female share in the textile sector by utilising industrial censuses. Fenoaltea (2003) argued that accepting the share of women in textile employment at face value can lead to a misinterpretation of what constitutes "modern" industry, and he suggested capping female employment at four times the level of male employment. The latter has received support from other scholars (A'Hearn & Venables, 2013; Ciccarelli & Missiaia, 2013). Mancini (2018) proposed an adjustment that combines quantitative data with qualitative sources, such as family monographs.

However, these adjustments do not fully account for the inherent differences between male and female labour. The qualitative literature emphasises the need for a comprehensive quantitative assessment of women's employment and a re-examination of Italian economic history through a feminist lens. This approach aims to eliminate the gender bias deeply entrenched in mainstream economics.[7]

2 What Do We Measure?

2.1 A Matter of Sources

The underreporting of women's work was not simply a result of the nature of their occupations but rather deeply rooted in ideological preconceptions regarding women's societal roles. Consequently, economic historians face significant challenges when attempting to uncover the extent of female employment in the past, as available sources prove inadequate. Population censuses, commonly relied upon to estimate female labour, largely underestimated women's paid work and left it "off the record" (Humphries & Sarasúa, 2012).

However, it is not only censuses that fall short in accurately recording female occupations. Other historical sources, including occupation surveys and household

[7] Spanish quantitative economic history has great examples of these efforts. Sarasua (2019) revisits the timing and the pattern of Spanish industrialisation including women by using data from the 1750–5 Cadaster of Ensenada. Muñoz Abeledo and Verdugo Matés (2023) focus instead on reassessing the occupational structure.

listings, also reflect the biases and prejudices of bureaucrats, enumerators, and individuals of the time concerning natural gender roles.[8] Zucca Micheletto (2013), recognising the "complex relationship between work and archival sources", advocates for the use of alternative sources and methodologies to explore women's work in the past. Scholars have heeded the advice of Carus and Ogilvie (2009) to convert qualitative evidence into quantitative data, utilising diverse qualitative sources that have thus far been overlooked in the study of female labour. These sources are transformed into a meta-source that can be analysed quantitatively. Examples of such alternative sources include diaries, monographs, court proceedings, records of poor relief requests, occasional or nonstandard censuses, and cadastres. In the case of Italy, Mancini (2023) re-evaluates the contribution of women's work in agriculture in the 1930s by using family monographies, whereas Zucca Micheletto (2013) uses registers of applicants for poor relief at the *Ospedale di Carità* in eighteenth-century Turin.

However, each type of source raises an epistemological question related to the concept of objectivity. Historians must inquire about the identity and background of those conducting the interviews. Scott (1988), in her analysis of the statistical representation of work in the *Statistique de l'industrie à Paris, 1847–48*, offers an insightful perspective on how historians should approach this epistemological issue. According to her,

> [a]n alternative approach situates any document in its discursive context and reads it not as a reflection of some external reality but as an integral part of that reality […]. Such an approach demands that the historian question the terms in which any document presents itself and thus ask how it contributes to constructing the 'reality' in the past. (203)

2.2 A Matter of Methods and Methodologies

Recent literature also reflects on the limitations of female labour force participation as a measure of work in pre-industrial societies, particularly women's work (Burnette, 2021). Female labour force participation is a binary measure, not suitable to capture changes in work intensity, unstable and precarious employment types, and forms of labour that fall between paid and unpaid categories. It assumes continuity in the employment relationship, disregarding the existence of precarious work. Betti extensively studied the emergence of precarious work in Italian history. While her work focuses on the second half of the twentieth century, she emphasises the need to re-examine the history of industrial capitalism through the lens of stability/precarity to shed light on the lives of marginalised individuals, such as women (2018). Recent research on the Global South has revived interest in the informal work debate by expanding the concept of work to encompass a "multiversum" of male and female workers (Petrungaro, 2013). (Fig. 1)

---

[8] Alberti (2011) acknowledges that in the 1835 Sicilian census, the Statistical Directorate had to explain to enumerators that they had to include women when accounting for occupations.

Fig. 1 Capitalism also depends on domestic labour, See Red Women's Workshop, United Kingdom, 1975

Alternative approaches to female labour force participation aim to provide a more comprehensive understanding of women's work. For example, Humphries and Thomas (2023) estimate women's unpaid work in historical coalmining communities and attribute them a working wage through a social reproduction framework. Contrary to the predictions of orthodox economics' "income effect" of male breadwinner families, pit women worked longer hours than women in factories, yet their households earned less overall.

It should now be apparent that the issue encompasses not only different measures but also diverse theoretical approaches. According to neoclassical economics, women's decision to participate in the labour market is a result of a rational choice, aimed at maximising utility or satisfaction. In these models, it is a matter of demand: women compare the wage they would earn from paid occupations in the market with the so-called "reservation wage", which represents the value of their time. Other sources of income, such as their husbands' wages, and various factors that may influence their participation, such as the number of children and their husbands' occupations, are taken into account. Such models are at the basis of the branch of economics known as *gender* economics, which integrates gender into mainstream economics by employing standard neoclassical analytical tools, mostly focused on markets, labour, and marriage, without adequately considering the impact of ideological and institutional factors (Horrell & Humphries, 1995). In contrast, *feminist*

Fig. 2 A Woman's Work Is Never Done, See Red Women's Workshop, United Kingdom, 1976

economics is a branch of heterodox economics that recognises the historical subordination of women's work and the discrimination of women and seeks to acknowledge the central role of care and unpaid labour in economic activities (Becchio, 2019). (Fig. 2)

In conclusion, these issues highlight the necessity of adopting new approaches to female employment, utilising sources that may sometimes appear impressionistic, employing mixed methodologies, and striving to capture the multifaceted dimensions of female employment and their complex role in the socio-economic life of past societies. The following section presents an empirical application of this approach.

3 Empirical Analysis: A Case Study

This section presents an empirical application to the case of nineteenth-century Italian women. Instead of estimating female labour force participation, I provide a snapshot of the occupational structure of women, employing an alternative scheme for categorising occupations. In this section, I am interested in identifying the women who did not report any occupation and exploring the intersection between the decision not to report an occupation and their social class. Additionally, I empirically examine whether this phenomenon can be attributed to the gradual spread of the male breadwinner model, thus corroborating the qualitative analysis of feminist scholars and the findings observed in other European countries.

3.1 My Sample

The primary source consists of individual-level occupational data extracted from marriage certificates, collected in the Civil Register (*Registro dello Stato Civile*) for two benchmark years, 1815 and 1866.[9] Marriage certificates provide socio-demographic details about the spouses, their parents, and their witnesses, including information such as birthplace, residence, age, and occupation.

In Italy, the Civil Register was introduced at the beginning of the nineteenth century by Napoleon and was subsequently adopted by all pre-unification States and in 1866 by the country, unified in 1861. This makes it an invaluable source, since, unlike many pre-unification censuses, it is homogeneous across pre-unification states, enabling comparisons between them and over time. Moreover, unlike census data, the information recorded in marriage certificates is at the individual level and self-reported, making it a more suitable source for investigating female employment. However, while marriage certificates provide a more nuanced understanding of female work by capturing unstable and informal types of labour, they do not allow for the differentiation of various tasks or the distinction between paid and unpaid work.

Relying on microdata, I employ a case-study approach selecting four areas with two objectives in mind: (i) to cover both the North and the South of Italy and (ii) to maximise differences between more industrial and rural municipalities within each macro-area. The two industrial areas are Brescia (in the region of Lombardy), encompassing both the cities and the surrounding municipalities that played a pivotal role in the province's industrial development, and Salerno (in Campania), following the same criteria. The two rural areas are Pisticci (in Basilicata), an agrotown, and the province of Udine (in Friuli).[10]

The case-study approach allows for the augmentation of information with secondary sources and local historical literature. This micro-historical approach proves significant when examining women, as contextual factors can significantly influence local labour demands (Zucca Micheletto, 2013), and it facilitates an exploration of how different economic systems may have shaped the types of jobs women engaged in, both within and outside the household. This approach aligns with Boserup (1970)'s hypothesis that the prevailing agricultural systems in the pre-industrial period had an impact on the gendered division of labour and, of utmost importance for this study, on the dissemination of gender norms.

---

[9] The data were collected for a joint project with Marco Martinez. See Freschi and Martinez (2024) for a detailed description of the source. We used scanned pictures of the certificates from the project Antenati, a Government-financed genealogical platform, where individual state archives upload the scanned pictures of their civil registers.

[10] See Freschi and Martinez (2024) for a detailed description of the selection criteria used to identify the case studies.

3.2 Occupational Categories and Structure

I categorise occupations using a standardised classification scheme called the Historical International Social Class Scheme (HISCLASS), as introduced by van Leeuwen and Maas (2011). I start from the classification of occupations in Freschi and Martinez (2024), which utilises a 5-catagroy scheme. This scheme is a modified version of HISCLASS, tailored to account for the specificities of the Italian labour market. However, I contend that HISCLASS fails to capture the multifaceted nature of female work. Departing from HISCLASS-5, I propose an alternative classification called HERCLASS. HERCLASS offers several advantages, including the incorporation of women who did not report any occupation and the flexibility to accommodate *ad-hoc* adjustments to align with diverse local economic systems (Fig. 3).

The case-study approach allows for the examination of specific scenarios, such as that of spinners in Pisticci. The number of women reporting themselves as spinners in Pisticci is remarkably high (over 60% of working women). If these data were used to estimate industrial production or productivity, adjustments would be necessary to prevent inflation. Reports from the time indicate that textile production in the province, both in factories and through the putting-out system, was almost non-existent (D. G. d. S. MAIC, 1880). However, the objective here is to describe female work in all its complexities and contradictions. It is plausible that women engaged

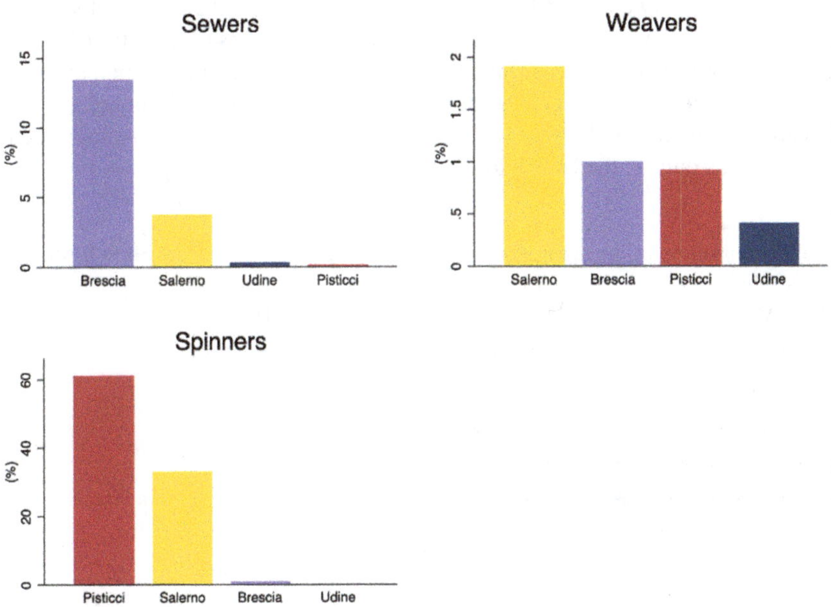

Fig. 3 % of women in textile over working women, by archive 1815–1866. *Source* author's elaboration. Note that the scale on the vertical axis for the upper and lower panel are different

in spinning, among various other domestic or non-domestic activities. If, among these activities, they chose to identify as "spinner", it is important for historians today to respect their choice. To address the large number of women in the textile sector in Pisticci and ensure comparability with other locations, I place them within the fifth occupational category, alongside farmworkers, although conventionally they are considered part of the fourth category. Pisticci was an agrotown, an agglomeration comparable to cities in terms of population and density but predominantly rural in its occupational structure, hence this adjustment is aligned with its economic structure. While the peak percentage of sewers across the entire population is around 13% and is reached in Brescia, the percentage of weavers does not even exceed 2%. However, the percentages of spinners are much higher. Unlike Pisticci, Salerno and its neighbouring municipalities played a central role in textile production, so the high figures of female textile workers there are not surprising (A'Hearn, 1998; D. G. d. S. MAIC, 1888) (Table 1).

Figure 4 illustrates the occupational composition of grooms and brides using both HISCLASS and HERCLASS. Over time, there was a notable transformation in the occupational structure for both men and women. The most significant changes occurred in Brescia, the most industrialised area in the sample. While men experienced a decline in the number of farmworkers, this was offset by an increase in the proportion of non-farm workers, artisans, and shopkeepers. Conversely, for women, the rural exodus resulted in a rise in the number of women who did not report an occupation. In the two rural areas of the sample, namely the provinces of Udine and Pisticci, men underwent a gradual occupational shift during the period. However, it appears that women were overlooked during the initial stages of industrialisation. It is now widely recognised that the decline in women's labour force participation was neither continuous nor uniform across occupations (Horrell & Humphries, 1995). However, non-reporting by women appears to be more nuanced than simply being categorised as outside the labour force.

Table 1 Comparison of the occupational classification schemes for women (HERCLASS) and HISCLASS-5

HISCLASS	HERCLASS
1. Landowners, managers, and professionals	1
2. White-collar workers	2
3. Artisans, shopkeepers, and small business owners	3
4. Lower-skilled and unskilled workers	4
5. Lower-skilled and unskilled farmworkers	5 + spinners in Pisticci
-	6 Outside the labour force

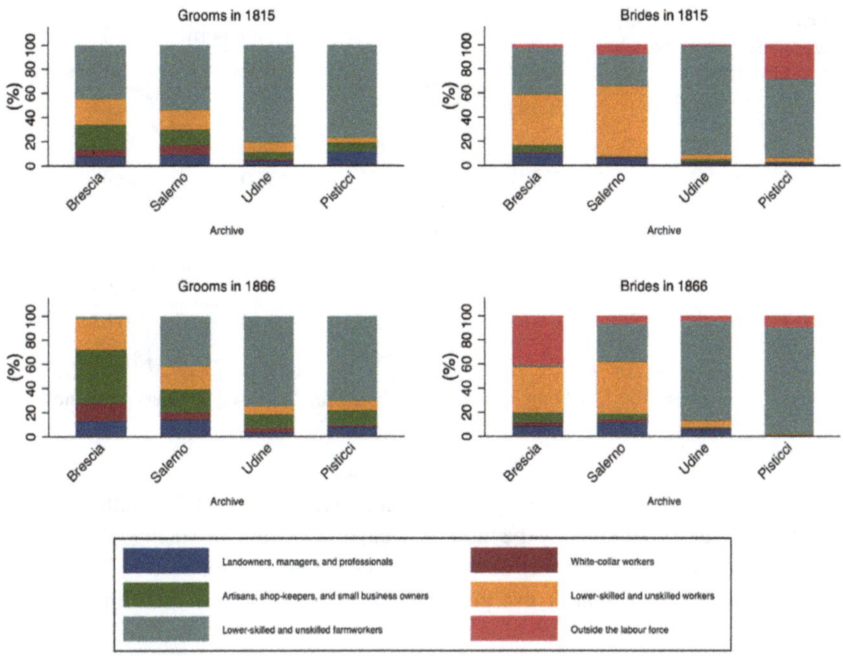

Fig. 4 Occupational structure of brides and grooms in marriage certificates by archive, 1815–1866. *Source* Author's elaboration

3.3 The Issue of Non-Reporting

Table 2 presents the percentage of women who did not report their occupation, disaggregated by year and location. The third column displays the non-reporting rate among brides, while the fourth column focuses on mothers. The pattern is consistent across all locations. In Brescia, Salerno, and Udine, non-reporting significantly rose over time, albeit with notable variations. Among these locations, Brescia experienced the most pronounced increase, reaching a peak of 66% for mothers in 1866.

This chapter aims to examine the prevalence of the social norm that women enter marriage without a job or, more specifically, *without reporting a job*. The methodology I employ is heavily influenced by Van Poppel et al. (2009) who utilise it in the context of Dutch marriage certificates. Table 3 presents the odds ratios derived from a set of logistic regressions, where the dependent variable is the likelihood of brides not reporting any occupation. My hypothesis posits that the probability of stating no occupation is closely linked to the socio-economic background of the brides. Within certain social classes, there was a distinct preference for women not to work, leading to a reduced likelihood of such work being mentioned in the source.[11]

[11] In the international literature, this pattern has been recognised by Davidoff and Hall (1987) and Ågren (2017).

Table 2 % of women not reporting their occupation by year and location

		Non-reporting (in %)	
Archive	Year	Brides	Mothers
Brescia	1815	6.96	24.04
	1866	26.66	75.10
Pisticci	1815	13.20	32.41
	1866	5.43	13.97
Salerno	1815	8.29	27.59
	1866	14.55	48.94
Udine	1815	3.20	10.65
	1866	5.90	18.55

Source Author's elaboration. Deceased mothers have not been considered

The probability that brides reporting no occupation is regressed on their fathers' social class, which is approximated by the father's occupational category using HISCLASS-5. This represents a key difference between this model and the one used by Van Poppel et al. (2009), which primarily use grooms' social class as their main independent variable.

Compared to the daughter of an unskilled farm worker, daughters from upper-class backgrounds were 6.4 times more likely to report no occupation at the time of marriage. The likelihood of reported non-participation in white-collar middle-class families was 2.57 times higher compared to unskilled farm workers, while daughters of shopkeepers and businessmen were 2.36 times more likely to report no occupations. The odds ratio for daughters of unskilled workers not in agriculture is positive but not statistically significant (Column 1, Table 3). Historical evidence suggests that women working was generally frowned upon in aristocratic circles (Pescarolo, 2019), and our empirical findings support this notion.

The model explores whether adherence to the social norm varied across locations and over time. The year dummy variable does not appear to have a significant impact, whereas geography reveals some differences. Women from Salerno, Udine, and Pisticci were more likely to report an occupation than those in Brescia, as indicated by the negative coefficient on the t statistics, although the coefficient for Pisticci is not statistically significant. Age at marriage does not seem to play a significant role, as the odds ratios are not statistically significant. Similarly, the age gap between spouses (measured as the difference between the groom's and bride's age) does not affect non-participation. This is surprising, as one might expect that women marrying older men, who are more likely to have been married before, would be more inclined to give up their jobs to take care of the household. One potential explanation is

Table 3 Logistic regression of not reporting an occupation at the time of marriage by brides, 1815–66

	(1)	(2)	(3)	(4)	(5)	(6)
	Model I	Model II	Model III	Model IV	Model V	Model VI
Father's status(farmworkers = 1) upper class	6.404***	2.759**	33.26***	7.381***	33.69***	28.48***
	[7.51]	[2.55]	[8.08]	[6.91]	[8.10]	[4.06]
White-collar middle class	2.573**	0.590	7.063***	3.287***	7.370***	6.110
	[2.38]	[–0.49]	[3.25]	[2.68]	[3.30]	[1.35]
Shopkeepers and skilled	2.256***	0.375	4.800***	2.664***	4.994***	0.374
	[3.14]	[–1.56]	[3.65]	[3.31]	[3.71]	[–0.90]
Unskilled workers	1.275	0.794	1.980	0.894	2.039	1.351
	[0.77]	[–0.45]	[1.44]	[–0.32]	[1.50]	[0.26]
Years (1815 = 1) 1866	1.157			1.294	5.722	
	[0.68]			[1.01]	[1.24]	
Location (Brescia = 1) Salerno	0.186***	0.210***	0.293	0.0786***	0.0420***	0.0604**
	[–6.15]	[–5.63]	[–0.67]	[–2.59]	[–2.72]	[–2.18]
Udine	0.0544***	0.0530***	0.103	0.230	0.0146**	0.0219*
	[–6.46]	[–6.51]	[–1.28]	[–1.05]	[–2.05]	[–1.80]
Pisticci	0.818	1.012	0.303	0.335	0.241	0.401
	[–0.90]	[0.05]	[–0.75]	[–1.07]	[–1.14]	[–0.71]
Age at marriage (20–24 = 1) less than 19	1.277	1.218	1.009	1.214	1.007	0.980
	[1.02]	[0.81]	[0.03]	[0.73]	[0.02]	[–0.06]
25–29	1.152	1.083	0.908	1.101	0.932	0.884
	[0.56]	[0.31]	[–0.27]	[0.35]	[–0.20]	[–0.34]
30–34	0.814	0.842	0.656	0.791	0.663	0.646
	[–0.53]	[–0.43]	[–0.80]	[–0.57]	[–0.78]	[–0.83]
35–39	1.780	1.666	1.093	1.611	1.101	0.968
	[1.29]	[1.13]	[0.13]	[0.98]	[0.15]	[–0.05]
40+	1.000	0.937	0.616	0.779	0.628	0.657
	[0.00]	[–0.15]	[–0.85]	[–0.55]	[–0.81]	[–0.73]
Gender age gap	1.000	1.000	1.000	1.000	1.000	1.000
	[–0.13]	[–0.13]	[0.03]	[0.13]	[0.04]	[0.03]
Interaction father's status × year upper class × 1866		4.920***				1.339
		[3.04]				[0.30]

(continued)

Table 3 (continued)

	(1)	(2)	(3)	(4)	(5)	(6)
White-collar middle class × 1866		10.24**				1.586
		[2.00]				[0.31]
Shopkeepers and skilled × 1866		15.60***				22.60***
		[3.85]				[2.59]
Unskilled workers × 1866		2.945				2.025
		[1.64]				[0.55]
Officers FE	No	No	Yes	No	Yes	Yes
Village FE	No	No	No	Yes	Yes	Yes
Observations	1672	1672	620	930	620	620

The coefficients are odds ratios; t statistics in brackets
$^{*}p < 0.1$, $^{**}p < 0.05$, $^{***}p < 0.01$

that the observations capture women at the time of their wedding, so they may be relinquishing their jobs immediately after getting married.[12]

As an initial step (Column 1), the model aims to investigate the origins of women who did not report their occupation. After discovering that these women belonged to the highest social stratum, the subsequent step involves examining the situation of all other women: did the trend of not reporting an occupation spread over time from the upper class to women in lower strata? By introducing interaction effects in the regression analysis (Column 2), it becomes possible to delve into the relationship between social class and the practice of reporting an occupation across different periods and locations. Considering two benchmark years, the first year, 1815, is utilised as the baseline. The odds ratios on the interaction term consistently indicate positive and statistically significant values, indicating a convergence over time among social classes in terms of the tendency to not report an occupation. Daughters of farmworkers in 1815 represent the baseline. In 1866, the probability of reporting no occupation is higher across all categories. The most significant increase in non-reporting over time is observed among daughters of shopkeepers and artisans, representing women from middle-class households. This finding corroborates the rich research on these categories and provides empirical support for the long-standing arguments suggesting that the male breadwinner model became a prevalent norm among the middle classes towards the end of the nineteenth century (Pescarolo, 2019).

This chapter empirically investigates the dissemination of a gendered ideology not only within families but also among the authors of the documents we currently study. In column 3, I have attempted to do so, by examining the influence of the

12 The inability to properly capture the age profile is a disadvantage of marriage certificates. However, historically women tended to remain in the labour force until their children grew older and could take their place in the labour market (Horrell & Humphries, 1997).

public officer responsible for preparing the marriage certificate. This also enables an investigation into whether women had limited agency in deciding whether to report their occupation or not, and whether the final decision to include it in the marriage certificate was made by a man: the public officer. Some officers may have considered women's occupations as unimportant or may not have even asked about them. Controlling for this factor reveals a significant heterogeneity in non-reporting across social classes. The odds ratios for wealthy women not reporting their occupation are over 30 times higher than for daughters of farmworkers. For women from white-collar families, the odds are 7 times higher, and for daughters of artisans or shopkeepers, the odds are almost 5 times higher.

Accounting for officers completely captures the geographical differences among different locations, although the sign of the t statistic suggests that non-reporting was less likely in every location compared to Brescia. The disparity between the first column and the third column indicates the presence of substantial omitted variable bias, implying that the choice of officer filling out the marriage certificate must have been correlated with the probability of non-reporting and/or the father's socio-economic class. The direction of the bias is noteworthy. Officers played a central role in perpetuating a gendered view of work across social classes, as some of them likely assigned all women the same occupational titles automatically. Moreover, women themselves had internalised a gendered perspective of their economic roles.

Controlling for village fixed effects indicates that there were geographical variations across villages, although their impact was not as significant as the heterogeneity across officers. In Column 5, I include controls for both officers and village fixed effects, and the results remain consistent. The coefficients for Udine and Salerno become statistically significant, although their effect sizes are small.

In the final column, the preferred specification is presented, which includes an interaction term with the time dummy. Several coefficients that were previously significant no longer retain their significance. This outcome is expected and likely attributed to the limited sample size, which can lead to collinearity issues arising from the inclusion of both officials' fixed effects and individual-level controls.[13] However, the coefficients on the interaction term for daughters of skilled workers remain positive, exhibit a high magnitude, and retain their statistical significance, which highlights the strength of convergence of middle-class families towards the practice of non-reporting, hence the progressive and pervasive diffusion of the cultural norm of the male breadwinner family.

A potential bias of the data arises from the fact that we are examining women at a specific moment in their lives, namely when they get married. Considering the life cycle is crucial as it plays a significant role. Therefore, investigating the status of mothers provides valuable insights into changes in female employment throughout their life course. The percentage of non-reporting among grooms' and brides' mothers

[13] In very small municipalities, it is not uncommon to have a one-to-one correspondence between officials and individuals. In such cases, when conducting a regression analysis, these observations are typically excluded to mitigate the potential issue of attributing variations solely to different public officers across municipalities. By removing these observations, the analysis aims to ensure that the observed variations are not solely driven by the idiosyncrasies of individual officials.

is considerably higher than among the brides themselves (Table 2). The underlying reasons for this discrepancy remain unknown: does it reflect a genuine trend of exiting the labour market as women age and establish families, or is it driven by cultural norms? I conduct a logistic regression analysis to examine the likelihood of mothers not reporting their occupations, conditional on their social class, which is now represented by their husbands' occupational status.

The results indicate a class effect, but with greater homogeneity compared to the case of brides, suggesting that social class may not have been the primary driver of non-reporting (Column 1, Table 4). Like the analysis for brides, when controlling for officers, the impact of social class becomes more pronounced, but still exhibits a more consistent pattern (Column 2, Table 4).

In the interacted regression analysis (Column 3), the group that exhibits a stronger convergence over time towards non-reporting of occupations is wives in white-collar occupations. This convergence can be attributed to the prevailing social norm that women should withdraw from the labour market after getting married. This finding helps explain why the differences across social classes among mothers are not as pronounced. Notably, in the regression analysis for mothers, the convergence towards the norm of non-reporting is more evident in the second-highest occupational category, specifically wives of white-collar workers, whereas among brides it is more prominent among the middle class. Since the mothers in 1866 likely got married in the 1830s, they represent a generation situated between the brides of 1815 and those of 1866. The higher coefficient on wives of white-collar workers suggests a gradual dissemination of the cultural norm across social classes, confirming that the practice of non-reporting developed in a class-specific manner. Initially, it was prevalent among the aristocracy, then spread to white-collar workers' families (as evidenced by the interacted regression on mothers), and eventually extended to daughters of artisans and shopkeepers, who likely substituted registered work with unregistered work.

4 Conclusions

This study delves into the realm of female employment in nineteenth-century Italy, aiming to provide a comprehensive understanding of women's economic culture within historical contexts. With a focus on four Italian locations during the period 1815–1866, this research combines theoretical, methodological, and empirical analyses to shed light on the intricacies of women's work and how they, and the society they lived in, perceived it.

The most innovative aspect of this study lies in the final section, where I employ logistic regression analysis to investigate the probability of women not reporting their occupations. This section does not claim to provide new evidence on the participation of female in the labour market, but it focuses on the ideology influencing the reporting patterns. Building upon the methodology of Van Poppel et al. (2009), this analysis delves into the underlying question of women's economic culture that

Table 4 Logistic regression of not reporting an occupation at the time of marriage by brides' and grooms' mothers, 1815–66

	(1)	(2)	(3)
Husband's status (farmoworker = = 1)			
Upper class	3.012***	8.152***	3.675***
	[6.89]	[8.10]	[2.82]
White-collar middle class	3.419***	5.708***	1.520
	[5.64]	[4.96]	[0.51]
Shop-keepers and skilled	2.707***	3.215***	1.626
	[6.65]	[5.08]	[1.26]
Unskilled workers	1.629***	2.150***	2.424*
	[2.78]	[2.84]	[1.90]
Years	2.007***	84,711,232.2	
	[6.03]	[0.01]	
Salerno	0.841	24.49***	23.32***
	[–1.26]	[2.73]	[2.72]
Udine	0.102***	1.88e–08	1.31e–08
	[–12.11]	[–0.01]	[–0.01]
Pisticci	0.322***	1.256	1.493
	[–7.12]	[0.19]	[0.34]
Upper class × 1866			3.264**
			[2.11]
White-collar middle class × 1866			5.789*
			[1.92]
Shop-keepers and skilled × 1866			2.875**
			[2.20]
Unskilled workers × 1866			0.939
			[–0.11]
Observations	2736	1684	1684

Exponentiated coefficients; t statistics in brackets
$^{*}\ p < 0.1$, $^{**}\ p < 0.05$, $^{***}\ p < 0.01$

permeates the entire book. By exploring the factors influencing women's decisions to report or omit their occupations, we gain valuable insights into the societal norms and attitudes towards female work during this period. The results of this logistic regression analysis not only provide empirical evidence regarding the prevalence of non-reporting among women but also offer glimpses into the complex interplay between gender, class, and cultural norms. In fact, this study examines the role of public officers in perpetuating cultural norms and stigma surrounding women's occupations. To the best of our knowledge, this is the first study to quantify the potential cultural stigma conveyed by these officers. Their influence on the reporting decisions of women underscores the intricate interaction between individual agency, societal structures, and the construction of economic reality.

Moreover, it contributes to the broader narrative of the book by uncovering the intricate layers of women's economic culture, challenging conventional interpretations, and inviting deeper reflection and future investigations into the rich tapestry of women's economic roles throughout history.

Bibliography

Ågren, M. (2017). *Making a Living, Making a Difference: Gender and Work in Early Modern European Society*. Oxford University Press.

A'Hearn, B. (1998). Institutions, Externalities, and Economic Growth in Southern Italy: Evidence from the Cotton Textile Industry, 1861–1914. *The Economic History Review, 51*(4), 734–762. https://doi.org/10.1111/1468-0289.00112

A'Hearn, B., & Venables, A. J. (2013). Regional Disparities: Internal Geography and External Trade. In G. Toniolo (Ed.), *The Oxford Handbook of the Italian Economy Since Unification* (1st ed., pp. 599–630). Oxford University Press. https://doi.org/10.1093/oxfordhb/9780199936694.013.0021

Alberti, M. (2011). Professioni, Arti e Mestieri in Sicilia Nel Censimento Della Direzione Centrale Di Statistica (1835). *Popolazione e Storia, 12*(1–2), 227–248.

Alberti, M. (2015). La disoccupazione delle donne nell'Italia liberale Realtà e rappresentazioni statistiche. *Italia Contemporanea, 277*, 7–33. https://doi.org/10.3280/IC2015-277001

Bateman, V. (2019). *The Sex Factor: How Women Made the West Rich*. Polity Press.

Becchio, G. (2019). *A History of Feminist and Gender Economics* (1st ed.). Routledge.

Bellavitis, A. (2002). Donne, cittadinanza e corporazioni tra Medioevo ed età moderna : ricerche in corso. In *Corpi e storia: donne e uomini dal mondo antico all'età contemporanea*, by Nadia Maria Filippini, Tiziana Plebani, and Anna Scattigno. I libri di Viella 33. Viella. https://doi.org/10.1400/170829

Bellavitis, A. (2016). *Il Lavoro Delle Donne Nelle Città Dell'Europa Moderna*. Storia Delle Donne e Di Genere 6. Viella Libreria Editrice. https://books.google.it/books?id=b2shEAAAQBAJ

Betti, E. (2012). Lo studio del passato e le fonti statistiche. Prospettive storiografiche a confronto. In M. Alberti (eds.), *Memoria E Ricerca* no. 40 (September): 111–44. https://doi.org/10.3280/MER2012-040008

Betti, E. (2016). Gender and Precarious Labor in a Historical Perspective: Italian Women and Precarious Work between Fordism and Post-Fordism. *International Labor and Working-Class History, 89*, 64–83. https://doi.org/10.1017/S0147547915000356

Betti, E. (2018). Historicizing Precarious Work: Forty Years of Research in the Social Sciences and Humanities. *International Review of Social History, 63*(2), 273–319. https://doi.org/10.1017/S0020859018000329

Borderías, C. (2018). The Statistical Construction of Women's Work and the Male Breadwinner Economy in Spain (1856–1930). In R. Sarti, A. Bellavitis, & M. Martini (Eds.), *What Is Work? Gender at the Crossroads of Home, Family, and Business from the Early Modern Era to the Present*, International Studies in Social History (Vol. 30, pp. 165–187). Berghahn Books.

Boris, E. (2018). Regulating Home Labors: The ILO and the Feminization of Work. In R. Sarti, A. Bellavitis, M. Martini (Eds.), *What Is Work? Gender at the Crossroads of Home, Family, and Business from the Early Modern Era to the Present*, International Studies in Social History (Vol. 30, pp. 268–294). Berghahn Books.

Boris, E., Hoehtker, D., & Susan, Z., eds. 2018. *Women's ILO: Transnational Networks, Global Labour Standards, and Gender Equity, 1919 to Present*. Studies in Global Social History (Vol. 32). Brill; International Labour Office.

Boserup, E. (1970). *Woman's Role in Economic Development*. Reprinted with new introduction. George Allen and Unwin Ltd.

Burnette, J. (2021). Why We Shouldn't Measure Women's Labour Force Participation in Pre-Industrial Countries. *Economic History of Developing Regions, 36*(3), 422–427. https://doi.org/10.1080/20780389.2021.1929602

Carus, A. W., & Ogilvie, S. (2009). Turning Qualitative into Quantitative Evidence: A Well-Used Method Made Explicit. *The Economic History Review, 62*(4), 893–925. https://doi.org/10.1111/j.1468-0289.2009.00486.x

Chisté, L., Del Re, A., & Forti, E. (1979). *Oltre Il Lavoro Domestico: Il Lavoro Delle Donne Fra Produzione e Riproduzione*. Felitrinelli.

Ciccarelli, C., & Missiaia, A. (2013). The Industrial Labor Force of Italy's Provinces: Estimates from the Population Censuses, 1871–1911. *Rivista Di Storia Economica, 2*, 141–192. https://doi.org/10.1410/74193

Corsi, M., & Zacchia, G. (2021). Il Femminismo Dei Dati. *INGENERE Newsletter*, 1–3.

Curli, B., & Pescarolo, A. (2003). Genere, Lavoro, Etichette Statistiche. In F. Bimbi (Eds.), *Differenze e Diseguaglianze: Prospettive per Gli Studi Di Genere in Italia* (pp. 65–100). il Mulino.

D. G. d. S. MAIC. (1880). *Annali Di Statistica. Statistica Industriale. Notizie Sulle Condizioni Inudstriali Della Provincia Di Matera*. Tipografia Eredi Botta.

D. G. d. S. MAIC. (1888). *Annali Di Statistica. Statistica Industriale. Notizie Sulle Condizioni Inudstriali Della Provincia Di Salerno*. Tipografia Eredi Botta.

Fenoaltea, S. (2003). Peeking backward: Regional aspects of industrial growth in post-unification Italy. *The Journal of Economic History, 63*(4), 1059–1102. https://doi.org/10.1017/S0022050703002535

Folbre, N. (2018). Family Work: A Policy-Relevant Intellectual History. In R. Sarti, A. Bellavitis, & M. Martini (Eds.), *What Is Work? Gender at the Crossroads of Home, Family, and Business from the Early Modern Era to the Present*. International Studies in Social History (Vol. 30, pp. 89–113). Berghahn Books.

Freschi, G., & Martinez, M. (2024). Intergenerational Mobility in 19th-Century Italy: A Case-Study Approach. *Rivista di Storia Economica, 1*, 43–76. https://doi.org/10.1410/109335

Groppi, A. (1990). Il Lavoro Delle Donne: Un Questionario Da Arricchire. In S. Cavaciocchi (Ed.), *La Donna Nell'economia Secc. XIII–XVIII*. Le Monnier.

Groppi, A., Ed. (1996). *Il Lavoro Delle Donne*. Storia Delle Donne in Italia. Laterza.

Horrell, S., & Humphries, J. (1995). Women's Labour Force Participation and the Transition to the Male-Breadwinner Family, 1790–1865. *Economic History Review, 48*(1), 89–117.

Horrell, S., & Humphries, J. (1997). The Origins and Expansion of the Male Breadwinner Family: The Case of Nineteenth-Century Britain. *International Review of Social History, 42*(5), 25–64.

Hudson, P. (2008). The History Construction of Gender: Reflections on Gender and Economic History. In F. Bettio & A. Veeraschagina (Eds.), *Frontiers in the Economics of Gender*, Routledge Siena Studies in Political Economy (pp. 21–41). Routledge.

Humphries, J. (1991). 'Lurking in the Wings...': Women in the Historiography of the Industrial Revolution. *Business and Economic History, 20*, 32–44.

Humphries, J., & Sarasúa, C. (2012). Off the Record: Reconstructing Women's Labor Force Participation in the European Past. *Feminist Economics, 18*(4), 39–67. https://doi.org/10.1080/13545701.2012.746465

Humphries, J., & Sarasúa, C. (2021). The Feminization of the Labor Force and Five Associated Myths. In G. Berik & E. Kongar (Eds.), *The Routledge Handbook of Feminist Economics*, Routledge International Handbooks (pp. 167–176). Routledge.

Humphries, J., & Thomas, R. (2023). 'The Best Job in the World': Breadwinning and the Capture of Household Labor in Nineteenth and Early Twentieth-Century British Coalmining. *Feminist Economics, 29*(1), 97–140. https://doi.org/10.1080/13545701.2022.2128198

Leeuwen, M. H. D. van, & Maas, I. (2011). *Hisclass: A Historical International Social Class Scheme*. G-Reference, Information and Interdisciplinary Subjects Series. Leuven University Press. https://books.google.it/books?id=Ol9EzJNLNYYC

Maitte, C. 2016. Le Travail Invisible Dans Les Familles Artisanales (XVIIe-XVIIIe Siècle). *Mélanges de l'École Française de Rome—Italie et Méditerranée Modernes et Contemporaines, 128*(1).

Mancini, G. (2018). Women's Labor Force Participation in Italy, 1861–2011. *Rivista Di Storia Economica, 34*, 3–68.

Mancini, G. (2023, May). Breadwinner, Bread Maker: The Gender Division of Labour in 1930s Rural Italy. *European Review of Economic History*, head009. https://doi.org/10.1093/ereh/head009

Muñoz Abeledo, L., & Matés, R. V. (2023). New Evidence for Women's Labor Participation and Occupational Structure in Northwest Spain, 1877–1930. *The Journal of Interdisciplinary History, 53*(4), 571–598. https://doi.org/10.1162/jinh_a_01906

Ortaggi Cammarosano, S. (1991). Labouring Women in Northern and Central Italy in the Nineteenth Century. In D. M. Smith, J. A. Davis, & P. Ginsborg (Eds.), *Society and Politics in the Age of the Risorgimento: Essays in Honour of Denis Mack Smith* (pp. 152–183). Cambridge University Press.

Patriarca, S. (1998). Gender Trouble: Women and the Making of Italy's 'Active Population', 1861–1936. *Journal of Modern Italian Studies, 3*(2), 144–163. https://doi.org/10.1080/13545719808454973

Pescarolo, A. (1990). I Mestieri Femminili. Continuità e Spostamenti Di Confini Nel Corso Dell'industrializzazione. *Memoria. Rivista Di Storia Delle Donne, 30*, 55–68.

Pescarolo, A. (2018). Productive and Reproductive Work: Uses and Abuses of an Old Dichotomy. In R. Sarti, A. Bellavitis, & M. Martini (Eds.), *What Is Work? Gender at the Crossroads of Home, Family, and Business from the Early Modern Era to the Present*, International Studies in Social History (Vol. 30, pp. 114–138). Berghahn Books.

Pescarolo, A. (2019). *Il lavoro delle donne nell'Italia contemporanea*. Storia delle donne e di genere 11. Viella.

Petrungaro, S. (2013). The Fluid Boundaries of 'Work'. Some Considerations about Concepts, Approaches, and South-Eastern Europe. *Sudost-Forschungen, 72*, 271–286.

Picchio, A. (1992). *Social Reproduction: The Political Economy of the Labour Market*. Cambridge Univeristy Press.

Prügl, E. (1999). *The Global Construction of Gender: Home-Based Work in the Political Economy of the 20th Century*. Columbia University Press.

Romero-Martín, J. (2016). Craftswomen in Times of Change: Artisan Family Strategies in Nineteenth Century Barcelona. *Mélanges de l'École Française de Rome—Italie et Méditerranée Modernes et Contemporaines, 128*(1).

Sarasua, C. (2019). Women's Work and Structural Change: Occupational Structure in Eighteenth-century Spain. *The Economic History Review, 72*(2), 481–509. https://doi.org/10.1111/ehr.12733

Sarti, R. (2018). Toiling Women, Non-Working Housewives, and Lesser Citizens: Statistical and Legal Constructions of Female Work and Citizenship in Italy. In R. Sarti, A. Bellavitis, & M. Martini (Eds.), *What Is Work? Gender at the Crossroads of Home, Family, and Business from the Early Modern Era to the Present*, International Studies in Social History (Vol. 30, pp. 188–225). Berghahn Books.

Sarti, R., Bellavitis, A., & Martini, M. (Eds.). (2018). *What Is Work? Gender at the Crossroads of Home, Family, and Business from the Early Modern Era to the Present. International Studies in Social History,* (Vol. 30). Berghahn Books.

Scott, J. W. (1988). *Gender and the Politics of History*. Columbia University Press. https://doi.org/10.7312/scot91266

Sharpe, P. (1995). Continuity and Change: Women's History and Economic History in Britain. *The Economic History Review, 48*(2), 353. https://doi.org/10.2307/2598407

Tilly, C., & Tilly, C. (1998). *Work under Capitalism.* New Perspectives in Sociology. Westview Press.

Van Poppel, F. W. A., & Van Dalen, H. P. (2009). Diffusion of a Social Norm: Tracing the Emergence of the Housewife in the Netherlands, 1812–1922. *The Economic History Review, 62*(1), 99–127. https://doi.org/10.1111/j.1468-0289.2008.00433.x

Various authors. (2021). *Angela Groppi e La Storia Sociale.* Vol. 20. Genesis. Rivista Della Società Italiana Delle Storiche 2. Viella Libreria Editrice. https://books.google.it/books?id=_yxjEAAAQBAJ

Vitali, O. (1968). *La Popolazione Attiva in Agricoltura Attraverso i Censimenti Italiani (1881–1961).* Tipografia Failli.

Whittle, J., & Hailwood, M. (2020). The Gender Division of Labour in Early Modern England. *The Economic History Review, 73*(1), 3–32. https://doi.org/10.1111/ehr.12821

Zamagni, V. (1987). A Century of Change: Trends in the Composition in the Italian Labour Force, 1881–1981. *Historical Social Research, 12*(4). https://doi.org/10.12759/HSR.12.1987.4.36-97

Zucca Micheletto, B. (2013). Reconsidering Women's Labor Force Participation Rates in Eighteenth-Century Turin. *Feminist Economics, 19*(4), 200–223. https://doi.org/10.1080/13545701.2013.842283

Zucca Micheletto, B. (2014). Only Unpaid Labour Force? Women's and Girls' Work and Property in Family Business in Early Modern Italy. *The History of the Family, 19*(3), 323–340. https://doi.org/10.1080/1081602X.2014.929528

Labour Market Segregation: Female Teachers in Southern Italy (1861–1937)

Vittoria Ferrandino, Marilena Iacobaccio, and Valentina Sgro

1 Women's Social and Working Conditions in Post-Unification Italy

Between the end of the nineteenth century and the beginning of the twentieth century, women's working conditions in Italy, as well as in the rest of Europe, became the subject of public debate. In the years immediately following Italian unification in 1861, the member of parliament Salvatore Morelli engaged in the fight for equality between men and women, both in the workplace and in social rights.[1] In fact, despite the increase in female work, women continued to be considered in a subordinate position to men: their main role remained within the family, dedicated to the home and to the children.

[1] It was only in 1902, however, with the so-called Carcamo law, that important women's rights were introduced in the workplace, as well as the obligation for companies with at least fifty female workers to set up special spaces dedicated to breastfeeding or to grant specific permits for this purpose. However, if on the one hand this rule sought to protect maternity, on the other hand it did not protect working women at all as it did not guarantee pay during the month of compulsory abstention, nor the retention of the job after that period. Only later, in 1910, was the Maternity Fund established to guarantee a subsidy to women on compulsory maternity leave. Finally, in 1919, the law which gave the husband the right to oppose the exercise of his wife's professional activity or access to public employment was repealed (Law No. 1176 of 17 July 1919). However, the effectiveness of the law was practically nullified by the limitations contained in the implementing decree (Semeraro, 1999).

V. Ferrandino (✉) · M. Iacobaccio · V. Sgro
Università degli Studi del Sannio, Benevento, Italy
e-mail: ferrandino@unisannio.it

M. Iacobaccio
e-mail: iacobacciomarilena@gmail.com

V. Sgro
e-mail: valentina.sgro@unisannio.it

M. Mosca (ed.), *Women at Work in Italy (1750–1950)*, Springer Studies in the History of Economic Thought, https://doi.org/10.1007/978-3-031-64281-4_6

With the outbreak of the First World War and the mobilization of the male population, both the needs of factories and offices and the needs of families gradually contributed to the increase in the number of women employed outside the domestic context. After the First World War, the greater role that women had in the workplace and in society during the conflict was soon forgotten. Those who managed to keep their profession had to fight against hostility and opposition—both ideological and effective—from a strongly male-dominated press and working men, who often failed to recognize and be grateful for the support that women had given during the war (Mondello, 1987, pp. 21–22). This was confirmed in the words addressed to women by the parliamentarian Luigi Federzoni[2]:

> to the many merits acquired they will want to add this other, no less worthy of their virtues: not to complicate the already numerous, very urgent and very serious problems of the war and of the post-war period by inappropriately and prematurely solving the question of "women's rights". (cit. in Gibelli, 2014, p. 211)[3]

During the fascist regime, despite its restrictions, women underlined their diversity from men, conceiving work as an element that had to coexist with the "natural" role of wife and mother; many affirmed it as a right to self-fulfilment, as an element of independence and of individual and social growth (Addis Saba, 1988, pp. 59–60). However, in this period the issue of women's work received little attention, also due to the great depression of 1929 (Scramaglia, 1997, pp. 51–52). It was only after the Second World War that various investigations were launched, focused on the political-institutional, legislative and social aspects of women's working conditions in Italy.[4]

As working women were predominantly teachers,[5] this chapter focuses on the employment of women in the school system, one of the professions considered as extensions of the domestic sphere. The feminization of the teaching profession was an important factor linked to the expansion of schooling, something that has been largely neglected so far in quantitative historical studies on the development of education. Arguably, a higher proportion of female teachers pushed more girls to enrol in primary education, with the expansion of overall enrolment rates (Cappelli & Vasta, 2021). The effect of feminization on enrolments was also driven by public education and influenced by institutional features: the Casati law of 1859,[6] by not

[2] Federzoni, among the founders of the Italian Nationalist Association, was an Italian politician and writer. He was President of the Senate of the Kingdom from 1929 to 1939. His work as Minister of the Interior was responsible for, among others, the laws relating to the establishment of the Governorate of Rome and the High Commission of Naples, the creation of the National Opera for the protection and assistance of maternity and childhood and the Opera Nazionale Balilla, the new public safety law, as well as various laws for the defence and improvement of public hygiene (Vittoria, 1995).

[3] Unless stated otherwise, the translations of quoted texts are our own.

[4] See Tomasi (1959), Bertoni Jovine (1963), Mayeur (1977), Porcheddu (1978), and Ulivieri (1978).

[5] See Albisetti (1993), Bertocchi and Bozzano (2019), Ciccarelli and Weisdorf (2019), and Federico et al. (2019).

[6] The Casati law was the institutional pillar of the reorganization of the new kingdom's school system and it organized the school system on the French plan of centralized control. The law on

explicitly mentioning women throughout most of its articles, inadvertently promoted full equality between boys and girls, as well as female and male teachers (Cappelli & Vasta, 2021).

In this chapter we examine the Italian national situation first, then we compare it with significant examples taken from Southern Italy. In economic history, the educational gender gap and the role of female teacher in Southern Italy has received very little attention. When considering inland areas, the need for historical research on the educational gender gap is even more compelling: indeed, the issue seems to have been neglected by coeval observers, historians and economic historians, with some notable exceptions (Ciccarelli & Weisdorf, 2019). By reconstructing the gender gap patterns in human capital in two inland areas of the Campania region (Avellino and Benevento), in comparison with the national data, this chapter aims to contribute to this line of research.

2 Development of Schools and Teaching Staff in Italy

2.1 School Development in Italy

In 1859 the Casati law had introduced compulsory education in Italy. In the twenty-five years that followed the first post-unification school year, 1861–62, the number of pupils in Italian public and private day primary schools increased from one million to a good 2,300,000. The doubling of the school population corresponded to a sharp decrease in the illiteracy rate (Ravà, 1906, p. 1732). For several decades public schools only rarely welcomed pupils from the most influential social classes, due to a widespread aversion by wealthy families to sending their children to school with pupils from more modest social backgrounds. Moreover, the content of the teaching was unsatisfactory and became a disincentive to attend school: the documents on elementary education collected and published between 1868 and 1873 recorded, for the municipal schools for girls, a truly alarming reality, namely that the teachers, rather than the rules of arithmetic and grammar or the correct pronunciation of Italian, limited themselves to teaching a little knitting and sewing and having prayers recited (Di Pol, 2002).

Tables 1 and 2 highlight a high number of private schools in the following decades, growing between 1888 and 1896, and equal to just over double the number in the decade 1927–1937. The private elementary schools had declined rapidly after the

public education of 13 November 1859 obliged fathers of families or those acting in their stead to provide the education needed by their children aged 6 to 12, taught in lower elementary classes in the way they deemed most convenient. The law included five sets of regulations dealing with higher education, upper secondary classical education, technical education, primary education and "normal schools" (for elementary teacher preparation). This system called for highly centralized administration and a clear division of upper secondary education between the *liceo classico* (a pre-university requirement) and vocational, "utilitarian" secondary schools for practical job training.

Coppino law of 1877, which had extended compulsory education,[7] although in some cities they remained quite numerous, and in some major cities they even grew in number.[8] This increase, especially in the period following 1882–83, was due to the fact that new schools, previously unidentified, were registered, since from that year also private schools had to fulfil, by law, the task of communicating any changes relating to the school activity.[9] Tables 3 and 4 show the number of public day elementary schools. It continued to grow so much that it increased by three thousand units between 1888–96 and doubled after thirty years, which means that the reforms to combat illiteracy, and to reorganize and improve the educational and training service at school level, were working. At the same time, however, two different scholastic realities continued to coexist: the elementary schools just described, in accordance with the law, and the optional ones,[10] which were maintained by the Municipalities in small villages or hamlets, where school is not compulsory. These schools do not have the characteristics of real primary schools, since they do not remain open every year, and even those that open only last a few months and are run by people without legal qualifications, paid by the municipalities with salaries lower than the legal ones or with very low remuneration. In most of them, teaching is limited to the rudiments of reading and writing, and so there are no fixed rules for enrolment or duration.[11]

Despite this, as we shall see, these schools were quite numerous and popular, particularly in small towns. We take them into consideration for statistical purposes because, although poorly organized and not compliant with the regulated schools, they still contributed to the reduction of the level of illiteracy.

2.2 *Development of Teaching Staff in Italy by Gender*

During the decade from 1865 to 1875 there was a significant increase in the number of female teachers in Italy, going from 10,541 to approximately 18,000, already

[7] The Coppino law "brought back the provisions of the organic law of 13 November 1859, prescribing that children aged 6 should be sent to the elementary schools of the municipality, if the parents, or those acting in their stead, did not provide them with elementary education or with teaching at home or in private schools. The obligation to attend school runs from 6 to 9 years and can extend up to 10 and even up to 12 years. [...] The implementation of that law was to begin with the 1877–78 school year: 1st in municipalities with fewer than 5,000 inhabitants, where there was one lower grade teacher for every 1,000 inhabitants; 2nd in municipalities from 5,000 to 20,000, where there was one every 1,200; 3rd in the larger municipalities, where there was one for every 1,500. In the other municipalities, the law was to be implemented when the number of teachers had reached the conditions indicated above" (Ministry of Agriculture, Industry and Commerce, 1891, p. XII).

[8] Note that for private schools, lower-level schools are not distinguished from higher-level ones. In private elementary schools, the distribution of courses and the distribution of classes and teaching staff are not uniform and do not correspond to those of public schools.

[9] Ministry of Agriculture, Industry and Commerce (1891, pp. XXIII–XXVII).

[10] As explained above, the law was not implemented in small municipalities.

[11] Ministry of Agriculture, Industry and Commerce (1892, p. XVII).

exceeding that of upper primary teachers in 1877, the first year of application of the Coppino law, and reaching 24,167 in 1882.[12] The higher presence of women in primary education was a consequence of the growing number of girls enrolled in normal schools,[13] intended as exclusively professional courses, in which the number of female students increased considerably in the last years of the nineteenth century. In 1870, there were 23 male and 36 female normal schools, while for schools training upper primary teachers the gap was as high as 13 to 43 (Saraceno, 2003, pp. 53–54). In the school year 1889–90 there were 3,788 private day schools with 49,366 teachers, of whom almost 29,000 were women. Five years later, there were 4,210 schools with 52,512 teachers, just over 32,000 of whom were women (see Table 1).

It is interesting to link the number of female teachers with that of kindergartens, both public and private, first of all because it highlights that there were 2.52 female teachers per kindergarten compared to 0.05 of men, but even more because it gives us a picture where the number of female teachers in kindergartens was higher than that of primary school teachers. In the year 1889–90 there were on average 1.64 women teachers per elementary school. In the years 1890–91 and 1891–92, there was a notable decrease in the number of public kindergartens, and an increase in private ones.[14] In the 1894–95 school year, the number of kindergartens increased to 2,799, of which 937 were private, with a total of almost 7,000 teachers, of whom 6,708 were women (see Table 5).

Marriage was considered an automatic cause for dismissal, as it was believed that a good educator could not devote herself to her own children and those of others. A further cause for dismissal, according to the provisions of the Casati law, was when the moral reputation of the teacher had been seriously compromised. The power exercised by the mayors, through the granting or refusal of the certificate of morality, was often configured as an instrument of discrimination, based on political motivations in the case of male teachers and on moral arguments in the case of female teachers. In terms of pay, too, the situation was no better: their salary was on average about a third lower than that of their male colleagues (Soldani, 1989).

In 1911, the Daneo-Credaro Reform[15] brought about a decisive improvement in female literacy. Even though the Reform was not aimed at girls specifically, it brought about the unintended consequences of more rapid human capital accumulation for

[12] The increase however was distributed very unequally among the various Italian regions: Piedmont and Lombardy represented 46% of the total (Ulivieri, 2012).

[13] From the eighteenth century, a gradual process of didactic, organizational and disciplinary standardization and homologation was spreading throughout Europe, in different forms and at different times. From these European models derived the adoption in Italy of the normal method, that is, responding to a norm, to a fixed programme, a method that also envisaged the practice of simultaneous schooling, with lessons given by a single teacher to several pupils. Thanks to the normal method, properly educated teachers could more effectively teach a curriculum previously set by the government (Schirripa, 2003).

[14] For 1891 it was not possible to obtain the information for some kindergartens of municipalities and private individuals in various provinces. Ministry of Agriculture, Industry and Commerce (1894, p. XII), tav. IV—Numero degli asili pubblici e privati e numero degli alunni dal 1872 al 1893.

[15] The reform implied a shift from a decentralized system towards primary-school centralization.

women and a reduced educational gender gap with important implications for Italy's economic history (Cappelli & Vasta, 2021).

With the outbreak of the First World War there was a notable increase in the presence of women in schools. The figure of the teacher became the ideal vehicle for increasing the literacy of the population, appreciated not only by the ruling class but also by the Church. The profession of women teachers became essential to guarantee a certain level of education for young people, but also to fuel patriotic support, since, among their tasks, there was also that of stimulating their attachment to institutions. During fascism women resisted the limitations imposed by the regime for their participation in the selection for teaching posts in schools and, in 1932, presented a petition to the Ministry of Education to ask for the readmission of women to the competition (Covato, 1996, pp. 49–51). And in fact, the data reported in Table 2 confirm that despite the reduction in the number of schools and teaching staff, the presence of female teachers did not undergo excessive variations, with female staff ranging between 86 and 88% of the total number of teachers. From 1926 to 1927, in a decade, the number of kindergartens increased from just over 7,000 to 9,589, with teaching staff increasing to 10,499 (see Table 6). As for the elementary schools, in 1936–37, there were 110,546 teachers, of whom 88,111 were women (see Table 7).[16]

2.3 *Roles, Grades and Qualifications by Gender*

Between 1889 and 1896 the number of female teachers in lower primary day schools exceeded male teachers in all years both for actual teachers and in the case of substitutes and assistants (see Table 7). There were approximately ten thousand more teachers every year, but this figure grew in the final three years. The same cannot be said for upper primary schools, where the number of female teachers was around 40% of the total, and in the last two years their number decreased. This data reflects the rather common idea that women had the ability to care for and educate children at a young age due to their maternal sense, in addition to the fact that they very often did not have the necessary qualifications to teach in higher grades. In fact, it can be seen from Table 8 that thirty years later, although the number of women with a degree or teaching qualification was significantly higher than that of men with 80% of women holding a magister qualification compared to 20% of men, this percentage dropped to 70% if a degree or diploma is considered. Furthermore, only a very small percentage of women managed to continue their careers and become principals. The percentage of women with a magister qualification who were qualified to be principals compared to the total number of qualified teachers is equal to 0.27%, while for men it is 3.4%. The percentage rises to 4% for female graduates and 32% for males. From 1929 to

[16] In the field of education, fascism began with the school reform promoted by Giovanni Gentile in 1923 of which one of the fundamental principles was the subjection of education to state control. The principle of state supremacy was reinforced by introducing at the end of each main course of studies a state examination to be taken by pupils from both public and private schools.

1935, female principals were always around 30% of the total, while they dropped to 23% in 1936 and 1937, due to fascist policies which restricted women's access to managerial positions. In the same year, most of them (approximately 27%) were between 40 and 44 years old (Tables 9 and 10).

3 Schools and Teaching Staff Development in Southern Italy

Focusing our analysis on the Southern Italian regions, we see that the data reported in Tables 11–30, while in some cases in line with the national percentages, in other cases show some specific differences.

3.1 Development of Schools in Southern Italy

In Southern Italy, during the post-unification decades the number of public schools rose, while the number of private schools decreased. From the school year 1888–89 up to 1895–96, there was a moderate growth of the number of schools, which is certainly the result of the already mentioned Coppino law. The situation changed radically in the period 1927–37, when the number of private schools was drastically reduced (around a third compared to forty years earlier) and consequently the same happened for the teaching staff. This also occurred at the national level. At the end of the nineteenth century, there was a moderate growth in both public and private elementary schools. Instead, from 1926 to 1937 there was a halving of private schools and a doubling of public ones.

3.2 Teaching Staff Development by Gender in the Southern Regions

In one of the provinces we examined, Avellino, the data regarding the work performed by men and women are not in line with the national and regional percentages. At the national level, male teachers vary between 50–65% compared to women in the years analysed, in the Campania region between 80 and 95%; in the province of Avellino the difference between the two sexes is reduced to a few units and in some years (1889–90 and 1891–92) male employees exceeded female employees. This suggests that in the South of Italy, although women were starting to enter the labour market, many of them still dedicated themselves only to domestic life and their family, therefore also in the teaching profession the male sex was predominant.

Just as happened in the rest of the country, female teachers had a significant role both in kindergarten and in lower elementary schools, where women reached a high percentage of positions as teachers and assistants. As for the higher-grade schools, the number of men was slightly higher, as there were few women who had access to higher education and universities and consequently could become teachers in higher education schools (Ulivieri, 1978). However, in the South of Italy, as well as in the rest of the country, there was an increase in female teachers in private schools that can be attributed to the fascist action which sought to exclude women from public competitions for teaching positions and therefore from public schools.

Fig. 1 A teacher with pupils in a second grade school (1921). *Source* Ferraro photographic archive

In the province of Avellino, consultation of archive data shows that the first women who embarked on a working career in the nineteenth century were either teachers or midwives. From statistical documents we learn that in 1838 there were 26 municipal teachers in the province of Avellino, who had to «teach to spin, sew, knit socks and be of Christian doctrine».[17] To these were added several private teachers. In this province we have identified many difficulties in the appointment of teachers. It is easy to find documents that attest to an obligatory choice, due to the lack of requirements in the other candidates.[18] It must be said that the qualities required were often of a

[17] State Archive of Avellino (hereinafter SAA), Statistical Summary on the Principality of 1838 on 1839, Avellino 1839, s.e., Chap. 1.

[18] As in the case of Caposele where the teacher Virginia Vitamore was the only one suitable to fill the role out of three candidates, the others lacking the qualifications required and the appropriate age (SAA, Intendenza P. U., b. 1108, fasc. 4694). Six years (1859–65) went by in the municipality of

moral nature and had to be certified by the mayor.[19] The prejudice towards women teachers was also the result of their economic independence (Covato, 1996, p. 28). From the beginning of the twentieth century, documents show that female teachers very often possessed either a teaching qualification or a degree.[20] In many cases they were single women, probably because it was believed that married women took time away from home life and above all from their children, to dedicate themselves to the education of children in the school environment (Bini, 1989; Covato, 1996, pp. 30–31; Dolza, 1987).

From the analysis of data on population censuses, in the twenty years following the unification of Italy, a rather limited participation of women in the labour market emerges also in the province of Benevento.[21] Here, the totality of the staff in kindergartens is made up of women, whose prevalence, albeit less marked, also emerges among the teachers of both lower and higher-grade compulsory schools (see Tables 28 and 29). The female presence was still strongly predominant in private day schools. In fact, from the archival data published in Table 30, it emerges that the number of female teachers was on average double that of male colleagues. During the period analysed, while the number of male teachers remained almost unchanged, the number of female teachers more than doubled (see Table 27), for the same reasons given in the Avellino province.

3.3 Roles, Grades and Qualifications by Gender

While for the national data in the period 1927–37 there was a constant presence of women in managerial roles, albeit to a considerably lesser extent than men (see

Grottolella to find a suitable woman for the position of teacher, in fact every time those who applied were lacking in the characteristics necessary to fill the role of teacher (SAA, Intendenza P. U., b. 1112, fasc. 4719). In the case of the municipality of Cairano, the Superintendent of Sant'Angelo dei Lombardi wrote to the Superintendent of the Province of Avellino informing him that in Cairano, pursuant to art. 226 of the law of 12 December 1816, the only woman who could carry out the function of teacher of the girls is Mrs. Donna Maria Michela Frieri because "educated in womanish virtues and in reading and writing" (SAA, Intendenza P.U. b. 1130, fasc. 4690, Sant'Angelo dei Lombardi, 20 November 1840). The same happened in the municipality of Santa Paolina in 1886, when there was only one candidate to fill the position of teacher (SAA, Municipality of Santa Paolina, b. 41, fasc. 3).

[19] The requirements were established from time to time by the city council and therefore sometimes appeared to have a discriminatory nature (Dolza, 1987, p. 34).

[20] SAA, Manzoni High School of Mugnano del Cardinale, b. 1, r.1.

[21] In particular, the 1881 census reveals for the municipality of Benevento alone, 1,183 women in the agriculture-hunting-fishing sector, against 2,670 men in the same sector, and the gap is even wider as regards those in the industrial sector (3,084 men and 276 women). Women also significantly outnumber men in the category of "domestic service workers" (223 women and only 64 men) and "non-professional conditions" (8,826 women against 2,769 men). Istat Historical Archive, Ministry of Agriculture, Industry and Commerce, General Directorate of Statistics, Census of the Population of the Kingdom of Italy on 31 December 1881, Population classified by profession and condition vol. III, Tipografia Bodoniana, Rome, 1884.

Table 8), in the regional school environment those roles were held by men, as shown in Table 20. They accessed the role of school principal at a much older age, often after the age of 55 (see Table 21). Instead, at a national level it appears that women were able to hold a managerial role especially between the ages of 40 and 44, therefore even younger than men (45–49 and 50–54 years, see Table 9).

For the reasons already explained, during fascism the female teaching staff in the province of Benevento experienced a period of stasis, and then grew significantly during World War II, when many men were called up to arms (Covato, 1996, pp. 49–51). The magister qualification appears to be the predominant qualification among principals and above all among teachers, followed by a degree or diploma, both for male and female staff (see Table 22).

4 Conclusions

In Italy, the issue of education certainly represents a very critical topic in the history of the country. Italy lagged some 50 years behind more advanced countries like France, Prussia and the UK. Moreover, its regional divide in gendered literacy was unparalleled in the rest of Europe.

As evidenced by the analysis and archival data, the presence of women in schools, especially in kindergartens and lower grade primary schools, can be traced back to emphasis on the role of "virtuous" educator, as an extension of the maternal mission» and it «represents both the formidable ideological coverage of a social devaluation of popular education and the will to consolidate an ambiguous educational model, which considered women suitable for educating girls or boys, but only in the lower course (Covato, 1996, p. 33).

And in fact, considering the data in tables showing the number of teaching staff in kindergartens and compulsory schools, we can clearly see that while for the lower grade public day primary schools and even more so for kindergartens, the number of male teachers is lower than that of the other gender, the opposite is recorded in upper elementary schools for both effective teachers and trainees. In private primary education, on the other hand, the cause of the gap between men and women employed could be found in the fact that this work activity for men was not particularly satisfactory and wages were lower than in other professions (Covato, 1996, p. 33), even more so in private institutions where the situation was characterized by greater precariousness and fewer protections.

Therefore, the history of the feminization of the teaching profession unfolds in a particular cultural and social context, with the access of women to teaching and at the same time to other professions marking on the one hand the start of a radically new process of acquisition of a social subjectivity through work, and on the other hand the attempt to bring this phenomenon back into a social dimension shaped by the characteristics and roles of family life.

From the analysis of schools and education institutions data relating to some internal areas of Southern Italy, it emerges that the situation was mainly in line with national data, with some significant differences such as the more limited participation of women in the labour market and their smaller number and older age in managerial roles.

The chauvinist model of teaching in schools continued to be challenged more incisively after the collapse of the fascist regime and the end of the Second World War (Bravo, 1991). In fact, a decree of the Council of Ministers issued in 1945 recognized not only women's right to vote, but also the constitutional provision which sanctioned the principle of equality between men and women, with other provisions aimed at protecting female employment and the role of women in society in general.[22]

Appendix

See Tables 1, 2, 3, 4, 5, 6, 7, 8, 9, 10, 11, 12, 13, 14, 15, 16, 17, 18, 19, 20, 21, 22, 23, 24, 25, 26, 27, 28, 29, and 30.

Table 1 Number of schools and teachers by gender in private day schools in Italy from 1889 to 1896

Years	Kingdom			
	Number of schools	Number of teachers		
		Male	Female	Total
1888–89	–	20,528	28,041	48,569
1889–90	3,788	20,550	28,816	49,366
1890–91	–	–	–	–
1891–92	3,891	20,447	30,372	50,819
1892–93	4,091	20,433	30,952	51,385
1893–94	4,168	20,269	31,591	51,860
1894–95	4,220	20,082	32,040	52,122
1895–96	4,210	19,968	32,544	52,512

Source ISTAT data processed by the authors

[22] See De Grand (1976), Perry (2002), and D'Amelio (2001).

Table 2 Number of schools and teachers by gender in private day schools in Italy from 1927 to 1937

Years	Number of schools	Number of teachers		
		Male	Female	Total
1927–28	2,551	839	5,737	6,576
1928–29	2,616	884	5,811	6,695
1929–30	2,563	724	5,649	6,373
1930–31	2,613	751	5,901	6,652
1931–32	2,656	764	5,905	6,669
1932–33	2,393	724	5,328	6,052
1933–34	2,302	740	5,042	5,782
1934–35	2,255	644	4,918	5,562
1935–36	2,798	688	4,855	5,543
1936–37	2,223	574	4,609	5,183

Source ISTAT data processed by the authors

Table 3 Number of regular and irregular public elementary day schools in Italy (expressed in number of classes) from 1888 to 1896

Year	Number of schools
1888–89	47,572
1889–90	48,198
1890–91	–
1891–92	49,217
1892–93	49,722
1893–94	50,151
1894–95	50,307
1895–96	50,526

Source ISTAT data processed by the authors

Table 4 Number of regular and irregular public elementary day schools in Italy (expressed in number of classes) from 1926 to 1937

Years	Number of schools
1926–27	110,606
1927–28	111,560
1928–29	108,093
1929–30	110,200
1930–31	114,344
1931–32	119,429
1932–33	123,612
1933–34	124,560
1934–35	126,934
1935–36	128,168
1936–37	129,580

Source ISTAT data processed by the authors

Table 5 Number of kindergartens and teaching staff in Italy from Unification to 1896

Years	Number of kindergartens			Teaching Staff		
	Public	Private	Total	Male	Female	Totale
1861–62	373	1,300	1,673	–	–	–
1862–63	457	1,349	1,806	–	–	–
1863–64	591	2,129	2,720	–	–	–
...	–	–	–	–	–	–
1868–69	853	–	853	–	–	–
...	–	–	–	–	–	—
1871–72	1,099	–	1,099	–	–	–
...	–	–	–	–	–	–
1876–77	1,287	–	1,287	–	–	–
1877–78	1,543	–	1,543	–	–	–
1878–79	1,566	–	1,566	–	–	–
...	–	–	–	–	–	–
1881–82	–	–	2,516	–	–	–
1882–83	1,379	362	1,741	–	–	–
1883–84	1,433	602	2,035	–	–	–
1884–85	1,428	655	2,083	–	–	–
1885–86	1,489	650	2,139	–	–	–
1886–87	1,553	671	2,224	–	–	–
1887–88	1,594	624	2,218	–	–	–
1888–89	1,618	602	2,220	–	–	–
1889–90	1,714	582	2,296	107	5,785	5,892
1890–91	1,676	556	2,232	–	–	–
1891–92	1,706*	642	2,348	117	6,018	6,135
1892–93	1,760	812	2,572	132	6,356	6,488
1893–94	1,792	835	2,627	174	6,512	6,686
1894–95	1,862	937	2,799	130	6,708	6,838
1895–96	–	–	2,813	114	6,770	6,884

Source ISTAT data processed by the authors
*"the decrease that is observed in the number of public kindergartens not set up as non-profit organizations and the increase of private kindergartens, for the years 1890–91 and 1891–92, depends on the fact that, for a better assessment of the juridical standing of the kindergartens, some of those formerly included in the category of kindergartens maintained by corporations, were classified among those maintained by corporations recognized as corporations; the other part was placed among the kindergartens maintained by private individuals, but in 1891 it was not possible to obtain information for some kindergartens of municipalities and private individuals in various provinces" Ministry of Agriculture, Industry and Commerce, *Statistica della istruzione elementare per l'anno scolastico 1892–93*, Rome, Tipografia Elzeviriana, 1894, p. XII, tav. IV—Numero degli asili pubblici e privati e numero degli alunni dal 1872 al 1893

Table 6 Number of kindergartens, managerial and teaching staff in Italy from 1926 to 1937

Years	Kindergartens	Out of 100 thousand inhabitants	Managerial staff	Teaching staff
1926–27	7,076	18	4,536	8,179
1927–28	8,165	20	5,163	9,051
1928–29	8,930	22	5,523	7,939
1929–30	9,546	23	5,903	10,851
1930–31	9,425	23	5,993	10,582
1931–32	9,371	23	5,889	10,469
1932–33	9,288	22	5,924	9,721
1933–34	9,218	22	5,720	10,168
1934–35	9,438	22	5,969	10,220
1935–36	9,691	22	6,837	10,257
1936–37	9,589	22	7,004	10,499

Source ISTAT data processed by the authors

Table 7 Number of teaching staff in compulsory schools (regular and irregular day schools) in Italy divided by grade and gender by school year 1889–90 to 1895–96

School year	Irregular school		Regular schools										Total		Total
			Lower grade				Higher grade				Trainees				
			Teacher		Substitutes and assistants		Teacher		Substitutes and assistants						
	M	F	M	F	M	F	M	F	M	F	M	F	M	F	
1889–90	1,735	1,173	15,558	24,108	223	801	2,872	2,053	80	173	82	418	20,550	28,816	49,366
1890–91	–	–	–	–	–	–	–	–	–	–	–	–	–	–	–
1891–92	1,698	1,285	15,145	25,145	312	974	3,064	2,141	70	189	158	638	20,447	30,372	50,819
1892–93	1,755	1,364	15,000	25,639	312	1007	3,070	2,174	63	156	233	612	20,433	30,952	51,385
1893–94	1,738	1,423	14,826	26,127	246	992	3,122	2,165	99	205	238	679	20,269	31,591	51,860
1894–95*	2,289	2,385	14,477	25,812	284	962	2,689	2,013	81	195	312	673	20,082	32,040	52,122
1895–96*	2,250	2,489	14,366	26,103	301	1004	2,649	2,058	108	177	294	713	19,968	32,544	52,512

Source ISTAT data processed by the authors

*The data refers to the optional and no longer to the irregular ones. Ministry of Agriculture, Industry and Commerce, *Statistica della istruzione primaria e normale per l'anno scolastico 1895–96*, Rome, Tipografia nazionale di G. Bertero, 1898, p. XV

Table 8 Principals in Italy in public elementary schools, years 1926–1937

School year	Male	Female	Total
1926–27	2,151	738	2,889
1927–28	*gender distribution is not available	*gender distribution is not available	2,868
1928–29	*gender distribution is not available	*gender distribution is not available	2,890
1929–30	1,734	780	2,514
1930–31	1,750	777	2,527
1931–32	1,700	790	2,490
1932–33	1,649	775	2,424
1933–34	1,595	694	2,289
1934–35	1,482	611	2,093
1935–36	1,538	470	2,008
1936–37	1,538	470	2,008

Source ISTAT data processed by the authors

Table 9 Principals and teachers in public, certified and subsidized elementary schools in Italy by age group and by gender (year 1936–37)

Age classes	Kingdom of Italy					
	Principals			Teachers		
	Male	Female	Total	Male	Female	Total
Under 30 years old	0	2	2	4,692	13,531	18,223
from 30 to 34 years old	33	15	48	2,420	15,252	17,672
35–39	189	73	262	3,110	18,445	21,555
40–44	279	125	404	3,755	15,468	19,223
45–49	321	76	397	2,940	9,420	12,360
50–54	338	76	414	2,415	6,580	8,995
55–59	263	61	324	1,668	5,523	7,191
60 and above	115	42	157	1,435	3,892	5,327
Total	1,538	470	2,008	22,435	88,111	110,546

Source ISTAT data processed by the authors

Table 10 Principals and teachers in public, certified and subsidized elementary schools in Italy, by educational qualification and by gender (year 1936–37)

Qualification	Kingdom of Italy					
	Principals			Teachers		
	Male	Female	Total	Male	Female	Total
Master's degree	140	55	195	370	910	1280
Other degree or diploma	591	195	786	1800	4740	6540
Magister qualification	766	218	984	19,927	81,755	101,682
Lower qualification	41	2	43	338	706	1044
Total	1538	470	2008	22,435	88,111	110,546

Source ISTAT data processed by the authors

Table 11 Number of kindergartens, public and private elementary schools, from school year 1889–90 to 1895–96, in Southern Italian regions

Years	Kindergartens	Number of public elementary schools	Number of private elementary schools
1889–90	351	14,623	2,987
1890–91	–	–	–
1891–92	361	14,831	2,519
1892–93	385	14,931	2,519
1893–94	380	15,057	2,761
1894–95	408	14,823	2,949
1895–96	411	15,038	2,870

Source ISTAT data processed by the authors

Table 12 Number of teaching staff in kindergartens of Southern Italy regions divided by grade and gender by school year 1889–90 to 1895–96

Years	Kindergarten		
	M	F	Total
1889–90	15	1,057	1,072
1890–91	–	–	–
1891–92	10	1,088	1,098
1892–93	8	1,147	1,155
1893–94	57	1,136	1,193
1894–95	38	1,106	1,144
1895–96	36	1,154	1,190

Source ISTAT data processed by the authors

Table 13 Number of teaching staff in compulsory schools (regular and irregular day schools) in Southern Italy divided by grade and gender by school year 1889–90 to 1895–96

School year	Irregular schools		Regular schools										Total		Total
			Lower grade				Higher grade				Trainees				
			Teachers		Substitutes and assistants		Teachers		Substitutes and assistants						
	M	F	M	F	M	F	M	F	M	F	M	F	M	F	
1889–90	114	51	5,997	5,195	76	141	1,207	876	37	57	35	34	7,463	7,354	14,820
1890–91	–	–	–	–	–	–	–	–	–	–	–	–	–	–	–
1891–92	119	56	5,977	6,341	177	172	1,258	906	10	18	83	62	7,624	7,572	15,196
1892–93	107	50	5,981	6,490	149	203	1,270	922	15	19	121	39	7,658	7,723	15,381
1893–94	108	52	5,940	6,631	117	170	1,272	896	31	26	104	26	7,572	7,801	15,373
1894–95*	386	213	5,829	6,642	125	161	1,141	858	21	22	139	36	7,555	7,679	15,434
1895–96*	220	120	5,858	6,690	139	155	1,178	887	27	31	116	29	7,171	7,912	15,390

Source ISTAT data processed by the authors

Table 14 Number of kindergartens, regular and irregular public day primary schools and private schools in the Campania region (expressed in number of classes) from 1888 to 1896

Years	Kindergartens	Number of public elementary schools	Number of private elementary schools
1888–89	148	3,673	–
1889–90	150	3,777	3,788
1890–91	–	–	–
1891–92	145	3,810	3,891
1892–93	156	3,823	4,091
1893–94	150	3,880	4,168
1894–95	165	3,893	4,220
1895–96	172	3,894	4,210

Source ISTAT data processed by the authors

Table 15 Teachers in kindergartens divided by gender in the Campania region from 1888 to 1896

Years	Teaching staff		
	Male	Female	Total
1888–89	4	467	471
1889–90	–	–	–
1890–91	4	469	473
1891–92	1	497	498
1892–93	48	509	557
1893–94	31	468	499
1894–95	27	494	521

Source ISTAT data processed by the authors

Table 16 Number of regular and irregular public day elementary schools in the Campania region (number of classes) from 1926 to 1937

Years	Number of schools
1927–28	8,416
1928–29	8,387
1929–30	6,706
1930–31	8,322
1931–32	8,335
1932–33	8,763
1933–34	8,883
1934–35	8,980
1935–36	9,081
1936–37	9,678

Source ISTAT data processed by the authors

Table 17 Number of schools and teachers by gender in private day schools in the Campania region from 1889 to 1896

Years	Number of schools	Number of teachers		
		Male	Female	Total
1888–89	–	560	904	1,464
1889–90	849	619	993	1,612
1890–91	–	–	–	–
1891–92	898	601	1,106	1,707
1892–93	976	553	1,074	1,627
1893–94	1,012	566	1,157	1,723
1894–95	1,019	569	1,146	1,715
1895–96	1,020	579	1,124	1,703

Source ISTAT data processed by the authors

Table 18 Number of teaching staff in compulsory schools (regular and irregular day schools) divided by grade and gender, in the Campania region from 1889–90 to 1895–96

School Year	Irregular schools		Regular schools										Total		Total
			Lower grade				Higher grade				Trainees				
			Teachers		Substitutes and assistants		Teachers		Substitutes and assistants						
	M	F	M	F	M	F	M	F	M	F	M	F	M	F	
1889–90	37	22	1,573	1,670	13	56	260	185	10	20	6	0	1,899	1,962	3,861
1890–91	–	–	–	–	–	–	–	–	–	–	–	–	–	–	–
1891–92	36	23	1,577	1,699	47	61	275	196	1	3	32	9	1,968	1,991	3,959
1892–93	27	17	1,570	1,716	51	59	285	212	4	7	32	15	1,969	2,026	3,995
1893–94	27	14	1,526	1,788	44	80	284	186	15	13	21	7	1,917	2,088	4,005
1894–95*	66	37	1,484	1,808	46	78	261	186	13	11	40	5	1,913	2,125	4,038
1895–96*	57	39	1,495	1,807	38	51	274	188	16	17	24	11	1,904	2,113	4,017

Source ISTAT data processed by the authors
*The data refers to optional schools and no longer to irregular ones

Table 19 Number of schools and teachers by gender in private day schools in the Campania region from 1927 to 1937

Years	Number of schools	Number of teachers		
		Male	Female	Total
1927–28	267	72	610	682
1928–29	271	75	615	690
1929–30	276	75	588	663
1930–31	307	81	656	737
1931–32	337	82	657	739
1932–33	366	86	670	756
1933–34	334	71	520	591
1934–35	329	63	477	540
1935–36	331	58	530	588
1936–37	217	58	467	525

Source ISTAT data processed by the authors

Table 20 Principals in public elementary schools in the Campania region from 1926 to 1937

School year	Male	Female	Total
1926–27	–	–	–
1927–28	–	–	250
1928–29	–	–	251
1929–30	134	66	200
1930–31	172	28	200
1931–32	108	29	137
1932–33	160	29	189
1933–34	148	23	171
1934–35	137	21	158
1935–36	111	40	151
1936–37	111	40	151

Source ISTAT data processed by the authors

Table 21 Principals and teachers in certified and subsidized public elementary schools by age group and by gender, in the Campania region (year 1936–37)

Age classes	Principals			Teachers		
	M	F	TOT	M	F	TOT
Under 30 years old	0	0	0	447	955	1,402
From 30 to 34 years old	1	0	1	196	1,033	1,229
35–39	9	2	11	274	1,169	1,443
40–44	20	6	26	397	1,070	1,467
45–49	21	4	25	329	748	1,077
50–54	23	2	25	285	583	868
55–59	19	9	28	179	456	635
60 and above	18	17	35	202	469	671
Total	111	40	151	2,309	6,483	8,792

Source ISTAT data processed by the authors

Table 22 Principals and teachers in recognized and subsidized public elementary schools by educational qualification and by gender in the Campania region (year 1936–37)

Qualification	Principals			Teachers		
	M	F	TOT	M	F	TOT
Master's degree	7	0	7	16	143	159
Other degree or diploma	50	12	62	257	649	906
Magister qualification	46	28	74	2,014	5648	7662
Lower qualification	8	0	8	22	43	65
Total	111	40	151	2,309	6,483	8,792

Source ISTAT data processed by the authors

Table 23 Number of kindergartens, regular and irregular public day primary schools and private schools in the province of Avellino (expressed in number of classes) from 1888 to 1896

Years	Kindergartens	Number of public elementary schools	Number of private elementary schools
1888–89	9	522	–
1889–90	14	561	17
1890–91	–	–	–
1891–92	15	562	22
1892–93	16	564	44
1893–94	14	569	61
1894–95	14	564	57
1895–96	14	560	52

Source ISTAT data processed by the authors

Table 24 Teachers in kindergartens divided by gender in the province of Avellino from 1888 to 1896

Years	Teaching staff		
	Male	Female	Total
1888–89	0	27	27
1889–90	–	–	–
1890–91	0	32	32
1891–92	0	32	32
1892–93	1	26	27
1893–94	0	23	23
1894–95	0	29	29

Source ISTAT data processed by the authors

Table 25 Number of teaching staff in compulsory schools (regular and irregular day schools) divided by grade and gender, in the province of Avellino from 1889–90 to 1895–96

School year	Irregular schools		Regular schools										Total		Overall
			Lower grade				Higher grade				Trainees				
			Teachers		Substitutes and assistants		Teachers		Substitutes and assistants						
	M	F	M	F	M	F	M	F	M	F	M	F	M	F	
1889–90	5	6	248	237	0	0	35	25	0	0	1	0	289	268	557
1890–91	–	–	–	–	–	–	–	–	–	–	–	–	–	–	–
1891–92	1	5	247	242	1	3	36	23	0	0	3	1	288	274	562
1892–93	2	4	246	248	0	1	34	22	1	1	10	1	293	277	570
1893–94	1	6	248	250	1	1	36	21	0	0	9	3	295	281	576
1894–95*	11	10	242	242	4	3	31	22	0	0	12	2	300	279	579
1895–96*	10	10	237	242	3	2	32	23	0	0	7	4	289	281	570

Source ISTAT data processed by the authors
* The figure refers to optional schools and no longer to irregular ones

Table 26 Number of schools and teachers by gender in private elementary schools in the province of Avellino from 1889 to 1896

Years	Number of schools	Number of teachers		
		Male	Female	Total male and female
1888–89	–	6	27	33
1889–90	17	6	27	33
1890–91	–	–	–	–
1891–92	22	14	18	32
1892–93	44	31	44	75
1893–94	61	42	56	98
1894–95	57	45	63	108
1895–96	52	36	64	100

Source ISTAT data processed by the authors

Table 27 Number of kindergartens, regular and irregular public primary day schools and private schools in the province of Benevento (expressed in number of classes) from 1888 to 1896

Years	Kindergartens	Number of public elementary schools	Number of private elementary schools
1888–89	4	206	–
1889–90	4	291	21
1890–91	–	–	–
1891–92	4	302	20
1892–93	7	302	21
1893–94	5	305	20
1894–95	6	304	24
1895–96	6	299	24

Source ISTAT data processed by the authors

Table 28 Teachers in kindergartens divided by gender in the province of Benevento from 1888 to 1896

Years	Teaching staff		
	Male	Female	Total
1888–89	0	10	10
1889–90			
1890–91	0	10	10
1891–92	0	13	13
1892–93	0	10	10
1893–94	0	12	12
1894–95	0	12	12

Source ISTAT data processed by the authors

Table 29 Number of teaching staff in compulsory schools (regular and irregular day schools) divided by grade and gender, in the province of Benevento from 1889–90 to 1895–96

School year	Irregular schools		Regular schools										Total		Total
			Lower grade				Higher grade				Trainees				
			Teachers		Substitutes and assistants		Teachers		Substitutes and assistants						
	M	F	M	F	M	F	M	F	M	F	M	F	M	F	
1889–90	2	1	127	129	0	0	20	10	0	0	5	0	154	140	294
1890–91	–	–	–	–	–	–	–	–	–	–	–	–	–	–	–
1891–92	2	2	125	142	0	0	19	11	0	0	6	1	152	156	308
1892–93	2	1	124	141	0	0	21	12	0	0	3	0	150	154	304
1893–94	3	2	127	138	0	1	19	15	0	0	5	0	154	156	310
1894–95*	4	2	121	141	2	1	19	12	0	0	5	1	151	157	308
1895–96*	7	1	123	137	0	0	18	12	0	0	9	1	157	151	308

Source ISTAT data processed by the authors
The figure refers to optional schools and no longer to irregular ones

Table 30 Number of schools and teachers by gender in private day schools in the province of Benevento from 1889 to 1896

Years	Number of schools	Number of teachers		
		Male	Female	Total male and female
1888–89	–	1	15	16
1889–90	21	12	23	35
1890–91	–	–	–	–
1891–92	20	13	27	40
1892–93	21	10	24	34
1893–94	20	13	27	40
1894–95	24	4	34	38
1895–96	24	12	34	46

Source ISTAT data processed by the authors

References

Addis Saba, M. (1988). *La donna "muliebre"*. In M. A. Saba (Ed.), *La corporazione delle donne. Ricerche e studi sui modelli femminili nel ventennio* (pp. 151–214). Vallecchi.

Albisetti, J. C. (1993). The feminization of teaching in the nineteenth century: A comparative perspective. *History of Education, 22*(3), 253–263.

Bertocchi, G., & Bozzano, M. (2019). *Gender gaps in education.* Centre for Economic Policy Research discussion paper DP14082.

Bertoni Jovine, D. (1963). Funzione emancipatrice ella scuola e contributo delle donne ll'attività educativa. In Società Umanitaria (Ed.), *L'emancipazione femminile in Italia; un secolo di discussioni (1861–1961)* (pp. 223–269). La Nuova Italia.

Bini, G. (1989). *La maestra nella letteratura: uno specchio della realtà.* In S. Soldani (Ed.), *L'educazione delle donne. Scuole e modelli di vita femminile nell'Italia dell'Ottocento* (pp. 331–362). Franco Angeli.

Bravo, A. (Ed.). (1991). *Donne e uomini nelle guerre mondiali.* Laterza.

Cappelli, G., & Vasta, M. (2021). *A "silent revolution": School reforms and Italy's educational gender gap in the liberal age (1861–1921).* Cliometrica.

Ciccarelli, C., & Weisdorf, J. (2019). *Pioneering into the past: Regional literacy developments in Italy before Italy.* European Review of Economic History.

Covato, C. (1996). Maestre e professoresse fra '800 e '900: Emancipazione femminile e stereotipi di "genere." In S. Ulivieri (Ed.), *Essere donne insegnanti, storia professionalità e cultura di genere* (pp. 19–46). Rosenberg & Sellier.

D'Amelio, D. A. (2001). Italian women in the resistance, World War II. *Italian Americana, 19*(2), 127–141.

De Grand, A. (1976). Women under Italian fascism. *The Historical Journal, 19*(4), 947–968.

Di Pol, R. S. (2002). *Il sistema scolastico italiano. Origine, evoluzione, situazioni.* Marcovalerio.

Dolza, D. (1987). Per un contributo allo studio delle classi medie in Piemonte nei primi decenni del secolo, il caso delle insegnanti. In U. Levra & N. Tranfaglia (Eds.), *Torino fra liberismo e fascismo* (pp. 15–118). Milan FrancoAngeli.

Federico, G., Nuvolari, A., & Vasta, M. (2019). The origins of the Italian regional divide: Evidence from real wages, 1861–1913. *Journal of Economic History, 79*, 63–98.

Gibelli, A. (2014). *La grande guerra degli italiani (1915–1918).* Rizzoli.

Mayeur, F. (1977). *L'ensegignement secondaire sous la troisième Republique, Paris*. Presses de la Fondation des Sciences polotiques.
Mondello, E. (1987). *La nuova italiana. La donna nella stampa e nella cultura del Ventennio*. Editori riuniti.
Perry, W. (2002). *Peasant women and politics in fascist Italy: The Massaie Rurali*. Routledge.
Porcheddu, A. (1978). La donna nell'insegnamento. Storia e prospettive. *Scuola e Città, 9*, 353–360.
Ravà, V. (1906). Attuazione delle disposizioni legislative sull'istruzione obbligatoria. *Bollettino Ufficiale del Ministero della Pubblica Istruzione, XXXIII*.
Saraceno, C. (2003). *Mutamenti della famiglia e politiche sociali in Italia*. Il Mulino.
Schirripa, V. (2003). *Insegnare ai bambini. Una storia della formazione di maestre e maestri in Italia*. Carocci.
Scramaglia, R. (1997). *Storia dei movimenti e delle idee. Femminismo*. Editrice Bibliografica.
Semeraro, A. (1999). *Il sistema scolastico italiano. Profilo storico*. Carocci.
Soldani S. (Ed.). (1989). *L'educazione delle donne. Scuole e modelli di vita femminile nell'Italia dell'Ottocento*. Franco Angeli.
Tomasi, T. (1959). La donna educatrice nella famiglia e nella scuola. *Scuola e città, 11*, 288–297.
Ulivieri, S. (1978). *I maestri*, in AA.VV., *L'istruzione di base in Italia* (pp. 163–212). Firenze.
Ulivieri, S. (2012). Le maestre elementari "apostole" dei valori del Risorgimento. Tra emancipazione politica e misoginia sociale. In V. Fiorelli (Ed.), *La nazione tra i banchi. Il contributo della scuola alla formazione degli italiani tra Otto e Novecento* (pp. 279–297). Rubettino.
Vittoria, A. (1995). Federzoni Luigi. *Dizionario biografico degli italiani, 45*, 792–801.

Archival Sources

State Archive of Avellino
Riassunti Statistici sul Principato Ulteriore del 1838 su 1839, Avellino 1839, s.e., Cap. 1.
Intendenza P. U., b. 1108, fasc. 4694.
Intendenza P. U., b. 1112, fasc. 4719.
Intendenza P.U. b. 1130, fasc. 4690, Sant'Angelo dei Lombardi, 20 novembre 1840.
Comune di Santa Paolina, b. 41, fasc. 3.
Liceo Manzoni di Mugnano del Cardinale, b. 1, r.1.
ISTAT—Italian National Institute of Statistics
Central Institute of Statistics of the Kingdom of Italy, *Intellectual statistics, Statistics of elementary education for the school year 1936–37 and statistical news for the school years from 1932–33 to 1935–36, Vol.* 14, Tipografia F. Failli, 1941 XIX.
Central Institute of Statistics of the Kingdom of Italy, *Intellectual statistics, Statistics of elementary education for the school years from1927–28 to 1931- and statistical news for the school years from 1932–33 to 1935–36, Vol.* 9, Tipografia I. Failli, 1936–XIV.
Istat Historical Archive, Ministry of Agriculture, Industry and Commerce, General Directorate of Statistics. (1884). Census of the Population of the Kingdom of Italy on 31 December 1881, Population classified by profession and condition, vol. III, Tipografia Bodoniana.
Ministry of Agriculture, Industry and Commerce. (1891). *Statistics of elementary education for the school year 1888–89*. Tipografia della cambra dei deputati.
Ministry of Agriculture, Industry and Commerce. (1892). *Statistics of elementary education for the school year 1889–90*. Tipografia della cambra dei deputati.
Ministry of Agriculture,, Industry and Commerce. (1893). *Statistics of elementary education for the school year 1891–92*. Tipografia della cambra dei deputati.
Ministry of Agriculture, Industry and Commerce. (1894). *Statistics of elementary education for the school year 1892–93*. Tipografia Elzeviriana.
Ministry of Agriculture, Industry and Commerce. (1895). *Statistics of elementary education for the school year 1893–94*. Stabilimento tipografico dell'opinione.

Ministry of Agriculture, Industry and Commerce. (1897). *Statistics of elementary education for the school year 1894–95*. Tipografia della casa editrice italiana.
Ministry of Agriculture, Industry and Commerce. (1898). *Statistics of elementary education for the school year 1895–96*. Tipografia nazionale di G. Bertero.

Incomes and Employment of Italian Women (1900–1950)

Giacomo Gabbuti and María Gómez León

1 Introduction

Within a long-run history of Italian women at work, and their broader economic culture, such as the one pursued in this book, the first half of the twentieth century inevitably stands out as a fundamental juncture. For most European countries, the so-called interwar decades, marked by two devastating global conflicts, but also the Spanish flu pandemic, the Great Depression, and all sorts of national economic and policy shocks, marked an important turn in women's work. As highlighted by works such as Curli (1998), even more than in practical aspects, female work in 'visible' occupations greatly affected its perception, structuring post-war debates on women's employment. This was the case, for instance, in public transportation, or in the "auxiliary factories" producing arms and munitions, where women rose from 23,000 to 198,000 between 1915 and 1918. Still, these were just a fraction of the women who had already been working in textiles, and were then making uniforms for the army (Willson, 2010, 53), not to mention the majority working in agriculture (Figs. 1 and 2).

This work expands a previous paper on inequality in Fascist Italy (Gómez León & Gabbuti, 2022). In this form, it has benefitted from comments by participants to the online workshops: "Women between economic facts and ideas in Italy (1750–1950)"; Università del Salento; the Inequality in Rome Seminars, Rome 3 University; and the fifteenth EHES Conference, Vienna University of Economics and Business. We also benefitted from the feedback by Francesca Bettio, Giuliana Freschi, Alessandra Gissi, Stefania Licini and Giulia Mancini. Unless stated otherwise, the translations of the quoted texts are our own.

G. Gabbuti (✉)
Scuola Superiore Sant'Anna, Pisa, Italy
e-mail: giacomo.gabbuti@santannapisa.it

M. Gómez León
Universitat de València, Valencia, Spain
e-mail: maria.gomez-leon@uv.es

M. Mosca (ed.), *Women at Work in Italy (1750–1950)*, Springer Studies in the History of Economic Thought, https://doi.org/10.1007/978-3-031-64281-4_7

Fig. 1 Office workers celebrating Women's Day at the Roberto Incerti & C. Villar Perosa,Turin, 1950s (*Source* Antonio Gramsci Piedmont Institute Foundation—Historical archive)

Fig. 2 Women's day at the Mazzonis factory, Corso Svizzera, Turin, 8 March 1949 (*Source* Antonio Gramsci Piedmont Institute Foundation—Historical archive)

As noted by De Grazia (1992, 3),

> In the interwar decades, all Western governments reacted to th[e] double challenge of democratization and demographic crisis. They responded at first by sanctioning female suffrage, and then by developing new public discourses about women, legislating about their place in the labour market, and recodifying family policies.

What De Grazia calls a "restructuring of gender relations" was, indeed, a crucial component of the broader recasting of bourgeois Europe, after the troubling experience of the War (Maier 1975). It was not only in Revolutionary Russia that the stereotype of the 'docile' nature of the female workforce was shown to be false, but also in Italy where women owners were at the frontline of popular unrest against the war and worsening living conditions (Pescarolo 2019, 199). While protests such as the 5 days in Turin of August 1917 were most often "begun by women angered by flour and bread shortages", "64.2 per cent of strikers in auxiliary factories were female" (Willson, 2010, 55), despite being a minority of the overall labour force. Informed economic agents, women realised soon that "Male strikers could be sent to the front whereas women were usually only fined, since prison would disrupt their families too much" (Willson, 2010, 55). Indeed, work is a crucial "concrete experience" from which we can study the economic culture of millions of Italian women under fascism.

As noted by Pescarolo (2019, 164), in this period science also concurred to a new attention to female bodies in the workplace: the discovery of the biological specificity of female gametes, and women's autonomous contribution to child generation, contributed to viewing women not only as sexual objects to preserve, under "traditional patriarchal protection", but "as a precious, delicate mechanism". "For the first time the labour effort became an object of attention in this new cultural framework", not only because of the danger to women's respectability, but also for the consequences on their reproductive capacity as mothers. Not surprisingly, then, "Never before was the sphere of gender relations more explicitly the focus of reformist zeal" (De Grazia 1992, 3). However, "both the scope and outcome of policies differed from country to country", depending on "whether government policies would take an authoritarian or democratic cast, repress labour or coopt it, allow women greater freedom or impose more restrictions on them. By and large, the outcomes varied according to the character of the class coalitions in power and their stands on broad issues of social welfare and economic redistribution" (De Grazia 1992, 3). Among the already controversial discussion of the 'modernising' developments of Italian society in the Fascist decades (Settis 2022), the reality of women's lives and the contrast with Fascist policy objectives and broader ideological claims are thus among the most crucial and difficult aspects. Within the growing attention devoted to these issues—including the international conference organised in November 2023 by the *Italian Association of Women Historians* (SIS)—this contribution aims at improving our quantitative understanding of women's paid work in this period, and the extent of the gap they faced in the remuneration for that work.

As noted by Pescarolo (2019, 219), "the role assigned to women in the economy has been relatively overlooked" by gender historians working on Fascist Italy. In a recent survey, Mancini (2022, 75) showed how, despite the crucial importance of quantifying employment and incomes of Italian women in history, and the "wealth of research on the history of female work throughout different eras of Italy's history", these dimensions are among "the least investigated in the Italian economic history literature", making it "extremely promising in terms of future research prospects". Indeed, the most comprehensive account of gender labour market gaps in modern Italy remains Bettio (1988). As for incomes, the only major advancement is represented by the estimates of gender wage gaps (henceforth, GWG) for agriculture and manufacturing during the liberal age, carried on by Federico et al. (2021). Mancini (2018) herself contributed to an upward revision of overall figures for female labour market participation, and to highlighting (in line with previous, more qualitative accounts by Salvatici 1999) the productive work by rural women not recorded by censuses (Mancini, 2023). However, the important focus on the complex nature of work (Sarti et al., 2018), on what official sources hide (Humphries & Sarasúa, 2012, 40) and the limitations of indicators such as female labour force participation (henceforth, FLFP)—better understood not as work "for the market", but rather as work "for pay" (Burnette 2021, 241)—possibly induced historians of this period to overlook what even official sources reveal about the evolution of gender gaps. In this chapter, therefore, we try to reconstruct trends in both GWG and FLFP, but also in major sectors, during a crucial period such as the first half of the twentieth century. Despite unavoidable limitations, this reconstruction fills major gaps in the literature, while contributing to the discussion of the economic culture of Italian women, as reflected by their actions as wage earners.

As highlighted in our earlier reconstruction of the overall income distribution in the period 1900–1950 by means of so-called "dynamic social tables" (henceforth, DST) (Gómez León & Gabbuti 2022), GWG were indeed among the major drivers of the specific Italian trajectory, within the compression of inequality that occurred in most European countries in that period (Piketty 2014). Normally overlooked by historical works on inequality (Bellavitis and Martinat 2022, 8), GWG show the crucial role of labour market dynamics, and unions' more or less 'inclusive' practices (Bettio, 1988), in driving inequality dynamics. By adopting this approach, we hope to fulfil Groppi's (1996, xiv) recommendation of not placing "the history of women, and of their work" in a lateral corner, but right at the centre of the productive economy under investigation. In this sense, our contribution here is complementary to Freschi's previous chapter. Modern Italy reveals how the same issues affecting the reliability of binary measures of labour market participation, that do not discuss work intensity (Burnette 2021, 424), undermine historical macroeconomic history, in view of the persistence of widespread unemployment and precarious employment (Alberti, 2018).[1] At the same time, Humphries and Sarasúa (2021, 170) reminded us that it is a "myth" to believe that "LFP will automatically lead to women's empowerment and independence", since "in the context of patriarchal and discriminatory economic and social institutions" (such as Fascist Italy), mere access to a job does

[1] For a discussion on the importance of precarious work in estimating labour shares, see Gabbuti (2021).

not imply economic independence. Nonetheless, even a 'lower bound' quantification of women's work for pay, and GWG, reveal the crucial role of women's work even in Fascist Italy.

To do so, the rest of the chapter is structured as follows: Sect. 2 briefly introduces the reader to the DST approach and discusses its suitability and limitations in discussing women's work in history; Sect. 3 presents our reconstruction of women's employment for pay, discussing its limitation, as well as the interesting trends we can observe in the data. Section 4 discusses surviving evidence on GWG. Section 5 concludes, trying to place women's work within the broader economic history of Fascist Italy.

2 Dynamic Social Tables and Women's History

Social tables are an established methodology in the historical literature on income inequality (Lindert & Williamson, 1982; Milanovic et al., 2011). Pioneered in Rodríguez Weber's (2014) doctoral dissertation, which aimed to explore income inequality in Chile between 1850 and 2009, the DST approach quickly spread to the analysis of long-run inequality in other Latin American countries (Gómez León 2021). This approach, which captures annual movements in both population shares and average incomes, provides us with insights into year-to-year inequality developments. Notably, its application played a crucial role in revealing the contrasting distributive histories of interwar Britain and Germany (Gómez León & De Jong 2019). Milanovic (2023, 293–295) recently listed this methodology among the "three remarkable developments in the work on inequality that … are most likely to have enduring impact on the economics profession and social scientists, at least for another half century".

But what are DST? First of all, economic historians refer to "social tables" when dealing with sources that provide an account of the number of people belonging to different social groups and the estimated average incomes that can be linked to these groups. Classic examples of these sources are the British social tables, adopted, for instance, by Lindert and Williamson (1982). Works such as Milanovic et al. (2011) established standard procedures in order to estimate Ginis based on these sources. When social tables are not available as historical sources, it is possible to build them, combining other sources on occupational structure (say, censuses) and on the incomes earned by different groups in society, as in Table 1. Conceptually, this procedure is very similar to the reconstruction of national accounts, when different items are compiled to eventually cover the entirety of national income. The novelty of Rodríguez Weber (2014) and later works was to let both population shares and incomes move on an annual basis to cover the evolution of income distribution over time.

The advantage of DST, compared to most available alternatives, is to capture the evolution of the whole range of the distribution, without limiting the discussion to partial indicators, such as top incomes or factorial shares of national income,

Table 1 An example of social table: Italy, 1913

Occupation	Work status	Gender	Number	Income
Industry	Salary-earners	Male	625,096	1233
		Female	239,986	604
	Self-employed	Male	54,947	2250
		Female	13,059	1212
Mining and Quarrying	Wage-earners	Male	99,295	772
		Female	2286	378
Bricks, cement, pottery	Wage-earners	Male	153,097	837
		Female	17,593	410
Metalworking	Wage-earners	Male	383,687	1075
		Female	17,758	526
Chemical industry	Wage-earners	Male	44,046	869
		Female	34,119	426
Wood and furniture	Wage-earners	Male	284,019	497
		Female	46,274	243
Paper industry, Printing, arts	Wage-earners	Male	55,168	608
		Female	24,083	298
Building	Wage-earners	Male	718,364	837
		Female	8886	410
Textile industry	Wage-earners	Male	104,436	451
		Female	434,212	221

Source Authors' elaborations on Gómez León and Gabbuti (2022)

or proxies such as the GDP wage-ratio, or the evolution of top income shares and labour shares. This is particularly important "when studying inequality in periods of rapid structural change (linked to sectoral shifts and inter-occupational inequalities), when changes in inequality are mostly linked to increasing differences between the middle and lower part of the income distribution" (Gómez León & Gabbuti, 2022). On the other hand, social tables will be imprecise when they encompass a restricted number of socioeconomic groups or fail to capture the internal income dispersion within these groups. Historically, however, it is standard to assume that the majority of income differentials can be attributed to inequality between major groups, such as capitalists and workers, white and blue collars, urban and rural sectors (Gabbuti 2021, 357–359).

In our work on Italy, we highlighted another overlooked advantage of this methodology: to overcome women's invisibility. In line with Bellavitis and Martinat (2022), we noted how most works on historical inequality "failed to include women's participation and pay gaps in the picture, due either to methodological issues, or source limitations" (Gómez León & Gabbuti 2022, 7). Social tables, instead, allow us to place gender gaps within the broader historical evolution of income inequality. In this chapter, by making a backward step—that is, by discussing the very construction of social tables, rather than the 'final', synthetic measures of inequality—we hope to contribute methodologically to the historical literature on female work. Surely, we have to be aware that by social tables we restrict the analysis to a fraction of FLFP—following Burnette (2021), we speak of "work for pay". Moreover, the underlying sources suffer, often substantially, from strong gender bias.[2] A women's history perspective highlights other limitations: at the present state of knowledge, we cannot take into account multi-activity, differences in work intensity and the number of hours worked in a year, and whether assumptions like the aforementioned irrelevance of within-group inequality are just another 'myth' to be debunked (Humphries & Sarasúa 2021). Despite the limited quantitative information available on these phenomena, the innovative approaches developed by feminist scholarship (see Humphries & Sarasúa 2012) should inspire future work on social tables, to better account for the reality of historical work, for both men and women.

Still, DST already represent a useful tool for women's historians. As we will show in Sect. 3, the harmonisation of occupational structures makes it possible to open the black box of FLFP to discuss the changing presence of women across sectors. On top of the sectoral GWG, discussed in Sect. 4, we could also highlight the relative evolution in the incomes of specific groups—say, of rural vs. urban working women.[3] Moreover, social tables make it possible to analyse at the same time women's work for pay and its remuneration: we will conclude Sect. 4 by showing an 'average' GWG, obtained by taking into account the weight of different sectors. Given that our DST have been built following as closely as possible Gómez León and De Jong (2019), we will also be able to compare Italian GWG with those of Britain and Germany. While the construction of the series is fully discussed in Gómez León and Gabbuti (2022), in the next section we will discuss the evidence we assembled on female employment in 1901–1950.

3 Female Participation to the Labour Market: What the Census Did Not Hide

To reconstruct social tables for Italy, it seems impossible to avoid population censuses to reconstruct the active population structure by professions. In population censuses individuals were asked about their main occupation and were grouped according to their work category and gender. Considering the various territorial changes occurring in the period, due to the territories annexed and lost as consequences of the World Wars, we followed the adjustment proposed by the statistician Vitali (1968), to obtain homogeneous series using current borders, making our series also consistent with

[2] For a discussion on the gender-bias of Italian censuses, see Patriarca (1998), and Freschi in this volume.

[3] In Gómez León and Gabbuti (2022), we took advantage of this possibility to show the relative position of the various (male) middle-class groups, compared to blue collar workers.

national accounts. The number of occupations was standardised to 18, as reported in detail in Gómez León and Gabbuti (2022). It is important to note here that, in line with the focus on work for pay, we aimed at excluding people living on a family wage, and thus left out a significant number of women, such as family assistants and housewives, together with students. We also re-classified work categories into three for agriculture (owners, self-employed, and wage earners); one for owners in industry, commerce and transport; three for industry (self-employed, salary earners and wage earners); three for commerce and transport (self-employed, salary earners and wage earners); two for public administration and services (salary earners and wage earners); one for liberal professions; and one for the unoccupied. They were all disaggregated, in turn, by gender (male and female), resulting into 60 classes. This disaggregation will be exploited to enrich, in line with Mancini (2023), the discussion on women's work in different sectors.

The vast literature on Italian censuses, and their biased representation of female work, has been surveyed by Freschi in this volume: although earlier censuses arguably better captured female work, by 1901 (the first census adopted for this chapter) a more 'masculine' definition of employment had been established (Patriarca 1998). This should of course affect the level of our series—arguably a lower bound of female labour force participation—but hopefully, not trends. As for the overall FLFP, Mancini's (2018) recent series tackled the major problem of censuses: the underestimation of women working in agriculture, addressed by looking at the differences between agricultural and population censuses. This led her to further increase FLFP, even compared to the previous correction by Vitali (1968), appreciated also by Patriarca (1998). Unfortunately, contrary to Vitali, who provided separate figures for peasants, sharecroppers, and other rural occupations, Mancini only estimated a sectoral FLFP: for this reason, in our social tables we had to rely on Vitali's lower figures.

For the secondary sector, an alternative to population censuses is represented by industrial ones: Italian economic historians have indeed heatedly debated the issue.[4] While those in favour of this source consider it, at most, a proper proxy of full-time equivalent workers, population censuses are the only source covering the whole Italian population (including those without any profession) and agriculture, still accounting for the lion's share of employment. Moreover, as pointed out by Fenoaltea (2015, 234–235), the differences between the two sources strongly 'discriminated' between the considerable domestic production by women, and that done for pay, in sectors such as textiles. As noted by Pescarolo (2019, 147), in 1911, the industrial census counted only 117,927 women in the clothing industry, less than a fifth of those counted in the population census; other sources, such as the early 1920s industrial inquiries, prove industrial censuses strongly underestimated female employment. We thus decided to not apply any corrections for female textile workers, contrary to the literature surveyed by Freschi.

FLPF resulting from our series are reported in Fig. 3, alongside Mancini's series. Before discussing the trend—reassuringly very similar—it is worth noting the

[4] See the discussion in Gabbuti (2021) and Gómez León and Gabbuti (2022), as well as in Freschi's chapter.

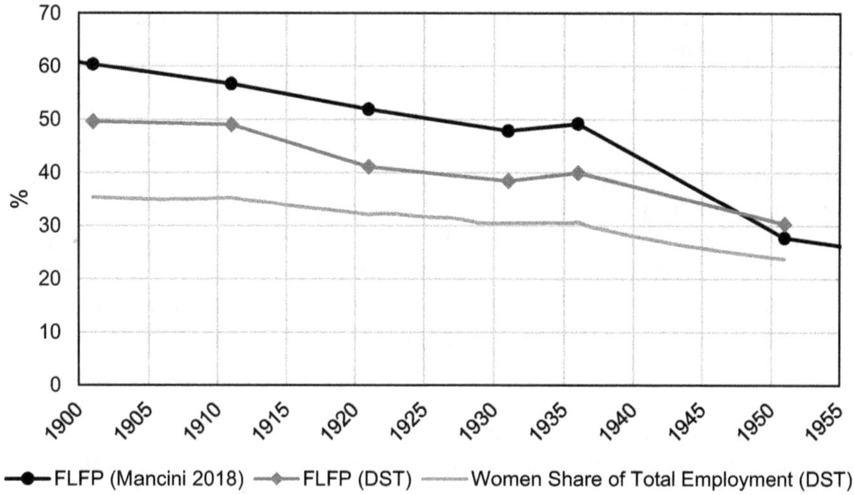

Fig. 3 Women and the labour force in Italy, 1900–1960 (*Source* Authors' elaborations on Mancini [2018] and Gómez León and Gabbuti [2022])

very high starting levels, even with 'limited' adjustment. As discussed by Ortaggi Cammarosano (1991, 152–155), "waged work for women did not have its origins in the factory system"; in Italy, even more than elsewhere, industrialisation "only reinforced and perfected tendencies" already present in agriculture, but also in the century-old putting-out system of textile manufacturing. Indeed, Italy was "a society in which the widespread employment of women and children in industry ... was considered a natural state of affairs, having its origins in the long-standing traditions of rural society". Unadjusted census figures show that in 1861, FLFP was higher in the newborn Kingdom of Italy than in France, Spain, Sweden, the UK and the US; in 1901, after decades of strong decline, Italy had just been 'reached' by France and the UK (Mancini, 2018, 25).

This secular decline, slower in Mancini's series, saw a sizeable reversal in the 1930s. The 1936 census registered a share of women in employment higher than in 1931, almost back to the 1921 level. The result is confirmed by industrial censuses, capturing the growth of women employed in industry between 1927 (11,2%) and 1937 (16,3%). This result, somehow overlooked in long-run reconstructions, is of major importance and deserves some discussion. Humphries and Sarasúa (2021, 173) noted how "in times of recession the scarcity of work justified prioritizing male 'breadwinners'". Surprisingly, however, the increase was especially marked among married women: 20.7% of them worked by 1936, from 12% in 1931 (De Grazia 1992, 186).[5] Mortara (1978, 68) had noted the increasing 'competition' of both women and children in the 1930s labour market, as a factor contributing to the decline in average

[5] According to some estimates, she adds, "40% of all Italian working women were married in the 1930s, a figure that was surpassed only in social democratic Sweden where working women benefited from a wide range of social services" (Ibid.).

wages. Cinnirella et al. (2017), indeed, detected increasing labour force participation for children between 14 and 18 in the same census years.

These results are clearly at odds with the standard view of women's work under Fascism—a view largely drawing on Fascists' own statements. A generous supplier of quotes such as Mussolini stated that "Work, where it is not a direct impediment, distracts from conception. It forms an independence and consequent physical and moral habits contrary to child bearing".[6] This view was shared by Fascist women themselves: for the mathematician Castellani (1937), the reduction of female employment before 1931 had been due to "living standard improvements"[7]; even for women workers in commerce, "work constitutes not a life goal for a woman, but a stage in her life, one to be finished up as soon as possible with her return to the home environment".[8]

According to De Grazia (1992, 7–9), however, Fascists had no "ready-made stance on 'the woman question'" at the time of the March on Rome: it was only in 1927, when Mussolini launched his demographic policies, that women became central for Fascists. Admittedly, like most interwar governments, they passed laws against female employment, marking a reversal with the great advancements of the post-war years. In particular, the Sacchi Law of July 1919 had abolished the husband's marital authorisation (see Licini in this volume) and decreed the legal equality of the sexes for professional and public employment, with the exclusion of "positions that involve the exercise of public judicial authority, political rights or power, or the military defence of the state". When reforming the school system, already in the early 1920s, instead, Fascists "determined that women lacked the prerequisite 'virile conception of life' necessary to direct upper-grade schools or to teach certain key subjects" (De Grazia 1992, 178). However, according to Musso (2019), Italian owners' willingness to "employing low-wage women" led in many cases to "stabilise higher shares of female workforce" after the war. It was only after the Great Depression, in 1933, that new laws restricting female employment were issued. Still, historians agree that they were really binding only in public employment, again, for not "harming private owners" (Pisoni Cerlesi 1959, 59). Women had certainly been affected by the firing of the public employees hired during the war; even in this sector, however, the main goal was to prevent them from reaching top positions, and 'quotas' were often set on the number of women already employed. Overall, historians agree the most sizeable effect of this legislation was to delegitimise women's professionality (Pescarolo 2019), reinforcing their segregation into low-paid jobs—a well-known issue in gender literature (Humphries and Sarasúa 2021, 176). More important were the measures introduced to protect working mothers that, when effectively applied, reduced the incentives to hire them. By 1931, "1,220,000 out of about 1,500,000 women employed in industry and commerce were insured" under the 1910 legislation on maternity funds; benefits and coverage were expanded in 1934, and in 1938 it

[6] 'Macchina e donna', *Popolo d'Italia*, 31 agosto 1934, quoted in De Grand (1976, 956).

[7] On Castellani, see Pagliai in this volume.

[8] First National Congress of Women in Commerce (1940), quoted in De Grazia (1992, 166).

was extended to women in agriculture (De Grazia 1992, 178), as similar measures were increasingly included in collective agreements (Musso 2019, pp. 113–114).

In any case, as shown by the third series in Fig. 3, until the mid-1930s women represented at least a third of the labour force. This series also makes it possible to see how we obtained the annual series, interpolating our series by means of the annual labour input figures by Giordano and Zollino (2015). Apart from agriculture, Giordano and Zollino relied on a great number of existing sources: however, their series are not disaggregated by gender. This is particularly unsatisfactory considering that both World Wars are in between census years, and especially in the later one, when the gap between the benchmark years is 15 years, any interpolation will arguably miss the specific dynamic of the 1930s and the war years—something that deserves a detailed discussion, in order to correctly interpret the graphs.

As for World War I, it is important to distinguish between reality and perception. In Italy, the war had a relatively modest impact on women's industrial employment: according to Musso (2019, 37–38), by the end of the war, 250,000 women were employed in auxiliary industries, compared to 800,000 in France, and 1 and 1.5 million in Germany and the UK. Rather than "replacing" men, women took new opportunities created by "the war economic diversification", mostly in clerical and office jobs, where the share of women rose from 11.6 to 16.6% (Curli 1998, 13). On the other hand, 'traditional' sectors already employed many women. In agriculture, in both conflicts male conscription determined an increased workload for women, especially those working in tenant or sharecropping families. In textiles, according to figures reported by Willson (2010, 52), some 600,000 women worked to provide uniforms for the army, in factories or from home.

In many areas, indeed, too many women (even middle-class ones) "queued up for th[is] work" (Willson, 2010, 52). Then, according to De Grand (1976, 949), "women were especially hard hit by the demobilization of wartime industries", with "thousands ... leaving the employment market after failing to find positions to replace those lost to veterans": this was reflected by the "higher than average female emigration rate" recorded in the first nine months of 1920, when women accounted for 60% of migrants to North America.[9] This gives us the opportunity to discuss the complicated issue of female unemployment—complicated even by the standards of historical unemployment (Alberti, 2018). According to Saraceno (1981, 209), women were hit "the most" by the scarcity of employment in this period, "in all sectors". Even official statistics reported lower rates for women in 1921–1922, equal in 1924–1925, and higher in 1926–1932. From then on, female unemployment was lower (even though, in the early 1930s, more than 250,000 women, including thousands of primary school teachers, were officially unemployed) simply because "females left the active population". Just as argued by Humphries and Sarasúa (2021, 173), in these situations, "women often became 'discouraged workers,' not registering for unemployment benefit or formally seeking work, their unemployment hidden

[9] As noted by Ertola (2017, 102–115), in the few years of Italian colonisation of Ethiopia, a sizeable number of Italian women (some 10,000) had already settled there; their lives (and work) clearly deserve more attention from the literature.

behind domestic roles". Indeed, the 1931–1936 censuses show the marked increase of women "without profession".

Much less information is available for World War II, whose impact on female employment "has not been properly studied" (Willson, 2010, 98). In June 1940, Italy's intervention led to the suspension of further "quotas on female recruitment in public sector white-collar employment" introduced in 1938; in April 1943, it was even forbidden to employ men in some jobs, such as waiters, cashiers, tram-conductors, where women were encouraged to work. Fascist outlets, of course, stressed that female work—an "attack to woman's health"—had to be used "only in necessity" (and in any case, was most "remunerative" and morally acceptable in "administrative and agricultural jobs"): after the period of necessity, it was important to go back to the "gradual, but systematic elimination of female work" (Dolmetta, 1940). Also in this case, however, the war mobilisation was much less effective than in the Great War. While some local studies revealed a sizeable increase in the female industrial workforce, these changes "were largely not officially co-ordinated by the authorities": by September 1941, "a mere 73,000 of the six and half million women and children the PNF had registered as available for war work were recorded as in employment" (Willson, 2010, 98).

With these limitations in mind, Fig. 4 allows us to see what the census did not hide. As shown by the upper panel, the majority of women working for pay were still employed in agriculture, accounting for two-thirds of women workers in 1918. By 1950, however, this sector fell to less than 50%. In the same period, women increased their presence in all other sectors, also increasing their relative share within those sectors, as shown in the lower panel. Even in services, middle-class women—according to Willson (2010, 71), the "main targets" of Fascists, given the "perennial oversupply of suitably qualified candidates for posts in state employment and the professions" that affected their male supporters—increased their relevance, even as physicians and pharmacists. The same trend, but with larger absolute numbers, can be observed for 'humbler' jobs in tourism, restaurants and cleaning services (Pescarolo 2019). Indeed, many authors noted the growth of domestic services, accounting for 10% of active women in 1936, with an absolute increase from 380,614 in 1921 to 554,076 in 1936 (Willson, 2010, 76). For De Grazia (1992, 190–191), even these "likely much underestimated" figures "put Italy on a different course from other Western nations in which declining middle-class wealth and new opportunities for employment in growing tertiary or consumer-oriented industries caused the servant population to decline".

As mentioned, even industrial censuses capture the increased share of women working in heavy manufacturing sectors (Fig. 5): women made up more than 20 per cent of metal production workers in 1937, compared to 8.5% in 1911, and went from 4.3 to 13.1% in machinery. On the other hand, trends in light industries (where the female share was already higher) seem to reflect business cycle dynamics: while women increased their share in the food industry (from 14.3 to 23.9% according to the same industrial censuses) or in tanning (from 9.8 to 15.6%), they suffered the most from the struggling cycle of the textile sector (Musso 2019, 37), hit by the collapse of global trade.

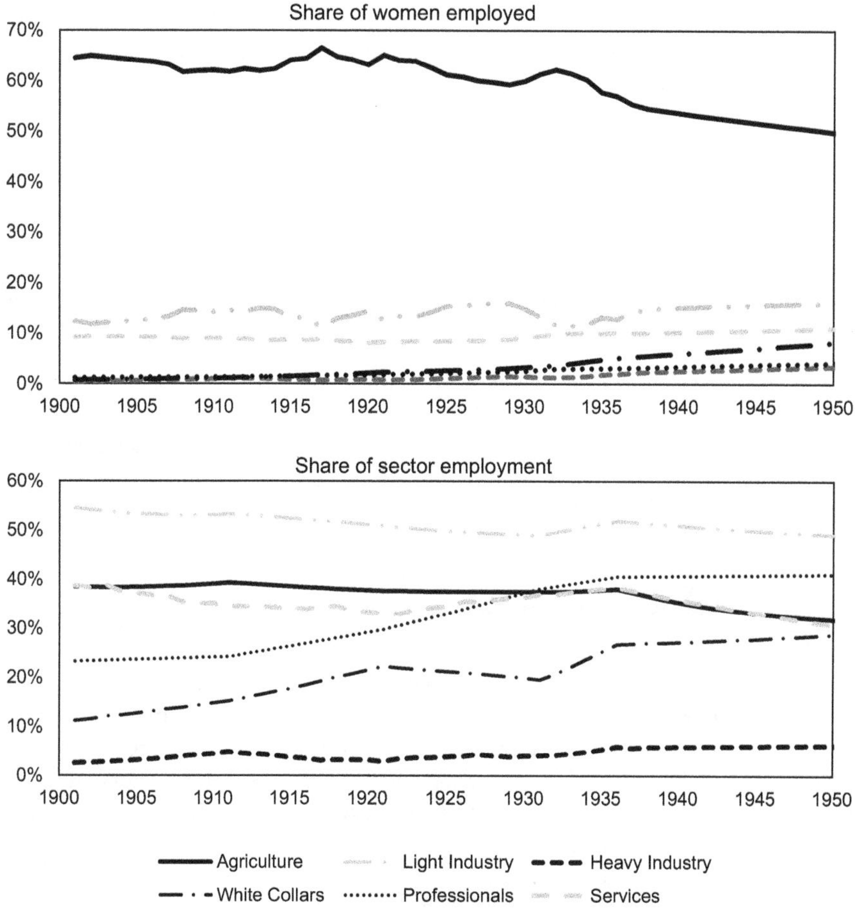

Fig. 4 Women working for pay in Italy, 1900–1950 (Source Authors' elaborations on Gómez León and Gabbuti [2022])

According to De Grand (1976, 968), "fascist policy toward women … can be seen as a struggle with no clear results". In this section, we confirmed this claim, discussing both women's participation in the labour force and their presence in increasingly more remunerative and visible sectors outside agriculture. What can we say, however, about their incomes? They will be the object of Sect. 4.

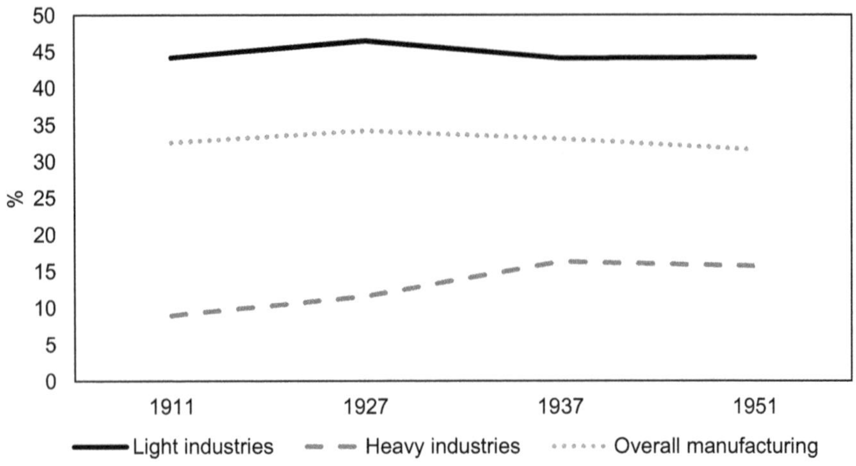

Fig. 5 Women in manufacturing according to industrial censuses (*Source* Authors' elaborations on Federico [2006])

4 The Incomes of Italian Women

As discussed by Mancini (2022), the historical literature on Italian women's wages is very limited: more archival research is needed to estimate levels and trends across the many sectors in which women worked. In this sense, while the evidence assembled for our social tables should be considered as a second-best, by documenting the limitations of existing sources, together with other sources not suitable to be included in the social tables, this section aims at stimulating further quantitative work.

As documented in detail in Gómez León and Gabbuti (2022), the main source for the estimation of average male incomes has been the various works on the matter by Vera Zamagni. We had to rely on a number of other sources to cover the whole period and to account for differences in work status. In the absence of comparable evidence of women's wages, we compiled estimates of GWG in agriculture, industry (here distinguishing between heavy and light industries), transport, commerce, public administration, liberal professions and services for the years 1901, 1911, 1914, 1918, 1925, 1938 and 1951. As listed in Table 2, they were compiled from both primary sources (as the *Annuario Statistico Italiano*) and secondary literature. Annual series were obtained by interpolating the ratios between available benchmark years, with the exception of agriculture, for which we have annual estimates from 1911 to 1950.

Apart from the aforementioned Bettio (1988), Felice (2005) deserves a discussion. In this paper, the author documented his regional disaggregation of value added, in which wages are adopted to proxy regional differences in productivity (Felice 2005, 273). Instead of imputing, as typical in Italian economic history, a fixed fraction of male wages to women and children, Felice (2005, 291–295) looked for sectoral GWGs, documenting the results in an appendix: notably, when a sector lacked consistent figures, he made informed assumptions, based on secondary literature. Further

Table 2 Sources for gender-wage-gaps behind italian dynamic social tables

Sectors	Estimated incomes:	Source
Agriculture	1911–1951 actual data on female wages	ISTAT (1953)
Heavy industry	1901, 1910, 1914, 1918, 1925, 1930, 1938, 1950 = 43, 47, 46, 65, 65, 52, 50, 71% (respectively) of men	MAIC (1900, 1905–1907, 1911, 1913, 1917–1918), Bettio (1988), Lasorsa (1931)
Light industry	1901, 1910, 1914, 1925, 1930, 1938, 1950 = 56, 64, 64, 77, 48, 50, 71% (resp.) of men	MAIC (1900, 1905–1907, 1911, 1913, 1917–1918), Bettio (1988), Lasorsa (1931)
Railway	1901, 1911, 1938 = 45, 50, 55% (resp.) of men	Felice (2005)
Commerce	1901, 1911, 1938 = 53, 55, 60% (resp.) of men	Felice (2005)
Credits	1901, 1911, 1938 = 38, 40, 60% (resp.) of men	Felice (2005)
Various serv	1901, 1911, 1938 = 55, 55, 60% (resp.) of men	Felice (2005)
Public Administration	1901, 1911, 1938 = 45, 50, 60% (resp.) of men	Felice (2005)
Liberal Professions	1901, 1911, 1938 = 50, 55, 60% (resp.) of men	Felice (2005)
Personal services	1911, 1938 = 70, 75% (resp.) of men	Felice (2005)
Salaried employees	1911, 1938 = 55, 60% (resp.) of men	Felice (2005)

Source Gómez León and Gabbuti (2022) (see there for the references)

work could expand this approach for more years, taking advantage of the wealth of secondary literature mentioned above. On the other hand, richer direct evidence is already available. For the liberal period, for instance, MAIC (1908) would enable us to discuss the evolution of GWG in sectors such as chemicals, food, typography, tobacco, wood and mining. For the Great War, Curli (1998, 303–311) reported interesting evidence on white-collar GWG in large firms, together with female wages in metalmaking and paper factories. Even for the Fascist period, when female wages disappeared from most official sources, scholarly works reveal the wealth of sources produced by Fascist bodies. For instance, for the period "just before the war". Alberti's (1943) work on the wage distribution in milling reported data by qualification, from the Provincial Unions of industrial workers. The gender segregation already mentioned, and its 'certification' by Fascist collective agreements, allows us to identify "women" as the 14th of 16 categories, just above under-age "Children" and "Apprentices between 18 and 20". The 462 women (out of 16,719 workers) earned 1.47 lire per hour—second lowest, just above children under 18 (1.33), but well below

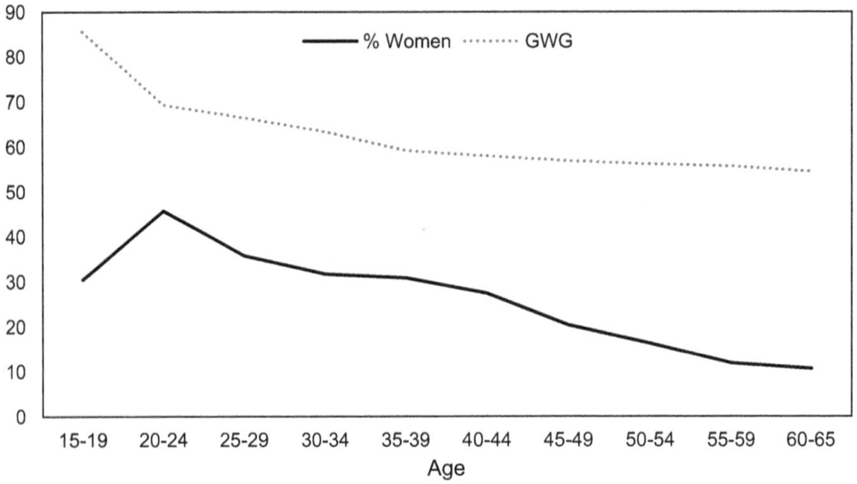

Fig. 6 Gender-wage-gap and female share of employment in commerce, by age (1930–1935) (*Source* Authors' elaborations on Pinghini [1935])

apprentices (2.03), and less than half of the industry average (3 lire). More interestingly, Pinghini (1935), "manager at the Commerce Workers' National Health Fund", took advantage of the extremely detailed data collected by this "typically Corporatist body" to discuss insured workers' wages. His work includes two tables on wages and employment by gender and age. As shown in Fig. 6, GWG are relatively low for under-age workers (above 85% in almost all sectors, and slightly above 100 in furniture, machinery trades, and auxiliary activities), but sharply declining in the 20–24 age bracket, the peak of female employment (more than 45 per 100 males on average, even 91 in clothing shops), consistently with the segregation of women in 'unskilled' jobs. Although biased towards more stable and visible forms of employment, similar evidence has definitely survived in social security archives.

In building social tables, however, our main effort was to cover most representative sectors throughout the whole period, covering the major turning points identified by gender historians. The resulting GWG, obtained as the ratios between female and male incomes in a given sector, are presented by sector in Fig. 7.[10] The room for improvement is clear, especially for the late 1930s but the figures already represent an important contribution for several reasons. First, the series reflects the equalising effect of the Great War: reduction in GWG was strongest in heavy industry, but was common to most sectors. The major exception was agriculture, where convergence took place only after the war. Indeed, most of the reduction in GWG happened between 1918 and 1925, encompassing both the two years of labour unrest known as "red biennium", the later Fascist reaction culminating in the March on Rome, and the first years of Fascist rule, characterised by laissez-faire policies, but also wage

[10] As discussed, gender segregation often makes it impossible or meaningless to compute ratios of workers performing similar tasks—see also Humphries and Sarasua (2021, 176).

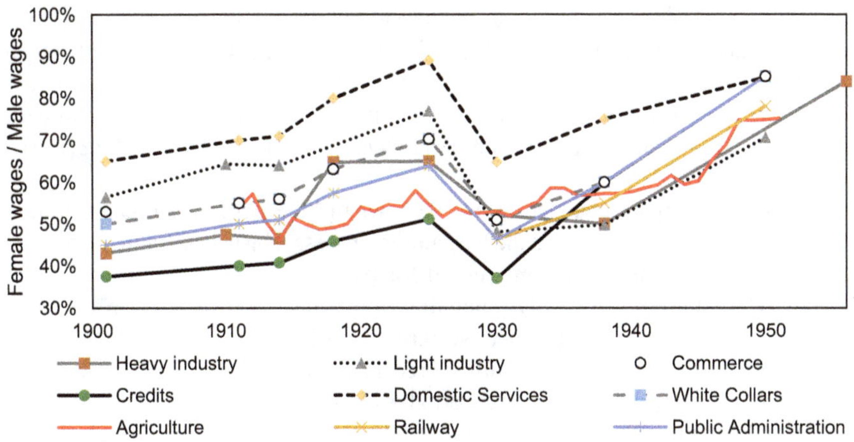

Fig. 7 Gender-wage-gaps across sectors in Italy (*Source* Authors' elaborations on Gómez León and Gabbuti [2022])

squeezes, falling labour share and rising within-labour inequality (Gómez León & Gabbuti, 2022).

Indeed, as discussed by Bettio (1988), two different forces—one 'benign', and one 'malign'—were driving this result. First, equalising union practices have been a partly overlooked 'tradition' of the Italian labour movement, at least with reference to remuneration. Both in the red biennium and in the post-WWII period, unions had often advocated wage compression (that is, more than proportional increases in unskilled wages), thus benefitting also women. De Grazia (1992, 172) attributes this strategy to weakness: the Italian labour movement, "never as strong as the British or German trade unions", could not promote reformist alliances "to pass protective legislation to eliminate low-paid female and child labor from the market", and thus had to "treat marginal female workers as full-fledged workers, involving them as much as possible in the labor movement". However, Bettio (1988) highlighted the importance of very similar tendencies in Republican Italy, when unions' strength and institutionalisation were considerably higher than in the liberal period. The first national contracts signed in 1945–1946 limited the maximum GWG for the same occupation to 30% (Bettio 2015, 234). In 1948, article 37 of the new Constitution—written, as stated by Rotondi in this volume, also by female delegates—recognised the "same rights and, for equal work, equal retribution" to the "working woman". Still, it would take 1977 for a law on equal work treatment, the culmination of three decades of campaigning by left-wing female organisations such as the Union of Italian Women, trade unionists and politicians (Betti, 2018).

Indeed, as shown by Fig. 5, the GWG went back to the early 1920s level only after 1945, driven by convergence also in agriculture. In this sector, female workers' conditions worsened during the interwar period, with the "return to semi-feudal situations" such as the landowners' right to authorise sharecroppers' marriages or evict them in case of variations in their household size, according to Pisoni Cerlesi

(1959, 84–85). There is no doubt that, "in the wake of the war, the Italian socialist trade unions, leagues, and chambers of labor, with their hundreds of thousands of female members, achieved the largest following of women of any labor movement in post-World War I Europe". Moreover, it was a woman, the socialist Argentina Altobelli, who led the single most numerous union branch, the rural workers' *Federterra* (De Grazia 1992, 172).

The unions' impact changed after 1922, when "the corporate organization of labor centralized and politicized the bargaining process. Unsuccessful in negotiating wage increases, the fascist unions settled for bargaining over benefits and special privileges" (De Grazia 1992, 174)—including, as we have seen, 'protective' measures against women. By examining collective agreements in Turin Manufacturing, Musso (1992) revealed the potential of this source in reconstructing GWG, at least for minimum levels. Figure 8 reports the ratio between a "first category" woman and a skilled male: in this case, contracts stabilised the GWG 'restored' in the early 1920s; on the other hand, we can observe the strong convergence in base pay from the early 1950s, leading to equality by 1963. On the other hand, this source reveals the impact of the introduction of family allowances for male household heads in 1934. This is one of the few cases in which we can quantify the discriminatory nature of the Fascist welfare state (Giorgi & Pavan, 2021), not captured by series like those in Figs. 6 and 7. National contracts also "codified sex-based differences. That women earned one-half of men's wages was nothing new; that skill levels and rate differentials were pegged to override local customs and market conditions perhaps more favourable to women was" (De Grazia 1992, 174). A similar development in agriculture was the widespread adoption of the so-called "Serpieri coefficient"—named after Arrigo, the foremost Fascist agrarian economist—that attributed to women 60% of male workers' productivity (Salvatici 1999, 16).

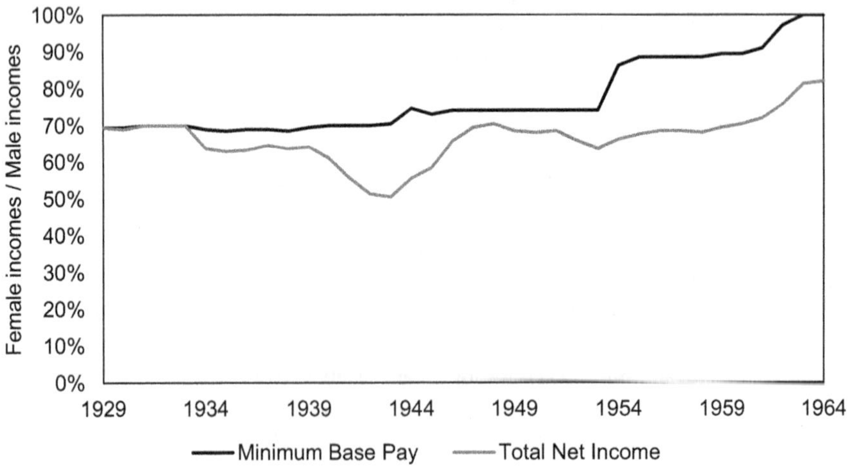

Fig. 8 The impact of family allowances on women's relative incomes in turin metalmaking (*Source* Authors' elaborations on Musso [1992])

A further element noted by De Grazia (1992, 174) was how "the corporate system prevented female workers from obtaining adequate representation": by grouping workers (and employers) by sector, it was "disarming … for any marginal or inchoate group, not least of all for women". Indeed, only one woman (the head of the all-female Midwives Corporation, Vittoria Maria Luzzi)[11] ever took part in the Superior Council of Corporations. Indeed, such discrimination against women found no opposition in Fascist unions: it was only in 1940 that 140 women delegates met to "illustrate in detail" restrictive legislation affecting 250,000 female commercial workers (De Grazia 1992, 200), in the meeting issuing the statement quoted in Footnote 9. While the available evidence does not allow us to deepen the class analysis of female work, it is interesting to note that convergence was lower for industrial workers, both in 'heavy' and 'light' sectors, compared to the (relatively) rising 'middle class' in the services. Even these 'white-collar' women, however, were effectively "confined" to the "lower ranks" (Willson, 2010, 72).

The change in union and bargaining practices, thus, contributed to the sizeable reversal, observed in most sectors from the mid-1920s (and the deflationary policy shift marked by the so-called *Quota 90*) until at least the Great Depression. Another element of convergence is what Humphries and Sarasúa (2021, 176) defined as the "dark side" of convergence in GWG—that is, the "levelling down" of men. Their analysis, related to the recent financial crises, applied very well to the Great War years—when the already low Italian labour share fell by almost 15 points in just a few years (Gabbuti 2021), with growing capital incomes driving inequality up, despite the collapse of the within-labour Gini index falling from 35 to 25 (Gómez León & Gabbuti, 2022). Even more, it perfectly fits the later Fascist experience. As long noted by historians, if anything of the Italian interwar economy emerges as truly 'Fascist', it is the unique level of control imposed over the labour force (Toniolo, 1980, xii–xiii). As noted by Zamagni (1975, 543–546), Italy was the only country where wages declined or stagnated throughout the whole interwar period: in these decades, wage squeezes (a characteristic feature of "Italian capitalism") became "a deliberate economic policy". This specific feature of Fascist domination affected women twofold. First, as workers for pay: according to De Grazia (1992, 174), by "enabling employers to slash men's wages", Fascists reduced the "incentive to substitute women for men" or to "mechanize firms, a process that elsewhere caused machine-tool enterprises and other light manufacture to increase the hiring of women". On the other hand, lower wages—and the resulting dramatic effect on the living standards of the working masses (Gabbuti 2020)—affected women in the reproductive sphere. Studies such as Salvatici (1999) and Mancini (2023) revealed the increasing burden imposed on rural women: but even in urban settings, women had to meet family needs with reduced means.

Figure 9, by showing average GWG, obtained as weighted averages, and thus 'summarising' the evidence presented in Figs. 2 and 5, allows us to conclude this section by placing GWG in Fascist Italy in a comparative perspective. First, with respect to the historical literature: according to De Pleijt and Van Zanden (2021,

[11] On midwives in Fascist Italy, see Gissi (2004).

614), in early modern Italy, the GWG "was about 50 per cent". For the first decades after unification, Federico et al. (2021, 13–14) estimated "remarkably stable" GWG in agriculture and industry, "oscillating between 0.4 and 0.5", rising to 0.55 before the Great War. Our evidence, thus, confirms the earlier assessment by Bettio (1988, 96): during the twentieth century, Italian relative wages converged "to an extent unparalleled in other industrialized countries". Indeed, in Gómez León and Gabbuti (2022), we showed that declining GWG were "one of the major 'equality forces' contributing to the Italian 'Great Levelling' throughout the first half of the twentieth century". Most of the action, however, took place in the years before and after fascism, and should rather be attributed to the labour movement. Both in the red biennium and in the late 1940s, in a context of low wages, egalitarian union ideology promoted pro-unskilled, pro-women wage compression, bringing Italian women closer to equality than British and German ones. Within this long-run convergence story, Fascism represented indeed the most striking, although temporary, reversal. While we need more research on the late 1930s, by then the Fascist control of the labour market had brought Italian wage gaps back to the 'old' low levels of 50%, below both Britain and Germany—another dimension of the reversal in living standards experienced by Italians under Fascism (Gabbuti 2020).

To conclude this section, it is worth mentioning that wage is not the only relevant monetary dimension of gender gaps. Groppi (1996) has long stressed the importance of "taking into account women's patrimonial dynamics, to remind how the relationship with the labour market—for both men and women—is always conditioned by social origin". As revealed by Stefania Licini, probate records are all but silent on women: despite the large literature devoted to their analysis in the liberal period, no study has so far investigated them in the interwar decades. 'Wealthy' women—traditionally receiving from their families' financial assets, instead of family firms or

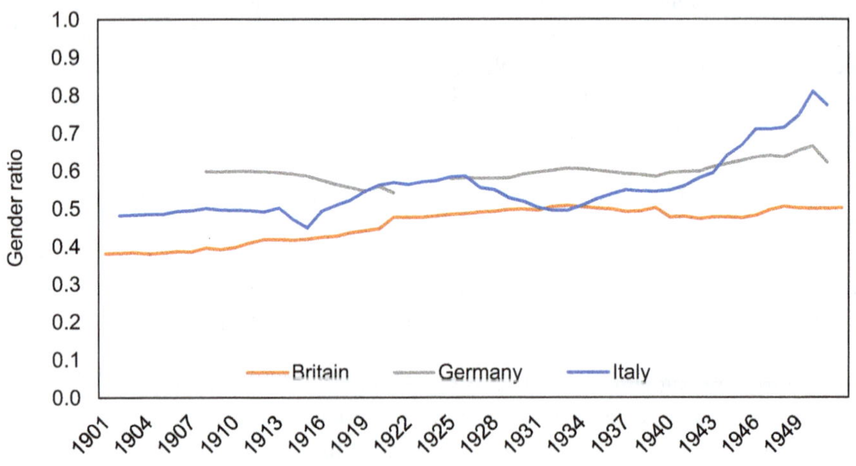

Fig. 9 Italian gender-wage-gaps in international comparison, 1901–1950 (*Source* Authors' elaborations on Gómez León & de Jong [2019] and Gómez León and Gabbuti [2022])

property destined to male heirs (Licini 2020)—arguably suffered from the turbulent macroeconomic environment of the period.

Some of these women, such as those investigated by Licini in this volume, were active as entrepreneurs: many more were running smaller businesses or working as self-employed. While in Gómez León and Gabbuti (2022), we were forced to rely on assumptions, also in this case we already have more detailed evidence. Gabbuti (2023) presents gender income gaps at the provincial level, from the lists of some categories of self-employed taxpayers, issued by the Finance Ministry in 1889, 1922 and 1933. In the latter year, women represented some 15% of these taxpayers, ranging from 7.5 to 27% across provinces. Even more interestingly, for a subset of provinces, we can appreciate the reduction of income gaps between 1922 and 1933, and the more sizeable contraction from 1889 (Fig. 10). The interpretation of similar gaps, for which we have few references in the literature, will require further investigation: still, it is interesting to use the source to highlight the extraordinarily diverse activities performed by women (from Elvira, tax collector, to Agnese the tinsmith), and indeed, the presence of few rich entrepreneurs, such as Turin's Gori Sisters, declaring 600,000 lire for their tailor's shops. As stressed by Licini (2020, 121), fiscal sources of this kind reinforce the impression that Italian women did not limit themselves to "trades, jobs, and occupations consistent with the ideology of gentility, domesticity, and 'respectability'", even in the Fascist period, as we have seen in this chapter.

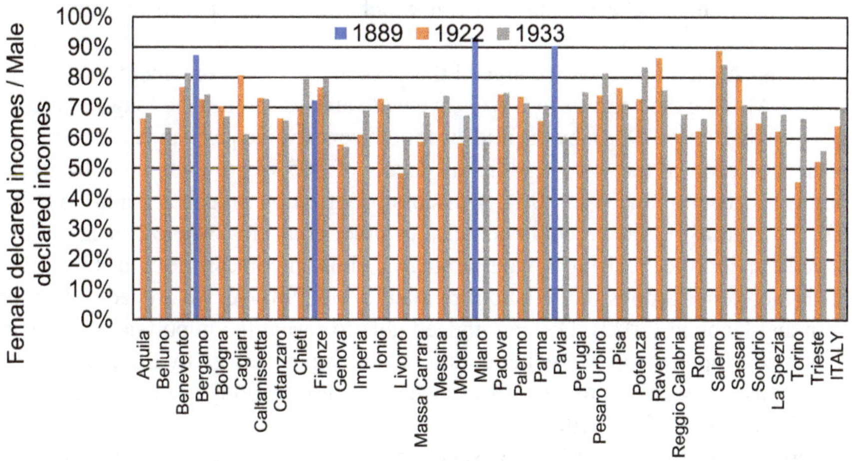

Fig. 10 Gender income gaps among Italian taxpayers (*Source* Authors' elaborations on Gabbuti [2023])

5 Female Labour in the Fascist Accumulation Model

In a 1936 speech to the National Assembly Corporation, Mussolini stressed how "in the fascist era, work … becomes the sole measure of the social and national utility of individuals and groups".[12] Fascist attempts to keep women outside the (official) labour force, and the degradation of their professionality, should thus be intended as an explicit attempt to undermine their contribution to society.

In this chapter, we made a twofold contribution. The first is methodological, since we demonstrated that social tables have the potential for casting new light on the history of women's work. Then, we addressed a major gap in the economic history of Italy, by discussing the overlooked topic of female work. In this sense, we have shown the growing gap between Fascist claims and the reality of women's work. In the Fascist period—and especially after the Great Depression—women increased their presence and visibility in industry and services: their presence declined (at least according to census data) only in "the very sector, agriculture, in which fascism wished to keep women occupied" (De Grand, 1976, 959). After applying standard adjustments proposed by the literature, even the distorted mirror of official statistics revealed how Fascism managed only to slow down the spread of female work outside traditional rural and textile jobs, and to segregate it into lower-paid unskilled positions. Employment figures capture, at a more aggregate but nonetheless insightful level, the same economic culture discussed in more detailed ways in Parts III and IV of this volume—the various ways in which women reacted to incentives and discrimination.

In this chapter, however, we argued that looking at the employment level is not enough. Moving the analysis to GWGs, we were able to confirm the long-run reconstruction by Bettio (1988): by the mid-twentieth century, the pay gap faced by Italian women, already at the low, 'traditional' levels of 50% registered since the Black Death, had been reduced to 80%. A discussion of union practices confirmed also that, "in contrast to the recent experience of other countries, where legislation has played a major role in raising female earnings …, this outcome in the case of Italy was much more endogenous to the labour market" (Ibid., 98). As we argued in Gómez León and Gabbuti (2022), DST are indeed able to reveal the importance of labour market developments in the reduction of inequality experienced by European countries in this period. This positive story, however, almost entirely occurred before and after the Fascist regime. After the turning point represented by the Great War, and the further push towards parity represented by the labour movement victories of the red biennium, Fascism represented a marked reversal in GWG terms. Drawing on women's history, we linked these developments to the change in union practices and labour market dynamics imposed by the Fascist domination. Unpacking the 'black box' of FLFP into sectoral series also allowed us to see how the history of women's work is better understood when intersecting with class and income differences.

[12] Quoted in De Grazia (1992, 166).

Indeed, looking together at employment and wage gaps allows us to understand how female work, both productive and reproductive, was crucial in the Fascist accumulation model of wage squeezes and reduced private consumption. As already highlighted by De Grazia (1992, 9),

> Mussolini's strategies of regime building inevitably had far reaching repercussions on the situation of Italian women, in particular on the working class and peasant majority. ... To sustain its pressure on wages and consumption, the dictatorship exploited household economic resources to an unusual degree for a country well advanced on the path of industrialization: it demanded that women act as careful consumers, efficient household managers, and astute clients to squeeze services out of an ever stinting social welfare system, in addition to being part time, oftentimes concealed wage earners who rounded out family incomes. ... To curb the use of cheap female labor in the face of high male unemployment, yet maintain Italian industry's reserve force of low cost workers, the regime devised an elaborate system of protections and prohibitions regulating the exploitation of female labor.

In this sense, also in Fascist Italy, demand for female labour seemed to have been more important than other factors (Humphries & Sarasúa 2012). In line with the first chapter of this volume, despite Fascist oppression Italian women remained active, autonomous agents, adapting to the economic environment. In post-unification Italy—a country well used to women and children working, at least in some sectors—this demand was mostly driven by the possibility of paying women lower wages. Despite Fascists' claims of placing the economy under the leadership of "politics", even crucial policy objectives such as demographic growth could not be pursued at the expense of private owners. Discriminatory laws mostly affected women in public services and reduced their ability to attain promotion—thus defending the status of male middle-class supporters of the Regime—while 'protective' legislation could be easily avoided by firms. "Equal pay for equal job", in order to prevent female work from being cheaper (Dolmetta, 1940), remained a mere slogan. Indeed, if we take seriously De Grazia's discussion on the importance of wage differentials in promoting female employment, we might even wonder if the rapid post-World War II convergence contributed to the strong decline of female employment which was extraordinary when seen in the long-run perspective. On the other hand, women faced a double burden in the interwar decades, exploited without representation and for lower wages at work—after all, as noted by Dolmetta (1940), women's work was a "duty", not a "right"—and under increasing pressure at home. This might have made many of them eager to focus on reproductive work when improved economic conditions made it possible to live on one wage.

References

Alberti, S. (1943). Distribuzione e salari contrattuali dei lavoratori dell'industria molitoria secondo le categorie professionali. *La Vita Economica Italiana, 16*(1), 4–8.

Alberti, M. (2018). The History of Jobless Italy. *Rivista Di Storia Economica, 34*(1), 69–106.

Bellavitis, A., & Martinat, M. (2022). Il valore delle donne. Saggio introduttivo. *Genesis, 21*(2), 7–14 (special issue). Disuguaglianze, il valore delle donne.
Betti, E. (2018). Unexpected Alliances: Italian Women's Struggles for Equal Pay, 1940s–1960s. In E. Boris, D. Hoehtker & S. Zimmerman (Eds.), *Women's ILO. Transnational Networks, Global Labour Standards, and Gender Equity, 1919 to Present* (pp. 276–299). Brill.
Bettio, F. (1988). *The Sexual Division of Labour*. Clarendon Press.
———. (2015). A un passo dalla parità? Mezzo secolo di differenziali salariali di genere. In S. Musso (Ed.), *Storia del lavoro in Italia. Il Novecento* (Vol. 2, pp. 232–253). Castelvecchi.
Burnette, J. (2021). Why We Shouldn't Measure Women's Labour Force Participation in Pre-Industrial Countries. *Economic History of Developing Regions, 36*(3), 422–427.
Castellani, M. (1937). *Donne italiane di ieri e di oggi*. Bemporad.
Cinnirella, F., Toniolo, G., & Vecchi, G. (2017). Child Labor. In G. Vecchi (Ed.), *Measuring Wellbeing: A History of Italian Living Standards Since 1861* (pp. 143–174). Oxford.
Curli, B. (1998). *Italiane al lavoro, 1914–1920*. Marsilio.
De Grand, A. (1976). Women Under Italian Fascism. *The Historical Journal, 19*(4), 947–968.
De Grazia, V. (1992). *How Fascism Ruled Women: Italy, 1920–1945*. University of California Press.
De Pleijt, A., & Van Zanden, J.-L. (2021). Two Worlds of Female Labour: Gender Wage Inequality in Western Europe, 1300–1800. *The Economic History Review, 74*(3), 611–638.
Dolmetta, F. (1940, July 15). Il lavoro femminile in guerra. *Critica Fascista, 18*(18), 293–295.
Ertola, E. (2017). *In terra d'Africa. Gli italiani che colonizzarono l'impero*. Laterza.
Federico, G. (2006). Industrial Structure (1911–2001). In R. Giannetti & M. Vasta (Eds.), *Evolution of Italian Enterprises in the 20th Century* (pp. 15–48). Springer.
Federico, G., Nuvolari, A., Ridolfi, L., & Vasta, M. (2021). The Race Between the Snail and the Tortoise: Skill Premium and Early Industrialization in Italy (1861–1913). *Cliometrica, 15*, 1–42.
Felice, E. (2005). Il valore aggiunto regionale. Una stima per il 1891 e per il 1911 e alcune elaborazioni di lungo periodo (1891–1971). *Rivista Di Storia Economica, 21*(3), 273–314.
Fenoaltea, S. (2015). Industrial Employment in Italy, 1911: The Burden of the Census Data. *Rivista Di Storia Economica, 31*(2), 225–246.
Gabbuti, G. (2020). When We Were Worse off. The Economy, Living Standards and Inequality in Fascist Italy. *Rivista Di Storia Economica, 36*(3), 253–298.
Gabbuti, G. (2021). Labour Shares and Inequality: Insights from Italian Economic History, 1895–1970. *European Review of Economic History, 25*(2), 355–378.
———. (2023). Fiscal Sources and the Distribution of Income in Italy: The Italian Historical Taxpayers' Database. *Annals of the Fondazione Luigi Einaudi, 57*(1), forthcoming.
Giordano, C., & Zollino, F. (2015). A Historical Reconstruction of Capital and Labour in Italy, 1861–2013. *Rivista Di Storia Economica, 31*(2), 155–224.
Giorgi, C., & Pavan, I. (2021). *Storia dello stato sociale in Italia*. Il Mulino.
Gissi, A. (2004). Between Tradition and Profession. Italian Midwives During the Fascist Period. In P. R. Willson (Ed.), *Gender, Family and Sexuality: The Private Sphere in Italy 1860–1945* (pp. 122–138). Palgrave-MacMillan.
Gómez León, M. (2021). The Kuznets Curve in Brazil, 1850–2010. *Revista de Historia Economica—Journal of Iberian and Latin American Economic History, 39*(1), 37–61.
Gómez León, M., & De Jong, H. J. (2019). Inequality in Turbulent Times: Income Distribution in Germany and Britain, 1900–1950. *The Economic History Review, 72*, 1073–1098.
Gómez León, M., & Gabbuti, G. (2022). Wars, Depression, and Fascism: Income Inequality in Italy, 1900–1950. *LEM Working Paper Series* 2022/26.
Groppi, A. (Ed.). (1996). *Il lavoro delle donne*. Laterza.
Iannello, A. (forthcoming). Le tessere previdenziali CNAS e INFPS: una fonte per la storia del welfare fascista?
Humphries, J., & Sarasúa, C. (2012). Off the Record: Reconstructing Women's Labor Force Participation in the European Past. *Feminist Economics, 18*(4), 39–67.
———. (2021). The Feminization of the Labor Force and Five Associated Myths. In G. Berik & E. Kongar (Eds.), *The Routledge Handbook of Feminist Economics* (pp. 167–176). Routledge.

Licini, S. (2020). Women, Business, and Finance in 19th Century Milan. *Journal of Modern Accounting and Auditing, 16*, 117–129.

Lindert, P. H., & Williamson, J. G. (1982). Revising England's social tables 1688–1812. *Explorations in Economic History, 19*, 385–408.

Maier, C. S. (1975). *Recasting Bourgeois Europe.*

Mancini, G. (2018). Women's Labor Force Participation in Italy, 1861–2011. *Rivista Di Storia Economica, 1*, 3–68.

Mancini, G. (2022). 'One Hundred Sixty Years of Gender Inequality in Italy. A Inequality Research Agenda. *Economia & Lavoro, 2*, 65–80.

Mancini, G. (2023). Breadwinner, Bread Maker: The Gender Division of Labour in 1930s Rural Italy. *European Review of Economic History*. https://doi.org/10.1093/ereh/head009

Milanovic, B., Lindert, P. H., & Williamson, J. G. (2011). Pre-Industrial Inequality. *The Economic Journal, 121*, 255–272.

Milanovic, B. (2023). *Visions of Inequality*. Belknap Press.

Ministero di Agricoltura, Industria e Commercio, Direzione Generale della Statistica (MAIC). (1908). *Annuario Statistico Italiano 1905–1907*. Tipografia Bertero.

Mortara, A. (1978). Osservazioni sulla politica dei "tagli salariali" nel decennio 1927–1936. In G. Toniolo (Ed.), *Industria e banca nella grande crisi 1929–1934* (pp. 65–71). ETAS.

Musso, S. (1992). II salario sessuato. Differenziali retributivi nell'industria metalmeccanica (1920–1900). In P. Nava (Ed.), *Operaie, serve, maestre, impiegate* (pp. 104–121). Rosenberg and Sellier.

———. (2019). Trasformazioni del lavoro e antidemocrazia negli anni tra le due guerre. *Studi di storia, 8*, 31–51.

Ortaggi Cammarosano, S. (1991). Labouring Women in Northern and Central Italy in the Nineteenth Century. In J. A. Davis & P. Ginsborg (Eds.), *Society and Politics in the Age of the Risorgimento: Essays in Honour of Denis Mack Smith* (pp. 152–183). Cambridge.

Patriarca, S. (1998). Gender Trouble: Women and the Making of Italy's 'Active Population', 1861–1936. *Journal of Modern Italian Studies, 3*(2), 144–163.

Pescarolo, A. (2019). *Il lavoro delle donne nell'Italia contemporanea*. Viella.

Piketty, T. (2014). *Capital in the 21st Century*. Harvard University Press.

Pinghini, C. (1935). I salari commerciali in Italia nel quinquennio 1930–1934 e nel primo semestre del 1935. *La Vita Economica Italiana, 10*(3), 25–41.

Pisoni Cerlesi, I. (1959). *La parità di salario in Italia*. Editrice Lavoro.

Rodríguez Weber, J. E. (2014). *La economía política de la desigualdad de ingreso en Chile: 1850–2009,* unpub. Ph.D dissertation, Universidad de la República.

Salvatici, S. (1999). *Contadine dell'Italia fascista: presenze, ruoli, immagini*. Rosenberg & Sellier.

Saraceno, C. (1981). La famiglia operaia sotto il fascismo. In *La classe operaia durante il fascismo. Annali della Fondazione Giangiacomo Feltrinelli* 20(1979/1980), 189–230.

Sarti, R., Bellavitis, A., & Martini, M. (2018). *What Is Work? Gender at the Crossroads of Home, Family, and Business from the Early Modern Era to the Present*. Berghahn.

Settis, B. (2022). Fascist Economy. Private Powers and State Intervention. In G. Albanese (Ed.), *Rethinking the History of Italian Fascism*. Routledge.

Toniolo, G. (1980). *L'economia dell'Italia fascista*. Laterza.

Vitali, O. (1968). *La popolazione attiva in agricoltura attraverso i censimenti italiani (1881–1961)*. Failli.

Willson, P. (2010). *Women in Twentieth-Century Italy*. Palgrave Macmillan.

Zamagni, V. (1975). La dinamica dei salari nel settore industriale, 1921–1939. *Quaderni Storici, 10*, 530–549.

Women in Education

Aurelia Josz, Educational Entrepreneur, and Her School of Agriculture for Girls

Giandomenica Becchio and Manuela Mosca

1 Introduction

Despite their traditional contribution to family businesses in a range of historical contexts and in different societies, the role of women in creating and managing firms and commercial activities has either been neglected or seriously under-reported. Nonetheless, the literature on women as entrepreneurs and managers has been increasing in recent decades, especially within women's studies (Butler, 2003). More recently, a few researches have been carried out by historians of ideas in order to show the role of forgotten women who were engaged in the spread of education in Europe and the United States in the timespan between late nineteenth century and mid-twentieth century (Bennet et al., 2020). Nevertheless, no research has explicitly focused on the role of women as creators of entrepreneurs and managers through their specific activity in education (Figs. 1 and 2).

This chapter scrutinizes the activities of a female educational entrepreneur, Aurelia Josz, who contributed to training women entrepreneurs and managers in agriculture. From 1902 to 1931 she founded, organized, and ran the first Female Practical School of Agriculture in Italy. Her purpose was threefold: to train modern agricultural entrepreneurs and managers in order to provide them with technical and economic instruments for farm management; to allow disadvantaged women to reach economic independence (the school initially was aimed at orphaned girls); to counteract the exodus and impoverishment of the Italian countryside due to urbanization as well as to the absence of men during the war.

G. Becchio (✉)
Università Di Torino, Torino, Italy
e-mail: giandomenica.becchio@unito.it

M. Mosca
Università del Salento, Lecce, Italy
e-mail: manuela.mosca@unisalento.it

M. Mosca (ed.), *Women at Work in Italy (1750–1950)*, Springer Studies in the History of Economic Thought, https://doi.org/10.1007/978-3-031-64281-4_8

Fig. 1 Aurelia Josz (*Source* Family Archive)

Aurelia was one of the many women who, driven by strong motivations, put their ideas into practice.[1] Luckily for us she was also a woman who wrote. She published several books on teaching agriculture, on her own experience as founder of the agricultural school for girls, and also on history, geography, and the woman question. As Kuiper (2022, p. 162) reminds us, women "wrote for an audience of women and girls, activists and politicians." Aurelia wrote to reach out to politicians, teachers, investors, "families from the countryside" (Josz 1910, p. 3), as well as the girls who attended her school and the board of the orphanage. Besides her published writings, our sources for her economic thought will include the scarce secondary literature on her figure, her private archive which is still in the hands of her family,[2] and—as mentioned—the ideas expressed through her activities.

Aurelia Josz (1869–1944) was born within a Jewish-Hungarian family who had settled in Florence. Her father, Ludovico, was an artist engraver, while her mother, Emilia Finzi, was a teacher. The artistic and pedagogical aura of her parents' personalities massively impacted her education and that of her siblings. A fundamental aspect of Aurelia's *Bildung*, coming from her family's influence, was a deep patriotism: in fact, her father left Trieste (at that time under the Austrian Empire) and

[1] The subtitle Josz gave to her 1932 book is "History of an idea and an endeavour". Unless stated otherwise, the translations of quoted texts are our own.

[2] Our thanks to Alberto Zylbersztajn, Aurelia Josz's grandnephew, for giving us access to the family archive.

Fig. 2 The dairy at the women's agricultural practice school of Niguarda, circa 1900 (*Source* Facebook page "Milano sparita e da ricordare")

moved to Florence right after the unification of Italy.[3] The importance of national identity was a constant element for the Josz family as well as their Jewishness, which was grounded in a secular vision that focused on the importance of education for both boys and girls.[4]

As a child, Aurelia attended the Liceo, and later graduated at the School of Magistero (Pedagogy) at the University of Florence. In 1890, the 21-year-old left Florence for Milan, where she worked as a teacher of History and Geography up to 1934 when she retired. During her long career as a schoolteacher, Aurelia realized the urgent need to get rid of the traditional pedagogical methods in order to create a new way of teaching that would increase creativity for children. Therefore, she published handbooks for secondary schools (Josz 1894, 1899, 1908a).

As a strong supporter of rural life, she overlaid her passionate love for agriculture with some patriotism, recalling Cavour's idea of "considering agriculture as the pillar of the new Italian nation" (Josz 1932, p. 50).[5]

In 1904 in Milan, she founded an agrarian school for girls (Scuola pratica di agricoltura femminile, SPAF). Then, she traveled to Switzerland, England, France, and Belgium to check out the teaching programs for agriculture in those countries and to find possible suggestions for her project. In the same year she moved the school to Niguarda, a village close to Milan where the agriculture was particularly

[3] The Italian unification occurred in 1861, but Trieste was reunited to Italy only in 1918.

[4] In the second half of the nineteenth century the battle for women's education was mostly 'a Jewish affair' in cities all over Europe (Freidenreich, 2002; Malleier, 2006; Rose 2008).

[5] The liberal politician Camillo Benso, Count of Cavour (1810–1861) was the main architect of Italian unification, and the first prime minister of Italy.

fertile. She lived there until 1933. The superiority of rural culture was a hot topic of Zionism, which was emerging in that period: Aurelia joined the Milan Zionistic Group, founded by Bettino Levi (Buseghin, 2012). As for socialism, her attitude was complex, as she wrote in her autobiography: "if I indulged, in theory, in the spirit of socialism, whose innovating influence I recognized, I also realized the dangerous sides of its manifestations and I disliked its too frequent formal vulgarity" (Josz 1932, p. 7). Aurelia's socialism was also mitigated by her genuine attachment for the already mentioned idea of national identity, almost nationalism, which emerged later on two occasions: she supported the involvement of Italy in World War I against Germany and Austria (although she was a pacifist) and, like many Italians at the beginning of the fascist regime (1925–1945), she trusted Mussolini and his agenda as a possible way to restrain the arrogance of parties, dramatically increased after the Great War. During World War I, the SPAF was very active in providing any form of help for soldiers, especially clothes and socks. Her attitude was revealed earlier on the occasion of the earthquake which destroyed Messina in 1908, and later during the Spanish flu pandemic in 1919. In 1932 the fascist regime shut down the school, which was re-opened one year later under new management and named after Mussolini's sister-in-law (Augusta).

The loss of her life-long project did not shatter Aurelia's attitude. In fact, she started to write more intensely than before by publishing a history of her school (Josz 1932), a critical edition of Boiardo's works (Josz 1936), and a historical novel (Josz 1937). Due to a broken arm, she was unable to escape to Switzerland with the rest of her family, to avoid the consequences of the racial laws introduced in Italy in 1938. In 1944, while hiding in a nunnery, she was arrested and deported to Auschwitz, where she was killed.

2 Schools for Girls and the Importance of Education: Pedagogy Versus Other Possible Fields

As is widely known, formal education for girls was precluded, either because they were denied access to universities, or to the lack of classes for girls within the high school system.[6] The unequal access to education between the sexes prevented women from getting involved in the formation of leadership. Their education only focused on female accomplishments whose major effect was the marginalization of women from public debates and the reinforcement of the doctrine of the separate spheres (Becchio 2020, 2024; Rostek 2014, 2019). Simply put, the doctrine holds that certain areas of life are best reserved for men, and certain areas of life are best reserved for women. Indeed, according to the doctrine, if society is to be at its most functional and prosperous, men and women should play the roles that their genders have suited them to play. Hence, supporters of the doctrine have accepted it in order

[6] For examples of preclusion to education for women in Europe, see Freidenreich (2002), Becchio (2020), Mosca et al. (2022).

to reinforce the gendered division of economic and social roles between men and women, while detractors of the doctrine have criticized it in order to promote gender equality (Eibach & Lanzinger, 2020), insisting on the need for women to become economically independent. As Kuiper wrote:

> Women have long fought for education as a fundamental right. Sound training and study enabled women to obtain the skills to get a job, earn a living, become economically independent, know their rights, defend themselves legally, control their own assets, and contribute to science and sociology at large … Women economic writers perceived education as starting from a very early age and encompassing all aspects of a person, including moral strength and skills required to lead a good and responsible life. (Kuiper 2022, p. 165)

In European countries, while boys might choose between two different high school systems which allowed them to get access respectively to academia and to engineering studies, girls were forced to enroll in very expensive private schools to extend their education beyond the basic level they had achieved at the compulsory school. The situation started to change in the second half of the nineteenth century, when several private institutions arose, mainly founded and led by women, and devoted to providing girls with six more years after their basic education. They were mainly boarding schools and they were private. However, they did not entitle their graduates to academic studies: they only allowed access to the teaching and healthcare professions (Holmes, 2012). The personal story of Aurelia's education perfectly fits this pattern. Pedagogy and health care were the female sectors that allowed women to work outside the home, making an exception to the doctrine of separate spheres. She stated that the teaching role for women was a kind of abuse: it became the only possible way for women to get a job (Josz 1932, p. 6). Traditional education, usually performed by women within the household, became paid work in the public spheres (Benjamin, 2023; Rostek 2021). Nonetheless, things changed when the first generation of highly educated women, like Aurelia, became active in their profession. Between the end of the nineteenth century and the beginning of the twentieth century, girls were trained in non-traditional female sectors: the phenomenon of female cultural entrepreneurs emerged. Several examples can be provided. In Vienna Ottilie Bondy (1832–1921) founded a private *Gymnasium* for girls, which offered a curriculum based not only on liberal arts, but also on mathematics and natural history. In 1907, Olga Steindler (1879–1933) and Olly Schwartz (1877–1960) established the first business school to prepare girls for a career in business (*Handelsakademie für Mädchen*). Eugenie Schwarzwald founded a school whose curricula included modern foreign languages and science and, influenced by Maria Montessori with whom she was in contact, Eugenie promoted girls' creativity as a fundamental educational principle. Aurelia belonged to this emerging group of cultural entrepreneurs. She devoted her activity to the foundation of her school for girls, going beyond the traditional educational fields.

3 The Female School of Practical Agriculture

The movement for women's agrarian education in Europe, which began in the last decade of the nineteenth century, grew at the beginning of the new century, thanks in part to "authoritative voices like Mrs. Crawford's" (Josz 1905, p. 15). Virginia Mary Crawford (1862–1948), a British Catholic journalist writing about art and literature, with obvious economic skills (Crawford 1901), was a great source of inspiration: committed to the women's rights movement, Crawford in 1911 founded the Catholic Women's Suffrage Society. For her, as for Aurelia, the teaching traditionally given to girls caused them to despise the countryside and desire a life in the city, where however "the openings for women [were] barely sufficient for the urban population, and [were] utterly insufficient for the vast yearly influx of would-be workers from the country" (Crawford 1898, p. 428).[7] The case of Daisy Greville, countess of Warwick (1861–1938), founder in 1898 of the first women-only collegiate center for agricultural education in England (Opitz, 2014) was quite similar to that of Aurelia.[8] Historiography provides us with other examples of women in Europe at that time who devoted their lives to the establishment of women's agricultural schools: Aurelia herself, in her account of her 1905 journey through some of the European countries, described many of them. This was a trip co-funded by the Ministry of Agriculture, Industry and Trade, specifically designed to visit and study women's agricultural boarding schools. Josz meticulously described the schools visited: the organization of the spaces, the social background of the pupils, their age of entry and their uniforms, the tasks performed, the syllabus, the agricultural goods produced, the teaching hours, the methods of financing, the budget, the employment prospects, the duration of the courses, the machinery used, the laboratories, and the fees. For her (Josz 1905, p. 1), as well as for Crawford (1898, pp. 428–432), the ideal example of women's agricultural schools was found in Belgium. But in Italy, a country with a strong agricultural vocation, despite the Minister of Education Guido Baccelli's willingness to help "the awakening of agriculture" (Josz 1900, p. 6),[9] Aurelia noted that for the country woman, "little or nothing had been done to make her conscious, modern" (Josz 1905, p. 18). In the words of Bisi Albini (1922, p. 96)[10]:

Italy unfortunately lacks the presence of the country lady, that is, the educated person who oversees with intelligence, who perceives with the heart, who finds new resources and studies innovations, and gets to where the husband busy with other

[7] It is interesting to see the list of jobs for women in that period: "teachers, governesses, typists, cashiers, bookkeepers, secretaries, shorthand-writers" (Crawford, 1898, p. 427).

[8] Warwick is cited by Crawford (1898), but also by Josz (1905, pp. 12, 14).

[9] The education minister Baccelli had proposed "making basic schooling the keystone of the desired progress in agriculture and of a revival of the values of rural Italy", but the project failed (Bidolli & Soldani, 2001, p. 458).

[10] Sofia Bisi Albini (1856–1919), writer and journalist, was the founder of *Vita femminile italiana*, a reference point for the Italian women's movements of the time, a publication to which Aurelia also contributed.

things, or with the more important chores of agriculture, could not arrive even if he wanted to.

What Aurelia wanted to achieve through her school was therefore a cultural change in the female world: "the great social benefit, which is expected from these schools, consists of raising the agricultural profession to the level of art" (Josz 1905, p. 4).

This marked the creation of the first women's agricultural school in Italy. The initial idea of founding it was present in the long review of Crawford's article (Josz 1898). From 1900, publicizing her project through lectures to journalists, philanthropists, intellectuals, and receiving encouragement even from Minister Baccelli, Aurelia began to obtain some private funding. The first concrete step was taken in 1902, with the activation of a single agricultural course in a well-known Milanese girls' orphanage (Josz 1903). More funding, including public funding, was added, and in 1904 a real school finally opened its doors, giving theoretical and practical lessons "in the garden, the stable, the silkworm farm, the chicken coop and the kitchen" (Vita Josz 1957, p. 11). Then in 1906 the school succeeded in becoming a boarding school, its diploma acquired legal value, and in 1913 a pedagogy curriculum in agriculture devoted to rural female instructors also began (1921).

During the Great War the school took in rural orphans and in 1918 received a gold medal for providing products to the army (Josz 1932, p. 68). The war as we know changed the very idea of women's possibilities and aptitudes: it revealed the "coefficient of resistance expressible by the forces that women draw from the mysterious roots of being" (Josz 1932, p. 10).[11] In the 1920s, Aurelia tried to reform the school according to the new rules advocated by Giovanni Gentile, the Ministry of Public Education under Mussolini's regime: in 1922 she met him in person in order to explain her ideas. Mussolini was quite dismissive, but after a few years, in 1926, opened a new agricultural school for girls in Rome which fascism strongly promoted, effectively draining the resources of the original school. For Aurelia, her venture ended in 1932, but in fact, as we shall see in the last section, it had a sequel.

In the field of innovation in teaching, Aurelia was a pioneer (Seveso, 2023). She was deeply impressed by the methods adopted by modern schools of agriculture, based on the daily outdoor activity of pupils who were encouraged to develop their own creativity rather than to focus on traditional learning through textbooks: a pedagogical methodology that was introduced in those years by Maria Montessori. Historiography acknowledges in every age the flair for innovative teaching shown by women, who are often "attacked for their less conventional attempts to broaden both pedagogical methods and research approaches and topics" (Jacobsen, 2020, p. 145).

The school targeted girls from country families belonging to the middle and higher class and sought to offer them an alternative after their elementary schooling. Until that time, the only education open to women who wanted to continue their studies encouraged them to work in the city or at least inculcated the desire to abandon the countryside. Instead, the women graduating from agricultural school could return to

[11] In 1915 Josz wrote an article in the *Secolo* on the organization of women's work to replace the male workforce during the war.

the country to administer the family landholdings, to introduce innovations in agriculture and animal husbandry, to teach agriculture, or to manage a farming business. At the same time, the school also aimed to educate women working as farm-hands, to give them better skills and prevent them from moving toward the cities.[12]

In Aurelia's words:

> we need to find a way to initiate the youthful spirits into the new fields of agricultural industry; to consider the value of female aptitudes, the purpose of the education of the rural woman, and to ensure that the existing agricultural institutes open their doors to women. (Josz 1908b, p. 15)

Let us now briefly focus on the economic subjects taught in girls' agricultural schools. The most commonly found subjects in all the European schools were certainly book-keeping: the administration of farming businesses, their budgets, accounts, and double-entry book-keeping (Josz 1910). There was also a rural economics program that is of interest to us, because it envisaged the study of factors of production, capital used in the agricultural industry, farm management systems, land credit, agricultural credit, insurance, consortia, and cooperative societies (Josz, 1910, p. 14). Finally, the school trained girls to study agriculture combined with the curricula of home economics. Home economics was a new research field that was emerging in the United States in the same period. It focused on the scientific management of the house; its central element was a strong expertise in economic matters which would help mothers to train their families as ideal consumers. Aurelia was an enthusiastic supporter of the introduction of home economics in American and European schools and universities (Josz 1908b, pp. 11–12). In the 1920s, "notions of Political Economy in Welfare Institutions" were also added (Josz 1932, p. 83).

4 First Aim of the School: Female Entrepreneurship and Management in Agriculture

Today's data on female entrepreneurship reveal that women "still appear less likely to take on investments with significant risk" (Jacobsen, 2020, p. 99). At Aurelia's time, the situation was much worse: businesswomen were limited by social barriers; they were recommended only for moderate credit and discouraged from making investments; the mainstream press belittled and disparaged women's entrepreneurial ambitions. Furthermore, legal restrictions against women often prevented them from becoming entrepreneurs (Le Chapelain & Baijot 2022). They were mostly seen as self-employed women who ran their own activities, however tiny or temporary (Gamber 1998). They could have been for instance "hucksters, saloon keepers, shoe shiners, laundresses, boarding house keepers, proprietors of private schools, street walkers, dancing teachers, organizers of charitable associations" (Phillips, 2006,

[12] According to Poggi (1907, p. 10), the women handling agricultural matters were administrators of their own properties, entrepreneurs "of small new female industries in the villages", agriculture teachers and writers, and lastly, farmers' wives.

p. 145). The phenomenon was common in European countries as well as in the United States. At the beginning of the twentieth century, things changed, and the number of female entrepreneurs increased dramatically. Many businesswomen of the time transformed their financial success into political strategies to advocate for women's empowerment (Yaeger, 1999; Yohn 2006). This was the case of Aurelia. She invested in her educational project in order to provide a formal education to girls, and to make women economically independent through their involvement in rural activity seen as a business.[13]

As has been said, Aurelia's educational plan was centered around the formation of two kinds of professionals: middle and upper-class rentiers who might work in their family business, and peasant women (Josz 1905, p. 19). For Aurelia, middle class included either an urban social group, whose main task was to get involved in the industrial system, or rural rentiers, i.e., landowners who never got involved in actually working on their farms, usually conducted by their farm overseers and peasants. Hence, Aurelia insisted on the importance of educating a new leadership of rural workers coming from the middle class. Women would be included in this new rural leadership, overturning the traditional discrimination against any possible active role of women in the rural sector, where financial access was possible only for men (Josz 1932, pp. 63–64, p.78), and "nobody would have thought to get girls involved" (Josz 1932, p. 13). She insisted on this: "[in Italy] we need middle-class girls to perform this professional task" (Josz 1905, p. 3).[14] As her good friend Ada Negri[15] wrote in 1904, she succeeded: "girls who followed the curricula of the agricultural school will be able to manage their own or someone else's farm or estate [as well as] to control balance sheets, performing a productive activity and getting an honorable income" (quoted in Josz 1910, p. 6).

Aurelia's school was not intended only as a cultural project: indeed, it was a no-profit business. Students were engaged in producing goods and selling them to obtain self-funding and to make some profits, which were invested in the school. It was therefore partially self-funded, though money mainly came from private and public funds. Again, this mixed form of co-funding was shared by the majority of the new schools of the time: Aurelia provided some examples, in Belgium and Great Britain, where agricultural schools were co-funded by public and private sectors, and she was well aware of the importance and the necessity of creating a synergy between the two sectors (Josz 1932, pp. 25–29).

[13] "Aurelia wanted to educate women to become entrepreneurs by getting acquainted with all the knowledge and technicalities which are necessary to production" (Schiaffelli, 2016, p. 79).

[14] She also wrote: "In Italy, when a father earns enough to provide everything to his family, he would never admit that his daughter might get trained for a profession that is not among those considered noble! Beyond the Alps, people are far away from this megalomaniacal mania, based on an old-fashioned vision, and they rightly think that every job is honourable, if done properly (Josz, 1905, p. 2).

[15] Ada Negri (1870–1945), poetess and writer, used her fame to support various initiatives in favour of women, also during the fascist regime. A former teacher as Aurelia and her close friend (Josz, 1932, p. 19), she introduced Aurelia to Mussolini in 1923 (Josz, 1932, p. 92).

5 Second Aim of the School: Economic Independence for Women

The second goal of the school was to allow disadvantaged women to reach economic independence through agricultural work, a goal also in line with Crawford's forecasts.[16] As we have seen, initially the school was aimed at orphaned girls, to offer them social redemption,[17] and one of its targets had always been to open the possibility for a remunerative job to women in agricultural sectors (Josz 1908b, p. 13). Financial autonomy for women was necessary also because, according to Aurelia, often "by the tyranny of circumstances, … they are called to roles of economic support for weaker members" (Josz 1905, p. 18). In short, for Aurelia's case, as for many other similar cases, "education, particularly professional or vocational instruction" was seen "as the key to women's economic emancipation" (Périvier & Rogers, 2022, p. 453).

Aurelia helped women to gain their economic independence without giving up their traditional complementarity with men, expected to persevere in heavier jobs (Josz 1898). She was convinced that women had specific abilities in rural activities:

> Women ... could, without taking over the attributions of men, bring to field work marked qualities of economy, diligence, constancy, and become a significant factor for the desired agricultural revival of our country. (Josz 1900, p. 12)

She insisted on the necessity of providing economic freedom for women without levelling the two genders: "I do not think good, true feminism tries to distort feminine inclinations, but to develop them and apply them appropriately: distorting them would be violence and would undoubtedly cause unhappiness" (Josz 1903, p. 13). Aurelia's feminism was definitively quite moderate,[18] as confirmed by her own words, when she hoped that her talk would be "acceptable in its premises for even the most lukewarm supporters of feminism" (Josz 1900, p. 3). Nevertheless, she was a feminist. She followed the European feminist conferences (Josz, 1900, p. 3), criticized the old conceptions of the woman, "the romantic morbidities that have done so much harm … to the female creature" (Josz 1900, p. 8), and encouraged girls to work hard since "your progress will give us all the strength to keep going in the task undertaken to your benefit and that of women in general" (Josz 1903, p.18).

---

[16] "Among women workers of all shades of thought, there appears to be a general conviction that it is in agricultural employment that the economic independence of our surplus female population is largely to be sought in the future" (Crawford, 1898, p. 435).

[17] On school as a means of personal and social redemption, see D'Annunzio (1999, p. 73; 2016, p. 25).

[18] She explicitly wrote: "The avantgarde women, although there were heartfelt and self-sacrificing ones, did not please me, indeed they even inspired something repulsive in me, the flaunting of feminism … as I have always aspired … to a hearth illuminated by the ideal light of love, firm as I was in the conviction that in it alone was happiness and the wifely realm" (Josz, 1932, p. 7).

In her time, Aurelia's was considered a feminism "of a new kind" (Panzini, 1903) and can be specifically linked to the widespread trend at that time of practical feminism,[19] aimed not only at obtaining the right to vote, but also precisely at emancipating women through work. Aurelia even went so far as to state in a critical tone that in the postwar period "women were ranting for the political vote, while Bolshevik echoes were stirring up the perverted, unruly crowds" (Josz, 1932, p. 74).[20] Her feminist militancy was based on action, and on teaching for action; it is no coincidence that she was also involved in 1908 in the First Congress of Women's Practical Activity, whose president was the Swedish writer Ellen Key (Josz 1932, p. 37).

This pragmatic conception of feminism, which saw charity not as "mere welfarism, but redemption through education" (D'Annunzio, 2016, p. 30),[21] was shared by a network of philanthropists mobilized by Aurelia to create and support the school, with open minds toward all her bold innovations. She invited them to "distinguish between charity that is alms-giving and true charity, which prevents evils" (Josz 1932, p. 37). Since its beginning, as we have seen, the SPAF was made possible by an intense fundraising drive that Aurelia was able to set up by involving this network, particularly in Milan.[22] She was especially in touch with well-known female activists, including Alessandrina Ravizza,[23] Alice Hallgarten Franchetti, the already mentioned Sofia Bisi Albini and Ada Negri, as well as with scientists like Paolo Mantegazza[24], and politicians such as Luigi Luzzatti[25] and Pasquale Villari[26], who were attentive to the rapid cultural transformation in a recently unified country. Among them, Alice Hallgarten Franchetti had a special role: she was not only a patron of Aurelia's school, she was also on its board (Josz 1910, p. 2), she sent some peasant girls to the school (Josz 1932, p. 30), and employed many graduates who were educated to become rural businesswomen or professional instructors devoted to teaching women living on her farms to lead and manage their business.[27] To Alice Hallgarten Franchetti she even dedicated a touching commemoration (Josz 1913).[28]

[19] The expression "practical feminism" was widely used at that time, as opposite to theoretical feminism (Laurenzi & Mosca, 2021, pp. 13 ss.).

[20] Aurelia used a similarly emphatic tone against the illusions of feminism regarding the rights of women workers (Josz, 1932, p. 20).

[21] On this topic see also Laurenzi and Mosca (2021, pp. 7 ss).

[22] The initial network in support of the school is to be found in Josz (1903, p. 17) and in Vita Josz (1957, pp. 7, 8). The names of those who helped the school over the years are given in Josz (1913) and in D'Annunzio (1999, pp. 75 ff., 2016, pp. 26–30).

[23] Alessandrina Ravizza (1846–1915) was a philanthropist, feminist, and pioneer in the field of social support based in Milan.

[24] Paolo Mantegazza (1831–1910) was a scientist, philanthropist and writer.

[25] Luigi Luzzatti (1841–1927) was Italian prime minister in 1910 –1911.

[26] Pasquale Villari (1827–1917), a well-known Italian historian, was also a senator and minister. Josz (1910, p. 30) reports Pasquale Villari and Paolo Mantegazza's praise for her school.

[27] Aurelia received written declarations from those who had employed the graduates on their behaviour and work (Josz, 1910, p.22).

[28] On Alice Hallgarten Franchetti see Buseghin (2021).

In 1914 also the school's ex-students created a network, the "League of new Home-makers," which planned to publish a journal and organize conferences, but the idea was then swept away by the outbreak of the Great War (Josz 1932, pp. 50–52).

6 Third Aim of the School: Women, Environment, and Urbanization

Inspired as we have said by Virginia Mary Crawford and Daisy Greville, Aurelia was convinced that Italy needed a school able to limit the phenomenon of leaving the countryside in order to get a job or simply to live in an urban setting. From the beginning of her enterprise, Aurelia was deeply influenced by Tolstoj's idea of a moral superiority of rural culture. As she wrote: "Let's get back to the land! Tolstoj advocates as a prophet let's get back to our mother [land]!" (Josz 1908b, p. 14). Later in her memories, she wrote that in those days she was "obsessed about the *georgical* idea" and added: "at that time Tolstoj was my idol and I totally accepted his call to get back to the land in order to be happy" (Josz, 1932, pp. 8–9). Besides Tolstoj, she also admired the Franciscan respect for nature and animals, combined with the application "of scientific progress to practical life" (Josz 1932, p. 87).[29] Another source of inspiration for her was Hermann Sudermann's popular novel *Es war*, in which Herta, a strong, gentle, and brilliant young lady who loved rural life, was able to save her land from being thrown into disorder (Josz, 1932, p. 11). As mentioned earlier, the role of agriculture was also central in Zionism of the time. Aurelia was acquainted with it, although she never explicitly acknowledged any influence from it. Common traits between Zionism and Aurelia's educational project were centered on the features of kibbutzim. They included: the central role of agriculture intended as a way to develop a new form of society, free from exploitation of workers; a modern version of agriculture aimed to improve the synergy between urban and rural contexts; gender equality; a combination of efforts between the private and the public spheres against the dichotomy between capital and labor (Abramitzy, 2018).[30]

The preoccupation about the rapid transformation of both the urban and rural environment during the second industrial revolution was commonly shared by many social scientists and scholars of the time. As Kuiper (2022, p. 168) wrote:

> while farmers used to have a direct interest in maintaining a healthy environment and supporting the commons, and while women, in running their household, were trained to make efficient use of resources and materials, the incentives in industrial agriculture and society at large changed over the centuries.

This means that there was a general underestimation of agriculture as a form of production of national wealth along with a snobbish attitude toward rural life.

---

[29] We will return to this point in Sect. 8.

[30] About the relation between Zionism and ruralism see also Bidussa and Meriggi (2000) and Misiani (2010). About the involvement of Italian Jewish women see Natterman (2022).

For instance, in the American Progressive Era, the society rapidly changed from an agrarian to an urban one, and a massive process of industrialization under large corporations and monopolies emerged: that quick process of transformation pushed progressive leaders and scholars to formulate a program of socio-economic reforms able to improve working people's living conditions. Many intellectuals of the time, especially located in big cities, such as Chicago and New York, focused their research on the rapid social changes of the urban environment, and the role of minorities as a fundamental factor of social transformation. Their research led them to conclude that the urban environment, not the family, was the source of the greatest social problems. This is the case of women economists such as Marion Talbot, Sophonisba Breckinridge, and Edith Abbott, to name but a few (Becchio 2020).

Aurelia shared those concerns, especially because of the peculiar Italian economic development and cultural framework, which had been traditionally firmly grounded on agriculture and rural values (Gardey et al., 2020). She mentioned the bias of rural rentiers who usually prevented their daughters from undertaking rural studies and activities: "our hope that middle-class women get involved in rural activity is vain as long as it is considered less noble than any other activity ... this belief is truly biased" (1900, pp. 18–19). Later, she spoke about a "medieval bias" against rural life (Josz 1932, p. 76), even stronger in the case of women. She was afraid that girls in the countryside "would believe they are disrespected by people ... demeaned in an occupation regarded vulgar... such a deadly prejudice!" (Josz 1900, p. 12).

Tolstoj's exaltation of traditional values related to rural activities was combined with a criticism of the frenetic life of cities. Aurelia realized soon that the new urbanism was having an enormous impact on the well-being of many workers, whose social and moral standards of life dramatically decreased. She denounced the effects of urbanization and the transformation of the traditional rural society into an industrial society dominated by a greed that would weaken human relations as well as destroy the connection between humans and nature. For her, urban life, with its air "corrupted by miasma and chimneys" (Josz 1903, p. 7), was the main enemy of the family (Josz 1932, p. 6). Nevertheless, women tended to be attracted to the city. Aurelia was always critical of it, and shared the concerns of those intellectuals who, as we said, saw in the urban environment the source of major social problems. In her words:

> while thinkers and lovers of the public good are calling for a return to the countryside and to a simple and modest life, albeit illuminated by the ray of civil progress, the exodus from the countryside is becoming ever more frequent, and the centralization more threatening. (Josz 1900, p. 5)

As a solution, Aurelia argued that gender discrimination in the rural sector had to be opposed by the mobilization of enlightened Italian women[31] and invited people, especially women, to "fall in love with the land. In today's terms 'to ruralize'" (Josz, 1932, p. 20). For her, women could "become initiators of activities advantageous for themselves, for the family, and a center of beneficial radiation in the circle of their

[31] In her words: "All the intelligent women in Italy must participate in the fight against the most disastrous prejudice that makes many think that farm work is not as noble as other kinds" (Josz, 1908b, p. 15).

rural neighbour" (Josz 1908b, p. 9). She saw the education given in her school as pivotal to improving the general conditions of society (Josz, 1905, p. 1).

7 Josz the "Economist"

As we have seen, Aurelia was certainly an educational entrepreneur, although she was often referred to simply as a teacher or educator. She was certainly never considered an economist. Did she formulate economic thought? The sources on which we have based the above description also enable us to derive her ideas on specifically economic topics, some of which have already been introduced.

Let us begin with her description of education as an economic choice, in which we find elements of human capital theory. According to Aurelia, fathers sent their daughters to school to provide them with "a small dowry …, a little capital from which they could draw at need enough earnings to suffice for life" (Josz, 1908b, p. 13). Husbands, too, would derive economic benefit from wives competent in the management of the marital home (Josz 1903, p. 10),[32] and the family economy would be revitalized (Josz 1932, p. 23). The economic effects of women educated in schools such as hers were reflected for Aurelia both in their production choices, that is, in their choice of agricultural products to grow (Josz 1900, p. 16), and in their consumption choices; on these issues it is worth leaving the floor to her:

> Our housewife educated in the experimental agricultural school ... would know ... how to survey the market to take advantage of every favourable opportunity, prepare ... for every eventuality, and even in the products that leave the narrowest margin of usefulness would know how to find the payoff, by the due appreciation of what to the uninitiated may appear negligible amounts. (Josz 1900, p. 17)

In addition to the economic advantage that would benefit her own family, at a time when due to economic conditions "all or almost all women of the middle class have to work to earn" (Josz 1900, p. 8), her female graduates could make their human capital pay off by finding work "on some neighbouring estate … or on any rural farm certainly with no less profit than they would make from a position as a schoolteacher" (Josz 1900, p. 14). Aurelia often insisted on the equivalence of remuneration in agricultural and typically female activities.

Mention has already been made of the new pedagogical methods introduced by Aurelia. Instead, here we want to focus on the agricultural school as a means of transmitting innovations from an economic, rather than pedagogical, point of view. Aurelia repeatedly mentioned the ability to innovate that her school provided: through agricultural education girls learned about and applied to the rural world new scientific

[32] Josz was already complaining that statistics on the participants in schools did not distinguish between genders (Josz, 1905, p. 14).

findings, and new technologies.[33] Only if modernity entered their work could the farm become competitive and profitable.[34] Aurelia's return to the land was thus not nostalgic and conservative, but was imbued with confidence in progress, and her school was intended to provide women with close and continuous contact with the world of science, leading to the formation of "an intelligent and productive rural femininity" (Josz, 1932, p. 7).

As well as the link between agriculture and progress, Aurelia clearly saw the connection between agriculture and national wealth. She wrote:

> In the more advanced European countries, the importance of agriculture has been recognized as a source of prosperity. When there is abundance of soil products, any other progress is possible: sciences, arts, military forces, and social advancement have only been able to take place where agriculture has advanced and been loved. (Josz 1903, pp. 8–14)[35]

Italy, even more than other European countries, was in her opinion a country with a rural calling, which should unquestionably specialize in agricultural production. Explicitly anti-industrialist, she argued that Italy could never reach "the industrial heights of France, England, and Germany" (Josz 1900, p. 5, 1903, p. 8), countries that, unlike her country, were able to sustain "ruthless competition" in the quality and prices of industrial products (Josz 1932, p. 49). Specialization in agricultural production would then lead to a profound change in international trade, which Aurelia specified in the following terms:

> [We Italians] through carelessness and ignorance, throw away millions and millions, either by neglecting the production of crops that we could perfectly well obtain at home, and which we are then forced to bring from outside, or by exporting foodstuffs of poor and depreciated quality to foreign markets. From the product of agriculture we draw only 5 billion annually, while, by improving the cultivation, we could get 15 billion! (Josz, 1903, pp. 11–12)[36]

In this scenario of economic valorization of Italian agriculture, a central role was to be played by women. She explicitly stated that this change could "give rise to great private and public utility" (Josz 1910, p. 3), and that to achieve this result, it was necessary to build upon their education:

> ... if country women knew how to understand the importance of education, if they knew how to intelligently avail themselves of the manuals and magazines dealing with the various agricultural industries ... a good deal of that wealth--which we foolishly lose today--would be produced and would remain in the country. (Josz 1903, p. 12)

[33] Aurelia believed her pupils "gain the ability to study and apply every new scientific proposal" (Josz, 1908b, p. 11). She cited England (Josz, 1903, p. 8) and Flanders (Josz, 1905, p. 17) as examples of schools that taught to apply scientific progress to agriculture.

[34] "Modern science ... has such great applications in agriculture ... farm work cannot continue with antiquated empirical habits, but must ... improve following modern criteria if it is to be profitable" (Josz, 1903, p. 9). And again: "this art cannot be practised today as it was a century ago, and only by animating it with the breath of science can it be made profitable today" (Josz, 1932, p. 76).

[35] Besides these quotations there are many other passages where the connection between agriculture and national wealth is very explicit, such as Josz (1903, p. 8, 1905, pp. 6, 10, 20, 1932, pp. 9, 88).

[36] In the same work (Josz, 1903) Aurelia gives further figures on harvests and population, on imports and exports, and on possible agricultural products.

Many economic arguments are also found in Aurelia's campaign against urbanization. Here she relied on opinions of economists, without naming them, who "complain about the damages of centralization".[37] As she wrote:

> the city reaps its victims; and in any case the exodus from the farms, while it impoverishes them, has as a natural consequence the excessive concentration of the population in the city centres, the damages of which are unanimously lamented by all economists. (Josz 1905, p. 18)

Economists also denounced the consequences of the concentration of people in the city on the labor market,[38] meaning the reduction of industrial wages according to the "economic law that oversupply reduces the value of the goods" (Josz 1908b, p. 9). Aurelia repeatedly criticized the worrying increase in migration toward the towns[39] and the excessive competition suffered by urbanized peasants.[40] The problem of concentration was especially serious in women's professions: Aurelia was well aware of the reduction of wages due to oversupply of the female workforce (Josz 1905, p. 15). Referring to the work of women in city centres, she wrote that the "fierce competition with the male workforce" (Josz 1903, p.13), certainly did not make the urban female workers free women. In agreement with Ada Negri, she was convinced that working in the city instead made them "slaves of the clock and of the price ... little by little crushed in the monstrous cogs of the greedy tumultuous city" (Negri 1904, p. 3).

8 Conclusions

Through her writings (Josz, 1932) one can reconstruct the influence of Aurelia and her work on her own generation and the following ones.

Her first publication,[41] appearing in a national cultural weekly magazine, gave her admittance to a female cultural circle where she delivered her first talk, which was

[37] She wrote: "All economists and all hygienists complain about the damages of centralization ... every work intended to oppose it, to curb the migratory flow, stopping the unaware people on their native soil ... is a patriotic and holy work" (Josz, 1908b, p. 9).

[38] She writes (Josz, 1905, p. 18): "the exodus from the farms, while impoverishing them, has as its natural consequence the overcrowding of city centres, the damage of which is unanimously lamented by all economists".

[39] In her words, "The competition in the city is becoming fiercer and fiercer because crowds of peasants disillusioned with farming come to offer a new workforce for industries and I could quote you here the statistics to show you that in Italy the population of cities is growing and that of the countryside is falling, in a way that would greatly concern those that hold science dear" (Josz, 1903, p. 6).

[40] "Every day the urban working class grows due to immigration and naturally this leads to the competition becoming terrifying, it ruins small industries and lowers the value of manpower: so while the land is deprived of its strong workforce, there is an increase in the multitude of the suffering, the malcontents, the poor" (Josz, 1900, p. 5, see also 1903, p. 8).

[41] The review of the article by Crawford (1898), already mentioned in (Josz, 1898).

reported in the leading Italian newspaper, the *Corriere della Sera*[42] and later also published (Josz 1900). This gave rise to a series of reviews and newspaper reports,[43] speeches at agricultural conferences[44] and talks on female education,[45] as well as articles that she published in widely circulating journals and papers.[46]

It was also the beginning of her contacts with politicians: from 1900 the already mentioned Education Minister Guido Baccelli became her supporter, along with the ministers for agriculture, whom she met repeatedly and from whom she obtained funding and authorizations. We have already mentioned her meeting with Mussolini in 1922: Aurelia believed it was due to her influence that he decided to make Italian agriculture one of the cornerstones of the regime's policy (Josz 1932, p. 94). Her last contact with the government was in 1925, when her request to transform the school from private to public was rejected.[47]

Right from her earliest scholastic initiative in 1902, the press was very supportive,[48] reporting her first course in 1902,[49] and the stand curated for the international exposition in Milan in 1906,[50] which was not only visited by Queen Margherita (Josz, 1932, p. 32), but was also awarded a gold medal (Josz 1932, p. 31). Also her proposal to erect a monument to peace in the city of Messina, destroyed by the 1908 earthquake, found a large consensus, even though in the end the substantial sum raised was used for other charitable purposes (Josz, 1932, pp. 42–43).[51] The fame of Aurelia's endeavor spread internationally as well: in the years 1911–14 the school's visitors' book records visits from Tokyo, Chile, the United States, England, and Spain. The network of influential names who supported the school has already been described.[52] The last articles mentioning the school, written at the height of the Fascist era by the future Minister of Agriculture, still call it "admirable" (Marescalchi,).

Thus, Aurelia was a well-known and influential educational entrepreneur and an activist of great impact on the realities of her time. But it is often the case that the

---

42 The woman in agriculture, *Corriere della Sera*, 20 May 1900.

43 Josz (1932, p. 11) cites in 1901 news in the Piacenza newspaper and in *Rassegna scolastica* of 13 April.

44 Besides those already mentioned, in 1901 the Agrarian Conference in Lodi, and in 1906 the National Agrarian Conference (Josz, 1932, p. 10).

45 Aurelia spoke at the third Conference of Female Education in Milan, and her talk was published in *Vita femminile italiana* (Josz, 1908b).

46 She wrote in *La nostra rivista* by Sofia Bisi Albini, as well as in the democratic daily newspapers the *Secolo* and *L'epoca.*

47 The arguments of the government's reply (given in Josz, 1932, p. 101) are in line with the free trade approach of the Minister Alberto de' Stefani, in office until July 1925.

48 As she herself points out, the "press of all shades was favourable, from the socialist *Tempo* … to the extremely moderate *Perseveranza*" (Josz, 1932, p. 16).

49 *Corriere della Sera*, 9 December 1902.

50 *Corriere della Sera*, 29 May 1906.

51 Among others to remember, Ferruggia and Manzi (1909), for their excellent photos of the school.

52 To these, one can add, among others, the pedagogist Giuseppe Lombardo-Radice (1879–1938), and Margherita Sarfatti (1880–1961), for whom see Chapter 12 in this book.

names of women even highly regarded in their time are not passed on to the next generation.[53] This is not the case with Aurelia. The school of agriculture she founded in fact still exists.[54] The last pages of her 1932 book imply that the school's history had sadly ended, but in fact it resumed its activities as early as 1933 with a new headmistress who was approved by the regime but who continued her methods.[55] However, the fact that it was named after Augusta Mussolini certainly made her suffer (D'Annunzio, 2016, p. 44). In 1942 the school was closed due to the war and only much later, in 1956, was it reopened, again with the same head, in a new city (Monza), still strongly preserving the imprint of its founder.[56] Today the school describes itself as having been founded in 1902 by Aurelia Josz,[57] so despite the trauma of fascism and racial laws, despite long interruptions and changes,[58] the memory connected to her education project certainly survives.[59] In addition to this, over the years both a literary prize on themes related to agriculture and the Niguarda botanical garden have been named after Aurelia, pacifist initiatives have been dedicated to her, events have been promoted in her memory on Memorial Day and theatrical performances on her figure, and finally a street in Monza (where the school is still located) will bear her name (Bon, 2023).

Nonetheless, her idea of enhancing agricultural production through women's labor was not followed up in Italy, which, in subsequent decades, continued to develop under the banner of industrialization at the expense of agriculture (Zamagni 1993, pp. 346–349). However, in the 1950s and 1960s, the management of a smaller number of agricultural properties became the task of higher-class women (Castagnoli 2013). In general, Aurelia Josz's entire project had two distinctly original, innovative elements: investing in women to avoid the enormous waste of talent and skills of half the Italian population and counteracting the impoverishment of the countryside with the "back to the land" ideology. Of these two innovations, only the first has gradually been achieved (Willson, 2010).

Besides Aurelia's role as an educational entrepreneur, it is possible to consider her also an economist, albeit not in the canonical meaning of the word. As we have seen, she had an economic culture, and she therefore wanted her actions to be effective in the Italian economy at micro and macro level. Aurelia's thinking was unquestionably

---

[53] Some of these cases are reconstructed in Mosca et al. (2022).

[54] The school's website is https://www.monzaflora.it.

[55] Maria Nicolini remained as head of the school until 1984.

[56] On visiting the school, Aurelia's sister writes, "I saw nothing that failed to reflect the ideal you pursued" (Vita Josz, 1957, p. 23). See also Nicolini (1946).

[57] In the school a plaque reads, "Let there be renewed among the young women who continue the work of encouraging love of the land, the memory of Prof. Aurelia Josz ... who in Niguarda in 1902 founded this school and for many years directed it with self-sacrifice, altruism and virgilian joy".

[58] Buseghin (2012) writes that the building was devastated by the partisans in 1945, and that in the 1980s the new head, Sergio Zerbini, opened it to boys as well.

[59] Such survival is not common in the history of women in Italy (Laurenzi & Mosca, 2021, p. 6).

economic, it was conscious, deliberate economic thought, which in the herstory of economic ideas is worth remembering.[60]

References

Abramitzky, R. (2018). *The Mystery of the Kibbutz: Egalitarian Principles in a Capitalist World.* Princeton University Press.

Becchio, G. (2020). *A History of Feminist and Gender Economics.* Routledge.

Becchio, G. (2024). *The Doctrine of the Separate Spheres in Political Economy and Economics. Gender Equality and Classical Liberalism.* Palgrave Macmillan.

Benjamin, M. (2023). *A Little Give. The Unsung, Unseen, Undone Work of Women.* Scribe.

Bidussa, D., & Meriggi, M. G. (Eds.). (2000). *Enzo Sereni. Emilio Sereni, Politica e utopia. Lettere 1926–1943.* Nuova Italia.

Bennett, R., Smith, H., Van Lieshout, C., Montebruno, P., & Newton, G. (2020). *The Age of Entrepreneurship.* Routledge.

Bidolli, A. P., & Simonetta, S. (Eds.). (2001). *L'istruzione agraria (1861–1928).* Ministero per i beni e le attività culturali.

Bisi Albini, S. (1922). *Le nostre fanciulle.* Vallardi.

Bon, M. (2023, September 21). Sì dell'aula: una strada nel nome di Josz, *Il Cittadino* (p. 27).

Buseghin, M. L. (2012). "Aurelia Josz". http://www.enciclopediadelledonne.it/biografie/aurelia-josz/

Buseghin, M. L. (2021). Alice Hallgarten Franchetti. A Woman Beyond Barriers. In E. Laurenzi & M. Mosca (Eds.), *A Female Activist Elite in Italy (1890–1920)* (pp. 59–92). Palgrave.

Butler John, E. (Ed.). (2003). *New Perspectives on Women Entrepreneurs.* Information Age.

Castagnoli, A. (2013). *L'imprenditoria femminile nell'Italia unita.* Istituto della Enciclopedia Treccani.

Crawford Virginia, M. (1898, September). Englishwomen and Agriculture. *Contemporary Review.*

Crawford Virginia, M. (1901). Philanthropy and Wage-paying. *Economic Journal, 11*(41), 96–105.

D'Annunzio, P. (1999). Aurelia Josz (1868–1944): un'opera di pionierato a favore dell'istruzione agraria femminile. In *Storia in Lombardia.* Angeli.

D'Annunzio, P. (2016). Biografia. In P. D'Annunzio, S. Heger, E. Heger Vita & C. Schiaffelli (Eds.), *Aurelia Josz* (pp. 19–52). Unicopli.

D'Annunzio, P., Simonetta, H., Eleonora, H. V., Carla, S. (2016). *Aurelia Josz.* Unicopli.

Eibach, J., & Margareth, L. (Eds.). (2020). *The Routledge History of the Domestic Sphere in Europe.* Routledge.

Ferruggia, G., & Alberto, M. (1909, September 20). Scuola di pratica poesia. *La Donna* (pp. 16–17).

Freidenreich Harriet, P. (2002). *Female, Jewish, and Educated: The Lives of Central European University Women.* Indiana University Press.

Gamber, W. (1998). A Gendered Enterprise: Placing Nineteenth-century Women in History. *Business History Review, 72*(2), 188–218.

Gardey, D., Margaret, M., Monique, M. (2020). Earning a Living in Europe During the 19th and 20th Centuries: A Question of Gender. *Encyclopédie d'histoire numérique de l'Europe* (online).

Holmes, D. (2012). Genia Schwarzwald and Her Viennese Salon. In G. Bischof, F. Plasser, & E. Maltsching (Eds.), *Austrian Lives* (pp. 190–211). Innsbruck University Press.

[60] As Rostek (2021, pp. 72–73) writes: "an implicitly androcentric definition of the economy impedes the acknowledgement of women's contributions to economic thought". Kuiper (2022, p. 5) adds: "Rather than engaging in the abstract reasoning that some of their male contemporaries excelled in, it was women's daily experiences that led them to write about how to run a household or estate".

Jacobsen Joyce, P. (2020). *Advanced Introduction to Feminist Economics.* Elgar.

Josz, A. (1894). *La storia di Roma, ad uso delle scuole secondarie.* Galli.

Josz, A. (1898). La donna nell'agricoltura. *Fanfulla della Domenica, 20*(46).

Josz, A. (1899). *La storia d'Italia nel Medio evo, conforme ai programmi governativi delle scuole complementari e tecniche.* Agnelli.

Josz, A. (1900). *La donna nell'agricoltura.* Agnelli.

Josz, A. (1903). *Prolusione al corso teorico pratico di agraria.* Agnelli.

Josz, A. (1905). *Le scuole femminili agrarie all'estero.* Bollettino ufficiale del Ministero di agricoltura, industria e commercio.

Josz, A. (1908a). *Lo studio della topografia nelle scuole primarie e secondarie.* Ferrari.

Josz, A. (1908b). L'istruzione agraria femminile. *Vita Femminile Italiana, I*, 5–15.

Josz, A. (1910). *Relazione e programma della scuola pratica agricola femminile in Niguarda.* Agraria.

Josz, A. (1913, March 16). Fiammella francescana. *Nuova antologia.*

Josz, A. (1932). *La donna e lo spirito rurale: storia di un'idea e di un'opera.* Vallardi.

Josz, A. (1936). *Matteo Maria Boiardo:1434–1494.* Paravia.

Josz, A. (1937). *Severino Boezio nel dramma della romanità.* Milano Treves.

Kuiper, E. (2022). *A Herstory of Economics.* Polity.

Laurenzi, E., & Manuela, M. (2021). The Political Philanthropy of the Female Elites. In E. Laurenzi & M. Mosca (Eds.), *A Female Activist Elite in Italy (1890–1920)* (pp. 1–27). Palgrave.

Charlotte, L. C., & Baijot, S. (2022). Reassessing Women's Participation in Entrepreneurial Activities in the Nineteenth Century: A Review of the Literature. *Oeconomia, 12*(3), 405–442.

Malleier, E. (2006). Making the World a Better Place. Welfare and Politics, Welfare as Politics? Activities of Jewish Women in Vienna Before 1938. *Aschkenas—Zeitschrift für Geschichte und Kultur der Juden, 16*(1), 261–268.

Marescalchi, A. (1927, June 22). La donna nelle campagne. *Corriere della Sera.*

Marescalchi, A. (1928, December 29). Le maestre rurali. *Corriere della Sera.*

Misiani, S. (2010). *Malio Rossi-Doria un riformatore del Novecento.* Rubbettino.

Mosca, M., Magdalena, M., & Astrid, A. C. (2022). Women, Economics and History: Diversity Within Europe. *Oeconomia, 12*(3), 371–378.

Nattermann, R. (2022). *Jewish Women in the Early Italian Women's 1861–1945, Movement, Biographies, Discourses, and Transnational Networks.* Palgrave Macmillan.

Negri, A. (1904, December 9). Scuola agraria femminile. *Corriere della Sera* (pp. 2–3).

Nicolini, M. (1946). L'alta Italia ha finalmente la sua scuola agraria femminile. *Pensiero Femminile, 2*(1), 3.

Opitz, D. L. (2014). "Back to the Land": Lady Warwick and the Movement for Women's Collegiate Agricultural Education. *The Agricultural History Review, 62*(1), 119–145.

Panzini, A. (1903, July 5). Una femminista di un nuovo genere. *La vita internazionale.*

Phillips, N. J. (2006). *Women in Business, 1700–1850.* Martlesham, Boydell & Brewer.

Périvier, H., & Rebecca, R. (2022). Writing Women Back into the History of French Economic Thought: The Case of Flora Tristan, Julie-Victoire Daubié and Clémence Royer. *Oeconomia, 12*(3), 625–661.

Poggi, T. (1907). *La donna e l'agricoltura.* Casale Monferrato.

Rose, A. (2008). *Jewish Women in Fin de Siècle Vienna.* University of Texas Press.

Rostek, J. (2014). Female Authority and Political Economy: Jane Marcet and Harriet Martineau's Contradictory Strategy in Disseminating Economic Knowledge. In R. Nischik & S. Mergenthal (Eds.), *Anglistentag 2013: Proceedings* (pp. 21–33).

Rostek, J. (2019). English Women's Economic Thought in the 1970s. In K. Madden & R. Dimand (Eds.), *Routledge Handbook of the History of Women's Economic Thought* (pp. 33–52). Routledge.

Rostek, J. (2021). *Women's Economic Thought in the Romantic Age.* Routledge.

Schiaffelli, C. (2016). La sorprendente attualità del pensiero e dell'opera di Aurelia Josz. In P. D'Annunzio, S. Heger, E. Heger Vita & C. Schiaffelli (Eds.), *Aurelia Josz* (pp. 73–89). Unicopli.

Seveso, G. (2023). Il ruolo delle donne ebree nel rinnovamento pedagogico dell'inizio Novecento: la sperimentazione educativa di Aurelia Josz. In E. Bianchi & P. V. Finzi (Eds.), *Donne ebree protagoniste* (pp. 29–46). Guerini.

Vita Josz, V. (1957). *Le origini della prima scuola agraria femminile italiana nel pensiero e nell'opera di Aurelia Josz*. Nervi, Ongarelli.

Willson, P. (2010). *Women in Twentieth-century Italy*. Palgrave Macmillan.

Yaeger, M. A. (1999). Will There Ever Be a Feminist Business History? In M. Yaeger (Ed.), *Women in Business* (Vol. I, pp. 3–43). Elgar.

Yohn, S. (2006). Crippled Capitalists: The Inscription of Economic Dependence and the Challenge of Female Entrepreneurship in Nineteenth Century America. *Feminist Economics, 12*(1–2), 85–109.

Zamagni, V. (1993). *The Economic History of Italy 1860–1990*. Clarendon Press.

Female Students and Graduates in Business and Economics in Turin (1906–1940)

Laura Giartosio and Giovanni Pavanelli

1 Introduction

The present chapter aims to shed new light on the dynamics of women's participation to university education in Italy in the first half of the twentieth century through the analysis of a significant case: the educational paths, achievements and constraints of the female students and graduates at the "Scuola Superiore di Studi Applicati al Commercio" (High School of Commerce) of Turin since 1906, when this was founded, until the second world war and after. From 1935 this business school became part of the University of Turin as the Faculty of business and economics.

This chapter draws mainly on the documentation stored in the historical archives of the University of Turin and on the data included in the "Annuari" (*Yearbooks*) of the High School of Commerce and, since 1935, of the University. It also utilizes the correspondence, stored at the "Fondazione Luigi Einaudi", of Giuseppe Prato, professor of political economy at the High School from 1911 till 1928, and of Luigi Einaudi, professor of public finance at the law faculty of the University of Turin.

Previous drafts of this chapter were presented at a workshop held at the University of Salento, April 2023 and at the AISPE-SISE Conference, Palermo, October 2023. We wish to thank Manuela Mosca, Marcella Corsi and an anonymous referee for their comments. We also extend our thanks to the staff of the historical archives of the University of Turin—in particular Paola Novaria—and of the archives of the Fondazione Luigi Einaudi for their support in retrieving and allowing us to consult the unpublished materials used in this chapter. The usual disclaimer applies. Unless stated otherwise, the translations of the quoted texts are our own.

L. Giartosio
Ispettorato del Lavoro, Cuneo, Cuneo, Italy

G. Pavanelli (✉)
Università di Torino, Torino, Italy
e-mail: giovanni.pavanelli@unito.it

M. Mosca (ed.), *Women at Work in Italy (1750–1950)*, Springer Studies in the History of Economic Thought, https://doi.org/10.1007/978-3-031-64281-4_9

2 The Institutional Framework

After the unification of Italy in 1861 Turin was, for a few years, the capital of the Kingdom of Italy. It then suffered a serious decline following the loss of its political and administrative role when the capital was moved to Florence and then to Rome. From the end of the nineteenth century, however, it was able to start a process of rapid expansion, particularly in the manufacturing sector (textiles and mechanics), driven by an increasing availability of abundant, low-cost hydroelectric power. A massive belt of factories and warehouses quickly arose around the historical urban perimeter, profoundly changing Turin's urban structure and consolidating its role as an industrial centre, the most dynamic, together with Milan, in north-western Italy (Castronovo, 1987; Levi, 2001).

Commercial activity and services, traditionally important sectors in Turin, also experienced a strong revival. The increase in employment and incomes led to renewed optimism and new initiatives, documented by numerous urban requalification projects and the creation of new infrastructures and services of public interest. Economic development, particularly in the manufacturing sector, was accompanied by the strengthening of labour organizations, mostly linked to the socialist movement. At the level of public opinion, there was a spread of new ideas and proposals for reform fuelled by widely circulated daily newspapers.[1] The new proposals included demands for a greater participation of women in political and economic activity.

This rapid economic and social development led to the need for higher education institutions capable of training the middle and managerial staff required by the new production activities.

The University of Turin, which had a centuries-old tradition, was the training centre for graduates in the traditional "liberal" professions (physicians, lawyers, notaries, pharmacists, teachers). In 1906 an institute of higher education in business and economics with the task of providing the administrative and management cadres required by the new productive sectors, began to operate with the title of "Scuola Superiore di Studi Applicati al Commercio" (from 1923 "Istituto Superiore di Scienze Economiche e Commerciali" and, from 1935, Faculty of business and economics at the University of Turin).[2]

The model adopted was that of the business schools, which had been active in Italy and in other European countries for several years: these were institutions endowed with a large degree of autonomy but nevertheless placed under the supervision of

[1] Among the most influential newspapers circulating in northern Italy at the beginning of the twentieth century, it is worth mentioning *La Stampa*, edited in Turin by Alfredo Frassati, an ambitious journalist who advocated social reforms and the extension of civil rights, and *Corriere della Sera*, published in Milan by Luigi Albertini, a brilliant journalist and manager who championed classical liberalism. An important role was also played by *Avanti!*, the official newspaper of the Socialist Party, published since 1896. Castronovo and Tranfaglia (1979), Forgacs (1990), Pavanelli (2023).

[2] On the High School of Commerce of Turin see Spadoni (1998), Allio (2008), Pavanelli (2008).

the government, which contributed to financing their activities, together with various local entities.[3]

The educational curricula, although structured with the objective of primarily training corporate administrators and managers, gave ample space to business disciplines, economic theory, mathematics, statistics, law and foreign languages. The course of study was for three years. At the end of the third year, in order to obtain a bachelor's degree, candidates had to submit a written dissertation, on a topic of their choice. It was also necessary to discuss two oral dissertations and demonstrate fluency in two foreign languages. At the end of the bachelor's examination, a diploma in business and economics was awarded, which opened the way to administrative and managerial careers in the private sector (industry, commerce and banking) but also in the public administration and as a teacher in secondary commercial and technical schools.

In 1922, the High School's educational offerings were expanded with the provision of a fourth year of specialization in accountancy, instrumental in obtaining the qualification to teach this discipline in the above mentioned schools. Advanced courses in actuarial studies, auditing and industrial economics were also established.

As will be seen, many of the women who graduated from the Turin High School would indeed become teachers in secondary schools in accountancy, law, economics and foreign languages (particularly English and French).

It is significant that the admission criteria to the High Schools of Commerce were less restrictive than those in force at the University: the latter required a diploma from a classical or scientific lyceum, a type of school generally attended by the (mostly male) children of the middle and upper bourgeoisie. Children of the lower middle class generally attended technical or commercial schools, which offered the possibility of a faster route to jobs, albeit less prestigious ones.

In the late nineteenth and early twentieth centuries, therefore, the High Schools of Commerce were an important factor of social mobility in Italy. As we shall see through the analysis of the Turin school, they became also a significant instrument of gender empowerment (Fig. 1).

[3] The first High school of commerce in Italy was founded in Venice in 1868, modeled on the *Handelshogeschool* of Antwerp (active since 1852). It was followed by similar business schools in Genoa (1884), Bari (1886), Milan (1902), Turin (1906) and Rome (1906). After the first world war other business schools began their activities in several Italian cities: Catania and Palermo (1919), Napoli (1920), Trieste (1924), Firenze (1926), Bologna (1929). A legislative measure approved by the Italian Parliament on 20 March 1913 established a common regulatory framework for all these institutions. In particular, the High schools of commerce were placed under the supervision of the Ministry of Agriculture, Industry and Trade, later renamed Ministry of National Economy. After 1928 they were placed under the supervision of the Ministry of Education and finally, during the 1930s, were incorporated into the university system as faculties of business and economics. See ISTAT (1933, pp. 21–23), M. M. Augello and M. E. L. Guidi (1988).

Fig. 1 The 'Istituto Superiore di Scienze Economiche e Commerciali' of Turin in the early 1930s

3 Female Students and Graduates from the High School of Commerce of Turin: An Analysis of the Data

At the beginning of the twentieth century, the Turin High School, as was the case with Italy's other business schools and universities, was predominantly a male institution: all the faculty were men, like most of the students. The presence of women (enrolled female students) although limited and, until now, scarcely studied, was nevertheless significant and worth a thorough accurate analysis.[4] During the period considered here (1906–1940) several female students won scholarships, graduated *summa cum laude* and presented dissertations which were considered worthy of publication. A significant number of female graduates continued their professional activity in the crucial educational role of secondary school teachers. In a few cases, overcoming difficulties and widespread prejudice, female graduates started to collaborate as teaching assistants and became professors at university level.

In 1909, among the first graduates from the High School (34 in total), two were women: Paolina Rinaldi and Caterina Rocco. Both were born in Turin (respectively in 1890 and 1881) and presented a dissertation on commercial law.[5] According

[4] On the case of female students and graduates in the faculties of mathematics, natural sciences and medicine in Italy between the 1870s and the early 2000s see Govoni (2009). On the admission of female students in the universities of Germany from 1865 to 1914 see Mazón (2003).

[5] *Archivio Storico dell'Università di Torino* (hence *ASUT*), *Economia, Verbali degli esami di laurea* and *Registri di Carriera.*

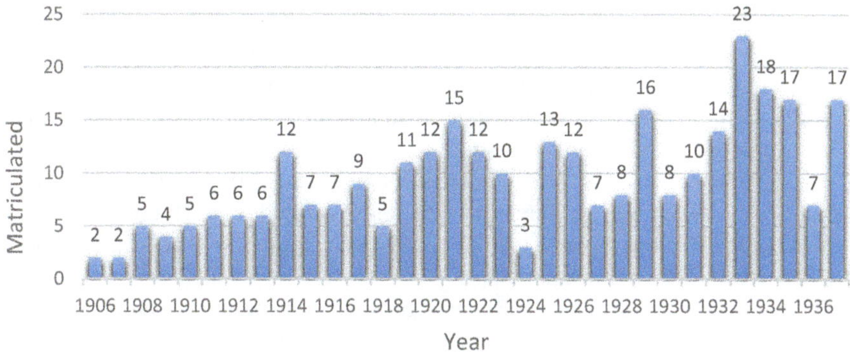

Fig. 2 Female students who matriculated at the High School of Commerce (since 1935, Faculty of Business and Economics) of Turin, between 1906 and 1937

to the Turin High School's yearbooks, after graduating both became teachers of accountancy.[6]

In 1910, out of 60 students enrolling, 5 were female, a percentage of 8.3%. This proportion increased until the first world war (in 1914 there were 12 female students out of a total of 62 enrolled, a ratio of 19.3%). As will be seen, in the years of fascism, a period undoubtedly not favourable to female enrolment at universities and more generally to their participation in the labour market, this percentage decreased considerably. As a result of systematic research carried out at the historical archives of the University of Turin and the consultation of the Turin High School yearbooks, we have been able to collect a large amount of data referring to female students and graduates at the Turin institution from 1909 to the end of the 1930s: among these, the data of the enrolments, subdivided by year; the region or country of origin of the female students and the qualifications they had obtained at secondary school level. With reference to female graduates, it was possible to identify the title and subject of the dissertation discussed, the graduation grade obtained and, in many cases, the professional activities carried out after graduation.

Based on the available data, it emerges that a total of 309 female students enrolled between 1906 and 1937. Of these, 219 (71%) had graduated by 1941 and 90 (29%) did not complete their studies. Based on the records stored in the archives, it is possible to reconstruct the annual data of female student enrolment. It is significant that, in absolute terms, the data of female students enrolled over the time period analysed, while varying considerably (in particular in 1924 the number of female students enrolled dropped to 3 and in 1927 to 7), do not allow us to identify a clear trend: in 1933, for example, we register the highest annual number of female students enrolled in the period considered (23). Three years later (1936), however, only 7 female students enrolled (Fig. 2).

[6] R. Scuola di Studi Applicati al Commercio in Torino, *Annuario, 1911*, Stab. Grafico Botta, Torino (1912, pp. 203, 213).

As in other cases, a comparison in percentage terms, rather than absolute terms, appears more relevant here. The fact is that, beginning in 1919–1920, the enrolment of male students, contrary to that of female students, increased exponentially. As a result of this, we observe a substantial reduction in the enrolment rate of female students out of the total number of students.

We have seen that in 1914 the female students enrolled in the first year were 12 out of 62. In 1923, however, the female students enrolled were 10 out of a total of 176: the ratio therefore dropped to 5.7%; in 1928 the figures are 8 out of 206 (3.8%); in 1929, 16 out of 287 (5.5%).

From 1935–1936, as noted above, the High School of Commerce was transformed into a faculty of business and economics. Starting from that year, the aggregate data collected in the University yearbooks refer to the total number of students enrolled to the faculty. Also in adopting this mode of calculation, the results are not significantly different: in the 1936–1937 academic year, out of 1489 enrolled, the female students were only 55 (3,7%)[7]; in 1939–1940, out of 1112 enrolled, female students were 43 (3,9%).[8]

To date, unfortunately, disaggregated data on the enrolment of female students in the other High Schools of Commerce in Italy are not available. A few surveys, carried out between the 1920s and the 1940s by the Italian Institute of Statistics (ISTAT) provide aggregate nationwide data on male and female students enrolled at Italian universities and Institutes of higher education, sorted by subject areas (ISTAT, 1933, 1936, 1948).[9] According to these investigations, female students enrolled in business and economics degree programs in Italy were in the 1926–1927 academic year 4.6% of total enrolment; 5.9% in 1936–1937 and 8.5% in 1939–1940 (ISTAT, 1948, pp. 40–42).

Based on these data, therefore, there would have been an increase, at a national level, in the presence of women in business and economics courses in the second half of the 1930s, a pattern that did not occur in Turin.[10] Apart from these differences, however significant, it is a matter of fact that the presence of women in business courses in interwar Italy appears in percentage terms to be rather small throughout the time period considered. What are the causes of this tendency?

A negative role was most likely played by the ideology of the fascist regime, which, particularly from the end of the 1920s, tried to impose a strongly conservative model

[7] *Annuario della R. Università di Torino. 1935–1936 e 1936–1937*, Tip. Villarboito, Torino (1937, p. 408).

[8] *Annuario della R. Università di Torino. 1939–1940*, Torino, I.T.E.R (1940, p. 382).

[9] For an overview of the statistical investigations on the universities and other institutions of higher education carried out in Italy since 1861 see Cammelli (2000).

[10] A new research project funded by the Italian Ministry of Education and coordinated by Manuela Mosca (*The Economic Thought of Italian Women: Methodological Issues, Ideas, Impact, International Links*) aims, among other objectives, to systematically reconstruct the data on female students enrolled in the various High schools of commerce and Faculties of business and economics in Italy from 1900 to 1950, so as to analyse possible regional differences in female student enrolment rates (e.g., between regions in northern and southern Italy) and to verify the accuracy of aggregate data published by ISTAT.

of the family in which women were mainly relegated to domestic work and childcare functions.[11] Having said that, it is legitimate to argue that, with reference to female enrolment rates, a gender bias specific to the fields of business and economics was occurring in Italy in the period under consideration, not only due to the influence of fascism: a bias that still persists today, albeit at a lower level.[12] This bias in economic subjects can be seen at the University of Turin itself by comparing the above-mentioned data with those of other disciplines. For example, the percentage of female students out of the total enrolled in the faculty of mathematics and physics, again in 1936–1937, was 35.2% (88 female students out of 250 total students) while in humanities it was 53% (216 out of 407).[13]

With reference to the country and region of origin, it appears noteworthy that 14 out of the 309 female students enrolled between 1909 and 1937, i.e., about 5%, came from abroad. Of these, 3 were from Argentina, 1 from the United States, 1 from Spain, 3 from Switzerland, 1 from Romania, 1 from Moldavia, 1 from Hungary, 1 from the Russian Empire, 1 from the Caucasus and 1 from Turkey. Referring to female students born in Italy, as was to be expected, the first region of origin was Piedmont (221 women enrolled). This was followed by Lombardy (18), Emilia Romagna (10), Liguria (9), Veneto, Lazio and Sicily (6), Tuscany (5), Marche (3), Friuli Venezia Giulia, Campania, Molise, and finally Umbria and Abruzzo (1). These figures appear to reflect an appreciable individual and family mobility in Europe and in Italy in the first decades of the twentieth century.

Let us now consider the female students (219 in total) who completed their studies between 1909 and 1941. Also in this case, it is significant to compare the figures for female graduates with those for male graduates: where the female component

---

[11] A decree of September 1938, converted into law in January 1939, stated that the recruitment of women in public administrations but also in the private sector had to be limited to 10 percent of the workforce. Moreover, public administrations were entitled to determine in public competitions even lower percentages of women in the case of jobs deemed for various reasons "unsuitable" for them (these included most executive positions). Women were also excluded from judiciary or diplomatic careers. In June 1939 a further decree stated which jobs were deemed "suitable" for women. These, as was to be expected, were all at lower levels: secretary, typist, telephonist, stenographer, file keeper (see Manfredini [1963, p. 184]). On the policies of fascism referring to women's participation in the labour market, see also de Grand (1976), De Grazia (1992).

[12] Based on the available data on the cohorts of graduates from Italian public universities between 2010 and 2019, recent research has established that the graduations in economics "are 41% less frequent among females than among males" and that "they are 35 and 30% less frequent, respectively, in business and STEM courses [science, technology, engineering and mathematics], while they are 71% more frequent among females in humanities" (Bertocchi et al., 2023, pp. 802–803; see also Govoni, 2009). Even more pronounced is the gender bias with reference to the academic staff composition of the departments of economics in Italy and elsewhere. See among others Lundberg and Stearns (2019), Zacchia (2021), Bateman and Hengel (2023).

[13] The percentage of female students enrolled in the faculty of law was on the contrary similar to that in business and economics (3.1 in 1936/37. See *Annuario della R. Università di Torino. 1939–1940*, p. 382. At a national level, the percentage of female students in the faculty of mathematics and physics was, in the academic year 1936–1937, 35% (1118 out of 3194); in humanities 51.2% (3978 out of 7756. See ISTAT [1948, pp. 40, 47]).

appears relatively constant, the number of male graduates registers a high increment, reflecting the sharp increase in male enrolments.

Table 1 below shows the total number of graduates for each academic year between 1909 and 1941, differentiated into males and females and by graduation session. For each year, the percentage value of the number of male and female graduates is shown.

As can be seen, the percentage of female graduates is always significantly lower than the percentage of male graduates, with the exception of the academic years 1916–1917 and 1917–1918. In these years, in which most of the male students had been called up for war, female graduates slightly exceed the male percentage, reaching levels between 57 and 53% (Fig. 3).

A piece of information that it has been possible to retrieve in the University archives and that is undoubtedly relevant is that relating to the graduation grade. It is interesting to note that 44 female students (20%) graduated with top marks (110/110), 36 (17%) with 110/110 and *summa cum laude* and 5 (2%) with 110/110, *summa cum laude* and recommendation for publication ("dignità di stampa"). It seems significant to compare these results with those of male graduates. In this case the available data are not completely overlapping, as we have data on male graduates only up to 1934–1935. In any case, considering a total of 1962 male graduates up to that date, we find that only 81 (4%) earned 110/110; 53 (2.7%) 110/110 *magna cum laude* and only 10 (about 0.5%) 110/110 *magna cum laude* and "dignità di stampa".

Further information on the excellent results achieved by the female students from the High School of Commerce of Turin is reported in the 1914–1915 yearbook: the previous year, the Turin chamber of commerce had established and financed scholarships for deserving students from non-wealthy families and the first four scholarships were awarded to female students.[14]

In an environment that was certainly not favourable to women's access to higher education, the completion of college careers by female students required them to have uncommon skills and strength. As a matter of fact, they were able to achieve excellent results, which were on average better than those of their male colleagues.

At the end of the fourth year, students had the opportunity to enrol in specialized courses. Among these, the most popular was that of accountancy, at the end of which students could take the exams to qualify to teach technical and economic subjects in secondary schools.

Based on data in the university archives, it emerges that out of the total number of female graduates, 70 decided to pursue a specialization in accountancy. Referring to the professional career paths of female graduates, although the available data are not complete, it is possible to state that a high percentage turned to teaching.

---

[14]. R. Istituto Superiore di Studi Commerciali in Torino, *Annuario 1914–1915*, Tip. Baravalle e Falconieri, Torino (1915, p. 123). The winners were Silvia Debernardi (who graduated in December 1914 with 90/90 *magna cum laude*), Adelina Peyrache (who also graduated in Dec. 1914 with 90/90, *magna cum laude* and "dignità di stampa"), Eugenia Villata (who graduated in Nov. 1915 with 80/80 *magna cum laude*) and Gemma Alliaud (who enrolled in November 1913 but, due to family problems, could not complete her course). *ASUT*, *Economia*, *Verbali degli esami di laurea* and *Registri di Carriera*.

Table 1 Number of graduates for each academic year between 1909 and 1941, differentiated into males and females

Academic Year	Total graduates	Female graduates	Female graduates/Total graduates (%)	Male graduates	Male graduates/ Total graduates (%)
1908–1909	34	2	6	32	94
1909–1910	16	0	0	16	100
1910–1911	23	4	17	19	83
1911–1912	26	3	12	23	88
1912–1913	33	3	9	30	91
1913–1914	31	6	19	25	81
1914–1915	7	2	29	5	71
1915–1916	8	2	25	6	75
1916–1917	14	8	57	6	43
1917–1918	19	10	53	9	47
1918–1919	49	3	6	46	94
1919–1920	125	11	9	114	91
1920–1921	92	4	4	88	96
1921–1922	60	7	12	53	88
1922–1923	62	5	8	57	92
1923–1924	119	12	10	107	90
1924–1925	78	5	6	73	94
1925–1926	89	6	7	83	93
1926–1927	92	8	9	84	91
1927–1928	77	3	4	74	96
1928–1929	102	14	14	88	86
1929–1930	156	5	3	151	97
1930–1931	143	4	3	139	97
1931–1932	133	3	2	130	98
1932–1933	156	4	3	152	97
1933–1934	202	10	5	192	95
1934–1935	174	4	2	170	98
1935–1936	211	10	5	201	95
1936–1937	216	21	10	195	90
1937–1938	164	11	7	153	93
1938–1939	180	10	6	170	94
1939–1940	ND	12	ND	ND	ND
1940–1941	ND	7	ND	ND	ND
TOT	2891	219		2691	

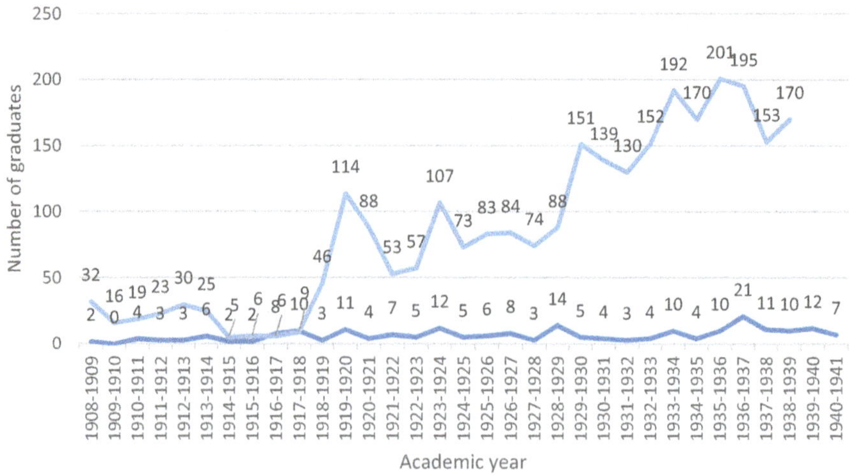

Fig. 3 A comparison of the annual data of female and male graduates at the High School of Commerce (since 1935, Faculty of Business and Economics) of Turin between 1906 and 1941

An important indicator of this is the fact that many female graduates passed public competitions to get the qualification to teach in secondary schools.

Of the total number of women graduates from 1909 to 1941, 55 (25%) were qualified to teach accountancy. In a context in which women were discriminated against in many areas of the labour market and were in fact excluded, with rare exceptions, from managerial roles in the private and public sectors, teaching at schools turned out to be one of the few careers that, while often requiring personal sacrifices due to frequent changes of the place of work, was not characterized, at least until the second half of the 1920s, by major legal or social barriers to entry and therefore played an important role in enabling women graduates to assert themselves professionally.[15]

In fact, it must be remembered that at the time secondary school teachers enjoyed considerable status, especially in provincial towns, and had a significant social role.[16] The marked participation of women in this sector therefore helped to promote in public opinion the image of women no longer just as housewives but as professionals involved in an important sector of the society. It was probably this aspect, along with

[15] In 1921, taking into account all primary and secondary schools in Italy, the number of female teachers was 128,266, or 70.4 percent of the teaching staff nationwide. In 1931 this proportion rose to 72.7 percent (Govoni, 2009, p. 228; See also De Grand (1976).

[16] It is also worth mentioning that, in contrast to what happens today, in the first half of the twentieth century it was quite common for scholars in economics and social sciences in Italy to start the first steps of their academic careers carrying out at the same time teaching activities in secondary schools, in order to supplement their income.

persistent gender-based prejudices[17] and the desire to increase male labour participation at a time of high unemployment even among graduates, that in 1934 led the fascist minister of education to introduce legal measures under which, starting from 1938, women were excluded from obtaining a permanent post in secondary schools in disciplines such as political economy, law and accounting.[18] Considering the fact that, already in 1926, a royal decree had excluded women from public competitions for posts in Italian literature, Latin, ancient Greek, history and philosophy in classical and scientific lyceums (the "élite" secondary schools that allowed access to university education),[19] it follows that at the end of the 1930s female teachers could obtain stable teaching positions only in such disciplines as humanities at a basic level, foreign languages, geography, natural sciences and a few other technical subjects.

4 Breaking the Academic Wall: Being a Female Economist in a Men's Faculty

As mentioned before, a significant number of female students at the High School of Turin won scholarships, graduated *summa cum laude* and, in a few cases, presented dissertations which were considered suitable for publication.

This section analyses a few cases of female graduates with a record of excellence. As we shall see, two of them, Olga Rivarono Deaglio and Costanza Costantino, were indeed able to start an academic career and to carry out innovative research activities in economics.

As a consequence of almost insurmountable gender-based obstacles, however, only Costanza Costantino was able to obtain a permanent position as professor of

[17] These prejudices were expressed as early as 1918 by Giovanni Gentile, a highly influential philosopher and intellectual closely linked to fascism and minister of education in the 1920s, in a work in which he deplored the gradual abandonment of teaching careers by men, who had been attracted to higher-paying professions, and their replacement by women "who are now crowding into our universities and who [. …] do not have and will never have either that vivacious originality of thought or that firm spiritual vigour which […] must be the cornerstones of the school, formative of the higher spirit of the country" (quoted in Govoni, 2009, p. 232).

[18] See the decree of 5 July 1934 n. 1185 "Regolamento per i concorsi a cattedre nelle Regie scuole e nei Regi istituti d'istruzione media tecnica", in *Gazzetta ufficiale del Regno d'Italia*, 28 July 1934, n. 176. According to this measure, the admission of women to permanent teaching posts in the disciplines of law, political economy and accountancy would be limited "to a four-year period" from the entry into force of the decree, i.e., till 1938 (art. 10). Moreover, the number of posts awarded to female candidates could not exceed one-fourth of those made available for competition. It is interesting to note that, again according to this decree, women were, however, allowed to participate in public competitions for the above subjects, but only for the purpose of obtaining a teaching qualification. With all evidence, in the face of a growing demand for teachers, mainly due to the increase of population in Italy, the fascist government was forced to recognize that this could not be met only by male candidates. Still, it relegated female teachers to an unfavourable status, characterized by precariousness (given the impossibility of obtaining tenure) and less favourable economic conditions.

[19] See on this point Manfredini (1963, p. 183), De Grand (1976, p. 949), Govoni (2009, p. 229).

public economics at the University of Turin. In this case, too, the promotion was hindered and occurred only shortly before Costantino's retirement.[20]

Proceeding in chronological order, the first significant case is that of Maria Clotilde Franchi. Born in Turin, Franchi had obtained a diploma in accountancy at a commercial school and had enrolled the High School in 1909, graduating in 1912 with 110/110 and *summa cum laude*. Her dissertation, entitled *La Banca d'Italia dopo l'atto bancario del 1893* ("The Bank of Italy after the 1893 banking law") had been supervised by Giuseppe Prato, professor of political economy at the Turin High School and was recommended for publication by the examining board. This work was then published the following year at the expense of the High School as a short monograph (Franchi, 1913).[21]

In his annual report the dean of the High School, prof. Vincenzo Vianello, congratulated Ms. Franchi and two other male graduates on their academic achievements and reported that the director general of the Bank of Italy himself, Bonaldo Stringher, had wanted to review the drafts of Franchi's publication and had offered "to give the graduates of our School the best possible terms of employment in the offices of the Bank of Italy".[22]

There were thus at first glance all the preconditions for Franchi's brilliant curriculum and well-documented publication to pave the way for her to have a promising career at the university or, alternatively, at the Bank of Italy. However, the obstacles arising from social conventions and prejudices to a woman's entry to university or to a banking institution in a managerial capacity were at the time almost insurmountable in Italy. Like many other promising female graduates from the High School of Commerce in Turin, therefore, Maria Clotilde Franchi spent her professional career teaching in secondary schools. In 1922 she started teaching business accounting at a technical school in Ivrea. Three years later she gained the qualification to teach this subject in secondary schools.[23]

The archives of the University of Turin contain other examples of dissertations written and submitted in the 1910s and 1920s by female high school students that

---

[20] As recalled by Giulia Zacchia, "In the period from the 1930s to the 1950s women represented a clear minority within the profession [of economist], with an almost total absence of female professors in the economics departments of Italian universities" (Zacchia, 2019, p. 93).

[21] In a letter to Giuseppe Prato dated March 6, 1913, Maria Clotilde Franchi, in announcing to the latter that she had received one hundred copies of her publication from the printer, thanked him for the "advice, support and encouragement" that had enabled her to complete her work and for supporting the publication of her thesis at the examining board. Fondazione Luigi Einaudi, Torino. Archivio Giuseppe Prato (hence *FLE, Giuseppe Prato*), *Correspondence,* letter of M. C. Franchi to G. Prato, Turin, 6 March 1913. On Giuseppe Prato's intellectual and professional biography see Pavanelli (2004).

[22] R. Istituto Superiore di Studi Commerciali in Torino, *Annuario, 1913–1914*, Tip. Baravalle e Falconieri, Torino (1914, pp. 11–12).

[23] We do not have much information on Maria Clotilde Franchi's professional biography. From a brief excerpt published in *La Stampa* in August 1939, we know that she taught computation and accounting for several years in a commercial school in Rovereto (in the Veneto region of Italy) and was then transferred in 1939 to teach the same subjects in a school in Novara, Piedmont. (see "Il movimento d'insegnanti medi", *La Stampa*, 31 August 1939, p. 2).

denote remarkable analytical potential and research skills. We will only mention here the case of Ada Costamagna, a student born in Venice in 1890 who had obtained a diploma from a technical institute in Turin. Enrolled at the High School in 1910, Costamagna graduated four years later with a thesis entitled *Il lavoro a domicilio per l'industria dell'abbigliamento a Torino* ("Homeworking in the clothing sector in Turin"), with Giuseppe Prato as supervisor.

After providing a general overview of the phenomenon of home-based work compared with factory work, the thesis expounded the results of a field research conducted in person by Costamagna at 54 small home-based workshops in the garment industry located in Turin, run mainly by women, who in most cases worked alone or assisted by a few female workers. In her work, accomplished mainly through direct field surveys and face-to-face interviews, Costamagna provided detailed data on the daily and weekly earnings of the women workers in the workshops examined, the duration of daily work (which often lasted over 12–14 hours), the environments in which the work was conducted, and the very poor hygienic conditions of the same.

Prato was very favourably impressed by this research and, as documented from his correspondence with Costamagna, offered to write to Giuseppe Toniolo, professor of political economy in Pisa and founder and editor of the *Rivista Internazionale di Scienze Sociali*, to advocate the publication in this journal of at least part of the dissertation. In a letter to Prato, Costamagna after thanking him, observed that in her opinion it would probably be necessary to revise some aspects of the thesis, that she had not been able to explore in depth due to lack of time. She nevertheless enthusiastically welcomed the initiative, which, she wrote, would enable her to relive for some time "the very enjoyable environment of the School" that she missed so much.[24] For reasons that could not be completely ascertained, however, the project was not followed through. Like others among her colleagues, Ada Costamagna continued her professional activity in the following years as an accountancy teacher at technical schools in Veneto.

Another outstanding graduate from the High School of Turin, this time in the 1930s, was Olga Rivarono (1908–2002; from 1939 Olga Rivarono Deaglio). After studying at the Liceo Cavour in Turin, Olga Rivarono enrolled at the High School in October 1927. She graduated in the summer session 1930–1931 with a dissertation entitled: *L'organizzazione scientifica del lavoro: tentativi di applicazioni reali nella prima fabbrica italiana di macchine per scrivere* ("The scientific organization of work: first applications in the first Italian typewriter factory"). Supervisor was Vincenzo Porri, then professor of economic policy and public finance at the Turin institution.[25]

Her excellent curriculum paved the way into what at that time was the initial rung of an academic career at an Italian university: in November 1931 she became a "volunteer" teaching assistant to the chair of political economy at the High School of Commerce. In the following years she decided to pursue a second degree at

---

[24] *FLE, Giuseppe Prato, Correspondence,* letter of A. Costamagna to G. Prato, 8 February 1914.

[25] The text of this dissertation, unfortunately, has not been located in the University archives. On the intellectual biography of Vincenzo Porri (1889–1934) see Di Fenizio (1934) and Castellino (1966).

the Faculty of law in Turin, which included a "Laboratorio di economia politica" (Laboratory of political economy), at that time one of the most important centres of economic research in Italy.[26] In 1935 she successfully discussed at this faculty a thesis on economic theory entitled *Leon Walras e le sue teoriche (in occasione del Centenario della sua nascita)* ("Leon Walras and his theories, on the centenary of his birth"). The dissertation, supervised by Pasquale Jannaccone, professor of political economy at the Faculty of Law and director of the Laboratory, stands out as an accurate reconstruction of the Walrasian theoretical system, preceded by a brief biography of Walras[27]. One section was devoted to a reflection on the relevance of the mathematical method in economics. The thesis included a careful analysis of Walras' contributions to "social" and monetary economics.

This dissertation, which addressed the theoretical core of neoclassical economics, was followed in 1936 by a well-documented article on applied economics. In this work, published in the *Rivista Internazionale di Scienze Sociali*, Olga Rivarono analysed the causes and economic effects of the decrease in the price of silver in the 1920s and 1930s (Rivarono, 1936). During the same year, probably in view of the barriers to women's access to the university, Rivarono entered a competition for teaching economics and law in secondary schools, one of the last in fascist Italy open to women that allowed to obtain a permanent post in these disciplines.[28] In spite of achieving positive results in this competition, however, Rivarono soon became convinced that in Italy economics had become a profession reserved exclusively to men (Paci, 2002). With the encouragement of her relatives, she then decided to perfect her knowledge of the English language by moving to the United Kingdom and enrolling in a phonetics course at the University College of London.[29]

Returning to Italy shortly before World War II she married, and during the war played an active role in the anti-fascist resistance. After 1945 she finally obtained a permanent position to teach English at a technical institute in Turin and published

---

[26] On the Laboratory of political economy at the University of Turin see Faucci (1995) and Becchio (2004). For an overview of Italian economic thought in the twentieth century see Faucci (2014).

[27] This brief summary is based on direct consultation of a copy of the dissertation, stored at *ASUT*, *Tesi di laurea.* In the first part of her dissertation, at page 13, Olga Rivarono expounded in synthesis the reasons that had induced her to deepen her analysis of Walras's work and that document, it seems to us, a stimulating interpretation of the French economist's work: "The importance of Walras and the sympathy that prompted me, after reading his main studies, to study him, is due to the contrast present in his figure as a thinker and teacher. Walras is an idealist; the impetus and sincere enthusiasm that impelled him to study the 'social question' and to embrace the noble part of socialist doctrine appear in sharp contradiction to his mathematical spirit, to his continuous effort to conduct his reasoning by the deductive method. I have spoken of contrast because it is the common opinion, and at one time it was also mine, that the mathematical concept, the clarity of the deductive method could not coexist with idealist views: but there is nothing to prevent a mathematician from making designs far from life and also lyrical. The science of numbers, of precision of measurement, does not conflict with sentiment".

[28] See *supra*, note 19.

[29] I owe this biographical information to the courtesy of Mario Deaglio, professor emeritus of economics at the University of Turin and son of Olga Rivarono Deaglio, whom I heartily thank. On Olga Rivarono's studies at University College of London see also UCL, *Calendar*, session 1938–1939, Taylor and Francis, London, p. 555.

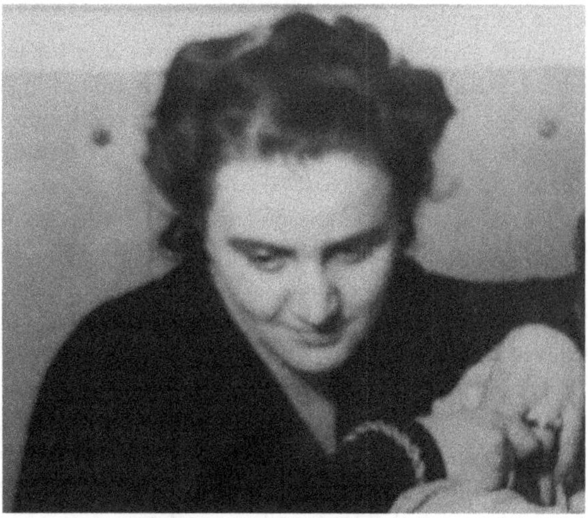

Fig. 4 Olga Rivarono Deaglio in the 1950s

a grammar of that language based on phonetics that established itself as one of the most widely used in the Italian schools (Deaglio Rivarono, 1946). For a few years she resumed her collaboration with the Faculty of business and economics of Turin as a volunteer assistant professor of English and as an appointee in the teaching of the same discipline. In the 1950s she also worked actively as translator of English texts.[30] Meanwhile she continued her teaching career at secondary schools, becoming dean of technical institutes, one of the first women in Italy to assume that position (Fig. 4).[31]

In the 1930s another graduate of excellence from the High School of Turin was Costanza Constantino (1913–1992). Born in Turin, Costantino had obtained a diploma in accountancy. After enrolling at the High School in November 1931, she graduated in July 1935 (110/110 *magna cum laude*) with a dissertation entitled *Ricerche sulle fluttuazioni economiche di lunga durata* (Research on Long-Term Economic Fluctuations). Her supervisor was Publio Mengarini, then professor of political economy at the Turin institution.

Her excellent thesis work, which formed the basis of an extensive article on the subject of economic fluctuations published in 1939 in the *Rivista Internazionale di Scienze Sociali* (Costantino, 1939), paved the way for her becoming, albeit only for one year (1935–1936), "voluntary" teaching assistant to the chair of "Economic history and policy", at the Turin High School, now Faculty of business and economics.

---

[30] We mention here, among others, the translation of the volume *Economic History of Europe (1760–1939)* by Ernest Ludlow Bogart published in 1953 by the publishing house UTET, Turin (Bogart, 1953).

[31] In May 1960 Olga Rivarono Deaglio presented at the 'Circolo della Stampa' in Turin the results of a survey promoted by the Italian government on married women's employment (see "Il lavoro della donna sposata", *La Stampa*, 6 May 1960, p. 4).

In November 1935, following a professional path that, as noted, was common at the time, given the barriers to entry, especially for women aspiring to an academic career, she started teaching at a secondary school in Alessandria, Piedmont, and the following year at a similar school in Imperia, Liguria.[32] In 1937, then, similarly to Olga Rivarono, Costantino took part in a competition to obtain a post as a school teacher of economics and law but, in spite of achieving an excellent result, was unable to get a permanent position. She could not, however, be denied a teaching qualification that in the following years allowed her to teach economics and law at a secondary school in Turin.[33]

These constraints notwithstanding, Costantino continued during these years an intense research activity: in 1941 she published in *Rivista di Politica Economica* a fairly bold and nonconformist article, given the censorship of the time, on the role of women's work in the context of the European reconstruction projects. After recalling that in modern societies most of the obstacles that prevented a male worker from improving his condition had been overcome, she noted that this was not the case for women: for them, several occupations remained precluded.[34] Where the more conservative exponents of fascism believed that women's participation in the labour market should be reduced, Costantino claimed the need to increase such participation, especially with reference to intellectual work (Costantino, 1941).[35] In a subsequent article she returned to the role of women in the labour market, this time analysing the causes of women's low wages and possible remedies (Costantino, 1943).

---

[32] The detailed information on Costantino's professional biography is taken from her personal file, which is stored in the historical archives of the University of Turin (*ASUT*, *Fascicoli personali docenti, Costanza Costantino*). Costanza Costantino is, along with Vera Cao Pinna, the only Italian female economist included in the *Biographical Dictionary of Women Economists* edited in 2000 by R. W and M. A. Dimand e da E. L. Forget. See Fontana (2000).

[33] In a letter to Turin school authorities dated 29 April 1952 and kept in her personal file, Costantino pointed out that "since 1938" [actually 1937] she had obtained a brilliant teaching qualification and that "she had been damaged by fascism in her career because she had been excluded, as a woman" from a post in economics and law (*ASUT*, *Fascicoli personali docenti, Costanza Costantino*).

[34] "Of course, the difficulties in climbing the social ladder are very great, but no man is prevented by law from changing status and reaching a better condition. No man. But how different is the condition of women. How many social functions remain closed and forbidden, how many obstacles to the free exercise of women's activities, which personal worth can hardly overcome" (Costantino, 1941, p. 678).

[35] Particularly since the 1930s, several fascist politicians and intellectuals believed that women's participation in the labour market and their consequent economic independence could weaken patriarchal family structures and reduce birth rates. Instead, these rates had to be increased to support the regime's foreign policy ambitions and fuel Italian colonial expansion. Among the most active propagandists of this point of view, which was fully shared by Mussolini, let us mention here Ferdinando Loffredo, author in 1938 of a monograph on the subject entitled *La politica della famiglia*, that had considerable circulation (Loffredo, 1938). It is interesting to note that Giuseppe Bottai, at that time minister of education and leading exponent of the fascist regime, expressed more moderate positions on this issue and wrote a rather critical preface to Loffredo's book. Bottai's preface was indeed quoted extensively by Costantino in her article to support her point (Costantino, 1941, p. 7). It is worth mentioning, furthermore, that the *Rivista di Politica Economica* in which Costantino's article was published, was the journal of the Italian industrial association, which traditionally had a more pragmatic view on the role of women in economic activities. On the topic

After World War II, during which she played an active role in the antifascist movement,[36] Costanza Costantino focused her field of research on issues of public finance, in which she went on to publish in rapid succession essays and monographs characterized by originality and remarkable doctrinal solidity. Her extensive academic production of these years includes, among others, a notable article published in 1951 in *Rivista Internazionale di Scienze Sociali* in which Costantino, using available statistical data, analyses the effects of economic fluctuations on consumption tax revenues in Italy from the 1920s to the 1940s, a subject addressed with greater extension, in the same year, in a monograph entitled *Imposte e congiuntura*, that was commented on favourably by Luigi Einaudi, one of the most influential Italian economists of the time and, in those years, president of the Italian republic[37] (1951b; Costantino, 1951a). Also noteworthy is an article issued by her in 1952 which critically analyses several *Public Finance Information Papers* published by the United Nations with reference to economic planning projects being carried out in several countries including Italy (Costantino, 1952). This was followed by an essay on the Danish tax system published in *Rivista di politica economica* in 1956, and by a further contribution to the counter-cyclical fiscal policies adopted in Denmark between 1945 and 1955 (Costantino, 1956, 1958a).[38] In 1958 she wrote a long article about the debate on the problem of the incidence of sales tax, published in the *Giornale degli Economisti* (Costantino, 1958b). This was followed by an article on the taxation of income, in particular labour income (Costantino, 1961). In the early 1960s, on behalf of the Union of Italian Chambers of Commerce she then conducted extensive

of women's participation in the labour market see also De Grand (1976), De Grazia (1992), Dittrich-Johansen (1994), Salvati (1997). On recent estimates of the female participation rates in the labor force in Italy between 1861 and 2011 see Mancini (2018).

[36] See in this regard a certificate issued by the Turin section of the National Liberation Committee (CLN), dated July 31, 1946, stored in *ASUT*, *Fascicoli personali docenti, Costanza Costantino.* This certificate is supplemented by a handwritten note drafted by Ada Marchesini Gobetti, leader of Turin's anti-fascist resistance and, at the time, deputy mayor of Turin: "I confirm from personal knowledge, Dr. Costantino having actively collaborated with me during the liberation fight with a spirit of true courage and self-sacrifice." During these years Costantino was also active on feminist issues, drafting a short 'manifesto' on women's legal and economic claims published by the Liberal Party.

[37] In thanking Costanza Costantino, in a letter of June 1951, for sending him her volume, Einaudi wrote: "The volume is good evidence of the care you have taken in studying individual taxes and their sensitivity to economic fluctuations. I hope that, by continuing your studies, the contributions you will want to give to science will become more and more important" (*FLE, Luigi Einaudi, Correspondence*, Letter of L. Einaudi to C. Costantino, Rome 30 June 1951). Luigi Einaudi (1874–1961) was professor of public finance at the University of Turin and a leading representative of political and economic liberalism in Europe. After the Second World War he became governor of the Bank of Italy and then president of the Italian Republic. On Einaudi's intellectual biography and work see, among others, Faucci (1986), Forte (1982), Forte and Marchionatti (2012), Nerozzi (2021).

[38] These contributions were the result of research carried out by Costantino at the University of Copenhagen between September 1956 and March 1957, thanks to a grant awarded by the Italian Foreign Ministry in collaboration with the Danish government. The letter of recommendation was written by Luigi Einaudi (*FLE, Luigi Einaudi, Correspondence*, Letter of M. Conti, director of cultural relations at the Ministry of Foreign Affairs to L. Einaudi, Rome, 6 April 1956).

research on public finance in Piedmont, with particular reference to withdrawals and payments made by the central government in the region. The first results were presented at a conference held in Rome in 1965 and were then developed into a monograph (1969a; Costantino, 1965a).[39] In parallel, she continued her research on the theory of public finance, publishing a short monograph on the notion of functional finance (Costantino, 1969b).

This renewed commitment to research enabled her to achieve significant academic recognition: from 1947 to 1952 Costantino was a volunteer teaching assistant to the chair of public finance at the Faculty of business and economics in Turin and, in 1954, assistant professor at the University of Genoa, where she worked with Aldo Scotto, a well-known Italian scholar in public finance. In 1960 she was awarded the qualification ("libera docenza") for teaching public finance at university, the first female economist to obtain this qualification in Italy in this field. Also in this case, the endorsement of Luigi Einaudi, who as mentioned esteemed Costantino's work, proved important, given the gender-based prejudices then still pervading academic promotions in the field of economics.[40] "I believe I am the first woman", she proudly wrote to Einaudi in announcing in May 1960 the attainment of the "libera docenza", "who can give you, our Teacher, the proof of having with dedication followed the exciting path of research in public finance".[41] Her qualification was confirmed in 1965 with a very positive judgement drawn up by Francesco Forte, at that time full professor of public economics in Turin.[42] In 1967–1968 and 1968–1969 she was then appointed to teach public finance at the Faculty of business and economics in Turin and, from 1969–1970, transport economics at the same institution.

These recognitions, although very significant, did not however result in the granting of a permanent position at the university, an award that she, on the basis of her academic curriculum, would have amply deserved. It appears difficult to deny that in this, as in other cases, a gender bias penalized Costantino in relation to other male candidates.

Costantino therefore had to continue in the 1960s and 1970s, in parallel with her academic activity, a demanding teaching job at secondary schools in Turin. Her

[39] In 1961, furthermore, at the invitation of a parliamentary committee charged with investigating the limits to competition in the Italian economy, she prepared an extensive report on the sugar industry in Italy in which she pointed out the poor efficiency of this sector as a result of decades of protectionism (Costantino, 1965b). See on this point Fontana (2000, p. 120).

[40] In January 1959 Costantino wrote to Einaudi announcing to him that she had applied for the qualification to teach public finance at university and asking for his support. "Although I am engaged for 17 hours a week in teaching law and political economy in the technical institute Quintino Sella of Turin", she added, "since 1950 I have spent every afternoon and all vacations studying" (*FLE, Luigi Einaudi, Correspondence*, Letter of C. Costantino to L. Einaudi, Turin, 22 January 1959).

[41] *Ibidem*, Letter of C. Costantino to L. Einaudi, Turin, 27 May 1960.

[42] See the minutes of the council meeting of the Law Faculty, October 25, 1965. The minutes, drafted by Francesco Forte as secretary, stated that the candidate "had produced valuable essays on excise taxes as well as extensive research in progress on the finances of Piedmont, confirming her qualities as a careful, accurate, serious scholar capable of original insights, as well as her qualities as a well-documented and up-to-date teacher on both theoretical and descriptive issues". *ASUT, Fascicoli personali docenti, Costanza Costantino.*

personal file, stored at the University archives, documents frequent (and sometimes unsuccessful) requests made by her to school authorities to obtain permits and leave that would have allowed her to devote more time to research and to teaching activity at the university. It was only in April 1983, on the eve of her retirement (which occurred a few months later), that she was given a permanent post at the university as associate professor.

For this to happen, however, a general reform of the Italian university system had been necessary, modernizing recruitment procedures and creating the role of associate professor.[43] A serious rethinking of the role of women in the country's professional and intellectual life was finally apparently beginning.

5 Concluding Remarks

In introducing this chapter on female students and graduates in economics in Turin in the first half of the twentieth century, we wrote that, in our opinion, this was a circumscribed but relevant case for the reconstruction of women's university education paths in Italy and the participation of female graduates in professional activities. We trust that the results presented here meet these expectations. This work, based largely on unpublished data and documents preserved in the historical archives of the University of Turin and, where available, on personal correspondence, has enabled us to reconstruct university curricula and professional paths of a significant number (more than 200) of women graduates in a period characterized by dynamics of profound transformation of Italian society but also by a regime, the fascist regime, which in the 1930s was totalitarian and which, with reference to gender policies, discouraged women's participation in the labour market and, on the whole, aimed at downsizing their role in Italian production sectors.

This difficult context weighed negatively on the enrolment rates of women students out of the overall total number of students, as well as on the number of women graduates in business and economics. However, many of the female students who were able to endure this unfavourable environment were able to achieve excellent results, on average better than those of their male counterparts. Several graduated *magna cum laude* and produced dissertations considered worthy of publication.

Referring to the female graduates' professional paths, it was observed that a high percentage devoted themselves to teaching in secondary schools. This choice was partly the result of an external constraint, in a context in which the professional opportunities at executive level open to women graduates, in the private and public sectors, were very limited. However, it should be remembered that especially in the early twentieth century, the role of the teacher held considerable prestige in public opinion and thus being a female teacher became in several cases an important factor in gender empowerment. This also explains why, as we have seen, the fascist regime, through a measure adopted in 1934 and enforced in 1938, tried to limit the teaching

[43] See decree 11 July 1980 No. 382 "On the reorganization of university teaching".

by women in disciplines characterized by greater visibility or prestige, such as law or economics.

We have also analysed some cases of female graduates who achieved results of excellence. Two of them, Maria Clotilde Franchi and Ada Costamagna, presented dissertations in 1912 and 1914, respectively, that denote remarkable analytical skill and aptitude for research. In Franchi's case, the dissertation was published by the Turin High School in the form of a monograph. Although there was every indication of a promising career in academia, for both of them the social barriers to entry proved insurmountable, and like many other female graduates, they continued their careers teaching in secondary schools.

Two other female graduates, Olga Rivarono Deaglio and Costanza Costantino were able, during the 1930s, to carry out innovative research and to start university work in the capacity of "volunteer" teaching assistants. Also in this case, however, gender-based obstacles proved almost impossible to overcome. Having said that, in a context that, as noted above, was in any case not favourable to women's entry into academic ranks, a gender bias specific to economics seems to be in place in this period. In the late 1930s Olga Rivarono decided to abandon the field of economics, which appeared to her de facto reserved to men, and to carry out her own study and research in the field of the English language. Costanza Costantino, while publishing, particularly in the 1950s and 1960s, several valuable essays and monographs in the field of public finance and while carrying out relevant teaching activity at the Faculty of business and economics, was able to obtain a permanent position at the University of Turin as an associate professor only on the eve of her own retirement.

From the point of view of gender-based barriers, the shift to a new democratic institutional setting after World War II, while undoubtedly constituting a crucial modernizing factor for the Italian society, seems to have brought an effective discontinuity only many years later.

References

Allio, R. (2008). Torino 1906. Una Scuola per la città che cambia. In *I primi cento anni della Facoltà di Economia di Torino* (pp. 11–40). L'Artistica.

Augello, M. M., & Guidi, M. E. L. (1988). I 'politecnici del commercio' e la formazione della classe dirigente economica nell'Italia post-unitaria. L'origine delle Scuole superiori di commercio e l'insegnamento dell'economia politica (1868–1900). In M. M. Augello, M. Bianchini, G. Gioli & P. Roggi (Eds.), *Le cattedre di economia politica in Italia. La diffusione di una disciplina 'sospetta' (1750–1900)* (pp. 335–384). FrancoAngeli.

Bateman, V., & Hengel, E. (2023). The Gender Gap in UK Academic Economics 1996–2018: Progress, Stagnation and Retreat. *Oeconomia: History Methodology, Philosophy, 13*(2), 163–200.

Becchio, G. (2004). Salvatore Cognetti de Martiis e il Laboratorio di economia politica (1893–1901). *Il Pensiero Economico Italiano, 12*(2), 11–23.

Bertocchi, G., Bonacini, L., & Murat, M. (2023). Adams and Eves: High School Math and the Gender Gap in Economics Majors. *Economic Inquiry, 61*, 798–817.

Bogart, E. L. (1953). *Storia economica dell'Europa* (trans. O. Deaglio Rivarono). UTET.

Cammelli, A. (2000). Contare gli studenti. Statistica e popolazione studentesca dall'Unità ad oggi. *Annali di Storia delle Università Italiane, 4*, 9–22.
Castellino, O. (1966). L'ordinamento monetario internazionale nel pensiero di Vincenzo Porri. In V. Porri, *Scritti vari di economia e di statistica* (pp. 61–68). Giappichelli.
Castronovo, V. (1987). *Torino*. Laterza.
Castronovo, V., & Tranfaglia, N. (1979). *Storia della stampa italiana* (Vol. III). *La stampa italiana nell'età liberale*. Laterza.
Costantino, C. (1939). Sulle fluttuazioni economiche di lunga durata. *Rivista Internazionale di Scienze Sociali* (Vol. X, pp. 794–809).
Costantino, C. (1941 August–September). Di alcuni aspetti del problema del lavoro femminile nel quadro della ricostruzione europea. *Rivista di Politica Economica, a. 31*(8–9), 677–684.
Costantino, C. (1943, May). Cause e rimedi dei bassi salari femminili. *Rivista Internazionale di Scienze Sociali, 51*(3), 152–160.
Costantino, C. (1951a, July–August). La sensibilità alla congiuntura delle imposte italiane sui consume. *Rivista Internazionale di Scienze Sociali, 22*(f. 4), 313–333.
Costantino, C. (1951b). *Imposte e congiuntura*. Giappichelli.
Costantino, C. (1952). Piani di sviluppo e pubbliche finanze. *Rivista Internazionale di Scienze Sociali, 23*(f. 2), 156–162.
Costantino, C. (1956). Finanze pubbliche in Danimarca. *Rivista di Politica Economica, 46*(12), 1123–1140.
Costantino, C. (1958a). Aspetti finanziari della congiuntura in Danimarca dal 1945 al 1955. *Studi Economici, 13*(1–2), 3–48.
Costantino, C. (1958b). Sulle moderne dottrine relative all'incidenza dell'mposta sulle vendite. *Giornale degli Economisti e Annali di Economia, n.s., 17*(5–6), May–June, 265–292; (7–8), July–August, 406–439.
Costantino, C. (1961). La tassazione del reddito e gli incentivi al lavoro. *Archivio Finanziario, 10*, 52–79.
Costantino, C. (1965a). La finanza pubblica in Piemonte. In *Annali di Statistica* (s. VIII, Vol. 16, pp. 233–239). *Studi statistici sulla finanza pubblica*.
Costantino, C. (1965b). *Il settore dello zucchero* (Studi e monografie, n. 7). In *Atti della commissione d'inchiesta sui limiti posti alla concorrenza nel campo economico*. Camera dei Deputati, Servizio studi legislazione e inchieste parlamentari.
Costantino, C. (1969a). *Le finanze pubbliche in Piemonte: La finanza erariale, provinciale, comunale, camerale e previdenziale piemontese, comparata con quella nazionale*. Giappichelli.
Costantino, C. (1969b). *Appunti sulla finanza neutrale e sulla finanza funzionale*. Giappichelli.
Deaglio Rivarono, O. (1946). *Grammatica della lingua inglese*. Ed. Palatine.
De Grand, A. (1976). Women Under Italian Fascism. *The Historical Journal, 19*(4), 947–968.
De Grazia, V. (1992). *How Fascism Ruled Women: Italy, 1922–1945*. University of California Press.
di Fenizio, F. (1934, September). L'opera scientifica di Vincenzo Porri. *Giornale degli Economisti e Rivista di Statistica, 74*(9), 589–603.
Dittrich-Johansen, H. (1994, January–March). Dal privato al pubblico: Maternità e lavoro nelle riviste femminili dell'epoca fascista. *Studi Storici, 35*(1), 207–243.
Faucci, R. (1986). *Luigi Einaudi*. Utet.
Faucci, R. (1995). Economia, storia, positivismo. Cognetti de Martiis e le origini del Laboratorio di economia politica di Torino. *Società e Storia, 69*, 599–618.
Faucci, R. (2014). *A History of Italian Economic Thought*. Routledge.
Fontana, M. (2000). Costanza Costantino (1913–1992). In R. W. Dimand, M. A. Dimand, & E. L. Forget (Eds.), *Biographical Dictionary of Women Economists* (pp. 118–121). Elgar.
Forgacs, D. (1990). *Italian Culture in the Industrial Era. 1880–1980*. Manchester University Press.
Forte, F. (1982). *Luigi Einaudi: Il mercato e il buongoverno*. Einaudi.
Forte, F., & Marchionatti, R. (2012). Luigi Einaudi's Economics of Liberalism. *European Journal for the History of Economic Thought, 19*(4), 587–624.

Franchi, M. C. (1913). *La Banca d'Italia dopo l'Atto Bancario del 1893.* Tesi di laurea pubblicata a cura della R. Scuola Superiore di Studi applicati al Commercio in Torino, Tip. Baravalle e Falconieri.

Govoni, P. (2009), "Donne in un mondo senza donne. Le studentesse delle facoltà scientifiche in Italia (1877–2005)", *Quaderni Storici*, n.s., vol 44, No. 130, April, pp. 213–247.

ISTAT. (1933). Statistica dell'Istruzione Superiore nell'anno accademico 1926–1927. *Annali di Statistica* (s. VI, Vol. 14).

ISTAT. (1936). Statistiche dell'Istruzione Superiore per l'anno accademico 1931–1932 e notizie statistiche per gli anni accademici dal 1927–1928 al 1930–1931. In *Statistiche intellettuali*, 11. Tip. Failli.

ISTAT. (1948). *Statistica dell'istruzione superiore nell'anno accademico 1945–1946.* Failli.

Levi, F. (2001). Da un vecchio a un nuovo modello di sviluppo economico. In U. Levra (Ed.), *Storia di Torino* (Vol. VII). *Da capitale politica a capitale industriale (1864–1915).* Einaudi.

Loffredo, F. (1938). *Politica della famiglia.* Bompiani.

Lundberg, S., & Stearns, J. (2019, Winter). Women in Economics: Stalled Progress. *Journal of Economic Perspectives, 33*, 3–22.

Mancini, G. (2018, April). Women's Labor Force Participation in Italy, 1861–2011. *Rivista di Storia Economica, 34*(1), 3–67.

Manfredini, G. (1963). Evoluzione della condizione giuridica della donna nel diritto pubblico. In *L'emancipazione femminile in Italia. Un secolo di discussioni 1861–1961* (pp. 171–193). La Nuova Italia.

Mazón, P. M. (2003). *Gender and the Modern Research University. The Admission of Women to German Higher Education, 1865–1914.* Stanford University Press.

Nerozzi, S. (2021). *Luigi Einaudi scrittore di banca e di borsa. Un saggio introduttivo.* Bancaria editrice.

Paci, F. (2002). L'economista 'esiliata' dal fascism. *La Stampa*, 1 giugno.

Pavanelli, G. (2004). Giuseppe Prato e il dibattito di politica economica e sociale del suo tempo. *Il Pensiero Economico Italiano, 12*(2), 167–189.

Pavanelli, G. (2008). Dalla Scuola Superiore di Studi Applicati al Commercio alla Facoltà di Economia. In *I primi cento anni della Facoltà di Economia di Torino* (pp. 41–69). L'Artistica.

Pavanelli, G. (2023, December). The Economists and the Press in Italy from the End of the Nineteenth Century until Fascism: the Case of Luigi Einaudi. *Journal of the History of Economic Thought, 45*(4), 576–602.

Rivarono, O. (1936, July). La svalutazione dell'argento nel periodo 1926–1932. *Rivista Internazionale di Scienze Sociali, 7*(4), 379–389.

Salvati, M. (1997, July–September). Tra pubblico e privato: gli spazi delle donne negli anni Trenta. *Studi Storici, 38*(3), 669–692.

Spadoni, M. (1998). Tra scuola e vita. La Facoltà di Economia di Torino dalle origini all'autarchia. *Quaderni di Storia dell'Università di Torino*, a. II–III(2), 91–116.

Zacchia, G. (2019, June). Alla ricerca del contributo perduto: (in)visibilità delle economiste nelle riviste italiane dal 1930 al 1970. *Moneta e Credito, 72*(286), 89–104.

Zacchia, G. (2021). What Does it Take to Be Top Women Economists? An Analysis Using Rankings in RePEc. *Review of Political Economy, 33*(2), 170–193.

Academic Research and University Careers of Women Economists During the Fascist Regime

Letizia Pagliai

1 Introduction

Italian women have given significant contributions to the field of economics throughout contemporary history.[1] This chapter examines the role of women economists during the fascist regime (1925–1945), which was characterized by the theory of corporatism (Guidi, 2000; Salvati, 2006), which was imposed in many different areas, from economic legislation to labour law, from economic policy to population statistics (Augello et al., 2019).

In the fascist university, female students in economic disciplines did gain more and more space but, despite graduating, they continued to have far fewer opportunities for advancement compared to their male counterparts (Rüegg, 2004, p. 248).[2] These women operated within the constraints imposed by the ideology of the fascist regime, which however needed them as qualified professionals to support its economic policies. As a result, some women were able to pursue economic careers, albeit with limited opportunities.

This research reconstructs the first steps of women economists on the academic scene, and also the profiles of those who, after some valid attempts at scientific research, were forced to abandon their university career. It also proposes different explanations for their under-representation at the highest levels of the academic career.

[1] No bibliographical entries referring to Italian women economists can be found in Madden et al. (2004).

[2] In 1930, the percentage of female students at Italian universities was lower than in France, the United Kingdom, Germany, the Netherlands and Austria.

L. Pagliai (✉)
Università di Torino, Turin, Italy
e-mail: letizia.pagliai@unito.it

M. Mosca (ed.), *Women at Work in Italy (1750–1950)*, Springer Studies in the History of Economic Thought, https://doi.org/10.1007/978-3-031-64281-4_10

2 Some Contextual Data in the Interwar Period

We start our analysis with a quantitative assessment of female students in economic and non-economic subjects in fascist Italy. The first available information on the gender distribution of enrolled and graduated students dates to 1911 (Ferraris, 1913). In the first decades of the twentieth century the presence of women economists increased very slowly.[3] An important acceleration was given in 1913 by the *Regolamento generale sugli Istituti Superiori di studi Commerciali* (General Regulation on Higher Institutes of Commercial Studies, Royal Decree No. 1223 of 1 August 1913),[4] which stated that women could be admitted as students and auditors under the same conditions as men. Between 1913 and 1932 the percentage of women in the total number of students increased by 299%, varying considerably in the different faculties and institutes (Istat, 1936b, p. 36). The most significant acceleration in women's access to university occurred, not surprisingly, in the years following the First World War. In 1939 the Italian activist Maria Castellani (Fig. 1), on whom we will focus later, gave a detailed account of the enrolment of female students in Italian universities after fascism came into power, noting 60.2% in Literature and Philosophy, 28.8% in Pharmacy, 17.4% in Mathematics and Physics, 11.3% in Law and Political Science, 9% in Economic and commercial sciences (Castellani, 1939, p. 92). The traditional gender dynamics of the early post-war period tended to be concentrated in courses of study relating to teaching, health, the humanities and, among the STEM disciplines (Science, Technology, Engineering and Mathematics), especially the latter.

The low presence of female students enrolled in Economics provides an initial explanation as to why their path as teachers in academia has been so bumpy. For quantitative data on the teaching staff by gender, legal status and university location, it was necessary to wait for the surveys carried out in the academic years 1926–1927, 1927–1928, 1931–1932 and 1945–1946 (Cammelli, 2000). However, while the surveys on the student component (enrolled and graduates) had a high degree of accuracy, the data on professors from 1926 to 1932 were much more incomplete.

In order to clarify this point, it is necessary to take an institutional look at the important reforms that were implemented in the post-WWI period. The changes contained in the 1923 law enacted by the Italian minister of education Giovanni Gentile (Colao, 1995), had indeed led to the recognition of the administrative, disciplinary and didactic autonomy of universities and colleges. However, the basic principles of autonomy affirmed in the Gentile law were modified in 1933 by the subsequent collection of regulations (called *Testo Unico*), which, while giving unity to the various laws enacted, introduced a limitation on teaching autonomy. The result was

[3] The two pivotal moments in the path of women's presence in the Italian university world were the right of access to the university, sanctioned in 1874, and the abolition of the institution of marital authorization for access to the university (1919).

[4] Chapter "Aurelia Josz, Educational Entrepreneur, and her School of Agriculture for Girls". On students and auditors. Art. 72. Women shall be admitted to the Institute as students and auditors under the same conditions.

Fig. 1 Maria Castellani, full professor in the United States

that in 1930s fascist Italy, the political supervision of professors and students became one of the main concerns of the new regime (Rüegg, 2004, p. 71). Law and Political Science were the faculties most subject to the strict controls of the Ministry of Corporations (Giuseppe Bottai), where professors were asked for regular reports on their graduates. The topics of theses in Corporative Law and Corporative Economics were not selected by professors according to the free criterion of scientific autonomy but suggested through ministerial circulars that listed them minutely.[5]

In short, the legislative reforms that regulated the university system and the structuring of the hegemonic discourse on corporatism not infrequently engaged professors to seek political legitimacy in the shadow of power. For this reason, it is useful to delve into the academic environment in which women economists in those years sought access.

[5] Archivio Storico dell'Università di Firenze, Carteggio e atti dell'amministrazione centrale, 1933.

3 Access to the Career of Women Economists

During the fascist period, economics courses in the faculties of Law and Political Science were greatly developed[6]: the number of courses in economic subjects increased in Italy by 82.2% from 1926 to 1931. The number of women studying economics (as a percentage of the total number of students) shows a significant increase between the pre-war period and the 1930s, rising from 2.5% in 1913 to 4.3% in 1931. However, the most significant figure is due to enrolments in Statistics (11.1%) (Istat, 1936a).

We do not have specific data on women graduates by economics degree programme in the various Italian faculties; in the same period, no female graduates appear in Statistical and Actuarial Sciences or in the Graduate School of Statistics. The university faculties of origin of women graduating between 1928 and 1943 were mainly Law and Economics and Business (Amore Bianco & Cini, 2021, pp. 45–209). As we shall see in Table 1, the women economists we cover in this study earned their degrees in Law and/or Political Science[7] and Statistics.[8] Looking at the specific academic year 1931–1932, the highest percentages of female graduates are recorded at the Higher Institutes of Economics and Commerce in Venice (11.6%) and Rome (6.2%).

As for the specific field of study, we have only the yearbooks of the various Italian universities to work with. Each yearbook presents at the end a list of graduates, their respective thesis title and their supervisor. Systematic reading of these lists constitutes the only means of knowing the graduation topics of women. It reveals that the largest number of female graduates in economics came from Law and Economics and the predominant fields of degrees were economic history and the history of economic thought.[9]

The most frequent employment outlet for these female graduates was teaching at technical and commercial institutes (see also §5.4). They were also enrolled in postgraduate courses at the most important School of Corporative Sciences in Italy, that of the University of Pisa; they were 3.5% of the total, although only a third of these women managed to earn their doctoral degree.

As for the academic career, according to Castellani (1939, p. 57), who in the mid-1930s was the Italian representative of International Professional Women's Organisation, there were 25 female full professors in the entire country and none of them in

[6] In addition to those taught at the nine Higher Institutes of Economics and Commercial Sciences and at the two private universities in Milan (University Luigi Bocconi and Catholic University).

[7] Paola Maria Arcari, Maria Luisa Boggeri, Anna Maria Calvi Sotgia, Nora Federici, Jenny Griziotti Kretschmann, Luisa Riva Sanseverino), Economic and commercial sciences (Vera Cao-Pinna, Costanza Costantino, Wanora Mancini, Olga Rivarono.

[8] Anna Maria Cao-Pinna, Nicolina Titolo. We will briefly illustrate their biographies in §5.1.

[9] National Education Yearbooks for the years 1923 to 1943 have been consulted for this research. For example, Corrado Barbagallo, professor of Economic History at the Higher Institute of Economic and Commercial Sciences in Naples, entrusted two female students in the academic years 1928–1929 and 1930–1931 with the following graduation topics: *A study of economics according to the theories of St. Thomas Aquinas*, and *The Economic Thought of Pellegrino Rossi*.

Table 1 Italian women economic writers

Women economic writers	Doctor's degree	Mentorship	Academic position	Research fields
Arcari, Paola Maria	• Philosophy of Law (Faculty of Political Science in Rome)	Corrado Gini	Full professor of History of political doctrines	• Economic statistics • History of Economic Thought
Boggeri, Luisa	• Finance (Faculty of Law in Pavia)	Benvenuto Griziotti	Lecturer of Finance	• Finance and financial law
Calvi Sotgia, Anna Maria	• Finance (Faculty of Law in Pavia)	Benvenuto Griziotti	Tenured lecturer of Finance	• Finance and financial law
Cao-Pinna, Anna Maria	• Statistics (Faculty of Statistical and Actuarial sciences in Rome)	Alessandro Molinari	Never enlisted	• Economic statistics
Cao-Pinna, Vera	• Economic statistics (Higher Institute of Commercial Studies in Rome)	Alfredo Niceforo	Lecturer of Economic Statistics	• Applied economics • Econometrics
Castellani Maria	• Mathematics (Faculty of Statistical and Actuarial sciences in Rome)	Francesco Paolo Cantelli	Lecturer of Mathematics	• Labour market • Social welfare • Actuarial sciences
Costantino, Costanza	• Economic policy (Economic and Commercial Sciences in Torino)	Alfredo Niceforo	Lecturer of Economic Policy	• Business cycle • Economic statistics • Finance and financial law
Federici, Nora	• Statistics (Faculty of Political Science in Rome)	Corrado Gini	Tenured lecturer of Statistics	• Economic statistics • Social statistics • Actuarial sciences
Griziotti Kretschmann, Jenny	• Political economy (Faculty of Law in Rome)	Maffeo Pantaleoni	lecturer of Political Economy	• Political economy • Business cycle

(continued)

Table 1 (continued)

Women economic writers	Doctor's degree	Mentorship	Academic position	Research fields
Mancini, Wanora	• Economics and Law (Higher Institute of Commercial Studies in Venice)	Alfonso De Pietri Tonelli	Tenured Lecturer of Economic Policy	• Political economy
Ratti Anna Maria	• Institute for Statistics and Economic Policy (Rome)	Corrado Gini	Never enlisted	• Demographic statistics • Emigration
Riva Sanseverino, Luisa	• Law and Political science (Faculty of Law and Faculty of Political Science in Rome)	Cesare Vivante	Full professor of Corporative law	• Labour Law • Corporative law
Rivarono, Olga	• Political economy (Higher Institute of Commercial Studies and Faculty of Law in Torino)	Vincenzo Porri	Lecturer of Economics	• Political economy • Financial and statistical science
Sensini, Francesca	• Law (Faculty of Political Science in Florence)	Gino Arias	Lecturer of Economic Policy	• History of Economic Thought
Titolo, Nicolina	• Statistics (Faculty of Statistical and Actuarial sciences in Rome)	Corrado Gini	Lecturer of Statistics	• Economic statistics

economics. In order to obtain reliable quantitative data in the 1930s, the only valid research method was to extrapolate economic subjects from the *National Education Yearbooks*, broken down by city of higher education. As already mentioned, it was only after 1933—the law which reduced the autonomy of universities and colleges (Raicich, 1989)—that the reporting of non-tenured professors became more efficient and credible. Further information can be found in the *Almanacco annuario Donne Italiane*, published by Silvia Bemporad (1878–1980) in Florence, which provides an annual survey of university women by category and discipline.

Despite the gradual increase of women enrolled in economics, in 1932 Istat recorded only a few volunteer assistants, and only at the Higher Institutes of Economics and Commercial Sciences in Catania, Florence, Genoa and Venice (Istat,

1936a, pp. 77, 85). Our initial findings illustrate that while there was an appreciable increase in economics courses offerings in the years 1926–1931, the most significant increase in female enrollment was at the School of Statistical Sciences in Rome. An extremely important fact is also the low number of women enrolled in the corporative specialization courses that could lead to leadership positions in the Fascist period.

The difficulty for women economists to enter the university career system as tenure-track assistants in economics, and the impossibility of climbing the hierarchical ladder is clear: no women obtained a professorship in economics until the 1960s. It was only the years of the so-called massification of the university in Italy in the 1970s (Fontana, 2015) that saw a consistent tendency towards its feminization. It is therefore almost a truism to point out how in the fascist period there was an overwhelming male dominance among professors, and how women economists never became full university professors.

4 Italian Women in Academic Institutions and Other Networks

Closing the gender gap in a subject such as economics was an important goal that proved remarkably difficult to achieve in the fascist period. However, our empirical investigations identified participation in international and national networks as the certain career path strategy, which was taken by at least a couple of women—Maria Castellani and Luisa Riva Sanseverino (Fig. 2)—who were characterized by a strong political and academic stance.

The *Almanacco* by Bemporad (Soldani, 2007) is a source for finding the various women's societies, including those of a more political nature, such as the Consiglio Nazionale delle Donne Italiane (CNDI), the Italian branch of the International Council of Women, which changed its leadership in favour of the government with the rise of fascism. This brings us to the topic of professional associations, whose formation was strongly accelerated by the ideology of corporatism, which became mandatory during the fascist regime. Corporative economy resulted from the will of the fascist regime, which—after an early ultra-liberal stage between 1922 and 1925—endeavoured to replace the classical liberal mechanism of political representation based on the individual vote, with a new model of representation based on the collective representation of professional and economic interests (Nardone et al., 2019).

As we know, women's networks are important platforms that provide support, resources and opportunities for professional development and collaboration. These networks aim to address underrepresentation and promote gender equality in the profession, including in academia. We explore here the existence of networks of Italian women economists in fascist Italy and discuss whether they were important in promoting diversity and inclusiveness in the field. Essentially, we distinguish the

Fig. 2 Luisa Riva Sanseverino, full professor in 1934

'relational' element, dependent on the networks created in socialization, from the 'structural' element (derived from belonging to a group, such as one's faculty).

Under the aspect of national networks that represented the interests of the category, women economists were strongly disadvantaged. This can be deduced from the comparison with female medical graduates, who were part of the Associazione Nazionale Fascista Dottoresse in Medicina (National fascist association of female medical graduates), or with female law graduates, represented by the Federazione Italiana Donne Giuriste (Italian federation of female law graduates) (Bemporad, 1938, pp. 341–349). The absence of a national institutional network among Italian women economists[10] was initially remedied by the Federazione delle laureate e diplomate degli istituti superiori (FILDIS, Federation of Graduate Women), a form of elitist, corporatist-professional associationism that arose in 1920 and survived until 1935 (Taricone, 1988).

Italian women economists were not included in the network of international associationism throughout the 1920s. The International Economic Conference (Geneva, 1927) promoted by the League of Nations made the absence of Italian women economists in top positions at the main economic institutions emblematically evident. The Conference can be seen as the pinnacle for the representation of women members of international organizations, who move in unison to nominate 'scholars with

[10] For an overview of Italian women's associationism since the early post-war period, see Gazzetta (2018, pp. 195–225).

expertise in economic issues'.[11] No Italian women were represented on the expert committee,[12] in spite of the existence of foreign women delegates for the International Federation of University Women. It was not until the 1930s that Italian women found their delegate at the international level in Maria Castellani. In fact, she became head of the League of Nations' Accounting Office in Geneva, the agency that promoted social justice in the workplace, producing in-depth research and studies on issues such as employment, social protection and gender discrimination. This change of pace in the 1930s did not however imply the recognition of women's special intellectual capacities in the most representative contexts of the international economic scene. Rather, it was an indication of the replacement of the traditional leadership of women's associations (professional or Catholic) with personalities legitimized by the regime's new directives.

It is therefore not surprising that Maria Castellani herself, together with another economist, Luisa Riva Sanseverino, became recurring names in international and national associations. Ideologically close to the fascist regime, models of the modern Italian fascist woman were both supported by the political and scientific legitimization of the Italian fascist politician Giuseppe Bottai, then undersecretary for Corporations. Castellani was an important female civil servant of the state, the first woman at the head of a state organization in Italy,[13] sent to promote the new dictatorship in the United States; during this period, she held a series of top roles in international women's associations and initiated the process of the loss of autonomy of the CNDI, which until then had been thought of as a possible bastion of Italian feminism.

As for the labour lawyer Riva Sanseverino, who had joined the corporative order in her youth, she was given a prominent role in the Mussolini regime's Associazione Nazionale Fascista Artiste e Laureate (ANFAL, National Fascist Association for Women Artists and Graduates), which replaced the already mentioned FILDIS, forced to disband for political reasons. Castellani was named by Mussolini at the head of ANFAL, and using this political leadership, she was active in representing professional women (Castellani, 1937) and promoting a nationwide network of 'cultivated' women employed in industry, professions, and state administration. Similarly, Riva Sanseverino (1927, 1931) was an effective advocate for the rights of working women.

The cases of Castellani and Riva Sanseverino are exemplary because this aspect of their careers reveals emancipatory purposes and a certain amount of awareness in covering female role models which could affect the young women's decision to major in economics (Porter & Serra, 2020). Our underlying hypothesis is that their pursuit of holding high visibility roles in women's associations increased the likelihood of young women coming into direct contact with successful and accomplished women working in attractive fields after they graduated from economics (Blau et al., 2010).

[11] United Nations Library Archives, Geneva, League of Nations, Period I (1919–1927) "International Economic Conference, 1927—Representation of Women".

[12] Chaired by the Italian Francesco Coppola D'Anna, then editor of the journal *Rivista di politica economica.*

[13] Istituto Nazionale Fascista della Previdenza Sociale (National fascist institute of social security).

5 Fifteen Italian Women Economists

The names of the fifteen women listed alphabetically in Table 1 were selected on the quantitative basis of their economic writings and not based on their specialization; therefore, it is natural to find women lawyers (Tacchi, 2004) among the women economists. These names were chosen from those belonging to different universities in the peninsula, from the 'basic' levels of the academic system, i.e., volunteers and tenured assistants, and extracted from the database of the Interuniversity Center for Documentation on Italian Economic Thought (CIPEI) at the University of Pisa.

The table below shows their educational qualification, mentorship, academic position attained during the fascist period, and their field of research.

5.1 Their Short Biographies

Here we add some biographical information on each of them, referring where possible to the existing secondary literature.

Paola Maria Arcari (1907–1967) (Fig. 3) graduated in Political Science in Rome, where she met Corrado Gini, who introduced her to the study of Statistics and Economic Policy, qualifying her to teach History of Political Doctrines in 1937. From 1936 to 1940 she taught History of Political Doctrines at the faculty of Law in Turin and from 1939 was tenured lecturer in Corporative Political Economy at the faculty of Law, University of Cagliari; here she became full professor of History of Political Doctrines (Alberti & Battente, 2024). In addition to her studies on labour and wages (see §5.2), Arcari published a statistical and historical survey on the role of women in political life (1957), in which she listed data from the Italian political elections of 1946, 1948 and 1953, analysing women's preferences to vote right or left.

Luisa Boggeri (1905–1972), Benvenuto Griziotti's student and international scholar (see §5.3), abandoned academic research after her marriage in 1940. Many years later, however, she became famous for editing the Italian translation of the third volume of *Capital* (Marx, 1954), which had numerous reissues until 1997 (Pagliai, 2024a).

Anna Maria Calvi Sotgia (1909–1975) graduated in Law in Pavia in 1932 and in the two academic years 1933–1934 and 1934–1935 she succeeded Ezio Vanoni as tenured lecturer in Financial Science and Financial Law at the faculty of Law in Cagliari, where he also taught Tax Law. Married to Sergio Sotgia, a professor of Commercial Law in Cagliari, she abandoned her academic career for the family (Pagliai, 2024b, f).

Anna Maria Cao-Pinna (1910–1986), economic statistician, did not belong to the university world but to that of research institutions. During the fascist regime she was a delegate of the Fascist Confederation of Trade Workers in Rome from 1939–1942; after World War II, she played an important role in international organizations, such

Fig. 3 Paola Maria Arcari, full professor in 1942

as the International Aid Administration, the *International Council on Social Welfare, the Italian Social Service Committee and the Parliamentary Commission of Inquiry into Poverty,* embracing the socio-political line of the Christian Democrats (Pagliai, 2024c).

Vera Cao-Pinna (1909–1986), economic statistician and Anna Maria's older sister, after receiving her degree in Economics with a dissertation in Economic statistics, qualified for university teaching only in her late forties and was appointed Lecturer in Economic Statistics at Rome in the academic year 1956–1957; she never won a chair but she is best known for having constructed, using Leontief's model, the first Input–Output table of the Italian economy (Corsi et al., 2017; Fornengo, 2000; Sunna, 2024).

We have already met Maria Castellani (1896–1985), a leading figure in the emancipation of women since the 1930s, when she represented Italy in international bodies dedicated to the advancement of women in education and their promotion in the most qualified sectors of society. Castellani graduated in Mathematics from the University of Rome in 1923 and had an interesting and varied career in Italy before moving to Kansas City, where she held the chair of Mathematics from 1946 to 1961, while in Italy she retained her academic position as lecturer until her death (de Grazia, 1992, pp. 258–259, 280; Hall, 2017; Pagliai, 2024d, f).

Costanza Costantino (1913–1992), liberal, catholic and anti-fascist scholar, was a lecturer of economic policy for the chair of Antonio Fossati in Turin; in that university she had graduated in economics in 1934 with a thesis *On Long-Term Economic Fluctuations* for which Publio Mengarini was supervisor. Qualified to teach law and economics subjects in technical colleges in 1937, she published her dissertation in 1939 after a study of the history of economics. Finally, in 1956 she obtained a scholarship from the Higher Institute for Social Workers in Turin, where she was a teacher of Statistics, to further her research on Economic Fluctuations (Fontana, 2000; Zacchia, 2024).

Nora Federici (1910–2001) was a tenured lecturer of Statistics at the faculty of Political sciences in Perugia and of Population development and race policy at the Faculty of Statistical Sciences in Rome. She was a scholar of demographic studies in the fascist period, trained in Rome with Corrado Gini. In 1962 she won the first competition in Italy for the chair of Demography. From 1966 to 1994 she was editor of the journal *Genus* and President of the Italian Committee for the Study of Population Problems (Rotondi & Pasotti, 2024).

Jenny Kretschmann (1884–1980), who married Benvenuto Griziotti, was a lecturer in Political Economy at the faculty of Law at the University of Pavia in the inter-war years, and in the years 1941–1943 she was a lecturer of History of Economic Thought (Parisi, 2007; Foresti & Parisi, 2024).

Wanora Mancini (born in 1904) matriculated at the Higher Institute of Economic and Commercial Sciences in Venice in 1921, graduating in December 1925 in Economics and Law with a dissertation on *Foreign Trade and Monetary Circulation in Italy* in 1924, for which Alfonso De Pietri Tonelli was supervisor. After winning a competition, she was appointed tenured assistant professor in February 1926 and affiliated to the Laboratory of Economic Policy directed by De Pietri Tonelli himself, whose textbook she edited in 1927.

Anna Maria Ratti was born in Palermo in 1905 and studied at an early age in Rome where she resided from 1919. She obtained a scholarship in 1929 from the Institute of Economic Policy and financial legislation of the faculty of Political Sciences at Rome that allowed her to complete her studies; after spending a year in the United States, she prepared a statistical study on emigration from the poorest part of southern Italy, edited by the National Bureau of Economic Research (Ratti, 1931), that received a large amount of international acclaim. Well entrenched in the mechanisms of the cultural strategies promoted by Giuseppe Bottai, she translated from German the miscellaneous economic works edited by Erwin von Beckerath that were published (1932) with a preface by Bottai from the School of Corporative Sciences of Pisa. Her statistical study did not open up an academic career for her, as she was hired on the editorial staff of the *Italian Encyclopedia*, where her scientific role, directed by Gustavo Del Vecchio, was instrumental in connecting Italy's leading scholars. Ratti worked on the largest series of biographical entries of economists ever[14] and, not least, that of 'J.M. Keynes', and on the entry 'Economics' (Ratti, 1929a), demonstrating a historical methodological approach. She was also editor of the academic journals *Economia* and *Rassegna Monetaria*, and other scholarly works (1929b, 1936). However, despite her activism, the intervening interactions with her institutional referents depict an author who abdicated her main field of research (the migratory currents) as a function of the power conferred on her by her role as the pivot of the network of Italian scholars. In the post-war period she was mainly known

[14] These entries included the very important 'Jean-Baptiste Say', 'Giuseppe Toniolo' and 'John Ramsay McCulloch'.

for writing the biography of the economist Riccardo Bachi (1961). In the absence of hard data, we assume she died in Rome in the mid-1970s (Pagliai, 2024f; Zanni, 1983).

The already mentioned Luisa Riva Sanseverino (1903–1985) graduated in Rome in Law (1925) and then in Political Science (1926); she became a labour lawyer embedded in the corporative system and in fascist power circles. A tenured lecturer in Labour Legislation (1932), she won a chair at the University of Sassari in 1934 (Battaglia, 2024).

Olga Rivarono (1908–?) graduated in economics in 1931 from the Higher Institute of Economic and Commercial Sciences in Turin with a thesis on *The scientific organization of work: Attempts at real applications in Italy's first typewriter factory.* In 1933 she became a free assistant to her supervisor, Vincenzo Porri, and, at the same time, matriculated in Law, graduating in 1935 in corporative economics with a dissertation on *Leon Walras and his theories: On the occasion of the centenary of his birth* (supervisor Pasquale Jannaccone). Shortly thereafter she published a monograph on agricultural economics (1936); we also refer here to the text by Giartrosio, Pavanelli.

Francesca Sensini (1905–?) graduated in Law in 1927 from the University of Florence, then qualified as a prosecutor (1928) and was registered to practice law on the same date. A lecturer of Economic policy for the chair of Gino Arias, in the academic years 1931–1933 she taught two courses that became treatises (1931, 1933) on the history of economic thought on the just wage and on the role of trade in the national economy (Bemporad, 1936).

Nicolina Titolo (1902–?), originally from Salaparuta in Sicily, won the competition (1939) for tenured lecturer of Statistics at the Institute of Statistics in Rome with a commission chaired by Corrado Gini, on the subject *Concept of concentration, its measures and applications in the field of economic statistics.* In 1940 she qualified in Statistics at the University of Naples, but her entire short university career took place in Palermo.

5.2 Their Economic Research Topics

With regard to women's research topics in the field of economics (Zacchia, 2017; Becchio, 2020), we have highlighted three macro areas: the labour market, the gender wage gap, and finance (see §5.3).

The first two topics, closely linked, were the centre of interest of the School of Statistics in Rome, fundamentally marked by the figure of the famous Italian statistician Corrado Gini. Meticulous investigations were undertaken into family budgets, consumption and food budgets (Cao-Pinna,1936, 1938, 1940b, Sotgia Calvi, 1966), the birth rate (Titolo, 1934), and generational turnover (Federici, 1940, 1941). Among the scholars belonging to this school of statistics, Vera Cao-Pinna, (1939), specializing in biometrics, analysed a Sardinian peasant family. She followed the model of the social survey conducted by the Lombardian reformer Maria Pasolini

Ponti (1892),[15] who can rightly be considered as the progenitor of family monographs based on quantitative data in Italy. Pasolini Ponti's model of analysis on family budgets was considered valid for many years: Pantaleoni continued to refer to it in his theory on the pressure of taxes on consumption (1910), in which he denounced the fragmentary and heterogeneous nature of statistics on family budgets in Italy (p. 309).

It was on the subject of labour that Italian women economists expressed their most original positions, using economic statistics (Favero, 2015) and the history of economic thought as their research method. Studies that highlighted the living conditions of the working classes and their variations over time were of particular importance from economic, political and social perspectives. Labour lawyer Riva Sanseverino (1931) focused particularly on the issue of the minimum wage, while Arcari (1932) turned her attention to gender discrimination in the labour market. The issue of the minimum wage had been the subject of extensive international debate since the late nineteenth century in labour and immigration treaties; in Italy it was studied to provide a legislative remedy for the abuses of home-based labour (informal work), which had been excluded from the scope of collective bargaining agreements. Vilfredo Pareto, before drafting his famous law of incomes, made it the subject of reflection in a lecture at the Accademia dei Georgofili (1886), establishing that the minimum wage should be a 'vital' portion such as to guarantee the reproduction of labour.

Thereafter, the fascist regime from the early 1920s inaugurated a long season of wage compression; as for the subsequent promulgation of the *Labor Charter* (April 21, 1927), which aspired to provide a definitive solution to the labour problem, it fuelled the debate among marginalists and corporatism theorists divided over the level of the solution to be given to the relationship between the state and the market.[16]

The subject of wages, included in the broader field of cost of living and industrial production, was addressed by labour lawyer Riva Sanseverino in a monograph (1931) presented in her first two university competitions.[17] The ambitious work, aimed at examining the legal problems of labour from a comparative and industrial law perspective, also dealt extensively with the economic side, emphasising the links

[15] For the links between Pasolini Ponti and Pantaleoni, established both in the preface to this paper (1892, pp. 311–315) and in the preface (Pantaleoni, 1925) to the speech on the 'Formation of a Social and Civil Culture' presented by Ponti in the education section of the first CNDI Congress in Rome in 1908 (already published in *Giornale degli Economisti*, May 1899), we refer here to Laurenzi and Mosca (2024).

[16] It had become the responsibility of the trade associations included in the corporative system to determine the minimum wage. At a higher level, the resolution of labour conflicts over wage conditions was referred to the judiciary; finally, the final say in the matter rested with the State, which had the right to intervene on behalf of the higher interests of production.

[17] Competition of November 1934 for the chair of Comparative Social and Labour Legislation at the Fascist Faculty of Political Science of the University of Perugia; competition for the chair of Trade union and corporative law at the University of Messina; Ministero dell'Educazione Nazionale (1935). *Bollettino Ufficiale*. II. *Atti amministrativi*, LXII(1), pp. 975–976, 1217–1218.

between social legislation and corporative law as theorized by Arias and Massimo Fovel.[18]

The subject followed the long debate on women's work—Arcari (1932, pp. 77–78) explains it very well—read in the light of gender conflicts, which had opened at the end of the First World War and which, in the desire for a restoration of normal life, had involved the whole of European public opinion. A scholarship holder at Istat, Arcari had been commissioned by C. Gini to extend the findings of the Labour Office on female industrial workers in the early twentieth century to the world of agriculture.

The issue had been raised by the transition of female wage-earners to be reintegrated into domestic life and the phenomenon of female labour redundancies in the post-war period. It had been an ideological issue that had seen different stances being taken: social Catholicism had been in favour of returning to work within the coordinates of the normality of 'natural' social laws; the women's world represented by the suffragists had attempted to show the non-competitiveness of women's work, while the socialist world had failed to fully interpret the political weight of women workers. In the end, the conflict had settled on the proposal of moderate Giolittian feminism, in favour of small cooperatives and home production structures. Finally, Fascism, without questioning the traditional mission of women, had turned the praise of domestic work into a wide-ranging instrument, in an interclassist key.

In her analysis, Arcari historically reconstructed the social advancement of female labour, which, benefiting both from the necessities of war and industrial evolution, had favoured women in the world of production. According to Arcari, this evolution had led to a level of rationalization of the ratio between female and male wages, improving the former.

It is interesting to note her research methodology's ability to range from statistics to the history of economic thought: Arcari reconstructs the evolution of economists' thinking[19] regarding women's entry into the productive life of the state, she analyses this thinking according to a specific value measure: the proportion between female emancipation and the right to work.

Anna Maria Cao-Pinna[20] is inextricably linked to her statistical surveys on food consumption and the measurement of poverty, yet she broke away from this by publishing a study on women's professions in 1936. In many ways, the text is to be considered fully aligned with the fascist ideology regarding the figure of the working

[18] Riva Sanseverino was indebted to the corporative theory by Gino Arias (*Il salario corporativo*, 1929) and by Massimo Fovel (*Rendita e salario nello Stato sindacale*, 1928).

[19] Arcari mentions the thought of the following economists: Paul Leroy-Beaulieu (*Le travail des femmes*, 1872), Michel Chevalier, John Stuart Mill (1869), Clemence-Auguste Royer (1868), Joseph Salway Eisdell and Théodore Fix.

[20] Cao-Pinna worked on a topic representative of Istat's research directions, namely the relationship between wages and the cost of living, working to determine the notion of real wages. In 1927, Istat was charged with promoting the formation of cost-of-living indices in all municipalities with more than 100,000 inhabitants. The researcher gave a talk on this topic in 1939 at the Naples Conference on Labour Statistics, promoted by the Italian Society of Demography and Statistics (Cao-Pinna, 1940).

woman; in fact, it accepted the principle of the need for women's work to be limited to certain professional activities, suited to the 'biosocial' function of women to ensure the continuity of the nation. What is relevant to note, however, is that she called for a levelling of women's wages to men's wages; such a solution would have had a twofold benefit: the mitigation of 'unfair' female competition and the affirmation of social justice through fairer labour protection. The issue of women's wages was indeed considered one of the most complex economic problems and only until a few years before the war, the suggestion to pay women the same as men would have been considered inconceivable. In the post-war period (1945–1962), her role became central to the U.S. Relief Program in Italy and the Christian Democratic government, particularly with regard to the Social Distribution Policy. Cao-Pinna's activities[21] unfolded mainly in the direction of the study service of the International Aid Administration, or AAI, a state body headed by Lodovico Montini (Ciampani, 2002). In the 1960s, Anna Maria Sotgia Calvi also collaborated as an appointee with the AAI, publishing a monograph on food in 1966, after ending a short and intense career in tax law in the inter-war period.

The issue of women's wages was also addressed by Castellani (1939), although the style of her reflections concurred to exalt the development of the corporatist state whose trade unions had pledged to put an end to the underpayment of women. Lower pay for doing the same work was considered by Castellani to be uneconomical as the world crisis had shown how men had been laid off and women hired because their wages were lower; later, Constantino (1941) also focused on equal opportunities in the labour market (Zacchia, 2024).

Few of these women economists taught those courses in Economics that fascist directives considered 'prestigious' in university teaching: since the decree of 28 November 1935, n. 2004—reforming the university system—transformed the teaching of 'political economy' into 'corporative political economy'. Wanora Mancini taught the course from 1926 to 1932 in Venice, Costanza Costantino in 1938 in Torino and Paola Maria Arcari in 1942. Only one of them, however, Jenny Kretschmann—a lecturer in Political Economy in Pavia from 1930 to 1961—dealt directly with economic policy in a monograph *Autarchia* in which the analysis on the nature of corporative economy gave her an opportunity to revise the aspects in international comparative terms.[22] According to the author, autarky would constitute the central pivot of the grandiose movement that would eventually transform the long-standing structural crisis. 'Therefore, autarky—is how she concludes the

[21] She also edited *Assistenza d'oggi* (1952–1964), the bi-monthly magazine of the International Aid Administration and, at the same time, she took part in the Parliamentary Commission of inquiry into poverty and the means of combating it, for which she carried out an investigation into the poor classes (1953).

[22] Autarkic policy was one of the most debated aspects of corporative economic doctrine (1935–1942) as it represented a model of a regulated economy that, through a change in domestic production, intended to transform the terms of international trade; indeed, autarky consisted of a set of production plans intended to guide Italy toward economic independence and was arrived at (1937) in response to the sanctions applied by the League of Nations against Italy, for its aggression against Ethiopia (Federico, 2002).

monograph—can become *a non-negligible coefficient of the prosperity* that will be represented by the equation of consumption and production, economic progress, and greater economic, social and international justice' (Kretschmann, 1937, p. 145).[23]

However, we wanted to ascertain the extent of women economists' adherence to the corporatist doctrinal discourse by consulting a source such as the *Bibliografia sindacale corporativa* (Gradilone, 1942). From this monumental collection we have expunged the names of those women who were formally recognized as convinced supporters of the corporatist system for the State. In addition to the already mentioned Jenny Kretschmann (1933b, 1937), and Francesca Sensini (see §5.1), there are also a few personalities who occupied a high level in the university system such as P. M. Arcari (1938) and Luisa Riva Sanseverino, but also a little-known figure that we find interesting to propose here. Maria Carolina Castellucci graduated in 1935 with a degree in economics from the Faculty of Law at the University of Palermo with a dissertation on the causes and remedies to unemployment and the 40-h working week.[24] A Catholic and an open supporter of corporatism, she took part in the 22nd National Conference of the Fuci (Italian Catholic University Federation) in Bari in 1936, called by Paolo Emilio Taviani and Giorgio La Pira. At the conference Castellucci (1937) addressed the theme of the relationship between individual and collective interest, analysing the figure of the entrepreneur according to Fascist morality.

In summary, we can now make a general observation: the themes of social enquiry addressed by women in academic research are rather homogeneous. They stem from contingent and primary problems (work and equal pay rights), but it is important to note that they were transversal to the political ideologies of the women authors, i.e. they are not indicative of a political 'faith'. Maria Castellani, Luisa Riva Sanseverino, but also Arcari, adhered to the fascist ideology, but this did not make them any less convinced in addressing issues involving workers and gender wage discrimination in the labour market.

5.3 *The Pavia School of Finance*

The Institute of Finance at the Faculty of Law in Pavia, directed by the Italian economist Benvenuto Griziotti in 1929 (Asta, 2024), constitutes a unique case in the Italian university system between the two wars because compared to other Italian faculties it gathered the largest number of female lecturers dedicated to financial research. In the 1930s at least two female lecturers under Griziotti's supervision (Auction 2023) did research abroad and produced writings of some significance.

Anna Maria Calvi, the scholar of financial law we have already met, graduated with Griziotti in 1932 and immediately won the Bank of Italy's Stringher Prize for further education abroad. She studied in Heidelberg (1932–1933), from then on, turning most of her work to the German economic situation and tax law; at the end

[23] Unless stated otherwise, the translations of the quoted texts are our own.

[24] Archivio Storico dell'Università di Palermo, Carriera scolastica degli studenti (1935–1937), 1317.

of her study period, she returned to the Institute of Finance in Pavia as a voluntary assistant. She later became lecturer in Science of Finance at the Faculty of Law in Cagliari but abandoned her academic career in 1935 after marrying Sergio Sotgia, professor of Commercial Law at the same faculty.

Luisa Boggeri, who was initiated to her studies by Griziotti and graduated from the Pavia Institute of Finance, had a short but highly varied international career. Winner of the Bank of Italy's Bonaldo Stringher Prize, she spent a period of study abroad in Vienna in 1933. After two years as a volunteer assistant at the Griziotti Institute, she moved to Columbia University on the Eleonora Duse Exchange Fellowship. There she worked (1935–1938) with the research group headed by Edward Lee Thorndike on the topic of Human Nature and the Social Order, considered among the most advanced in the Psychology Department of the Institute of Educational Research. It was at this time that she wrote (Boggeri & Sundelson, 1938), together with Jacob Wilner Sundelson of Rutgers University, one of the best known texts in the literature on fiscal studies, in which she synthesized the theories of the Italian economic tradition on the problems of public finance, followed by a study (Shoup & Boggeri, 1938) on the tax system in the United States. As Italy's delegate, she participated in the New York Conference of the Institute of Pacific Relations (Columbia University) in 1939 with a contribution on 'Italy and the Far East' (Boggeri & Shoup, 1940); however, she abruptly abandoned her academic career after getting married the following year.

Jenny Kretschmann must of course also be added to this core of the Pavia School, although she was already an independent scholar in the 1930s and did not gravitate under the scientific shadow of her husband Benvenuto Griziotti. Kretschmann was the only woman who lectured in economics at that time at Pavia; she had got to know her future husband in 1906 while studying with Pareto at the faculty of Social Sciences in Lausanne. After graduating in Rome under Pantaleoni's supervision, she was directed by him to the analysis on system dynamics factors and became the only woman studying cyclic phenomena since the Thirties (Kretschmann, 1933a, 1935; Parisi, 2007).

5.4 Non-Recognition and Exclusion

In the long path taken by women economists, the interruption of their university careers was due to the lack of or partial recognition of their merits in the scientific field, which led them to teaching at higher commercial institutes,[25] as can be seen in

[25] We cannot suppose, in the absence of certain data, whether teaching at higher institutes became the alternative path for a number of women economists who had a very brief presence as voluntary assistants. We can mention the cases of Laura Davico (Finance Science, University of Turin, 1940), Anna Del Buttero (Economic Policy, University of Rome, 1937), Bice Ferrari (Political Economy, University of Rome, 1937–1941), Irene Giardina (Political Economy, University of Palermo, 1938), Emilia Leitenberger (Political Economy, University of Venice, 1938), Maria Luigia Lelmi (Political Economy, University of Perugia, 1934–1935), Renata Pes (Finance, University of Trieste, 1940), Eugenia Zappi (Economic Policy, University of Palermo, 1938).

the cases of Wanora Mancini,[26] Olga Rivarono and Nicolina Titolo.[27] Furthermore, it was common practice for scholars—without gender differences—to also qualify to teach law and economics subjects at technical and commercial institutes. Costanza Costantino, for example, obtained this qualification in 1937, while she was a lecturer of Economic Policy in Torino; therefore, she cultivated a dual career path, also embarking on a teaching career at high schools, first in Pinerolo, then in Torino.

The same fate was shared by personalities not linked to a university career, but with scientific profiles of a certain continuity and consistency such as Anna Maria Ratti, who held an important position in the *Enciclopedia Italiana* the most famous Italian encyclopaedia, a private initiative supported by fascist government and promoted by Giovanni Gentile that was also the most important cultural grouping under the dictatorship. After its collapse, she was forced to teach in the province of Rome and to carve out a very marginal role for herself in the group of intellectuals once gathered around Gentile.[28]

The lesser-known Amelia Dainelli graduated in 1932 from the School of Corporative Studies in Florence with Gino Arias with a dissertation on *Politics and Economics in G.D. Romagnosi* in which she examined the theme of corporatism in terms of its historical evolution, which was then presented in various publications up to 1936 (Pagliai, 2024e). Her scholarly career was short, but among various publications, her most important scholarly contribution (Die faschistische korporative Wirtschaftsordnung/The fascist corporative economic order, 1933) appeared in the *Weltwirtschaftliches Archiv*, founded in 1913 as the world's first journal focusing on international economics. Nevertheless, she ceased her production of scholarly works to teach in technical schools in Rome, where she had moved after her marriage.

Marriage in women's biographies introduces the theme of further self-exclusions to academic careers, as already observed in the cases analysed by Sotgia Calvi and Boggeri. At the time, it was often customary, if not the rule, for married women not to pursue professional careers and thus, after marriage, to give up university research positions.

Considering all levels of university posts, two women—Maria Castellani[29] and Costanza Costantino[30]—were involved in the fate of the anti-Semitic laws that made the expulsion of Jewish teachers inevitable in the Italian academic world in 1938 (Finzi, 2005). Although Costantino was excluded from the voluntary position of

[26] Wanora Mancini, already a tenured assistant in Venice, left her position in 1935 to teach Institutions of civil law at the Technical and Commercial Institutes in Forlì, Rovigo, Bologna and finally in Milan.

[27] The continuation of N. Titolo's professional career alternated between the Technical Commercial Institute in Palermo and teaching Methodological Statistics at the Higher School of Social Work in Palermo.

[28] In 1944 Ratti went to teach at the Technical Commercial Institute in Velletri History of Institutions of Law, Political Economy and Financial Science, while continuing to collaborate with the Institute of *Enciclopedia Italiana*.

[29] Daughter of Paolo Costantino and Elisa Namias.

[30] Cessazione di Costanza Costantino (cattedra di Storia economica). In Archivio Storico Università di Torino, Corrispondenza. Carteggio 1938, 2.4 "Assistenti volontari pratiche generali".

assistant professor of Economic policy at the faculty of Economics in Turin, which she had obtained in 1937, she continued her studies independently publishing an article based on her thesis on long-term economic fluctuations (1939) and on the right of women to work (1941, 1943).

Castellani, for her part, was forced to resign from the Italian branch of the International Federation of Business and Professional Women in 1940 as a result of the worsening racial persecution. In 1944 she was a visiting professor in Switzerland and in 1945 she became an economist for the United States Armed Forces Institute. She then embarked on a brilliant career in the United States, where she became a citizen in 1953.

6 Conclusion

The analysis carried out in this chapter sheds some light on the academic careers of women economics writers from the beginning of Mussolini's prime ministership until the end of World War II. We have seen that the fields of their economic research, which had to confront the 'new economy' (corporatism), ranged from economic legislation to labour law, from economic policy to population statistics. Most women focused their research interests during the years of fascism in subdisciplines oriented toward family budgets, nutrition and the labour market (minimum wage) (Finoia, 1991). In particular, this study documents the same scientific interest in conducting social surveys on wage discrimination with respect to men, and on the professional orientation of women. Beyond our expectations, therefore, the fields of interest of women economists, except for the scholars belonging to the Pavia School, appeared to us to be rather uniform in addressing social issues. The common foundation of their research was value-based and thus underpinned what was perceived as a demand for a possible renewal of the society of the time.

The second aspect that we have identified in the intellectual biographies of women economists consists in the coherence and continuity of the research objectives with which they approached their scientific path, as can be seen in the developments of their studies in the post-war period in a context of institutional transformation. This element consequently excludes institutional pressures or pressures from the scientific community in selecting topics during the fascist regime for women economists that were unrelated to the scholars' scientific predilections. From this point of view, women economists highlight some possible strategies of resistance that could be expressed within the university context, which, in the field of economics, was pushed in the direction of a flattening on corporative doctrine. In one of the best books on the sociology of the professions (Abbot, 1988, pp. 67–88), some insights clearly explain the phenomenon of this period when it is argued that high-prestige occupational groups (i.e. full professors) maintained and emphasized jurisdictional boundaries towards subordinates by controlling and emphasizing the importance of theory (typical of the corporative doctrine). By underlining theory, high-prestige academic groups established prestige and legitimacy to their teaching by accrediting themselves in government and driving a wedge between themselves and the phalanx of women economists doing applied economics and statistical economics on socially relevant topics.

As we have seen, women economists were able to defend their intellectual and scientific independence during the fascist period, although very few were able to reach the rank of full professor (only Nora Federici and Costanza Costantino) and only achieved this in the 1960s.

References

Abbot, A. (1988). *The system of professions: An essay on the division of expert labor*. University of Chicago Press.

Alberti, M., Battente, S. L. (2024). Arcari, Paola Maria. In *Scrittori e scrittrici di economia nel Regno d'Italia* (pp. 42-43). Roma: Bancaria Editrice.

Amore Bianco, F., & Cini, M. (Eds.). (2021). *La Scuola di scienze corporative dell'Università di Pisa*. Pisa University Press.

Arcari, P. M. (1932). Il rapporto tra salari femminili e salari maschili secondo le prime risultanze di una inchiesta sul bracciantato agricolo, La Vita Economica Italiana. *Indici del Movimento Economico d'Italia, 7*(4), 64–78.

Arcari, P. M. (1938). *Lineamenti di storia delle dottrine economiche in rapporto all'idea di Stato. (Lezioni)*. Tip. V. Ferri.

Arcari, P. M. (1957). *Le rôle des femmes dans la vie politique* (Vol. 39). Cedam (Studi economico-giuridici, Università di Cagliari, Facoltà di Giurisprudenza).

Asta, M. (2024). Griziotti, Benvenuto. In *Scrittori e scrittrici di economia nel Regno d'Italia* (pp. 319–321). Bancaria Editrice.

Augello, M. M., Guidi, M. E. L., & Bientinesi, F. (Eds.). (2019). *An institutional history of Italian economics in the interwar period*. Volume I. *Adapting to the fascist regime*. Palgrave Macmillan.

Battaglia, M. R. (2024). Riva Sanseverino, Luisa. In *Scrittori e scrittrici di economia nel Regno d'Italia* (pp. 497–498). Bancaria Editrice.

Becchio, G. (2020). *A history of feminist and gender economics*. Routledge.

Bemporad, S. (ed.) (1936). *Almanacco annuario Donne italiane*. Giannini e Giovannelli.

Bemporad, S. (ed.) (1938). *Almanacco annuario Donne Italiane*. Giannini e Giovannelli.

Blau, F. D., Currie, J. M., Croson, R. T. A., & Ginther, D. K. (2010). Can mentoring help female assistant professors? Interim results from a randomized trial. *The American Economic Review, 100*(2), 348–352.

Boggeri, L., & Shoup, C. S. (1940). Problemi di oggi e di domani alla Conferenza 1939 dell'Institute of Pacific Relations. *Asiatica, 6*, 368–376.

Boggeri, L., & Sundelson, J. W. (1938). Italian theories of fiscal science. *Political Science Quarterly, 53*(2), 249–267.

Cammelli, A. (2000). Contare gli studenti. Statistica e popolazione studentesca dall'Unità a oggi. *Annali di Storia delle Università Italiane, 4*, 9–23.

Cao-Pinna, A. M. (1936). La preparazione della donna all'esercizio delle professioni che le sono proprie. *Assistenza Fascista, 2*(1–2), 461–464.

Cao-Pinna, A. M. (1938). La razione alimentare giornaliera delle famiglie di lavoratori del commercio nella città di Napoli. *Il Lavoro commerciale, 7–8–9*, 20–21.

Cao-Pinna, A. M. (1940a). Sulla rappresentatività e compatibilità degli indici del costo della vita calcolati in Italia. In *Atti della V riunione dedicata alla statistica del lavoro* (Vol. 1, pp. 299–313). Tip. dell'Unione Arti Grafiche.

Cao-Pinna, A. M. (1940b). Consumi normali e consumi razionati: Italia, Inghilterra, Francia. *Rivista Italiana di Scienze Economiche*, 808–814.

Cao-Pinna, A. M. (1953). Le classi povere. In Camera dei Deputati, *Atti della Commissione parlamentare di inchiesta sulla miseria in Italia e sui mezzi per combatterla, 2. Indagini tecniche. Condizioni di vita delle classi misere* (pp. 9–111). Camera dei Deputati.

Cao-Pinna, V. (1939). *Monografie di famiglie agricole. XV. Contadini Sardi. Provincie di Cagliari e Nuoro*. Tip. Operaia Romana.

Castellani, M. (1937). La donna fascista nell'assistenza sociale. *L'assistenza Sociale, 21*(2), 450–453.

Castellani, M. (1939). *Italian women past and present*. Società editrice di Novissima.

Castellucci, M. C. (1937). *L'imprenditore nell'economia corporative*. Studium.

Ciampani, A. (ed.) (2002). *L'Amministrazione per gli Aiuti Internazionali. La ricostruzione dell'Italia tra dinamiche internazionali e attività assistenziali*. FrancoAngeli.

Colao, F. (1995). *La libertà di insegnamento e l'autonomia nell'università liberale: Norme e progetti per l'istruzione superiore in Italia, 1848–1923*. Giuffrè.

Corsi, M., D'Ippoliti, C. & Zacchia, G. (2017). Gendered careers: Women Economists in Italy. *Working Papers CEB*, n. 17-003, Université Libre de Bruxelles.

Costantino, C. (1939). Sulle fluttuazioni economiche di lunga durata. *Rivista Internazionale di Scienze Sociali, 47*(5), 794–809.

Costantino, C. (1941). Di alcuni aspetti del problema del lavoro femminile nel quadro della ricostruzione europea. *Rivista di Politica economica, 31*(8–9), 677–684.

Costantino, C. (1943). Cause e rimedi dei bassi salari femminili. *Rivista Internazionale di Scienze Sociali., 51*(3), 152–160.

de Grazia, V. (1992). *How fascism ruled women, Italy 1922–1945*. University of California Press.

Dimand, R. W., Dimand, M. A., & Forget, E. L. (Eds.). (2000). *A biographical dictionary of women economists*. Elgar.

Favero, G. (2015). La statistica nell'Università italiana tra le due guerre. In P. Barucci, S. Misiani, & M. Mosca (Eds.), *La cultura economica tra le due guerre* (pp. 339–347). FrancoAngeli.

Federici, N. (1940). L'intervento dello stato nel campo demografico. *Il Giornale economico, 18*(5–12).

Federici, N. (1941). *Politica della popolazione; prefazione di Corrado Gini*. F. Failli.

Federico, G. (2002). Autarchia. In V. de Grazia & S. Luzzatto (Eds.), *Dizionario del fascismo* (pp. 116–120). Einaudi.

Ferraris, C. F. (1913). Statistica delle Università e degli Istituti Superiori. In *Annali di Statistica* (Vol. 6). Tip. Nazionale di G. Bertero.

Finoia, M. (1991). La questione femminile attraverso il "Giornale degli Economisti", 1975–1935. *Giornale degli Economisti e Annali di Economia, 50*(9–12), 525–538.

Finzi, R. (2005). The damage to Italian culture: The fate of Jewish University professors in fascist Italy and after, 1938–1946. In J. D. Zimmerman (Ed.), *Jews in Italy under fascist and Nazi rule* (pp. 96–113). Cambridge University Press.

Fontana, M. (2000). Costanza Costantino. In R. W. Dimand, M. A. Dimand, & E. L. Forget (Eds.), *A biographical dictionary of women economists* (pp. 118–121). Elgar.

Fontana, R. (ed.) (2015). *Le donne nell'accademia italiana. Identità, potere e carrier*. Mondadori.

Foresti, T., & Parisi, D. (2024). Griziotti Kretschmann, Jenny. In *Scrittori e scrittrici di economia nel Regno d'Italia*. Bancaria Editrice.

Fornengo, G. (2000). Vera Cao-Pinna. In R. W. Dimand, M. A. Dimand, & E. L. Forget (Eds.), *A biographical dictionary of women economists* (pp. 343–346). Elgar.

Gazzetta, L. (2018). *Orizzonti nuovi. Storia del primo femminismo in Italia, 1865–1925*. Viella.

Gradilone, A. (1942). *Bibliografia sindacale corporativa (1923-I-1940-XVIII)*. Istituto Nazionale di Cultura Fascista.

Guidi, M. E. L. (2000). Corporative economics and the italian tradition of economic thought: A survey. *Storia Del Pensiero Economico, 40*, 31–58.

Hall, L. M. (2017). Founders, feminists, and a fascist. Some notable women in the Missouri section of the MAA. In *Women in mathematics: Celebrating the centennial of the Mathematical Association of America* (pp. 121–140). Springer.

Istat. (1933). *Statistica dell'Istruzione superiore nell'anno accademico 1926–27* (Annali di Statistica, Vol. 14). Tip. Failli.

Istat (1936a). *Statistica dell'Istruzione superiore per l'anno accademico 1931–32 e notizie statistiche per gli anni accademici dal 1927–28 al 1930–31* (*Statistiche intellettuali*, Vol. 2). Tip. Failli.

Istat (1936b). *Indagine sugli studenti iscritti nelle Università e negli Istituti superiori nell'anno accademico 1931–32* (Statistiche intellettuali, Vol. 13). Tip. Failli.

Kretschmann, J. (1933a). Ricerche sulle fluttuazioni economiche di lunga durata. *Giornale degli Economisti e Rivista di Statistica., 73*(7), 461–508.

Kretschmann, J. (1933b). *Lo Stato come soggetto economico: Studi metodologici sull'economia politica.* Treves.

Kretschmann, J. (1935). *Il problema del 'trend' secolare nelle fluttuazioni dei prezzi.* Treves.

Kretschmann, J. (1937). *Autarchia economica e finanziaria ed economia mondiale.* Cedam.

Laurenzi, E., & Mosca, M. (2024). Il pensiero economico di Maria Ponti Pasolini (1856–1938) tra femminismo e percorsi di lettura. *Il Pensiero Economico Italiano, 32*(1), 127–147.

Madden, K. K., Seiz, J. A., & Pujol, M. (2004). *A bibliography of female economic thought to 1940.* Routledge.

Madden, K. K., & Dimand, R. W. (Eds.). (2019b). *The Routledge handbook of the history of women's economic thought.* Routledge.

Marx, K. (1954). *Il capitale: Critica dell'economia politica.* 3.1: *Libro terzo: Il processo complessivo della produzione capitalistica*; transl. by L. Boggeri. Rinascita.

Nardone, P., Ridolfi, N., Laureti, L., A., & Di Nucci. (2019). Corporatism: Dynamics and contradictions in fascist economic policy. *Il Pensiero Economico Italiano, 27*(2), 61–78.

Pagliai, L. (2024a). Boggeri, Luisa (Maria Primina). In *Scrittori e scrittrici di economia nel Regno d'Italia* (pp. 92–93). Bancaria Editrice.

Pagliai, L. (2024b). Calvi Sotgia, Anna Maria. In *Scrittori e scrittrici di economia nel Regno d'Italia* (p. 122). Bancaria Editrice.

Pagliai, L. (2024c). Cao-Pinna, Maria. In *Scrittori e scrittrici di economia nel Regno d'Italia* (pp. 127–128). Bancaria Editrice.

Pagliai, L. (2024d). Castellani, Maria. In *Scrittori e scrittrici di economia nel Regno d'Italia* (pp. 139–141). Bancaria Editrice.

Pagliai, L. (2024e). Dainelli, Amelia. In *Scrittori e scrittrici di economia nel Regno d'Italia* (pp. 188–189). Bancaria Editrice.

Pagliai, L. (2024f). Ratti, Anna Maria. In *Scrittori e scrittrici di economia nel Regno d'Italia* (pp. 485–486). Bancaria Editrice.

Pantaleoni, M. (1910). L'identità della pressione teorica di qualunque imposta a parità di ammontare e la sua semiotica. *Giornale degli Economisti e Rivista di Statistica, 21*(3), 293–324.

Pantaleoni, M. (1925). Della divisione del lavoro in attribuzioni maschili e femminili. In *Erotemi vari di economia* (Vol. 1, pp. 361–375). Laterza e Figli.

Pareto, V. (1886). Se convenga fissare per legge un minimo al salario guadagnato e un massimo alla ricchezza speculata, memoria letta nell'adunanza ordinaria del 4 aprile 1886. *Atti della Reale Accademia economico-agraria dei Georgofili di Firenze, 9*, 103–130 (now in *OEuvres Complètes.* 17. *Écrits politiques. Lo sviluppo del capitalismo, 1872–1895*; texts collected with an introduction by G. Busino. Droz, 1989, pp. 191–213).

Parisi, D. (2007). Una lunga vita da economista: l'itinerario biografico e scientifico di Jenny Kretschmann Griziotti (1884–1980). *Il Politico, 72*(2), 145–165.

Pasolini Ponti, M. (1892). Monografie di alcuni operai braccianti nel Comune di Ravenna. *Giornale degli Economisti, 5*, 245–277, 316–343, 411–427.

Porter, C., & Serra, D. (2020). Gender differences in the choice of major: The importance of female role models. *American Economic Journal: Applied Economics, 12*(3), 22–254.

Raicich, M. (1989). Liceo, università, professioni: un percorso difficile. In S. Soldani (Ed.), *L'educazione delle donne. Scuole e modelli di vita femminili nell'Italia dell'Ottocento*. F. Angeli.
Ratti, A. M. (1929a). Economia. In *Enciclopedia Italiana di scienze, lettere ed arti* (Vol. 2, p. 118). Istituto della Enciclopedia Italiana.
Ratti, A. M. (1929b). La bilancia dei pagamenti internazionali negli economisti italiani dei secoli XVII e XVIII. *Economia, 4*(2), 103–118.
Ratti, A. M. (1931). Italian migration movements, 1876 to 1922. In W. F. Willcox (Ed.), *International migrations*, II (pp. 440–470). NBER.
Ratti, A. M. (1936). Le vicende dell'economia albanese e le fortune del franco. *Rassegna Monetaria, 7–8*, 252–263.
Ratti, A. M. (1961). *Vita e opere di Riccardo Bachi*. Dott. A. Giuffrè.
Riva Sanseverino, L. (1927, September 7). L'organizzazione del lavoro femminile nei sindacati. *Il Giornale della donna*, 39–47.
Riva Sanseverino, L. (1931). *Salario minimo e salario corporative*. ARE.
Rivarono, O. (1936). *Monografia di podere*. G. Giappichelli.
Rotondi, C., Pasotti, I. (2024). Federici, Nora. In *Scrittori e scrittrici di economia nel Regno d'Italia* (pp. 249–250). Bancaria Editrice.
Rüegg, W. (Ed.). (2004). *A history of the university in Europe, 3. Universities in the nineteenth and early twentieth centuries, 1800–1945*. Cambridge University Press.
Salvati, M. (2006). The long history of corporatism in Italy: A question of culture or economics? *Contemporary European History, 15*(2), 223–244.
Sensini, F. (1931). *Il giusto salario nella storia delle dottrine economiche: Corso di esercitazioni di Economia politica*. Poligrafica universitaria del dott. C. Cya.
Sensini, F. (1933). *Il commercio nell'economia nazionale: dai mercantilisti ai nostri giorni*. Poligrafica universitaria.
Shoup, C. S. & Boggeri, L. (1938). La disorganizzazione fiscale negli Stati Uniti d'America. *Rivista di Diritto finanziario e Scienza delle Finanze, 2*(2), 32–45.
Soldani, S. (2007). Almanacco annuario della donna italiana nel 1938–1939. In S. Franchini, M. Pacini, & S. Soldani (Eds.), *Giornali di donne in Toscana. Un catalogo, molte storie, 1770–1945*. 2. *1900–19445* (pp. 562–568). Olschki.
Sotgia Calvi, A. M. (1966). *L'alimentazione nelle collettività infantili*. F. Failli.
Sunna, C. (2024). Cao-Pinna, Vera. In *Scrittori e scrittrici di economia nel Regno d'Italia* (pp. 128–129). Bancaria Editrice.
Tacchi, F. (2004). Dall'esclusione all'inclusione. Il lungo cammino delle laureate in Giurisprudenza. *Società e Storia, 103*, 97–125.
Taricone, F. (1988). La Fildis (Federazione Nazionale laureate e diplomate) e l'associazionismo femminile, 1920–1935. In M. A. Saba (Ed.), *La corporazione delle donne. Ricerche e studi sui modelli femminili nel ventennio* (pp. 127–169). Vallecchi.
Titolo, N. (1934). Alcuni dati sulla fecondità in Sicilia. *Rivista italiana di economia, demografia e statistica, 8*(3–4).
Zacchia, G. (2017). Diversity in economics: A gender analysis of Italian academic production. *INET Working Paper Series*, 61, Institute for New Economic Thinking.
Zacchia, G. (2024). Costantino, Costanza. In *Scrittori e scrittrici di economia nel Regno d'Italia* (pp. 178–179). Bancaria Editrice.
Zanni, A. (1983). Gli economisti e l'Enciclopedia Italiana, con notizie e documenti inediti sulle "voci" Keynes e Cournot. *Quaderni di Storia dell'economia politica, 1*(3), 169–196.

Women in Politics

Anna Kuliscioff's Labour Economics

Luca Michelini, Paolo Passaniti, and Luigi Vergallo

1 From Anarchism to Socialism

Anna Kuliscioff, or rather Anna Rozenstejn,[1] was born in Simferopol, Crimea, most likely in early 1854, to a prosperous family of Jewish merchants. At the age of seventeen, in 1871, she moved to Zurich to enrol for an engineering (technical sciences) degree, which in her home country was an opportunity still closed to women. There was a substantial Russian expatriate community in Zurich, and many women who contributed to reflections on socialism, anarchism and the backwardness of Russian society. Anna Kuliscioff's husband, the Russian nobleman Pëtr Makarevič, was also an anarchist and was arrested when, with Anna, he was forced by a decree of Tsar Alexander II to return to Russia. Makarevič later regained his freedom, but he and Anna parted ways forever. Kuliscioff redoubled her efforts and her revolutionary planning, repeatedly evading the tsarist police, until once again she had to return—for refuge—to Switzerland. It is certain that she lived there from 1877 onwards, and

[1] Anna changed her surname when living in Paris.

Sections 1, 2, 8 and the first part of 7 are by Luigi Vergallo; 4, 9 and 10 by Luca Michelini, 3, 5 and 6 and the second part of 7 by Paolo Passaniti. We thank Fiorenza Taricone and Manuela Mosca for their comments on the text. Unless stated otherwise, the translations of the quoted texts are our own.

L. Michelini (✉)
Università Di Pisa, Pisa, Italy
e-mail: luca.michelini@unipi.it

P. Passaniti
Università Di Siena, Siena, Italy
e-mail: Paolo.passaniti@unisi.it

L. Vergallo
Fondazione Feltrinelli, Milan, Italy
e-mail: luigi.vergallo@fondazionefeltrinelli.it

M. Mosca (ed.), *Women at Work in Italy (1750–1950)*, Springer Studies in the History of Economic Thought, https://doi.org/10.1007/978-3-031-64281-4_11

met revolutionaries such as Mikhail Bakunin, Carlo Cafiero, Benoit Malon, Andrea Costa and many other political exiles from across Europe, as well as activists of the Paris Commune.

Kuliscioff's encounter with Costa was a pivotal event in her life story, not only for the love that bound them from that moment and for several years, but also for the indispensable connection that she then forged with the Italian revolutionary movement. On 22 March 1878, Anna and Andrea were arrested together in Paris: she was acquitted but deported, and he was sentenced to two years in prison. In October, Kuliscioff was again arrested in Florence but freed in November of the following year. In 1880 Kuliscioff and Costa signed the programme of one of the first theoretical journals of Italian socialism, *La rivista internazionale del socialismo*, which encouraged not only men, but also women, to play a part in social issues. On 27 July 1879 Costa published a letter entitled *Ai miei amici di Romagna* (To My Comrades in Romagna), a key text in the history of Italian socialism and anarchism. As Giorgio Candeloro has written, with that letter Costa distanced himself from the anarchists, though he did not take a stand against them. He did however support the abandonment of insurrection and championed instead the imperative of creating a political party representing the workers' movement (Candeloro, 1994, p. 176). Kuliscioff's role in the letter by Costa—whose afterthought, as is known, can represent and be taken as the turning point of the entire Italian labour movement—was clear to all the protagonists of the time. Eduard Bernsten wrote that:

> I remember a specific incident of our life as exiles in Lugano. There were many of us. Cafiero was present, Kuliscioff had been in Italy for some time. And one day, news arrived that Andrea Costa had abandoned the Bakunian ranks and ideas and converted to parliamentarism. We were all more than a little surprised. But Cafiero put his hands in his hair; then, chopping the air with them and shaking his long beard, exclaimed: 'Anna, Anna, what have you done?' Just like that. We all immediately understood that the persuasive words of Anna Kuliscioff had won the day. (Kuliscioff, 1978, p. 43)

The centrality and relevance of the intellectual and political exchange between Andrea Costa and Anna Kuliscioff is thus clear, as is the effect—not to be underestimated—of the intimate, inseparable connection between her and Italian socialism. Costa became the first parliamentarian (elected in 1882) to win election on behalf of the Italian socialist movement. For Anna, however, the doors of the institutions were closed and would remain so.

2 Socialism and Feminism

In the Spring of 1881, Kuliscioff—living covertly because she still had an expulsion order hanging over her—joined Costa in his hometown of Imola, and in December 1881 their daughter Andreina was born. The newspaper *Avanti!*, which would later become the official newspaper of the Socialist Party, was already being published, having been founded in 1896, and Anna contributed to it with her "correspondences from Russia." However, her relationship with Costa soon began to fracture, in part because she was again constrained to seek refuge in Switzerland due to the difficulty, as a new mother, of living clandestinely in Imola.

In 1884, suffering from tuberculosis, she moved with her daughter to Naples in search of a better climate. When Costa, now a deputy, was with her again, having gone to Naples to help with the treatment of the illness, the close contact precipitated their final separation. But by then Anna, still in Naples the following year, had met Filippo Turati, a younger comrade in Costa's struggle (Boggio & Cerliani, 1977, p. 109), who was destined to become her lifetime companion. Back in Italy, she resumed her studies, this time in medicine, specialising in gynaecology at Turin in 1888. Her thesis was on puerperal fever, which she deduced to be of bacterial origin, opening the way to discoveries that would later save many women's lives. She practiced medicine in Milan, where she had the opportunity to meet key figures in Italian feminism.

In that city, Anna lived openly and publicly with Turati, outside of any legal tie and bound only by their mutual feelings, thus exemplifying a rejection of the bourgeois family structure. Alongside her medical work—often going up and down the stairs of the homes of working women, wives, and mothers—she developed a strong desire to champion working-class women. During this period, the "*dottora*," as she was called in Milan, made the city's poorest workers and children the centre of her care and attention. "Her work, however, was also sought out and respected by the most notable families of the upper middle class, thanks to her influential friends within the League of Women's Interests founded by Anna Maria Mozzoni, Paolina Schiff and Norma Casati" (Pillitteri, 1986, p. 73).

In 1891, the most important and longest-running theoretical journal of Italian socialism, *Critica Sociale*, was launched thanks to the initiative and guidance of Kuliscioff and Turati. It was intended to have both a political and cultural approach, surveying not only the world of socialism but also the bourgeois forces capable of abandoning narrow class ideas. The magazine's contribution to the birth of the Socialist Party was of fundamental importance, as also were Kuliscioff and Turati's political endeavours.

Between 1890 and 1891, Linda Malnati, Giuditta Brambilla and Carlotta Clerici founded the Women's Section of the Chamber of Labour in which Kuliscioff became involved, having placed a commitment to feminism at the forefront of her activities (Taricone, 1992). In short, the birth of the party was closely connected to the debate on the female question, albeit difficulties and tensions would remain significant for decades.

On 17 April 1890, Anna delivered a lecture at the Milan Philological Circle entitled *The Monopoly of Man*. This became one of her key writings, republished many times, and it addressed a question that still captivates the world of international progressivism today: "How can we," the author asked, "isolate the woman question from other social problems that originate from injustice and are based on the privilege of sex or class?" (Kuliscioff, 1890, ed. 2021, p. 35).

The lecture was undoubtedly influenced in some way by August Bebel's essay *Woman and Socialism* (Bebel, 1879). Following the teachings of Friedrich Engels, who, in the volume *The Origin of the Family, Private Property and the State*, had

Fig. 1 Anna Kuliscioff, 1907

attacked head-on every notion of women's natural inferiority and duly revisited the historical and social causes of female oppression, Bebel, in his writing, outlined what he saw as the historical transition from ancient matriarchal communism to the contemporary bourgeois paternalism. On the basis of these interpretative suggestions, Kuliscioff focused on the still essential theme of the *autonomy* of the woman question within the broader struggle against every form of economic and political oppression (Fig. 1).

The lecture conference thus set out two long-term themes in the author's approach to the woman question. On the one hand, that of inter-classism, because the subordinate condition of women concerns every social class (Casalini, 1978, p. 99). On the other hand, that of the autonomy of the struggle of women within the broader confrontations of the proletariat, or, as we might say today, *with* the working class and *against* male power. In this regard, Kuliscioff made a particularly significant reflection on the revolution:

> I don't want to be a bird of ill omen, but I firmly believe that not even a socialist republic, even if it should come soon, would do us the justice we deserve. Even if an economic revolution took place, woman would be considered by the majority of men as an ignoramus, a straw brain; the same as the bourgeoisie did with the working class, after all the revolutions made with blood of the worker, in the name of freedom and equality – triumphant, it left the worker with the freedom to starve and placed his equality in Paradise [...]. The emancipation of the proletariat can only take place through the work of workers of both sexes. But the emancipation of woman can only take place through the work of woman herself. (Kuliscioff, 1892a, ed. 2015, p. 74)

Kuliscioff sought to broaden the alliances of the world of labour by adhering "to some demands typical of bourgeois feminists who, starting from the 1890s, had begun to establish a series of leagues engaged not only in assistance and educational activities but also in an interclass battle for women's political and legal rights" (Casalini, 1978, p. 99). According to Franca Pieroni Bortolotti, who unquestionably deserves credit for reviving studies on feminism, Kuliscioff's greatest limitation—and, in reality, that of the entire European social democratic movement—between 1890 and 1906 was the presumption that the establishment of an independent democratic women's movement dedicated to their liberation was unnecessary after the foundation of the class-based party (Pieroni Bortolotti, 1978, p. 6). As Maurizio Degl'Innocenti has observed, "for Kuliscioff, the idea of an autonomous movement achieving the desired emancipation above everything and everyone could be a generous idea, to which she did not deny importance, but it remained abstract, condemned to substantial impotence, and politically ambiguous" (Degl'Innocenti, 2017, pp. 15–16). In effect, in Kuliscioff's view, the female proletariat was at the vanguard of the political struggle:

> While middle-class women are compelled to engage in a vital competition to secure professions so far monopolised by the male sex, the female worker has long since won, or rather suffered, the right to be exploited on an equal footing with the male worker. As a result of the evolution of industry, she already finds herself facing men in conditions of much greater independence than the vast majority of women from other social classes. (Kuliscioff, 1897, p. 105).

Kuliscioff did not rule out a political and cultural dialogue with the bourgeois female world, but at the same time she recognised and criticised its conservative traits and its limited aims of expanding suffrage and job opportunities only for affluent women. This is what drove her to establish an organic connection between the socialist movement and the woman question. She subsequently reiterated these positions, and eventually they culminated in another of her essential texts, which was also indispensable for the Italian socialist movement. This was published as a pamphlet under the title *Proletariato femminile e Partito socialista* (The Female Proletariat and the Socialist Party), conceived as a report for the Socialist Congress of 21–25 October 1910:

> In the proletarian battlefield, in the daily struggle of the dispossessed against economic exploitation, in the class struggle to achieve a higher standard of living that facilitates their upward path toward complete emancipation, the woman question no longer has the character of a reaffirmation of those 'rights of man' proclaimed for over a century and from the exercise of which women were always excluded in practice. Instead, it emerges on the stage of history as one of the aspects of the great economic, political, and social revolution that began with the rise of industrial civilisation. (Kuliscioff, 1910a, p. 165)

On 23 September 1911 she wrote in *La battaglia socialista*:

> Now, we female socialists not only cannot embrace the minimum programme of the feminists, but our parliamentary group would unanimously revolt if any government proposed a reform that, in reality, by favouring women of various bourgeois ranks, would be equivalent to arming the natural adversaries of the proletariat with multiple voting rights. (Kuliscioff, 1911, p. 177)

3 For a New Anthropology

Building on the ideas of Marx, Engels had argued in *The Origin of the Family, Private Property and the State* that the liberation of women would become possible when they participated in production, and when the demands of their domestic labour were reduced to an insignificant level. August Bebel saw legislative injustices as the consequence of economic and anthropological features to be corrected at a social level. The working woman portrayed by Anna Kuliscioff perfectly aligns with the vision of women in the future society imagined by Bebel: "In the new society woman will be entirely independent, both socially and economically. She will not be subjected to even a trace of domination and exploitation but will be free and man's equal, and mistress of her own lot" (Bebel, 1879, ch. 28). This is clearly a view of emancipation that aims at a radical anthropological transformation, where labour becomes the basis for the emergence of free love, a concept explicitly theorised by Anna Kuliscioff in 1892 in *Critica Sociale*:

> When women can suffice in themselves and have no need to be maintained legitimately or illegitimately, then the form of relationships between man and woman will become a simple accessory: they can cohabit without marriage, they can unite with a simple notice to the local authorities, they can conjoin in eternal life if they wish, and all the better for them; and no one will think of establishing control over such intimate relationships that concern only the two freely contracting parties. (Kuliscioff, 1892b, p. 64)

In this context, it becomes evident that the battle waged for the protection of female labour is by no means an economic idea but rather the practical application of the ideas underlying the *Monopoly of Man*.[2] Kuliscioff aims to change the presence of women outside the home to transform their role within it, where conditions would be created for their effective liberation from male dominance by shattering the mechanism that combined male-productive work and female caregiving. The protection of female labour constitutes the first step towards legitimising the female subject in terms of gender equality. Legal protection should be exerted not only, and not predominantly, in the workplace, but rather in the domestic context: in industrial society these "spheres" were in no way separate but closely connected and overlapping (Bock, 2000).

Legal recognition removes female labour from the submerged state to which it had been relegated: a form of work entirely devoid of protections that is authorised and directed by the husband. Legislative protection would enable women to reconcile their roles as mothers with economic self-determination, allowing them to have children and continue working with or without the presence of a male figure. The safeguarding of motherhood means safeguarding a natural and existential role that women cannot and should not relinquish in order to be economically independent. On the other hand, such independence is a precondition vital to enabling women to decide how and when to become mothers (Fig. 2).

---

[2] As highlighted by Maurizio Degl'Innocenti in a reflection fundamental (Degl'Innocenti, 2017) to reconsidering the liberating nature of the centrality of labour and understand the relevance of Anna Kuliscioff's contribution to feminist theoretical constructs.

Fig. 2 Anna Kuliscioff and Filippo Turati together in a very rare photo

Only by separating traditional family roles, where the male is recognised as the sole productive subject and head of the family, and the female is destined to be a caregiver, can the actual liberation of women be achieved. In the *Monopoly of Man*, Kuliscioff writes:

> Hence, by cooperating on an equal footing with man in any aspect of social labor, women will make current laws impossible, laws that put them in a position of inferiority with regard to political rights – among minors and people incapacitated because of imbecility or madness – and assign them such an inferior status within the family with regard to civil rights. However, it is certainly the case that until woman becomes self-sufficient and stops depending on man in order to survive, the law considers her as a property of the husband – whereby the wife has to follow him wherever he goes – will remain fully in force. And should the legal articles in question, so offensive to woman's dignity, be abolished, this abolition will remain a dead letter owing to the economic dependence of the great majority of women. (Kuliscioff, 1890, ed. 2021, pp. 55–56)

It should be remembered that the law that Kulisciof referred to is a legacy of the Napoleonic code which, having been transposed line-by-line into the civil code of 1865 and then into that of 1942, was in force for much of the Italian twentieth century.[3]

The future that Kuliscioff prophesied is one that has clear echoes in contemporary life. Her thought helps us to understand the connections between patriarchal legal superstructures and anthropological structures built upon the division between productive work and caregiving. In particular, it helps us to grasp the relevance of cultural mechanisms that appear invisible to the law.

4 Marxist Disseminator

Before writing *The Monopoly of Man*, Kuliscioff had been developing an increasingly Marxist conception of socialism. When the essay *Socialism* by Napoleone Colajanni was published in 1884, Anna wrote to him:

> Don't you think that we should seek the cause of political and social transformations in the changes in modes of production and trade, that is, in the economy of a certain given era, rather than in ethics and abstract philosophy? I know that many, countless factors influence social evolution and perhaps I am too influenced by the German socialist school that considers the historical-economic process as the higher law of modern socialism. Don't you think that the economic condition of every era determines the entire social aspect from the standpoints of politics, justice, religion, philosophy, art, etc.? (Kuliscioff, 1978, p. 64)

If we were to adopt some of the criteria that inform the history of economic thought, we might assert that Anna Kuliscioff was involved in propagating Marx's economic thought, which she interpreted politically and socially in a reformist light. However, even staying within the history of Marxism, which is not entirely aligned with the history of economic thought, Kuliscioff's writings cannot be likened, for instance, to those of Rosa Luxemburg, who was viewed as a "theorist" and admired by those within and outside her intellectual tradition. Kuliscioff's writings include nothing as complex and substantial as *The Accumulation of Capital*, which in any case did not gain any theoretical and political prominence in Italy until after the Second World War.

Anna Kuliscioff's work of dissemination belongs to the period when the Italian socialist and anarchist movements were deeply influenced by the works of Karl Marx and Friedrich Engels, which were subjected to many different interpretations. It should be remembered that in the context of the division between the anarchists and "Marxists" in the First International, the most important exponent of Italian and international anarchism, Carlo Cafiero, still chose to write a *Compendium of Capital*, a work intended to popularise Marx's economic thought that was appreciated by Marx himself. Moreover, the final two decades of the nineteenth century in Italy were

[3] Article 133 of the Civil Code of 1865 is reproduced in the Civil Code of 1942 as Article 144, with changes to punctuation, under the title "potestà maritale" (marital authority): "The husband is the head of the family; the wife takes his civil status, takes his surname, and is obliged to accompany him wherever he deems it appropriate to establish his residence." This article was only rendered obsolete with Law No. 151 of 19 May 1975.

characterised by an intense passion for interpretation. This produced, for example, the analytical disputes between Achille Loria and Engels on Marx's theory of value, as well as the reflections of the philosopher Antonio Labriola, which were later revisited in Antonio Gramsci's *Prison Notebooks*. In the late nineteenth century, Italy also witnessed a spirited debate on so-called revisionism, which would give rise to the Italian neo-idealism of Benedetto Croce and Giovanni Gentile. Additionally, there were more political and political-science-oriented readings of Marx by such figures as Georges Sorel, Vilfredo Pareto and Benito Mussolini—all of whom were attracted (the third based on the readings of the first two) to the figure who Croce termed the "Machiavelli of the proletariat." This was a foundational moment for all Italian culture and has been meticulously analysed by Paolo Favilli in the volume *The History of Italian Marxism: From Its Origins to the Great War* (Favilli, 2018).

It is in this context that we should consider some of the characteristics that distinguished Kuliscioff's intellectual work. In the first instance, it is important to remember that *Critica Sociale* sought to support dialogue with liberal forces by remaining open to theoretical debates with anti-Marxist and anti-socialist formulations, such as that of Pareto, who indeed collaborated with the magazine, engaging in several celebrated disputes, including with Turati. This dialogue brings to light two fundamental characteristics of the reformist socialism of Turati and Kuliscioff.

On the one hand, reformism proved to be the main organised political force of any significance directed towards fighting openly and devotedly for the construction of a modern political democracy in the country, as Engels had in fact advised the Italian socialists to do. On the other hand, the magazine's two founders did not prove up to the challenge posed by the discussion on Marx's scientific work, which, as is well known, was enhanced by the sections (the so-called volumes II, III, and IV) of *Capital* published after Marx's death, first by Engels and later by Kautsky. Turati and Kuliscioff were unable, on a strictly theoretical level, to break down the barrier against Marx (Michelini, 1997) erected, especially in Italy, by both socialists (Loria) and anti-socialists (Pareto). However, it is also true that despite the considerable and authoritative theoretical opposition to his ideas,[4] Marx remained an indispensable reference point for both Kuliscioff and Turati.

Kuliscioff saw Marx, in particular in Volume I of *Capital*, as the historian and sociologist of the industrial revolution, and felt little attraction or interest in issues then deemed to be purely matters of economic theory, such as the theory of value or the laws of motion of capitalism. Indeed, she admitted to not being proficient in these subjects (Kuliscioff, 1893, pp. 75 ff.). Industrialisation and the rise of capitalism were, on the other hand, fundamental events that profoundly changed the human condition, specifically that of women. It is to this transformation that Kuliscioff paid attention, setting out an analysis of the situation of Italian female workers but, even

[4] The only author who was able to oppose them was the philosopher Antonio Labriola, who did not share the cultural and political openness to the liberal universe that Turati and Kuliscioff imparted to *Critica Sociale* and the party. When republishing *The Monopoly of Man* in the United States, Jamila Mascat recalled how the Italian philosopher had great disdain for the Milanese socialist group, with one obvious exception, given his somewhat sexist conclusion: "In Milan there is only one man, who on the contrary is a woman, Kuliscioff" (Mascat, 2021, p. 11; see Marx & Engels, 1964, p. 489).

before that, indicating that the chief task of the socialist movement was to study the economic and social reality of the country in order to transform it. The analysis of the Italian female working class, including its importance in agriculture, was indeed a prerequisite for proposals for the social reform of female labour, such as those regarding the limitation of the work of women and children and those designed to support maternity.

On the political level, Kuliscioff's position was clear: the emancipation of women was part of a more comprehensive emancipation, meaning it had to take place through the transformation of women into workers, subject to exploitation but in a new form that rendered them protagonists of a new phase of political struggle and social transformation. The point was not to escape the world of capitalist labour but to become a central figure within it, and Marx pointed out that the exploited had a heroic and revolutionary task, that of creating a new society. Such a society would be new above all because of its ability to put an end to the age-old subordination of women to men, irrespective, as we might say today, of the existing mode of production: "In all the ages of human development, woman's destiny has always been to be considered by man as his working tool," Kuliscioff wrote (1890, ed. 2021, p. 42). In order to break free from a condition of servitude and economic and moral subjugation, it was necessary to recognise the "great and fundamental truth of modern ethics," (Kuliscioff, 1890, ed. 2021, p. 49):

> labor alone, of whatever nature, divided and remunerated with equity, is the actual source of the enhancement of the human species. And, indeed, if every individual belonging to either sex, of the appropriate health and age, perceived the entire moral range of such an ideal and independently obtained their means of subsistence, participating in any way possible in the division of social labor, one of the greatest scourges of modern society would disappear, namely, parasitism – which is so rare among inferior animals of the same species and, unfortunately, so pervasive among the superior animals of the human species. (Kuliscioff, 1890, ed. 2021, p. 49)

It should be noted that Kuliscioff based her argument on the observation, which would be reinforced through study and direct involvement with the world of Italian labour (lectures, meetings, discussions, political activism), that the Italian factory proletariat was predominantly female, particularly in the regions that were more industrially developed:

> The statistics from 1892 already counted one million six hundred thousand women employed in Italy in large industries, over a million of whom were in the textile industry alone. In the province of Milan, one of the most industrialised, we have 67,561 men and 74,793 women in large industries; in the textile industry in the same province, compared to 60,677 women we count only 16,314 men. (Kuliscioff, 1898, p. 115)

It is important to bear in mind the level of exploitation of female labour to which she referred:

> If the male worker endures all the hardships in the world to make ends meet, the female worker is truly a martyr: after working for 12, 13, 14 hours for a meagre salary, returning home, she must think about preparing food, taking care of the children, and mending the few miserable rags. And how many Saturday nights do the women see dawn without going to bed? And how lucky she is if she has a decent husband. But if he is brutal, violent, and

> overbearing, who defends her? The legal code, perhaps. Ah, yes! In the legal code, you will find numerous articles for the defence of movable and immovable property, and woe to those who touch them! The bourgeois is too jealous of his property and has an arsenal of laws to defend it. The violence suffered by women is much less important than the slightest attacks on property. (Kuliscioff, 1892a, ed. 2015, p. 73).

The inhumane exploitation in the workplace typical of Italy at that time is thus matched by the exploitation of women by men, which, even when perpetrated by working men, was effectively bourgeois in anthropological and legal terms.

Kuliscioff observed that it was mainly small businesses that were responsible for the most pronounced forms of exploitation, and the labour legislation she sought to promote explicitly encouraged the creation of larger companies: a theme, as is known, that still holds sway in contemporary Italian economic and political debate. The virtues of the Italy of the Marshallian "industrial districts" have in fact been the subject of meticulous evaluation, including by those who have praised their economic and social merits, because they may in fact have been based more on the hyper-exploitation of labour than on technological innovation. Even so, unlike Anna Maria Mozzoni, Kuliscioff maintained that the protection of female labour would not result in a fall in female employment, as happened in England (Kuliscioff, 1898).

5 Reformist Action in the Social Field

The popular uprisings in Milan in 1898, the declaration of a state of siege by the Italian government, and the arrest of many socialist leaders, including Turati and Kuliscioff (initially sentenced to twelve and two years in prison, respectively), did not break their determination or that of the Italian socialist movement. The latter still struggled to find unity of purpose, entangled as it was in its contradictions and the emerging dialectic between "reformists" and "revolutionaries," which developed while one side of Italian liberalism looked for ways to involve the socialists in government, albeit much more timidly than elsewhere. Despite Kuliscioff's deep commitment, especially during Turati's imprisonment, to reorganising the party between 1900 and 1902, her concern continued to be focused on the condition of female workers. This is evidenced, among other things, by the text signed by Kuliscioff-Turati, *Pel lavoro delle donne e dei minorenni* (For the work of women and minors), published in *Critica sociale* on 16 June 1901 (Kuliscioff & Turati, 1901). On the other hand, the political development of theoretical reflection regarding the central role of labour was made clear by the inclusion of the female-labour question in the socialist party's programme and in the subsequent presentation of a draft law clearly inspired by Kuliscioff and endorsed by the entire socialist parliamentary party. This became the subject of extensive political campaigning by socialists around the country, even in sectors excluded from its provisions, such as agricultural labour. Turati would declare in the Chamber of Deputies:

those between eight and eleven hours, and two hours for days exceeding eleven hours. Rest periods would be partly negotiable with the workers, but in any case women and children could not work more than six hours without a break. Women and children were entitled to one day off per week.

Nevertheless, socialist pressure had forced the liberal political class into action by passing a law which, while containing modest provisions, nevertheless marked a genuine recognition of the female subject: a turning point in Italy's social and civil progress. The maternity fund was eventually established with the law of 17 July 1910,[5] thanks to the parliamentary initiative of the reformist socialist Angiolo Cabrini, and this would be designed to make the law on women's labour fully effective: the fund provided every female worker with a subsidy of thirty lire on the occasion of childbirth or involuntary abortion.

6 The Struggle for Universal Suffrage

One of the major themes of the citizenship of women is that of the right to vote, and the fight for women's suffrage. The socialist programme adopted at the 1900 congress in Rome envisaged "legal and political equality of the two sexes," and at the top of the list of "political transformations" required to achieve a "democratic state" is "universal simple, direct, and secret suffrage for all adults of both sexes" (Cortesi, 1969, pp. 132–134).

For Anna Kuliscioff, the right to vote had to be a consequence of the integration of women into the workforce, and more of an endpoint than a starting point. Kuliscioff was wary of great leaps forward, fully understanding the strength and limitations of bourgeois feminism, as we have already seen. The vote could therefore not be limited to bourgeois ladies, but had to constitute "the defence of labour, and labour has no gender" (Kuliscioff, 1910b, p. 146). In the appeal directed at her female "comrades, workers, and mothers," the right to vote thus became the means to combat exploitation: "this limitless exploitation is not rooted only in the insufficiency of our resistance organisations. It arises even more from the fact that we are outside the law and the nation. We are the pariahs, the foreigners, the perpetual minors; equated by law with idiots, imbeciles, and those condemned for the most shameful crimes" (Kuliscioff, 1913, p. 1). The vote therefore became the political representation of the moral self-sufficiency connected to economic self-sufficiency: the closing of the circle of female citizenship.

Within the socialist party, Anna Kuliscioff played a decisive role in supporting a political campaign capable of influencing the struggle for suffrage and ensuring that attention to the problem of women's rights remained high whenever the party's focus might have wavered.

---

[5] On the law, and on the socialists' collaboration in the social legislation of the period, see see Minesso (2016).

The socialist party did not prioritise the battle for women's suffrage, and in fact took advantage of the government's lack of progress to set the issue to one side, sensing the potential danger of engaging with the female masses in the South, who had scarcely been exposed to any form of socialist discourse. However, the party could not turn its back on its commitment to gender equality affirmed in the Rome congress of 1900 and reiterated in the Florence congress of 1908, which made explicit reference to women's political suffrage. The bill proposed by the republican Roberto Mirabelli, debated in 1905, was endorsed by the socialists Andrea Costa and Camillo Prampolini. Theirs was not a full and unconditional endorsement, but rather a desire to detach a long-term plan from immediate tactics. Despite this context, Anna Kuliscioff was not cowed by the party, and translated her dissatisfaction and disappointment into political action. The response to the aforementioned tactical manoeuvres was a level of political organisation by women in years that proved decisive years for international feminism. The right to vote was granted in the Australian Commonwealth in 1902, in Finland in 1906, and in Norway in 1901 for municipal elections and in 1907 for parliamentary elections. In the same year, English women were granted voting rights in municipal elections. The right to vote was therefore a topic for debate all around the world. In this context, a family dispute arose between Filippo Turati and Anna Kuliscioff. While Turati was wary of the political risks inherent in expanding suffrage, Anna responded sharply, reminding the party of the historical significance of women's suffrage for the socialist movement at the international level, and she listed unsparingly and in great detail the resolutions passed by the socialist movement across Europe (Kuliscioff, 1910b).

However, the year 1912 represented a missed opportunity for women's suffrage: the socialist proposal, signed by Turati and Claudio Treves, to extend voting rights to women on the basis of Article 24 of the Albertine Statute, which established the equality of all subjects without making any reference to gender, was rejected. What in hindsight appears to have been a failure to rise to the historical moment, however, was seen at the time as merely another political step towards an achievable goal. Claudio Treves's 1913 draft bill for women's suffrage at the local level would not reach the debate phase due to changes in the parliamentary agenda caused by the war, just as the target seemed within reach (Passaniti, 2015, p. 173). The issue was raised in increasingly emphatic terms at the socialist congress in Ancona in 1914 (Casalini, 1978, p. 284).

In short, the second phase of Kuliscioff's political journey in Italy, the one which has attracted the most criticism due to a perception that she yielded to the party, brought women (and the socialist party) one step away from achieving female suffrage. This was not achieved due to the outbreak of world war, which reset all the previous work and restarted and aplified contradictions still in search of an answer. The result was a grossly contemptuous situation when, after winning approval from parliament in 1919, with the socialists voting in favour, in 1925 the fascists granted women the right to vote in local elections, one year before revoking this right from both men and women.

7 "La Difesa Delle Lavoratrici"

In 1912, Kuliscioff was one of the participants and the main organiser of the first congress of female members of the Socialist Party, with a platform that included, in particular, a series of demands relating to social legislation: maternity benefits for women farmers; protections for home-based work, including a request for a minimum wage; and the extension of safeguards for female industrial workers. More importantly, January 1912 saw the birth of the newspaper *La Difesa delle Lavoratrici* (The Defence of Female Workers), the first official organ of Italian socialist women and "a genuine political forum for the new generation of socialist women" (Pironti, 2010, p. 166).

La Difesa delle Lavoratrici was headed by Anna Kuliscioff for the first two years, after which she had to limit herself to the no less valuable role of advisor, for health reasons. As Fiorenza Taricone recalls, the newspaper gave particular prominence to the analysis "of the living conditions and problems of women workers," in industry, agriculture, domestic work, and also in new clerical and school occupations. The newspaper, Taricone has also pointed out, was the forum for the most intense arguments within the Italian feminist world: on one side were the socialists, and on the other the so-called "bourgeois feminists," accused by the former of wanting to restrict the right to vote to certain categories of women. Among the most outspoken socialist women was Giselda Brebbia, "who reproaches bourgeois feminists for a basic lack of political commitment, adding that if they were forced to make a party choice, it would undoubtedly be conservative" (Taricone, 2020, p. 119; Brebbia, 1912).

On behalf of the National Committee of Socialist Women, an appeal was published in the newspaper for women to intensify their electoral campaigning in the run-up to the elections, even though they were excluded from voting. This was because only the Italian Socialist Party (PSI) demanded that they be given the right to vote, and "the struggle alongside the male proletariat is in this sense justified" (Taricone, 2021).

Taricone has written:

> The argument between socialist feminism and bourgeois feminism reaches its climax during the Pro-Suffrage Conference of 1913. The Socialist Women's Group in Milan calls for Linda Malnati and Carlotta Clerici, who have strong connections with various women's associations in which an interclass alliance prevails, to distance themselves from bourgeois-oriented movements. Both comply, demonstrating their selflessness. (Taricone, 2021, p. 29)

We have seen how and when the issue of universal women's suffrage was resolved:

> After the parliamentary session concluded, Anna did not hide her resentment over the defeat when refuting the false justifications contained in the Giolitti bill. The law cited the following reasons for excluding women from universal suffrage: illiteracy, the presumed lesser needs of women, and finally, the fact that men serve in the military. (Pillitteri, 1986, p. 189)

Despite its title, the magazine was not a trade union bulletin but an authentic programme for the liberation of women from the social and economic systems that determined their unacceptable subjugation. In the first issue of *La Difesa delle Lavoratrici*, Argentina Altobelli, the historic leader of the farmers' union Federterra, presented a detailed political programme aimed at protecting women in the home and at work, aspects of life destined to intertwine in the "family redemption that must transform the housewife into a woman, the female into a companion, the slave into the citizen who will better understand and love her man, and better educate the children for the new society that we socialists are working for every day" (Altobelli, 1912). Another author wrote: "If working women want to prepare themselves and prepare a future of joy and freedom for their daughters (the workers of tomorrow) along the paths of redeemed and respected labour, they must organise in leagues, and strengthen the class party: the socialism that defends them, that fights for their rights" (Zanetta, 1913).

The home-work directive, moreover, had been the fundamental axis for understanding the meaning of Anna Kuliscioff's reflection. A meaning that was captured with exemplary clarity by Pietro Costa:

> For Anna Kuliscioff the family is once again the place that establishes and consecrates female dependence and subjugation: it is in the family that the woman identifies with her role as a compliant handmaid to an omnipresent man; it is in the family and for the family that that much praised female altruism, incapable of overcoming the private sphere and responsible for conformity and indifference, develops. The 'real' (and ideal) element destined to cut through the tangle that ties a woman to the family and hinders her autonomy and independence is work. (Costa, 2001, pp. 390–391)

Following in the footsteps of Kuliscioff, Margherita Sarfatti—the future fascist and biographer of Benito Mussolini—published in *La difesa delle lavoratrici* her theory of the "sexual responsibility of the male," the consequence of which was the breakup of the family legitimacy that would legitimise every emotional aggregation around the procreative fact, the true essence of family legal discourse:

> ~~The future […] lies in the union of a man and a woman, which the state acknowledges and in which it intervenes only with regard to the wellbeing and protection of innocent and blameless third parties, the children, who must always and in every case be protected from the weakness, carelessness, or culpable thoughtlessness that too often taints the parents, especially the fathers, in their selfish treatment of these innocents.~~ (Sarfatti Grassini, 1914)

La Difesa delle Lavoratrici followed the different fronts of family law reform, consistently supporting progressive demands on the tactical level, and always looking ahead to the future of free emotional unions (Brebbia, 1914) while downplaying the significance of bourgeois achievements. This was the case in 1919 with the abolition of the requirement for women to gain marital authorisation to enter certain professions, a measure which established women's legal competence and opened some professional doors, such as the legal profession, but kept many others closed, including access to the judiciary (Bartoloni, 2021). This was a law that socialist women considered to be something that belonged to the bourgeois world.

8 The Great War and Fascism

The cause of reformism suffered a setback with the Great War. Hatred of German and Austrian imperialism was for Kuliscioff stronger than any neutrality and pacifism, and she therefore followed and sided with the "democratic" phase of the Russian revolt with great conviction and emotion, while remaining strongly critical of the Bolsheviks. The separation between the two currents within the socialist party (revolutionaries and reformists) became even more pronounced, and Turati and Kuliscioff both believed that the October Revolution would bring back the pre-Marxist conditions of utopian socialism. In the final years of her life, Kuliscioff's polemical verve and fighting spirit were not diminished, especially in her writings, although she did withdraw somewhat from her involvement in immediate political life and from public exposure, partly for health reasons. She was naturally also opposed to fascism, but, like Turati, did not immediately grasp its implications. At the beginning of 1923 fear and concern pervaded their correspondence, but they continued to hope that regular parliamentary work could resume following a normalisation of fascism (Addis Saba, 1993, pp. 394–395). Even so, they were already describing it as a "regime," and showing themselves determined to counter the fascists blow by blow in Parliament, where the socialists still had a strong presence. The deputy Giacomo Matteotti, as history records, would pay the price of this approach when he was killed by the fascists.

These were the months when Kuliscioff, aware of the difficulty, and perhaps even the impossibility of an agreement between the left factions, still hoped to collaborate with the People's Party, but even in that party the pro-fascists prevailed over the anti-fascists. In mid-May 1923, the IX Congress of the International Alliance for Women's Suffrage was held in Rome, but she did not participate, while Turati conveyed the greetings of the socialists. Kuliscioff, always somewhat sceptical of "bourgeois feminists," still saw a contradiction in the need for herself and all socialist activists to go through their male comrades or party colleagues to give a public and "represented" (in the institutions) voice to their words. Moreover, Benito Mussolini received more than one round of applause at that congress, promising administrative voting rights to a broad category of women.

The relationship between Kuliscioff and Turati in this period was intense. Although they looked with equal concern at fascism, their analyses were in part divergent, not least with regard to how best to respond on the political front. A few months before her death in Milan on 29 December 1925, Kuliscioff had written to Turati that they could at least find comfort in the knowledge that they had been "present in their time" and had done everything in their power to oppose fascism (Casalini, 1978, p. 288). Her funeral, as noted, was "opposed by the fascists and watched over by an incredible deployment of police" but also "attended by all the socialists and democrats in the city, and by many people who came from afar" (Boggio & Cerliani, 1977, p. 112).

9 Labour Economics

Kuliscioff was an integral part of that historical process wherein the worker, both male and female, defines their own autonomous political consciousness, a distinct economic and social horizon of their own, which is to say their own cultural autonomy and original worldview. As we have seen, she advanced this cause on multiple fronts, in the first place by developing a close intellectual relationship with two key figures in Italian socialism, Andrea Costa and, more so, Filippo Turati. The emotional bond, which became a political manifesto in itself by rejecting the norms of bourgeois family life of the period, became an essential part of her political development. The relational space was one of the few in which women of that era could actively engage, since a political role in the institutions of liberal Italy was largely denied them. The extensive correspondence between Kuliscioff and Turati fills nine volumes (Turati & Kuliscioff, 1977), serving as a mine of political reflections on every salient aspect of Italian political life. Their correspondence is a lively and often anguished testimony to the attempt, sometimes thwarted by the political fatuity imposed on the role of women, to direct socialist policy and, thereby, the political life of the country. Their reflections often reveal a remarkable realism that drove socialism to become deeply rooted in society and political reforms, to embrace parliamentarism, to formulate proposals for social reform, and to acknowledge that one cause of the crisis in the Socialist Party was its remoteness from the world of female labour. Perhaps it might have been realistic for the party to adopt a more nationalist position at the start of the First World War, as was the opinion of Antonio Gramsci, who remained isolated in the PSI for about a year. Realism also meant foreseeing that fascism, having evolved into a military organisation, would soon seize power, and that Mussolini would become the country's despot.

Kuliscioff's second great contribution was to the birth and organisation of the Socialist Party, one of the essential instruments of political action in her era, and within which she successfully carved out a space for women. The third front on which Kuliscioff played a decisive role was the establishment and leadership of the most significant publications in Italian socialism. First and foremost was *Critica Sociale*, the result of collaborative work with Turati, and then came *La Difesa della Lavoratrice*, which, despite the unfavourable political and social climate in Italy, strove to affirm the autonomy of socialist feminine thought. The fourth front of Kuliscioff's work was her role as a lecturer and writer who studied the reality of Italian labour and of women's work in particular. The purpose of her studies was quite clearly to improve working conditions, not only for women but also for the entire labour force. Study and social reforms constituted the fifth front on which the Russian exile played a key role.

Considering the diverse and demanding impulses behind Kuliscioff's political activities, it might seem somewhat restrictive to place her contribution within the conventional parameters of the history of economic thought that might lead to her being labelled a "disseminator". Even looking solely at the number of pages of volume I of *Capital* that Marx dedicated to historical and sociological analysis makes it clear that this constituted a fundamental part of his frame of reference. What Marx referred to in those pages as "the holocaust of the English working class" is certainly no mere peripheral detail within the reasoning encapsulated in his seminal work. In this sense, then, it is both possible and legitimate to interpret Kuliscioff's reflection as a proposition of labour economics: in other words, she was involved in the construction of the "political economy of labour" that on the political, social and economic levels Marx wished to establish in opposition to "bourgeois" political economy. Some time ago an interesting anthology, *Scrittori di economia* (Economic Writers), was opportunely published in Italy (Bocciarelli & Ciocca, 1994), and this emphasised that those engaged in economics could not be confined to the realm of that economic science which, from time to time, proclaimed itself as the sole custodian of truth. Economics is not a subject written about only by those who at various times are considered or, most importantly, consider themselves to be economists. Unfortunately, Kuliscioff is conspicuously absent from the anthology, as are contributions from any other female economic writers: a sign that a certain tradition carries on.

In any case, if we consider the writings of some of the most renowned economists of Kuliscioff's era in Italy, such as Vilfredo Pareto, Maffeo Pantaleoni and Enrico Barone, we would struggle to find in their pages of "pure economics"—that is, their self-proclaimed theory—even a single reference to the economic reality that intrigued Kuliscioff.[6] The three illustrious economists effectively distanced themselves from the Italian socialist movement and began to align themselves with reactionary political currents, of which they became eminent spokesmen. This shift occurred exactly when Italian socialism, and reformism, started to demonstrate their ability to influence the country's political life, promoting the first social reforms, endorsed by Kuliscioff, with the support of a bourgeoisie that Pareto vehemently criticised for failing to resist the impetus of these new socialist elites. Political democracy and social democracy, the embryonic forms of the welfare state based on wealth redistribution, in Italy had an indispensable cornerstone in socialism. Similarly, the socialist movement played an essential part in the struggles for fundamental political freedoms, as the aforementioned "pure" economists acknowledged before withdrawing their support for the liberalism that was disposed, albeit with numerous reservations, to open the path to progress.

It should also be noted that just at the point when the Italian economic culture was rapidly coming to the conclusion that a definitive showdown with the socialist movement was necessary—well before, it is important to say, the Russian Revolution exacerbated social and political conflict in Italy—the correspondence between Kuliscioff and Turati bore witness to exasperated divisions and personal issues within the Italian socialist movement.

However, the dialogue between them also bore witness to a loss of analytical momentum that led Kuliscioff not only to grapple with the contradictions within the socialist movement but also to try to influence a parliamentary debate that was firmly

---

[6] It was observed that the magazine in which the three cited authors wrote, i.e. *Giornale degli economisti*, manifests a clear closure towards the legislation on the protection of women's work (Finoia, 1991). The author does not mention Anna Kuliscioff.

in the hands of the liberal ruling classes and extremely tentative and cumbersome when tackling social issues. As we have seen, reformism in particular suffered a reverse of fortune with the Great War, which authors like Barone and Pantaleoni, key voices in the nascent Italian nationalist movement, extolled both in its own terms and as a means of restraining any form of political and social democracy. The electoral and social explosion experienced by the Socialist Party in the post-war period found the party essentially unprepared and unable to face the challenges facing it, as well as exhausted by new divisions, primarily the one caused by the October Revolution.

But this was not the only occasion in which the Italian labour movement was called upon to perform that historical function which liberal culture and society, and the forces of democracy—those defined as completely bourgeois by Marxism—had fulfilled or would fulfil in other countries. In a letter of May 1923, while presenting her usual press review to Turati,[7] Kuliscioff emphasised how a well-known Italian journalist and writer, Mario Missiroli, opined that "for the past twenty years, there has been but one true liberal in Italy, and that is Filippo Turati" (Turati & Kuliscioff, 1977, vol. VI, p. 25): in the Italy of that era, using the term democracy was extremely problematic. Moreover, in the aftermath of the war, the Italian bourgeoisie found its guardian angel in the national fascist Pantaleoni, and in Mussolini the political instrument for the creation of a new, freedom-crushing political regime where socialism, having completely lost its political autonomy under the blows of the *squadristi* and the fascist laws, would be kept on an altogether tighter rein (Michelini, 2020).

Given the importance of Pantaleoni's role in the rise to power of national fascism, it is worth recalling his reflection on the topic of feminism, not least because it might be interpreted as the inverse of that of Anna Kuliscioff, being an explicit justification of the "monopoly of man." While acknowledging that the division of labour between men and women had been and remained at the mercy of the whims of history and customs, he nonetheless identified a genuine "monopoly" of each gender, "scientific inventiveness" being the one belonging to men:

> History shows us that scientific and technical inventiveness, as well as originality of behaviour, are qualities inherent only in the male mindset, to the extent that they are even repugnant to that of women. Similarly, the female mindset recoils from hypothetical reasoning: it is inclined to the observation of reality and to analysis. This observant and analytical spirit is notably manifested in the ability to decipher psychological nebula, which materialises in the form of rapid and accurate intuitions. Scientific advancements have never yet been credited to women, as history attests, despite their greater involvement in arts compared to men (Pantaleoni, 1908, p. XVIII).

And what of female suffrage? Even "while it may be doubtful that women will ever make great and lasting conquests in the political arena," perhaps the day would come when "certain types of political vote may also be granted to women," and one might imagine that these "types" concern the area typically occupied by women, namely that instinct of motherhood, which, according to the economist's reasoning,

[7] This was another thing that Kuliscioff did: she read an astonishing amount of newspapers and magazines to maintain an understanding of the political situation of the country.

distinguishes the female monopoly.[8] However, there is no doubt that "political rights are pure and simple *indicators* of the existence of *forces*," and force, as Pantaleoni's reasoning implies, is the monopoly of men (Pantaleoni, 1908, p. XXI). To put it in Sorel's words, Pantaleoni was one of the first to transform the "violence" of the fascist squads into the "strength" of the fascist state.

10 Conclusions

When considering the various issues addressed by Kuliscioff, one cannot help but be struck by their astonishing relevance today. One of the many reprints of *The Monopoly of Man* features a concise yet significant introduction by Rita Levi Montalcini, who states that Kuliscioff proposes a:

> passionate denunciation of the millennia-old subjugation and exploitation of women by men, regardless of the country or caste to which they belonged, but especially those of the lower ranks. The possibility of making decisions has been denied to them, as has always been too well known, and even if today they may enjoy civil rights equal to those of men, they do not participate in these decisions even in the most advanced societies, except to an extent irrelevant to the governance of them. (Levi Montalcini, 1995, p. 1).

Kuliscioff's analysis "remains painfully valid today, as it did then, especially concerning women in underdeveloped countries, where approximately three-quarters of the human population lives" (Levi Montalcini, 1995, p. 1). We might add that many decades of "bourgeois labour economics" have only slowly changed, and only in a few areas and in the period that marks the life of the so-called First Republic (approximately 1945–1990), the *relative* positions of the social classes and genders vying for power. Rita Levi Montalcini's words warn us that the disappearance of the socialist movement in Italy in the early 1990s, following the fall of the Berlin Wall, has in no way given a boost to the realisation of gender equality, nor has it given rise to an autonomous and robust feminist political movement. As stated in the third article of the Italian Constitution,[9] which owes a great deal to the Italian socialist culture of which Turati and Kuliscioff were the utmost expression, social democracy is, for Italy, the cornerstone and fundamental driving force of political democracy.

---

[8] Pantaleoni took part in the political enterprise of Fiume, led by Gabriele D'Annunzio. The so-called "Carnaro Charter", i.e. a constitutional charter, provided for women's suffrage (Taricone, 2020, p. 55). The economist criticised this for its socialist connotations but did not intervene on the point.

[9] "All citizens shall have equal social dignity and shall be equal before the law, without distinction of gender, race, language, religion, political opinion, personal and social conditions. It shall be the duty of the Republic to remove those obstacles of an economic or social nature which constrain the freedom and equality of citizens, thereby impeding the full development of the human person and the effective participation of all workers in the political, economic and social organisation of the country".

References

Addis Saba, M. (1993). *Anna Kuliscioff. Vita privata e passione politica.* Mondadori.

Altobelli, A. (1912). Difendiamo la donna nella casa e nel lavoro. *La Difesa delle Lavoratrici*, 7 January, p. 2.

Bartoloni, S. (Ed.). (2021). *Cittadinanze incompiute, La parabola dell'autorizzazione maritale.* Viella.

Bebel, A. (1879). *Die Frau und der Sozialismus*, Zürich-Hottengen: Verlags Buchhandlung. Engl. transl. *Woman and Socialism.* Socialist Literature Company.

Bocciarelli, R., & Ciocca, P. (Eds.). (1994). *Scrittori di economia.* Laterza.

Bock, G. (2000). *Frauen in der europäischen Geschichte.* München: Verlag C. H. Beck. Engl. transl. *Women in European history.* Blackwell, 2002.

Boggio, M., & Cerliani, A. (1977). *Anna Kuliscioff. Con gli scritti di Anna Kuliscioff "Sulla condizione della donna".* Marsilio.

Brebbia, G. (1912). *Le signore suffragiste.* In La Difesa delle Lavoratrici, 4 febbraio 1912, p. 1.

Brebbia, G. (1914). La precedenza del matrimonio civile. *La Difesa delle Lavoratrici*, 15 February, p. 1.

Candeloro, G. (1994). *Storia dell'Italia moderna, Lo sviluppo del capitalismo e del movimento operaio* (Vol. VI). Feltrinelli.

Casalini, M. (1978). *La signora del socialismo italiano. Vita di Anna Kuliscioff.* Editori Riuniti.

Cortesi, L. (1969). *Il socialismo italiano tra riforme e rivoluzione. Dibattiti congressuali del Psi 1892–1921.* Laterza.

Costa, P. (2001). *Civitas. Storia della cittadinanza in Europa, La civiltà liberale* (Vol. III). Laterza.

Degl'Innocenti, M. (2017). *L'età delle donne. Saggio su Anna Kuliscioff.* Lacaita.

Degl'Innocenti M., Taricone F., Passaniti P., & Tomassini, L. (2015). *Anna Kuliscioff. Il socialismo e la cittadinanza della donna.* Agra.

Favilli, P. (2018). *The history of Italian Marxism: From its origins to the great war.* Haymarket Books.

Finoia, M. (1991). La questione femminile attraverso il *Giornale degli economisti*: 1875–1935. *Giornale Degli Economisti e Annali Di Economia, 50*(9/12), 525–538.

Kuliscioff, A. (1890). *Il monopolio dell'uomo.* Milan: Galli. Engl. transl. *The monopoly of man.* MIT Press, 2021.

Kuliscioff, A. (1892a). Proletariato femminile. In *Scritti*, Fondazione Anna Kuliscioff, 2015, pp. 68–74.

Kuliscioff, A. (1892b). Il sentimentalismo nella questione femminile. In *Scritti.* Fondazione Anna Kuliscioff, 2015, pp. 62–65.

Kuliscioff, A. (1893). Appunti per una conferenza su *Il Capitale.* In *Scritti.* Fondazione Anna Kuliscioff, 2015, pp. 75–81.

Kuliscioff, A. (1897). Il femminismo. In *Scritti.* Fondazione Anna Kuliscioff, 2015, pp. 103–107.

Kuliscioff, A. (1898). In nome della libertà della donna. In *Scritti.* Fondazione Anna Kuliscioff, 2015, pp. 116–119.

Kuliscioff, A. (1910a). Proletariato femminile e Partito socialista. In *Scritti.* Fondazione Anna Kuliscioff, 2015, pp. 161–176.

Kuliscioff, A. (1910b). Suffragio universale? In *Scritti.* Fondazione Anna Kuliscioff, 2015, pp. 144–146.

Kuliscioff, A. (1911). Femminismo e socialismo. In *Scritti.* Fondazione Anna Kuliscioff, 2015, p. 177.

Kuliscioff, A. (anonymous). (1913). Alle donne del lavoro. *La Difesa delle lavoratrici*, 19 October, p. 1.

Kuliscioff, A. (1978). *Immagini, scritti testimonianze*, Edited by F. Damiani and F. Rodriguez. Feltrinelli.

Kuliscioff, A., & Turati, F. (1901, June 16). Pel lavoro delle donne e dei minorenni: un buon sintomo. *Critica sociale, XI*(12), pp. 177–179.

Levi Montalcini, R. (1995). Anna Kuliscioff, un secolo dopo. In A. Kuliscioff (Ed.), *Il Monopolio dell'Uomo* (pp. 1–2). Zephiro.

Marx, K., & Engels, F. (1964). *Corrispondenza con italiani 1848–1895*, edited by G. Del Bo. Feltrinelli.

Mascat, J. M. H. (2021). Introduction: Portait of a socialist lady. In A. Kuliscioff (Ed.), *The monopoly of man* (pp. XI–XXV). MIT Press.

Michelini, L. (1997). La modernizzazione secondo Pantaleoni e Pareto (1887–1905). *Il pensiero economico italiano, 2*, 81–118.

Michelini, L. (2020). *Il nazionalismo economico italiano*. Carocci.

Minesso, M. (2016). *Madri figli welfare. Istituzioni e politiche dall'Italia liberale ai nostri giorni*. Il Mulino.

Pantaleoni, M. (1908). Della divisione del lavoro in attribuzioni maschili e femminili. In Maria Ponti Pasolini (Eds.), *Per la formazione di una coltura sociale e civile* (pp. V–XXII). Forzani.

Passaniti, P. (2015). Anna Kuliscioff e i diritti di cittadinanza delle donne. In Degl'Innocenti et al. (Eds.), *Anna Kuliscioff. Il socialismo e la cittadinanza della donna* (pp. 25–46). Agra.

Pieroni Bortolotti, F. (1978). Prefazione. In A. Kuliscioff (Ed.), *Immagini, scritti testimonianze* (pp. 1–13), edited by F. Damiani and F. Rodriguez. Feltrinelli.

Pillitteri, P. (1986). *Anna Kuliscioff. Una biografia politica*. Marsilio.

Pironti, T. (2010). *Femminismo ed educazione in età giolittiana. Conflitti e sfide della modernità*. ETS.

Sarfatti Grassini, M. (1914). Le nuove leggi sull'ordinamento della famiglia. *La Difesa delle Lavoratrici*, 8 March, p. 1.

Taricone, F. (1992). Cronologia per una storia sociale femminile: Dall'unità al Fascismo. *Il Politico, 57*(2(162)), 341–364.

Taricone, F. (2020). *Politica e cittadinanza. Donne socialiste fra Ottocento e Novecento*. FrancoAngeli.

Taricone, F. (2021). La Difesa delle Lavoratrici: Socialiste a confronto. *Laboratoire italien. Politique et societé, 26*. https://journals.openedition.org/laboratoireitalien/6920

Turati, F. (1901). Come regolare il lavoro delle donne e dei fanciulli, discorso tenuto nella tornata del 21 maggio 1901. In F. Turati (Ed.), *Discorsi parlamentari* (Vol. I, pp. 33–56). Camera dei deputati, 1950.

Turati, F. (1950). *Discorsi parlamentari* (Vol. I). Camera dei deputati.

Turati, F., & Kuliscioff, A. (1977). *Carteggio*, 6 vols., Einaudi.

Zanetta, A. (1913). Il lavoro martirio ed emancipazione della donna lavoratrice. *La Difesa delle Lavoratrici*, 7 December, p. 1.

Margherita Grassini Sarfatti, the Economic Thought of the Jewish Woman Who Popularized Fascism

Francesco Poggi

1 Introduction

The twentieth century ideally began with the death of Nietzsche (25 August 1900). The German philosopher's *God is Dead* (1882) encapsulated and synthesized an era which was exceptional, and unrepeatable for the European continent, with a marked revolutionary and avant-garde character. Until the outbreak of the First World War, dozens of cultural and social movements arose. Meanwhile, the pictorial, literary, and musical avant-gardes published their thematic manifestos, from Abstractionism (1907) to Futurism (1909), from Metaphysics (1911) to Expressionism (1912), from Vorticism (1913) to Dadaism (1916) and Cubism, to name but a few. The same period also saw the articulation of new philosophical and social movements with a strong non-conformist impact. From Sorel's revolutionary syndicalism to the strong roots of socialist movements across the continent, from anarchist movements to feminist movements, from the new sociological proposals to the birth of innovative editorial proposals. The second industrial revolution was underway with its main corollaries, such as mass production, urbanization, the development of large cities, and the widespread diffusion of the social question, which led to the birth of trade unions, both socialist and Catholic, while the new productive and financial bourgeoisie, however elitist, was replacing the old aristocratic class, by then in free fall. The process of the formation of modern nation-states was being completed, with the territorial definition of Germany and Italy as the last of the great European areas. This progressive settlement led to two major consequences, fundamental for understanding the events of the new century: the end of the great universal empires (Habsburg, Russian, Turkish-Ottoman), and the progressive affirmation of nationalism and protectionism in the economy, in tandem with the colonial dream, seen as economic hegemony, demographic control, and military power.

F. Poggi (✉)
Pisa University, Pisa, Italy
e-mail: francesco.poggi@ec.unipi.it

M. Mosca (ed.), *Women at Work in Italy (1750–1950)*, Springer Studies in the History of Economic Thought, https://doi.org/10.1007/978-3-031-64281-4_12

Fig. 1 Margherita Grassini Sarfatti

Margherita Grassini, born in 1880, lived in this extraordinary atmosphere from a very young age. Many of the future protagonists of international politics and culture were her contemporaries. The year 1883, for example, is a symbolic crossroads of the change of generation: in that year, Marx died, and Mussolini, Keynes, and Schumpeter were born. In the present work, we will use secondary literature to reconstruct the period of her education and the cultural environment in which she developed her personality and her activities as journalist, art historian, event organizer, and artistic group leader. The original contribution of this work concerns the figure of Margherita Grassini, later Sarfatti, from the point of view of the history of economic thought, on which there is a gap in the literature. Our sources are her writings, articles, essays, and volumes as well as archival material (Fig. 1).

2 Education and the Spirit of the Times: The Artistic and Social Avant-Gardes

The first twenty years of Margherita Sarfatti's life were spent in Venice, in the circles of the Jewish upper middle class, in a conservative family, with her mother (Levi) a cousin of the father of the writer Natalia Ginsburg. This first period was characterized by the development in Margherita of the attraction for art history, accompanied by an early business sense.[1] In her teenage years she had no less than three tutors, Pietro Orsi, Pompeo Molmenti, and Antonio Fradelletto (Urso, 1994), all of whom were involved in both academia and politics. The first left her with a decisive lesson, which she always tried to keep to, namely that social and intellectual progress is the mirror

[1] On the first part of Margherita Sarfatti's life, it is possible to consult the archives and papers indicated at the end of this chapter. As for literature on the same period, see Barisoni (2018), Basilico Pisaturo (1990), Bini (2009), Cannistraro and Sullivan (1993), De Grazia (1993), Ferrario (2015), Festorazzi (2010), Marzorati (1990), Urso (1994), Wieland (2006) and Zapponi (1996).

of a nation, on a par with politics. The third, the creator of the Venice Biennale, made her breathe in the emotions of art and its protagonists from the very beginning. In a profoundly male-dominated culture, she showed herself, still in her teens, determined not to follow the traditional pattern. Thus, she began her first journalistic experience as an art critic at the 4th Venice Biennale. In 1898, she married the lawyer Cesare Sarfatti, also from a Jewish family, a militant socialist, who brought her closer to socialism. They then moved to Milan (1902), seen by the couple as an industrial, cosmopolitan city in full evolution, a destination for intellectuals and artists, and the natural seat of the socialist party. Margherita began to deal simultaneously with political economy (in particular Marx) and art history, identifying a model in the figure of John Ruskin who, in the midst of the Victorian era, had developed the concept of the connection between the labour of art and the state of society. She thus changed from an aesthetic critic to a critic of society, devoting the last forty years of her life to expounding her theories on social and industrial problems and on the role of art as a means of raising the tone of spiritual life. Margherita's early socialism was dominated precisely by the need for an aesthetic transformation, in the Aristotelian meaning of the beautiful and therefore the good, accompanied by a profound critique of capitalism that turns man into a machine incapable of thinking (Ruskin, 1851–1853, vol. I). Commitment to politics then followed as a natural outlet, seen as the possibility of realizing a "future city," from the title of one of her later columns in the pages of the journal *La difesa delle lavoratrici* (Defence of women workers). From 1909 she ran a column in *L'Avanti*, the press organ of the Socialist Party. This activism gave rise to a nickname by which she was often remembered: "The Red Virgin," in honour of Louise Michel, the feminist of the Paris Commune of 1871. As a journalist, she also moved in her other privileged sphere: art. Among the Futurists she befriended above all the famous artist Umberto Boccioni, who also painted her a portrait that remained unfinished, and with the Futurists she fervently advocated intervention in the First World War. The Futurists in this period also chose social confrontation, and with them she collaborated on the drafting of the *Technical Manifesto of the Futurist Movement* (1910). Absolute protagonist, Margherita defined her identity by becoming patroness, inspirer, and architect of the success of many artists. She was the first woman to deal with art criticism and the organization of artistic events in a managerial role, at the same time creative and administrative, while, in the social sphere, she was among the first women journalists to publish nationwide research and surveys, as well as directing magazines and periodicals.

3 From l'*Avanti* to the Direction of *Gerarchia*[2]

It was her husband Cesare Sarfatti who spoke to her, for the first time, about the young teacher and journalist Benito Mussolini, in 1911, and it was her husband again, present at the 1912 socialist party congress, who wrote to his wife about his oratorical skills (Urso, 1994), while it was the journalist Giuseppe Prezzolini who introduced him to her. Their meeting took place in 1912 in Anna Kuliscioff's drawing room. As we know, Margherita Sarfatti collaborated with the socialist newspaper *l'Avanti,* which from 1912 was directed by Mussolini. She also collaborated with *Utopia*, a theoretical magazine of revolutionary socialism, founded and directed by Mussolini in 1913. They soon became lovers.[3] Following Mussolini, who in 1914 had been expelled from the socialist party for his position in favour of the Italian intervention in the Great War, in 1915 Margherita sided with the interventionists through the publication of a small booklet entitled *La milizia femminile in Francia* (The women's militia in France), which led to her abandonment of the socialist party. During these years, she introduced Mussolini to the upper middle class in Milan, then began to look after his appearance and corrected his impetuous ways. With the founding of the journal *Il Popolo d'Italia* by Mussolini himself (1914), she became a regular contributor (from 1918 until the end of the 1920s), reserving articles on art and a literary review column. Meanwhile, on 28 January 1918, her son died at the front. She had a memorial monument (*The sacred enclosure*) built for him by architect Giuseppe Terragni, who later became one of the leading architects of the fascist revolution. At this stage, in continuity with her son's patriotism and sacrifice, Margherita strengthened her anti-Germanic spirit, which she kept alive even during the subsequent rapprochement between Mussolini and Hitler.

From 1922 to 1933 she was co-editor and later director of the journal *Gerarchia*,[4] founded by Mussolini and destined to be the theoretical organ of his thought. A

[2] On the second part of Margherita Sarfatti's life, it is possible to consult the archives and papers indicated at the end of this chapter. As for literature on the same period, see Balabanoff (1976), Bini (2009), Boschiero (2018), Cannistraro and Sullivan (1993), De Felice (1961), Festorazzi (2010), Kuliscioff (1949–1959), Macciocchi (1976), Marzorati (1990), Navarra (1946), Scurati (2018), Urso (1994), Wieland (2006) and Zapponi (1996).

[3] The love affair with Mussolini remained as the strongest and longest for both of them. Countless letters were exchanged, a total of 1272, some unequivocal: "as your friend, your woman, your wife. With absolute loyalty and devotion as a partisan, as an Italian, as a citizen, as a mother, and as a lover [...] I am proud of you to the point of fanaticism [...] but for your intrinsic value, not for the fetishism that the crowd have for you" (Scurati, 2018, p. 629). Unless stated otherwise, the translations of the quoted texts are our own.

[4] *Gerarchia* was born at the end of January 1922 and for two years was co-edited by Sarfatti and Mussolini; from 1924 this burden remained with Sarfatti alone, but it can be assumed with good certainty that the editorial line of the journal was decided by both. The famous historian of fascism Renzo De Felice (1966, p. 228) commented as follows: "Collaboration [with *Gerarchia*] almost always remained confined to 'Mussolinians' of strict observance and new collaborations were generally accepted only on the basis of precise political considerations". The journal, precisely because it reflected an official position, had good sales success. The average circulation was in fact around 17,000 copies per issue.

select group of contributors, including the economists Gino Arias and Arrigo Serpieri, worked around the journal. On the tenth anniversary of the regime (1932) Margherita wrote an editorial in *Gerarchia* entitled *Orientamenti e presagi* (Orientations and omens). At stake was the future of Italy and of fascism itself, which she wanted to shape in the fusion of philosophical ideas, political forms, economic innovations, and free artistic expression, clearly identifying the adversary, the "old" to be defeated, as individualistic liberalism and statist socialism, America and Russia. It was Margherita again, in *L'Universalità della politica italiana* (The Universality of Italian Politics, 1932), who succinctly summarized the key concepts that Mussolini developed in his main document, *La dottrina del fascismo* (The doctrine of fascism)[5] in the same year:

> Fascism, capable of evolving and assimilating […] neither towards liberalism nor towards Bolshevism, neither to the right nor to the left, neither towards the Western degenerations of unbridled individualism, nor towards gloomy slavery […] this is provided for by the youthful maturity of its duce. (Mussolini & Gentile, 1932, in Susmel & Susmel, 1951–1974, vol. XXXIV, pp. 117–138)

Thus, the idea of the fascist state took shape. It was precisely in her house on Lake Como, where she returned for the rest of her life, that the march on Rome[6] in October 1922 was planned and financed.[7] The first months of government were full of commitments for both Mussolini and Margherita, with the latter acquiring unparalleled influence and a primary role in the journal, also due to her command of languages. Mussolini relied on her for opinions and judgements, he entrusted her with relations with the foreign press, and he let her manage the search for sponsors for the journal, such as the payment of articles signed, for American newspapers, by the leader himself.

In 1924 Margherita's husband died, so her relationship with Mussolini became official. That year emerges from her papers as having been difficult, a year of suffering, of worry. On politics she wrote: "How much better and greater is art even in its most rudimentary manifestations than politics even the most brilliant".[8] On the murder of the socialist deputy Giacomo Matteotti[9] she wrote: "What and how

---

[5] The first part of the work, the fundamental ideas of fascism, was written by the philosopher Giovanni Gentile, former Minister of Education in the Mussolini government. The second part of the work, the political and social doctrine, written in Benito Mussolini's own handwriting, has a more direct language that continuously compares societies, nations, ideas and political and economic systems of previous centuries and the twentieth century with the emerging fascism; it explains a new concept of the State-Individual and its responsibility in the evolution and elevation of man.

[6] The march on Rome by thousands of fascists was an armed demonstration organised by the National Fascist Party (PNF), aimed at a *coup d'état* with the objective of facilitating the rise of Benito Mussolini to the leadership of the government in Italy. It was touted in the following years as the prologue of the 'fascist revolution' and its anniversary became the countdown to the years according to the fascist era.

[7] As recorded in the archives of Baron von der Schulenburg and in Schulenburg (2010).

[8] Letter to painter Arturo Martini, 1924, Margherita Sarfatti Archive, Mart Rovereto; Scurati (2018, p. 740).

[9] Giacomo Matteotti, secretary of the United Socialist Party, was abducted and murdered on 10 June 1924 by a fascist squad led by Amerigo Dumini, because of his denunciations of electoral fraud

many sad things around us, what a fabric of snares [...] the finding of this wretched corpse will silence the tumult and the turncoats who follow it".[10]

It was also in this year that the propaganda-communication project of the nascent fascist regime took shape; she was among its architects, inspiring the idea of the myth of Rome, inventing the "lictor fasces"[11] and making the image of the "Duce" credible outside Italy. She published in England in 1925 a highly successful biography of Mussolini (*The Life of Benito Mussolini*), later reprinted in Italy (1926) with the title *Dux*, a term that became the leader's emblem. The book was sold and translated into eighteen countries. It served to make Mussolini and his idea of society known in the world. It was Margherita herself who in 1925 launched the idea of the renovation of the entire archaeological area of Rome. Her words pronounced during her meeting with the historian of fascism Renzo de Felice in 1961, a few months before her death, confirm the fundamental, strategic role she played at this stage in the construction of the myth of Romanity, including Catholicity (De Felice, 1975, p. 12). She was more and more a heeded advisor, a confidant, and for some even a protector, but later she became the object of attacks and criticism: as we shall see, she had too much influence on the regime and its leader.

4 The *Novecento* Movement

In 1922 Margherita launched her group of artists, originally composed of seven painters,[12] which went down in history as *Novecento*. Born as a follow-up of the more moderate Futurism, it was, in the founder's expectations, the reformulation of painting on the basis of a "compact, bare, almost monumental style" (Sarfatti, 1925a), in a classical sense. It was the poverty of 1919, with sons returning from the front, the countryside without arms, the cities destroyed and in general the early post-war period, that brought down the vague Futurist hopes. *Novecento* presented itself as a return to order, but also to concreteness and the reality of things. Sarfatti became the mastermind and ultimate expression in art of fascism's will to power.

and the climate of violence implemented by Benito Mussolini's nascent dictatorship in the elections of 6 April 1924. According to some historians, the murder was also a consequence of Matteotti's investigations into government corruption.Rome.

[10] Letter to Mussolini, August 1924; Scurati (2018, p. 740).

[11] The lictor's fascio was, in Ancient Rome, the weapon carried by the lictors, which consisted of a bundle of wooden sticks tied with leather strips, usually around an axe, to represent the power of life and death over the condemned Romans.

It then became a symbol of power and greater authority, the imperium, later taken up as a symbol in heraldry by revolutionary political movements and ideologies (in the French Revolution together with the Phrygian cap as a symbol of public order, led by the liberated people) and then by Fascism, which in 1926 made the fascio part of the coat of arms of the Kingdom of Italy.

[12] The painters were Marussig, Funi, Dudreville, Malerba, Sironi, Oppi, Bucci. In a letter to Mussolini, their support for the cause of fascism emerges: 'Our applause for the young head of government [...] the man who will know how to rightly evaluate the forces of our dominant art in the world', signed by Carrà, Funi, Marinetti, Sironi and others (Scurati, 2018, p. 643).

She organized an international exhibition at the 1924 Venice Biennale, the first in the fascist era. Taking back the past and making it eternal was among the main slogans, as she wrote for another exhibition opened in 1926 in Milan, where Mussolini was present:

> for the first time in the history of Italian artistic events, the head of government inaugurates with a memorable speech an exhibition of young fascist artists, that is, revolutionaries of the modern restoration. (Scurati, 2020, p. 436)

Mussolini was well aware of Margherita's intentions to make Novecento the leading expression of an aesthetic and political revolution, a synthesis of traditional values and avant-garde spirit, of classicism and modernism. It was her most powerful and lofty moment, but, as in all high points, her decline also began here. First jealousies in the party with rumours circulating about her alleged profits accumulated through speculations. Mussolini too began to distance himself, as shown in this quotation:

> Dear Madam […] this attempt to make people believe that the artistic projection of fascism is your '900 is now pointless and is trickery […]. Because you still do not possess the elementary modesty of not mixing my name as a politician with your artistic inventions or self-styled such, do not be surprised if at the first opportunity and explicitly, I present to you my position and that of fascism in the face of the so-called '900 or what remains of the late '900. (Scurati, 2020, p. 440)

In 1931 she was also excluded from the organizing committee of the exhibition being prepared for the tenth anniversary of the March on Rome. The *Novecento* group broke up, but the ideas remained strongly present in the Italian art scene, as in the case of national rationalist architecture, a boast of the regime, with its great masters Giuseppe Terragni and Giovanni Michelucci.[13]

5 *Gerarchia* and the Corporate Economic Way

Margherita's approach to economics was affected deeply by the ideological core of her thought. Her ideas about art, politics, philosophy, or religion were bound together in an all-encompassing *Weltanschauung*, always in flux. Economic thought became an essential part of it. As editor of the journal *Gerarchia,* she regularly intervened in current economic issues, domestic or international. Meanwhile with a column containing the chronicles of the month, titled *Speculum*, she brought together brief comments, insights, and analyses. Sometimes they were signed with the initials S. and we do not know if it was Sarfatti's signature, but certainly the editor shared its contents, which she discussed with some experts. These included the well-known Italian economists Alberto de' Stefani, Gino Arias, Carlo E. Ferri, Arrigo Serpieri, Giuseppe Bastianini, Giuseppe Bottai, Gino Borgatta and Corrado Gini. On some

[13] They were all members of the Accademia d'Italia and absolute protagonists in the regime's major projects.

occasions, Sarfatti mentioned themes and authors from the history of economic thought, as in the article commemorating Luigi Luzzati, which she wrote in *Gerarchia* in 1927:

> The lineage of great economists loses in him perhaps its posthumous epigone. The lineage was great for scholars of Ricardo, Marx, Malthus and Smith, through the ebb and flow of gold, of more subtle and complex problems in the ebb and flow of peoples. Luigi Luzzati did not, like those illustrious ones, create enduring systems, he did not discover principles […] but like them he had his eye on the moral purposes of man, and political economy did not serve him to construct the aberrant monstrosities of economic man, but well to trace […] those lights of eternal ethics that can make it, Virgilianly, sacred. (Sarfatti, 1927, p. 252)

She shared Luzzatti's call for the subordination of classes to the nation, while reproaching him for not understanding the need for the strong state: relying "on the weak utopia of the fraternity of men […] Luzzatti considered the wealth of nations and the prosperity of commerce as instruments to diminish material labors and social contentions among individuals, classes and peoples" (Sarfatti, 1927, p. 253). Many topics were covered in the journal, which was published quarterly. For example, in 1930 it focused on monetary issues, particularly on the achievement of "quota 90" in the exchange rate of the Italian lira against the British pound. As we shall see the regime declared this goal to prevent inflation from continuing to produce its evil consequences on the life of the country. Sarfatti's journal took a sharp stance: "an issue that in a liberal regime would have toppled governments […] the question of the not inconsiderable wage cut (12 percent), was met with serene composure".[14] Clerks and workers, the fixed-income categories, were under attack and, according to her, in this scenario, "a nominal wage, even a very high one, is useless if the purchasing power of the currency is minimal; or it is illusory, if there is no possibility of employment in the country".[15] For her the state structure seemed to hold up because of the effectiveness of ideas and the corporate movement. There transpired a constant reference to politics seen as the possibility of achieving a New State, the aforementioned "future city," the harmony of strength, beauty, emancipation and destiny, identified initially with socialism, then in the resurgent homeland with the Great War, and, finally, with the fascist state:

> It seemed at first a movement of anti-Bolshevik reaction […] it seemed an Italian national fact […] but it created a new model of national society, corporatism. It restored substance to the values of social justice and labour, to the formation of new ruling classes. And, overall, it implements a form of social justice and tempered collectivism. (Sarfatti, 1931a, pp. 787–788)

The corporate state, with its interclass, ethical, trade unionist economic model developed from the first founding ideas (disjointed and even contradictory, in a mixture of references to Marxism, revolutionary syndicalism, nationalism, and the first liberal orientations of management of the economy[16]) to the final arrangement

---

[14] *Gerarchia*, 1930, p. 1948–1050.

[15] Idem.

[16] On the liberal phase with economist Alberto de' Stefani at the Ministry of Finance and Treasury (1922–1925), see Mattei (2017).

that definitively clarified the contours of a fascist, organic and complete ideology. In her words:

> Socialism was the first strong school of educational and collective discipline perpetrated in the masses of the Italian people, to correct the anarchist individualist instinct [...]. [To] us Italians it came above all from German Marxism and reflected (and fortunately for us) the 'Prussian' character of the trade and political organizations proper to the German sozial-demokraten, [...] to make people understand the necessity of organization, solidarity, subordination, in a word, discipline. (Sarfatti, 1931b, p. 225)

The goal declared fundamental by Margherita was social justice:

> millions of men are suffering, the cries of economic inequality between classes are becoming more ominous every day [...] but the gentlemen who rule the world fiddle with paperwork, votes, ministries and parties [...] they grow plump behind the talismanic power of the fetish, now so old, the Holy Card. (Sarfatti, 1932a, p. 41)

For her, the focus of the corporate system seemed to be work rather than wages. "Optimistic and easy" finance was the real enemy, while "inflation and unemployment are two fearful spectres" (Sarfatti, 1930c, p. 1050) The way was to control public spending and the state budget. With the already mentioned "quota 90" launched by Mussolini on August 18, 1926, to stop the dizzying run of the pound, which had reached 160 Italian liras, the aim was precisely to restore the accounts. After a year, the lira again achieved full convertibility to gold, but the revaluation triggered restrictive monetary measures, such as restriction of circulation and credit cuts, further igniting fiscal austerity measures: financial austerity was in fact a precondition to compensate for the rising balance of payments deficit. Thus, wage deflation constituted a crucial variable of an economic policy, consistent with currency revaluation. The corporatist system, vertical and participatory at the same time, succeeded in making economic categories digest major sacrifices for the good of the nation and public finances in the long run. A stronger lira required lower labour costs, leading to lower prices and thus greater international competitiveness (Sarfatti, 1930c, pp. 1048–1053). Finally, in 1927 the *Carta del lavoro*[17] was signed, enshrining the goal of excluding any possibility of class conflict or any bargaining power for workers. It was the period of the transition to the new corporatist structure that characterized the governing structure of more mature fascism and of the close of the first phase called by many historians "authoritarian neoliberalism" (Mattei, 2017). The corporatist project took its first steps, while the state became "ethical" and took over the market.

A constant in Mussolini's own thought, after the first phase of his government, was his aversion to liberalism. In *La Dottrina del Fascismo*, written by Mussolini and Gentile, in setting out the fundamental ideas, an entire paragraph was devoted to the evolution of political economy and the various movements. There were many references to the classical school, many fewer to the marginalist school, despite the

[17] *The Labour Charter* is one of the fundamental documents of fascism, passed on 21 April 1927: it expressed its social principles, the doctrine of corporatism, the ethics of fascist trade unionism and fascist economic policy.

deep relationship of closeness with Pareto and Pantaleoni.[18] As Sarfatti pointed out, the limit was individualism: "Fascism represses unbridled, seditious and dissolving individualism" (Sarfatti, 1931b, p. 227). At the centre was precisely the critique of liberalism and the goal was its overcoming. A diriment issue was the individual-state antinomy, on which there was a continuous reversal of position. A new approach was codified that contradicted the previous one: "If he who says liberalism says individual, he who says fascism says state" (Susmel & Susmel 1951–1974, vol. XXXIV, p.125). In contrast to Adam Smith who originally, albeit cautiously, acknowledged a role for the state, she thought that more mature liberalism gradually moved away from this approach, cutting off any space for the state itself. The fascist state, on the other hand, claimed the field of economics to itself, with the individual being not annulled, but rather multiplied, with the state becoming an absolute, before which individuals and groups are relative. Sarfatti wrote:

> Number and mass bring man closer and closer to the social regime of the bee, and further away from that of the lion [...] the man whom Aristotle called a 'political animal' today is increasingly a 'social animal' [...] Montesquieu's thought: it is so that others may not get in the way of my freedom, that I consent to sacrifice a part of it [...] Modern life is quantitative and mechanical, and cannot leave to the individual that boundless freedom, which was proper to the patriarchal ages, from the individual economy of craft and family. (Sarfatti, 1931b, p. 226)

She was certain that corporate fascism also stood as a negation of that doctrine, first advocated by Mussolini himself, which formed the basis of Marxian scientific socialism. For

> historical materialism, the history of human civilization can be explained only by the struggle of interests between different social groups and by the change of means and instruments of production. (Susmel & Susmel, 1951–1974, vol. XXXIV, p. 128)

She thought that, by denying historical materialism, one comes to deny the class struggle itself, which is the natural offspring of this economicist conception. This was the heart of fascism: man was conceivable only when placed in a hierarchically ordered and functional community. It was a true metaphysics of the people, an organic, unitary, and metapolitical level. Already the 1919 *Charter of Carnaro*, by which the poet-soldier Gabriele D'annunzio governed the autonomous city of Fiume (now Rijeka) for 16 months,[19] stated that the state had not to recognize property as the absolute dominion of the person over the thing, but considered it as the

[18] Pareto, repeatedly mentioned by Mussolini in his articles as a Maestro (Susmel & Susmel, 1951–1974; Megaro, 1947), accepted the nomination as senator in 1923, equally with Pantaleoni, already active in the nationalist ranks during the First World War and already a minister in the aforementioned Fiume corporative experience of the Carnaro republic (1919), also appointed senator in 1923. In October 1922, Pareto urged Giovanni Preziosi to invite Mussolini to seize power, with the appeal "now or never!". In a letter to Pareto dated 17 October 1922, Pantaleoni wrote: "That foxy Giolitti is preparing the defeat of fascism. I believe that if the fascists allow themselves to be tamed they are finished [...] it is therefore necessary to make the revolution before they give up, because otherwise it's over".

[19] The *Charter of Carnaro* was the trade unionist constitution of the Italian Regency of Carnaro, written by the socialist trade unionist Alceste de Ambris and revised by the poet Gabriele

most useful of social functions. The Charter envisaged a new system of relations between capital and labour, a new method for regulating the conditions under which the social relationship between employers and workers was conducted, in the light of the principle of cooperation between the categories, in the interests of individuals and the community as a whole. These ideas referred to integral state unionism, to the organic state, which reconciled and harmonized opposing interests. At the heart of the project was the need to make the economy part of a comprehensive theory of society, an antidote to the socialist class struggle and an overcoming of the inability of liberal regimes to guarantee effective labour participation. However, the corporatist movement was by no means united and in agreement, as there were several main lines: from those who saw corporatist theory as a natural development of classical theory, as its natural consequence, to those who saw such doctrine as new and revolutionary.[20] Of this second current, the so-called corporative left, the philosophical soul was represented by the philosopher Ugo Spirito. The stated goal was to reunify economics and sociology kept separate by the refinements of pure theory, with the demolition of the individualistic premises of classicism and the creation of *homo corporativus*, a merging of *homo oeconomicus* and *homo civis*. One of Sarfatti's most important collaborators, Gino Arias, belonged to this second movement which stood in perfect antithesis to the systems advocated by economic science.

Another of her key collaborators in the economic pages of the journal was the agrarian economist Arrigo Serpieri, who was the protagonist of the proposals related to a new idea of coexistence of tradition and modernity, of redesigning both the city, its spaces and its architecture, and the countryside, its rurality. Mussolini's dream was accompanied by an attempt to imitate the great civilizations of the ancient or medieval past, which left an unrepeatable imprint precisely in the original interpretation of the city. Parallel to the city theme was the development of agricultural policy, of which Serpieri was the interpreter par excellence. His stated goals were the following: expropriation of latifundia, land reclamation, colonization, modernization of agriculture and land policy, transformation of sharecroppers into landowning colonists, national agricultural independence, and sovereignty. Already a member of the party since 1923, then elected to Parliament, he would be vice-minister for integral reclamation. A fundamental principle of Serpieri's policy, in line with the corporatist idea, was the application of the principles of co-participation and class collaboration, as opposed to the regime of continuous confrontation inherent in the

D'Annunzio, and promulgated by him on 8 September 1920 in Fiume (present-day Croatia); see Negri and Simoni (1990). Articles 13 and 14 of the *Carnar Charter* defined the corporations, made up of workers (with small artisans and small landowners), technical and administrative personnel, employees of commercial enterprises, employers, civil servants, teachers (together with students), and professions.

[20] The corporate movement was by no means united and concordant. Within it we can distinguish several main lines. From the ethical-catholic one of Francesco Vito and Jacopo Mazzei, to the social, 'left-wing' one of Gino Arias and Ugo Spirito, to the more moderate one with Giovanni Demaria and Alberto Bertolino.

Marxist and capitalist visions.[21] Margherita Sarfatti shared the Serpieri line, but two attitudes coexisted in her that came into conflict: the strong national appeal on the one hand and her innate inclination to frequent high society on the other. Much of her own future as well as that of the entire regime was played out on this tension.

6 Internationalism and Economic Nationalism

6.1 International Relations and Protectionism

During the 1920s and 1930s there were numerous destabilizing factors including monetary imbalances (inflation until 1927 and deflation thereafter) and the monopolistic transformation of capitalism, while the legacy of World War I threatened already highly unstable balances. There was a transition from a single world organization of the economy, based on a gold standard, to a world of separate markets, in which international trade was continually threatened by contingencies, bilaterality and offsets, exchange bans, and exchange monopolies. Thus, the nation-state became increasingly the protagonist, with exchange used once again as a weapon of dependence and domination. Among the economic determinants of a state's power, it was foreign trade that played a role in the first order. Indeed, from this time on, the overriding theme of international politics was the search for a possible coexistence among states. The Locarno Peace Conference (1925) had opened a positive, albeit short-lived phase, which culminated in Germany initially being denied entry to the League of Nations. Against this unstable backdrop, fascism sought to position itself among the international powers by looking especially to England and the United States. In December 1922 Mussolini was in London, while the British King returned the visit on May 4, 1923. In this same year the *Daily Mail* presented Mussolini as "the statesman who saved not only his country but probably all of Europe from Bolshevism" (Scurati, 2018). This was followed by a letter from the Duce to the British people on May 25, 1924, in which he extolled the English role: "for its virtues and its wonderful history of civilization and government, a perfect example without parallel since the days of Rome."[22] Mussolini "synonymous with Italy," the *Times* wrote in November 1925, while Winston Churchill declared in two separate statements, the first in 1926 and the second in 1927, at the British embassy in Rome:

> Italy increases more and more in importance under the virile and enlightened leadership of its present government, which has secured for it a magnificent position in Europe and the world. (Scurati, 2020, p. 106)
>
> I could not fail to be fascinated by Mussolini [...] His only thought is the lasting welfare of the Italian people [...] if I had been Italian, I am sure that I would have been entirely with you from the beginning to the end of your struggle against the bestial appetites and

[21] See A. Serpieri, *La Guerra e le classi rurali italiane*, Yale University Press and Laterza, Bari, 1930.

[22] The journal Il *Popolo d'Italia*, 24 maggio 1924.

> passions of Leninism […] externally your movement has rendered a service to the whole world. (Scurati, 2020, p. 248)

This was a real endorsement, with a view to a common fight against communism. But, surprisingly, fascism's greatest feeling was born overseas, not because of Mussolini, but because of another quadrumvir, Italo Balbo, triumphantly welcomed in Chicago (Guerri, 2017). He had the cover of *Time*, they named a street after him (the Seventh renamed General Balbo Avenue), and he was even welcomed by the Indian community (Guerri, 2017). Ambassador Richard Washburn Child wrote reassuringly, three days after the march on Rome (31 October 1922): "Here we are witnessing a beautiful revolution of young people. No danger, it is full of colour and enthusiasm" (Scurati, 2018, p. 600). Six months later, on June 28, 1923, it confirmed the first sensations:" the conception of life and history that inspires fascism finds gallant and numerous partisans even overseas".[23] The great American press came to bless the Italian scenario. *The Washington Post* wrote on November 1, 1926:

> It is an institution inspiring fanatical devotion just as fanatical opposition, but despite its repressive tendencies it is transforming Italy into a productive and prosperous nation […] Mussolini is a brave man who defies death by doing his duty. He wins and deserves the admiration of the world. Anyone who abhors communism and the murderers it produces must fervently hope that Benito Mussolini will continue his miraculous life. (Scurati, 2020, p. 218)

Evident in this scenario is the key strategic role played by Margherita Sarfatti, both on British and American soil, in fostering the rapprochement of the two countries to the cause of fascism and, above all, to the enhancement of its leader. She personally curated Mussolini's presence in the British and American press. She emphasized the diplomatic success in some of her comments concerning the growing attention to the regime's economic policy:

> When our finance ministers went on official visits to London, as poor relatives of the provinces, and returned after the humiliating pilgrimage, without having obtained the interview, one would not have foreseen that, a few years later, the course of the powerful pound, in London and in the markets of Europe, would be influenced by the single word that the minister of Italy, without asking advice and permission from anyone, dictated from his desk. (Sarfatti, 1932a, p. 42)

However, the crisis of 1929 sowed seeds for future confrontations. The new tariff and customs systems introduced in some countries, the policies of imperial and colonial preference, and the detachment from the gold standard of several national currencies, undermined the very foundations of the classical theory of international trade, based on free competition, international division and stability of monetary systems. With the year 1932, protectionism ran rampant and international trade volumes were halved (De Rosa, 1981). A redistributive scenario of wealth opened up, which placed in front of a great many debtor countries a few great creditor countries, with irrational blockades to immigration of the latter, while the mass production moved in search of vast markets, causing overproduction and unemployment. On the same

[23] Ibidem.

wavelength, Sarfatti wrote still in 1930: "The United States with its customs barriers forbid us their markets and now limit our emigration [...] unemployment in Italy is far less worrying than abroad" (Sarfatti, 1930c, p. 1052). Italy actually delayed in following the customs policy of other European nations: the fascist government initially limited itself to granting certain incentives, such as forms of subsidized credit or guarantees for exporters, however the growing tension led to a response with the identical weapons of protection, until autarky was officially proclaimed in 1936.

6.2 *Travel Chronicles, Colonies, and Economic Inquiries*

Perhaps the most significant area for bringing out the contradictions in Margherita's thinking between the nation, international economics and the mission of fascism was that of the colonies, about which fascist Italy positioned itself in line the ambitions of previous governments. Italian colonialism began in the late nineteenth century with the purchase of the African ports of Assab and Massawa on the Red Sea. Following the partition of Africa by the European powers (1881–1914), the Kingdom of Italy held control of Eritrea and Somalia, as well as Cyrenaica, Tripolitania, and the Aegean Islands, which had been taken from the Ottoman Empire during the Italian-Turkish war (1911–1912). There was also an Italian concession in Tientsin, China, since 1901. During the First World War, an Italian expeditionary force preemptively occupied southern Albania to prevent its conquest by the Austro-Hungarian Empire and established a protectorate there (1917–1920). The Fascist regime of Benito Mussolini, who came to power shortly after the World War, expressed the intention to reconquer some of these territories and further expand the kingdom's possessions. The inclined plane of international relations underwent a decisive shift in the Duce's Abyssinian and Eritrean campaign and to the subsequent economic sanctions that France and England, through the League of Nations, applied to Italy in 1935.[24] From the traditional anti-Germanic positions of the 1910s and 1920s, the regime gradually slipped towards an alliance with Hitler, who came to power in 1933, and Sarfatti was not able to prevent this. Before this stage, she moved across the world reporting chronicles and travel notes, from Africa and South America to some European countries, and the themes were the colonies and the national mission, European culture, and its economy. Margherita began her travels to North Africa as they were territories historically disputed with France, and her reports were a test case for the regime. The first, related to the "Tunis issue," recalled the demographic tragedy, one of the driving topics of fascist policy. On the one hand, it was a sign of military strength and possible economic supremacy, while on the other, the clash between Italian demographics and the lack of available territory was becoming, as Mussolini wrote in the introduction to Sarfatti's 1923 volume *Tunisiaca*, an issue "acute especially

[24] The economic sanctions against Fascist Italy were decreed by the League of Nations against Italy in response to the attack on Ethiopia that led to the ensuing Ethiopian War. The sanctions remained in force from 18 November 1935 until 14 July 1936.

since the large overseas markets, which used to absorb our surplus labour, are practically barred" (Sarfatti, 1923c, p. 69). The case of Tunis was emblematic for the times, adding to the many tensions already present among major European nations. At issue here was the relationship between Italy and France, but it was only one of many: France's denunciation of the conventions (1896) had jeopardized the role and presence of the important Italian community in Tunis. Great interests were simultaneously played out on the Germany-England-France-Italy axis, interests that resulted in the two world wars. France went and stayed in Tunis, similarly to other powers in other countries. Sarfatti in her trip to Tunis retraced the route of the approximately 90,000 Italians living in Tunis (as opposed to 46,000 French). She travelled to the extreme limits of the desert, as far as the oasis of Tozeur, retracing the path of that large group of Italian families, particularly from Tuscany, most of them Jewish, who had settled in the capital in the latter part of the previous century. On the great theme of immigration and emigration, and of colonialism, Sarfatti presented an extraordinary account in terms of breadth of references and modernity of language:

> France and Italy have the same imperious need to colonize, but for diametrically opposite reasons: we to pour the surplus of the metropolitan population into the colony; France to make up for the shortfall. The ideal, for us, would be a fertile, deserted colony; for France, a super-populated colony. (Sarfatti, 1923a, p. 1138)

The old Italo-Tunisian Treaty of 1868 granted Italy most-favoured-nation treatment. The subsequent convention of 1896, after France's seizure of Tunisia, left the right to recognize the Italian-ness of its subjects and associations. But the strongly absorbing French law on nationality violated many of the rights, both in the commercial field and in the educational field, in which the final blocking of possible new openings came. Sarfatti knew well the encompassing character of French nationalism: "that patriotism which knows no sects, classes or categories, and unites them all, freemasons and priests, socialists and anarchists […] when it comes to France" (Sarfatti, 1923b, p. 1190). The transalpine country always resorted to the blackmail of denouncing the very treaties between Italy and France in order to strengthen its presence in North Africa:

> Pressed by the Lombard silk merchants or the Piedmontese wine growers or the southern citrus growers, for a rebate or facilitation of commercial exports, the Italian government ceded ground on the rights of the colony, sacrificing Tunisia. (Sarfatti, 1923a, p. 1140)

However, the new French colonialism in the land of Tunisia also became a model of European colonization. France had learned from its mistakes in Algeria a few decades earlier, where it "distorted, rebuilt, Europeanizing without regard or plan, at random" (Sarfatti, 1923b, p. 1196). In Tunis, on the other hand, "the whole old, Arab part of the city was immediately declared as a monumental zone and planned with a rational method" (Sarfatti, 1923b, p. 1196). The comparison for Sarfatti even here was to post-1870 Rome, devastated by "vandalism, destruction, remaking and contamination" (Sarfatti, 1923b, p. 1196). Interestingly, it was in line with the corporate project, the model of relations between ownership and management:

> The European concessionaire gives an Arab settler family the land free of charge, provides the planting capital, and from season to season maintains it at his own expense until the end of five years. The olive tree [...] on the sixth year must bear fruit. One half of the profitable farm remains with the European concessionaire and the Arab pays him the rent, and the other half passes into the ownership of the Arab settler, equalizing first a portion of the advances already provided. If the farm does not yield, the bad farmer has lost his labours, the unwary hireling the capital advanced. (Sarfatti, 1923b, p. 1197)

This was an atypical agricultural contract, a mixture of sharecropping and small-holding, which fit well with the hypotheses that fascism was beginning to design, such as "foundation towns," corporate towns. Moreover, the Tunisian model might be useful for Italy in Libya.

> it would seem that the two colonies of Cyrenaica and Tripolitania, rationally organized and cultivated, can lead themselves in not long to the same degree of prosperity as Tunisia [...] Cyrenaica indeed is even more fertile: France and Italy have on the opposite shore of the Mediterranean rivalries and competitions of influences and interests [...] But it is well not to hide from us that, apart from the antagonisms and perhaps above them, there is the necessary solidarity of Christians in the face of the Saracen East. (Sarfatti, 1923b, p. 1198)

Sarfatti often entered into topics concerning Islam, with a mixture of admiration for the philosophy and a further reminder of the tendential superiority of European civilization:

> The program of Arab life, a minimum of needs for a minimum of effort, may be a philosophy of moral and spiritual superiority [...] but if it is true that mankind is an undead, the undead glories of Rome above the soil, where nothing is ancient that is not Roman, admonish us Europeans: it is worth living and the penance of working, if vestiges of us remain on earth. (Sarfatti, 1923b, p. 1199)

Contradicting her Risorgimento background, however, Margherita's criticism went to the pacifist preaching of the Presbyterian American president Wilson, but especially to his words about "peoples, arbiters freely of their own actions" (Sarfatti, 1923b, p. 1199). This idea of European "superiority" also returned in accounts of travel to South America, where the theme was "poverty in rich lands," from the title of one of her 1930 articles. On this continent "in four or five different and distant countries, they have made revolution [...] for four or five different orders of reasons" (Sarfatti, 1930b, p. 1016). But for her, the real issue was South America's relationship with the United States. According to her, the Europeans had "the wrong of suffering too many Yankee influences in judging Latin America" (Sarfatti, 1930b, p. 1017). With the Monroe Doctrine, the Americas belonged to the United States. Regarding the Argentine case, she thought that the fascist regime was the first to recognize the new government born of the revolution. Margherita brought to Argentina the *Novecento italiano* exhibition, a

> friendly act and homage to Argentine culture [...] which greatly served to strengthen the current of Latin and Mediterranean sympathies [...] the inevitability of whiteness, the superiority of the clear European dynamic, against romantic nostalgia and confused regrets toward the cruel, hieratic and immobile Indian civilization (Sarfatti, 1930b, p.1018).

This was followed by her trip to Brazil. She said that while in Argentina "there is unemployment and poverty, in Brazil there is even unemployment and misery" (Sarfatti, 1930b, p. 1019) and added: "Two countries so rich, is it possible? They are two very rich lands [...] but one suffers more than in our poor lovely Italy" (Sarfatti, 1930b, p. 1019). Argentina exported grain and meat, while Brazil was a leader in coffee, but also had bananas, cotton, rubber, timber, and important gold deposits. For Sarfatti, the problem was profoundly economic:

> both Argentina and Brazil are suffering from the crisis of overproduction that is strangling the entire planet [...] it is not clear by what paradox of our farrago mechanical and industrial capitalist age, if at one time mankind trembled beset by the nightmare of famine, it now lives threatened with the fearful spectre of abundance. (Sarfatti, 1930b, p. 1021)

She then asked why greater wealth of material goods generated greater misery for people. Her analysis, argued and incisive, captured an issue that Argentina relives in contemporary times, as in the great crisis of the 1990s that went down in economic history as poverty in abundance. Thus, for rubber and coffee, this mistake of aiming for too high-profit margins allowed the emergence and development of competition from other countries:

> the paradox that while the consumption of the aromatic grain is continually growing in the world, as a much sought-after commodity [...] in Brazil huge quantities of it lie unsold [...] The construction of the Panama Canal already provided very valid reasons and pretexts [...] for the United States to take virtual economic and political possession of that region. (Sarfatti, 1930b, p. 1017)

Her attention then shifted to comparisons with other European countries. On *Gerarchia* she mentioned negotiations to regulate international trade with France, Germany, Spain, the USSR, and Yugoslavia, countries with which domestic trade was severely deficient. But the country chosen for an all-out confrontation was Spain, a true model for good and bad. In 1924 the Iberian Peninsula was plagued by the same long-standing dualisms, conflicts, and separatisms as Italy in the late nineteenth century, with an agricultural south, badly cultivated, with large absentee landowners tied to parasitic rent rather than production. She compared Primo de Rivera to the Italian prime minister Francesco Crispi, and juxtaposed the similarities between Catalonia and Lombardy, with Barcelona and Milan considered as the industrial, industrious, liberal, and revolutionary capitals, as opposed to the political and bureaucratic capitals Madrid and Rome. But she envisaged some differences: while Spain was rich because of large agricultural areas and large mineral deposits, it seemed an old country if compared to a poor but younger Italy. Some of Sarfatti's analyses deliberately fell into the narrative of the new fascist state, such as the relationship between central state and autonomies, between state and individual, between state and bureaucracy, between national solidarity and collective discipline, and between rent and labour. In several articles she dwelled on this last topic, strongly present in the objectives of the regime:

> Much of the most fertile and richest land in Spain [...] is in the hands of great lords. These [...] do not care at all for the latifundia, collecting lavish rents from it and paying derisory

> taxes [...] There is no sharecropping; the land is generally rented for money to people who then have it cultivated by hand, by laborers at work. (Sarfatti, 1924a, p. 620)

Writing about Spain, she referred to Italy: it was the subject of land reform, one of the flagships of Mussolini and his already mentioned contributor to *Gerarchia*, Arrigo Serpieri. A direct consequence of this behaviour of local landowners was the suffocating presence of foreign capital: "the big profitable businesses are in the hands of French or partly Belgian capitalists [...] gas companies, tramways, steamers, hotels and especially railways [...] the exploitation of hydroelectric forces is all in the hands of Canadian capitalists" (Sarfatti, 1924a, p. 621). The foreign entrepreneurs themselves were considered more experienced and more capable, but above all, they were seen as willing to invest unlike the locals devoted to rent. Sarfatti's appeal went to southern Italy, grappling with the same atavistic problem on which the fascist regime had to intervene and in her analysis she moved carefully, aware that she was on a minefield. She lucidly foresaw the strategic importance of international relations and, in perspective, the potential economic and military risks they conceal. She knew that for the regime, as for herself, this was the crucial, decisive, moment.

7 The Post-War Period and Oblivion

Margherita Sarfatti did not approve of the new colonial enterprises in Abyssinia (1935) as the intensification of relations with Nazi Germany ("Nazism is ugly, unsightly, demagogic")[25] and she became increasingly an unwelcome figure. Meanwhile, by 1929, following rapprochement with the Vatican and the signing of the Lateran Pacts,[26] Mussolini married his historical partner Rachele Guidi, while three years later a young Claretta Petacci became Mussolini's official mistress until they both died in 1945. By 1933 Margherita was no longer director of *Gerarchia* and the downward parabola took her far from fascism and Italy. It was Mussolini's historical footman, Quinto Navarra, who reminded us of this in his memoirs: "What was the most unpleasant order I had to execute? It was to announce to Mrs. Margherita Sarfatti, after two hours in the antechamber, that the Duce would not receive her" (Navarra, 1946, cit in Scurati, 2020, p. 618). Despite, or perhaps precisely because of the esteem in which she was held internationally, she could no longer guide the regime's political-cultural choices. Nor could she any longer underestimate the

---

[25] Margherita Sarfatti (1937). Under the guise of a chronicle of a trip to the United States, *America* contained a negative judgement on the political failure of the fascist regime and, perhaps, also the hope of finding in America the new Rome, the 'future city', for which Sarfatti was constantly searching.

[26] The Lateran Pacts were the agreements signed between the Kingdom of Italy and the Holy See on 11 February 1929 containing a treaty, a convention and a concordat. Subjected, in the concordat part, to revision in 1984, they still regulate relations between Italy and the Holy See today. To the Pacts we owe the establishment of Vatican City as an independent State and the full formal reopening of relations between Italy and the Holy See, interrupted in 1870 but gradually re-established in the following decades until their final settlement with the stipulation of these agreements.

growing anti-Semitic climate. New trips abroad came, in northern Europe and the United States especially, then the final departure to Uruguay in 1937, when the Racial Laws (adopted by fascism in 1938) were just around the corner. She returned to Italy only when the war was over. Her last years were spent in the house on Lake Como, totally forgotten. It was oblivion, interrupted only by the aforementioned visit, a few months before her death, of the young scholar De Felice, who wrote (Fig. 2):

> From this conversation, actually, in terms of documents, I did not get anything out of it. It served me very much, however, to understand this woman, to understand […] the kind of influence she must have had for some years. After that conversation I wondered, for example, how much of the myth of Roman-ness was Mussolini's baggage. And not instead rather the product of Sarfatti's influence. For I have never in my life known a person as obsessed with Roman-ness as she was (De Felice, 1975, p. 12)

Fig. 2 One hundred thousand copies of her biography of Mussolini

In another interview with journalist Stefano Folli in *Corriere della Sera* in 1993, De Felice recalled:

> She never spoke of Mussolini in the last years of her life. She told me that even Augustus, after Livia's death, set out to become a Tiberius [...] she identified with Livia. As if to say: as long as he stayed with me, I knew how to keep him on the right path [...] the guiding ideas of her life had turned into obsessions. The main one was Roman-ness. That is, the sense of classical forms as the dominant motif of artistic civilization. (Folli, 1993, 1 Febbraio)

All this was further transformed by the study of De Felice's most important disciple, Emilio Gentile, who in 1993 published *Il culto del littorio. La sacralizzazione della politica nell'Italia fascista*, where he devoted a great deal of space to the role and contribution of Margherita Sarfatti in the growing "euphoria for the new era," evident in the "monumentalist imagination of architects" and beyond (Gentile, 1993, p. 240). Already outside her country, two of her articles appeared in the newspaper *La Stampa*, in 1937 "Leopardi's Mother" and in 1938 "D'Annunzio." They dealt with poetry, not politics. Her name remained unpronounceable for decades: she was a Jew to former fascists, a traitor to Jews, and fascist to the new republic born of the Resistance. To make an exhibition about her one had to make a public profession of anti-fascism. There is a Via Sarfatti in Milan, but it is in memory of her son Roberto. Only a few decades after her death, the Museum of Contemporary Art in Milan and the Museum of Modern and Contemporary Art of Trento and Rovereto (MART) dedicated events to her, and the latter started the archival fund that bears her name.

What remains of Margherita Sarfatti? A unique female personality who inspired an era of great artists. Called derogatorily muse, courtesan, vestal, and uncrowned queen,[27] in our opinion she was more demiurge, and *Deus ex machina* of Italian art. She was certainly the protagonist of a great season of art and the press, of politics and thought, of culture as meaning and not just as business and custom, and even of economic thought, as we have shown in this chapter. She was a complex personality who influenced an evidently male-dominated regime for years. In her last writings *Acqua passata* (Thing of the past of 1955) the word fascism recurred only once, and Mussolini was entirely absent. The Duce's fault in her eyes was that of not having created the true alternative of civilization she expected and of having turned fascism into the tragic antithesis of itself.

Writings, Articles, Essays, and Volumes by Margherita Grassini Sarfatti

1913. Le suffragiste inglesi. *La Voce*, 2 October.
1915a. Lettera ad un giovane italiano. *La Difesa delle Lavoratrici,* 15 March.
1915b. *La milizia femminile in Francia.* Ravà & C.
1917. Le arti plastiche. *Gli Avvenimenti,* 2, 21–28 January.

[27] Wieland (2006).

1919. *La fiaccola accesa. Polemiche d'arte*. Istituto editoriale italiano.
1921. *I vivi e l'ombra* (lyrics). Facchi Editore.
1923a. Tunisiaca. *Gerarchia, 6*, 1134–1140.
1923b. Ancora il problema di Tunisi. *Gerarchia, 7*, 1190–1196.
1923c. *Tunisiaca,* preface of Benito Mussolini (alias "Latinus"). Mondadori; Handwritten copy in Central State Archives, Autographs of the Duce, envelope 7, file 6.5.2.
1924a. Cinema Spagna. *Gerarchia, 10.*
1924b. Spagna mistica. Avila di Santa Teresa. *La Rivista Illustrata del Popolo d'Italia, 8*, 32–36.
1925a. *Segni, colori e luci.* Zanichelli.
1925b. *Achille Funi.* Hoepli.
1925c. *Dux.* Butterworth (ediz. It. Mondadori, 1926).
1927. Luigi Luzzati. *Gerarchia.*
1929. *Il Palazzone* (novel). Mondadori.
1930a. *Storia della pittura moderna.* Paolo Cremonese.
1930b. La povertà delle terre ricche. *Gerarchia.*
1930c. Speculum. *Gerarchia.*
1931a. Decennale. *Gerarchia.*
1931b. Individualismo e Fascismo. *Gerarchia.*
1932a. L'universalità della politica italiana. *Gerarchia.*
1932b. Orientamenti e presage. *Gerarchia.*
1935. *Daniele Ranzoni.* Reale Accademia d'Italia.
1937. *America, ricerca della felicità.* Mondadori.
1950. *Casanova contro Don Giovanni.* Mondadori.
1955. *Acqua passata* (memoir). Cappelli.
1958. *L'amore svalutato.* ERS.

Documentary sources

Archive A. F. Formiggini, authors (3 letters), Biblioteca Estense, Modena.
Archive Casciola (35 letters, 1916–25), Ispettoria salesiana sicula, Messina.
Archive Sarfatti Margherita, 35 letters, 4 telegrams by D'annunzio, General Archive of Il Vittoriale degli Italiani, Gardone Riviera.
Arnoldo Mondadori, Authors' Archive, Margherita Sarfatti (57 letters, 1922–25), Mondadori Foundation, Segrate.
Duse Eleonora archive (9 letters, 1918–24), Cini Foundation, Venice.
Fogazzaro-Roi Archive, Grassini Margherita, 3 letters, 1908, and Grassini Vivanti Lina, 4 letters, 1907–09), Bertoliana Library, Vicenza.
Gerarchia (1922–1943), National Central Library, Rome.
Historical and art critics' competition 1903, Biennale contemporary art historical archives, Venice.
Margherita Sarfatti archive, 51 envelopes, 16 binders, 1 folder (including 884 files, 234 photographs, 15 notebooks, etc.), Mart, Rovereto.
Martini F. papers, b. 20, f. 33, 11 letters 1921–1933, Archivio Centrale dello Stato, Rome.
Orvieto Angiolo archive (13 letters, 1902–13), Gabinetto Viesseux, Florence.
Panzini-Sarfatti Archive, 52 letters, 1914–37, Sovrintendenza ai beni librari e documentari della regione Emilia-Romagna, Bologna.
Paolo Buzzi archive, coll. Margherita Grassini Sarfatti-Buzzi, (3 letters, 1924–33), Biblioteca comunale Sormani, Milan.
Papini archive (20 letters, 1926–48), Primo Conti Foundation, Fiesole.
Prezzolini Archive, 38 letters, 1904–38, Cantonal Library, Lugano.

References

Balabanoff, A. (1976). *La mia vita di rivoluzionaria*. Feltrinelli.

Barisoni, E. (2018). *Viaggio alle fonti dell'arte: il moderno e l'eterno. Margherita Sarfatti 1919–1939*. Zel Edizioni.

Basilico Pisaturo, A. (1990). *Margherita Grassini Sarfatti. Tra futurismo e metafisica*. La Buona stampa.

Bini, M. (2009). *Sull'ondivaga prora. Margherita Sarfatti: arte, passione e po*litica. Centro editoriale toscano.

Boschiero, N. (2018). *Il Maestro e Margherita. Marinetti, Sarfatti e il futurismo negli anni del regime*. Mart.

Cannistraro, P. V., & Sullivan, B. R. (1993). *The Duce's other woman*. Morrow.

De Felice, R. (1961). *Storia degli ebrei sotto il fascismo*. Einaudi.

De Felice, R. (1966). *Mussolini il fascista, I, La conquista del potere (1021–1925)*. Einaudi.

De Felice, R. (1975). *Intervista sul Fascismo* (by M. Leeden). Laterza.

De Grazia, V. (1993). *Le donne nel regime fascista*. Marsilio.

De Rosa, L. (1981). *La rivoluzione industriale in Italia*. Laterza.

Ferrario, R. (2015). *La regina dell'arte nell'Italia fascista*. Mondadori.

Festorazzi, R. (2010). *Margherita Sarfatti. La donna che inventò Mussolini*. Angelo Colla Editore.

Folli, S. (1993, February 1). Intervista a Renzo De Felice. *Corriere della Sera*.

Gentile, E. (1993). *Il culto del littorio. La sacralizzazione della politica nell'Italia fascista*. Laterza.

Gentile, G. (1925). *Che cosa è il fascismo*. Vallecchi editore.

Bruno Guerri, G. (2017). La trasvolata di Balbo. *Il Giornale.it*, 28 giugno.

Keynes, J. M. (1932). "State Planning", radio address on 14 March. In *The collected writings* (CWK. 1971–1989) (vol. XXI, pp. 84–92). Royal Economic Society.

Kuliscioff, A. (1949–1959). *Carteggio* (by A. Schiavi). Einaudi.

Marzorati, S. (1990). *Margherita Sarfatti*. Biographical essay. Nodo Libri.

Mattei, C. E. (2017). Austerity and repressive politics: Italian economists in the early years of the fascist government. *The European Journal of the History of Economic Thought, 24*(5), 998–1026.

Megaro, G. (1947). *Mussolini. Dal mito alla realtà*. Istituto Editoriale Italiano.

Mussolini, B., & Gentile, G. (1932). La dottrina del fascismo. In E. Susmel & D. Susmel (Eds.), 1951–1974 (Vol. XXXIV, pp. 117–138). La Fenice.

Navarra, Q. (1946). *Memorie del cameriere di Mussolini*. Longanesi.

Negri, G., & Simoni, S. (1990). *Le costituzioni inattuate*. Editor Colombo.

Ruskin, J. (1851–1853/1987). *Le pietre di Venezia*. Rizzoli.

Schulenburg, von der S. (2010). *Il barone*. La nave di Teseo.

Scurati, A. (2018). *M. Il figlio del secolo*. Bompiani

Scurati, A. (2020). *M. L'Uomo della provvidenza*. Bompiani.

Serpieri, A. (1930). *La guerra e le classi rurali italiane*. Yale University Press and Bari.

Susmel, E., & Susmel, D. (eds.) (1951–1974). *Opera Omnia* di Benito Mussolini (1951 [36 vols.], 1974 [8 vols.], pp. 18,000). La Fenice.

Urso, S. (1994). La formazione di Margherita Sarfatti e l'adesione al fascismo. *Studi Storici, 1*, 153–181.

Wieland, K. (2006). *Margherita Sarfatti, l'amante del duce*. Utet.

Zapponi, N. (1996). L'oracolo azzittito: Margherita G. Sarfatti. *Storia Contemporanea, XXVII*(5). Ottobre.

In the Name of Equality. Women's Action to Shape the Right to Work in the Italian Constituent Assembly

Claudia Rotondi

1 The Tip of the Iceberg

Investigating women's actions in the Constituent Assembly on the affirmation of rights to equal pay and access to all professions, requires starting from a consideration of the role and identity women had in that specific historical phase. It is, therefore, worthwhile considering how women became—or rather longed to become—active participants in the Reconstruction of their country from the Resistance until obtaining the right to vote on the ratification of the Constitution (§2) (Fig. 1).

The Constituent Assembly was in effect the institutional stage in which issues already present in the political debate were addressed, and the place where their implementation into strategies could be—to some extent—influenced by the constitutional dictate that women helped define when acting as a unified group, even if bearers of different political stances and cultures (§3). Work was the one issue around which they rallied, where they were most cohesive and thus contributed in unison to clarifying important articles of the Constitution by participating in crucial debates on equal rights (§4).

The difficulty in countering a culture that was frequently misogynistic, sometimes unconsciously so, emerged with a certain frequency in the Constituents' debates. It reached a climax in the debate on access to the professions, in particular to the judiciary (§5). The debate not only covered entrance to all professions—the wording of which had not yet been established in the constitutional dictate—but also the issue of equal pay—which, on the contrary, was already affirmed in the Constitution. It emerges as an issue requiring a transformative outlook and mentality not only among the major parties but also in the trade unions, where women have been active for decades, and where they expect to be listened to attentively, but which is not often the case in practice (§6).

C. Rotondi (✉)
Università Cattolica del Sacro Cuore, Milan, Italy
e-mail: claudia.rotondi@unicatt.it

M. Mosca (ed.), *Women at Work in Italy (1750–1950)*, Springer Studies in the History of Economic Thought, https://doi.org/10.1007/978-3-031-64281-4_13

Manifestazione dei Gruppi di difesa della donna a Milano.

Fig.1 Demonstration of Women's Defense Groups in Milan (1945)

The reflections expressed in this work are linked to several research questions, in particular, if the women's actions in the Constituent Assembly were effective in terms of achievements and ideals; if so, in what terms, if not, for which reasons. Although only the tip of the iceberg is touched upon in this chapter, a few aspects can be highlighted (§7).

2 A Matter of Role and Identity

An issue that in my view should be considered to gain a better grasp of the role of women in post-World War II Italy is the gap between two aspects: on the one hand, the data on their presence in the workforce, let's call it their role; on the other hand, the cultural model of the woman with which Italian culture is permeated, and thus the difficulty of constructing a new, more wholesome identity.

Factual data alone are not sufficient to define the role of women in the Italian economy and society, although they do help for a better understanding of the situation.

The data show that women had already been an active part of the productive workforce for several decades.

World War I had forced a shift in women's employment patterns and by 1936 there were more than five million female workers in Italy, more than half were employed in agriculture. In the secondary sector, there were more than 1.2 million women, mainly employed in textiles, wool and cotton production. In the tertiary sector, the activity women were significantly involved in was teaching.

In percentage terms, women were 29.2% of the total number of workers employed in agriculture, 25% of those employed in industry, and 30% of those employed in the service sector (Istat, 2011, p. 470).

During World War II, women once again were present in every productive sector replacing men off at war. In the post-World War II period, while the presence of women in the labour force was not substantially different from what it had been in the 1930s, there was a significant difference. Empowered by their participation in the country's struggle for Liberation, women had become increasingly aware of their role and wanted to play a more active part in the reconstruction of Italy's economy and society.

During the Resistance, women were a fundamental presence in various spheres: in civil Resistance (with tasks of assistance, logistical support, dissemination of information, proselytism) and in the armed Resistance.[1] Within the GDD (Gruppi di Difesa della Donna, Women's Defence Groups)[2] and also in intermediate bodies—i.e., trade unions, university student associations; women's associations—a political consciousness was spreading that led to the determination to engage in the process of socio-cultural equalising, the conquest of civil rights and obtaining a political voice (Bravo & Bruzzone, 2000, Dau Novelli, 1995).

This dynamic poses problems in defining the role and identity not only of women but also of men.

Politics and society must provide answers to this demand for equality, which intertwines—and clashes—with no small opposition to changing the existing model. In fact, it is hard to reconcile it with the 'feminine mystique' with which the role of women in Italy is imbued: a woman is first and foremost the caretaker of the family (Bellassai, 2000; Mafai, 1979). Nevertheless, since women have had the right to vote since February 1945, obtaining their support becomes important.

The two major parties in Italy—Christian Democrats and Communists—and all parties in general, did not deny the importance of women's active participation. 'The parties are courting us' stated the Constituent Nadia Gallico Spano.[3]

---

[1] On women's participation in the Resistance, the historical reconstruction is still incomplete, and figures are underestimated. The most consolidated data refer to 70,000 women belonging to the Women's Defence Groups; 35,000 recognised partisans; 4600 arrested; and 2750 deported as resistance fighters. More than 600 women were shot or died in combat. Only about 15 were awarded the medal for military valour (Rossi-Doria, 1994, p. 781). Once the war ended, there was a tendency to consider the female presence in the Resistance as having had a sort of mass "maternage" effect (Bravo & Bruzzone, 2000; Casalini, 2007). In the Resistance, the woman supposedly showed her maternal side by caring for the disadvantaged. It was more difficult to accept women as female partisan fighters. This role was hardly reconcilable with the role of 'woman-mother'. Some personal testimonies by female partisans clearly show that this fact was difficult to preserve as a collective memory and was even concealed during the initial moments following Liberation. See, for example, the testimony of Trottolina in M. Casalini (2005, p. 75).

[2] More than 40,000 women with different political views joined the GDD. What brought them together was not only their opposition to the Nazi-fascist occupation but also their desire to contribute to the rebirth of their country (Orlandini 2018; Betti, 2020). Unless stated otherwise, the translations of the quoted texts are our own.

[3] See D'Amico and D'Amico (2020, p. 19). But beware of the transitory nature of this courtship.

The attitudes of the major parties as well as the political climate can be inferred from the words of their leaders, both of whom were attentive to the involvement of women, albeit with different nuances.

On the one hand there was Palmiro Togliatti, the leader of the Communist Party; in his speech to the Communist Women's Conference in June 1945, he encouraged them and in a certain sense offered a bit of 'constructive' criticism:

> It seems to me ... that you have not yet put in the right perspective that all our work in the field that interests you is aimed at bringing about the emancipation of women, or what the value of emancipation is in today's society in Italy, or what the fundamental demands are of the struggle that must be conducted for the emancipation of women [...]. If we actually want to carry out a democratic revolution in Italy, which will transform our political institutions, economic life and customs, we must solve the problem of women's emancipation and solve it in all its aspects, namely in its economic, political, social and moral aspects, in the broadest sense of the term. (Togliatti, 1973, pp. 37–39)

On the other hand, De Gasperi, the leader of the Christian Democrats since 1908 and after World War II (De Gasperi, 1949), saw no obstacle to what he called reasonable feminism, and considered opposing positions as anti-historical.[4] His view was quite clear:

> We are in favour of the participation of women in public affairs in such forms and to such extents as the status of woman as mother, woman as wife, woman as mistress of the family permits. (De Gasperi, 1908)

On women's suffrage, however, both major parties had their worries. The Communist Party's greatest concern revolved around how the monarchy and the Christian Democratic Party attracted greater electoral support from women, who were more receptive to the messages of traditional institutions such as the monarchy and the Church. Moreover, there was the conviction that the cultural lag in southern Italy played more in favour of the Christian Democrats.

Catholics feared abstentionism and considered women as 'less educated in the exercise of political rights'. These fears were at the origin of the battle that the Christian Democratic Party waged in favour of compulsory voting and the remarkable dedication of the women in the party on that issue.

In Italy, as is well known, the position of the Catholic Church is very influential. A reference to Pope Pius XII's thoughts on the role of women and their summons to vote, expressed on the eve of their participation in the Constituent Assembly, shows how women—particularly female Christian Democrats—unequivocally received a message on their involvement with the institutions.

One often finds reference to how Pius XII encouraged women with a quote summarised as *tua res agitur* (i.e., it is your concern) in a speech addressed to

---

It is interesting to note what women delegates did after this political experience. Very few remained parliamentarians for a prolonged period, some became active in trade unions, others in local government, and some returned to their previous occupations. The term 'political seasonal workers' (Fiume 2007) fits this example well.

[4] On De Gasperi's early steps in politics and his presence in the Habsburg Parliament, see Pombeni (2007).

women associations on 21 October 1945. In summary, in the message he states that: public life needs women to preserve the 'dignity of women also in the legislation', a dignity which is fulfilled in motherhood and is realised within the family. This was a campaign that, by virtue of the right to vote, was played out at the political level.

Urbanisation, the growth of larger companies at the expense of smaller ones, challenges faced by artisans and farmers, unemployment, and women abandoning their households to support their husbands were all extremely worrying issues. What was the Catholic woman to do in this situation? She must act. The Pope stated:

> Will you perhaps leave to others, to those who promote or who are accomplices in the ruin of the domestic hearth, the monopoly of social organisation, of which the family is the principal element in its economic, juridical, spiritual, and moral unity?

This is the meaning of *tua res agitur*. The destiny of humanity was at stake. Hence:

> the ballot paper in the hands of the Catholic woman is an important means of fulfilling her rigorous conscientious duty, especially in the present time. (Pio XII, 2003, p. 222)

The positions of the major parties and the Church were well known to the women Constituents (Bizzarri, 1980; Corghi, 1979). It is therefore legitimate to ask how and to what extent these stances influenced their actions in the Assembly.

3 At the Constituent Assembly: Women as a Group

After a tiny representation in the *Consulta Nazionale i.e.* National Council (September 1945-May 1946), a non-elective body entrusted with preparing the guidelines for the Constitution where parties nominated 13 women out of the 440 members,[5] after an absolutely minor presence—one could even call it invisible—in the *Ministero per la Costituente* i.e. Ministry for the Constituent Assembly, another non-elective body tasked with preparing the needed elements for a new Constitution,[6] and after the first experience with active and passive participation of the

[5] The Consulta Nazionale i.e. the National Council was active from 25 September 1945. On it there were thirteen women members who shared an anti-fascist culture and partisan experience. Five would be elected to the Constituent Assembly. These 13 women out of 440 members represented 2.9% of the total. They actively participated in the committees on industry and commerce; education and the fine arts; labour and social security; political and administrative affairs; agriculture and food. The proposals of the National Council committees were in appearance technical; however, they played an important political and social role. The proposals made by the women constituents were especially on issues concerning school, work, integral education of the person (Camera dei Deputati, 1948).

[6] The only woman on the *Commissione economica del Ministero per la Costituente* (a committee expressly dedicated to studying the economic issues for the Constituent Assembly), headed by Giovanni Demaria, was Maria Luisa Boggeri, a pupil of Benvenuto Griziotti's, who was called to serve on the sub-committee for the study of labour problems chaired by Antonio Pesenti from January to June 1946. In this role Boggeri - who subsequently would be the translator and editor of volume III of the Italian edition of Karl Marx's Capital - drafted a memoir on the problem of

electorate in the municipal elections of March 1946,[7] on 2 June 1946, 21 women, out of the 556 members, were elected to the Constituent Assembly.[8] Nine were from the Communist Party; nine from the Christian Democrats; two from the Socialist Party; and one from the *Uomo Qualunque* Party—i.e. Everyman's Party—a populist, anti-Communist group.[9] Five were also part of the smaller *Commissione per la Costituzione* or *Commissione dei 75,* a 75-member committee with the task of drafting and proposing a Constitution to the Assembly.

This group of women shared some commonalities. They were all 'politicised' women, between the ages of 25 and 65, with different experiences but in no sense naive or unprepared. They were well acquainted with the views of their parties of reference, and even with the different active currents within them, as in the case of the Christian Democrats. These women had assimilated and embraced the climate of renewal within the country, firmly believing in their right/duty to contribute to the reconstruction of Italy. They were acutely aware of their responsibility to represent a vast electorate and advocate for women's rights to be included in the Constitution: in the workplace, family, and society.

unemployment which she signed with her husband's surname, Ambrosini (Ambrosini, 1946). On the activities of the sub-committee on labour problems see: Rotondi 2011. On the work of the Ministry for the Constituent Assembly see: Fondazione Pietro Nenni (1995). Further useful information on Boggeri's academic career can be found in Letizia Pagliai's chapter in this volume.

[7] After an initial, politically unimportant possibility for women's active participation—though subject to their husbands' consent—envisaged by the Crispi Charity Law of 1890, and after the failed promises of Mussolini's initial programmes, women were finally allowed to vote in 1946. The right to vote was already enshrined in Decree No. 23/1945, but the same contained a serious omission. The text, in fact, did not mention passive suffrage, and Italian women were thus in the anomalous position of being able to vote but not to be candidates. The issue was not remedied until more than a year later. With Decree No. 74/1946 entitled Norms for the Election of Deputies to the Constituent Assembly, women were fully equalized with men in the political rights of active and passive suffrage (Camera dei Deputati, 1965). In the local elections of March 1946, female participation was close to 90%. The first female mayors elected numbered less than a dozen, but they were well distributed throughout the territory, in the north, centre and south of Italy; in addition, more than 2000 female members were elected to municipal councils (Rossi-Doria, 1996; Weber, 1977).

[8] On 2 June 1946, a referendum was held on the institutional form of the state (Republic or Monarchy). At the same time elections for 556 deputies to the Constituent Assembly were held. 25 June 1946 was the Assembly's first meeting. On 31 January 1946 the Project, i. e. the draft constitution, was presented to the Constituent Assembly. Discussions and debates on the articles were held from 4 March to 22 December 1946. The Constitution was approved on 22 December 1947 and came into force on 1 January 1948.

[9] Of these 21 women, 9 belonged to the Christian Democrats: Laura Bianchini; Elsa Conci; Filomena Delli Castelli; Maria De Unterrichter Jervolino; Maria Federici Agamben; Angela Gotelli; Angela Maria Cingolani Guidi; Maria Nicotra Fiorini; Vittoria Titomanlio; 9 to the Communist party: Adele Bei Ciufoli, Nadia Gallico Spano, Leonilde Iotti, Teresa Mattei, Angiola Minella Molinari, Rita Montagnana Togliatti, Teresa Noce Longo, Elettra Pollastrini, Maria Maddalena Rossi; 2 to the Socialist group: Bianca Bianchi and Angela Merlin; and 1 woman belonged to *Uomo Qualunque* (Everyman's Party): Ottavia Penna Buscemi (Serantoni, 2009; Sarsini, 2021).

We could ask what experience these twenty-one constituents had of the realm of employment and its problems? Well, their backgrounds were in themselves representative of different worlds: they were factory workers, housewives, teachers, trade unionists, journalists, scientists. Fourteen were university graduates. Many suffered prison, exile, or deportation, and participated in the Resistance.

In the Constituent Assembly they spoke not only on typically women's issues—such as family and gender equality—but also on themes not directly related to the status of women, such as the school system, property rights, the role of regions, the inclusion of workers on company boards, and land reform.

On 'women's' issues, in general, they worked together irrespective of the party to which they belonged. On other issues, their political identity emerged more clearly, and they spoke in a manner consistent with the views expressed by their party.[10]

4 A United Action on Equality and Access to Work

Let us examine the united actions of the women elected to the Constituent Assembly.

Two topics of particular interest took centre stage in discussions where women exhibited a united and proactive stance: equality—including equal wages—and the right to work along with access to more employment opportunities.

Women strived to secure greater access and enter domains previously inaccessible to them including politics, productive activities, and institutions. In this regard the case of the magistracy, as we will see, is emblematic.

We can consider various articles on this subject. Women Constituents took part in many debates and their contributions to Articles 3, 37, 51, and 106 of the Constitution are of particular interest.[11]

Let us consider Article 3, on the equal social dignity of citizens:

> All citizens have equal social dignity and are equal before the law, <u>without distinction of sex</u>, race, language, religion, political opinion, personal and social conditions.
>
> It is the task of the Republic to remove economic and social, which, <u>in fact</u> restrict the freedom and equality of citizens, prevent the full development of the individual and the

---

[10] It is important to highlight not only the areas of convergence but also of divergence, so as to distance from a distorted portrayal of these women as an indivisible group, as often conveyed by the literature. Indeed, these women showed differences in political sensitivity, political culture, and life experiences, despite belonging to the same party. On the other hand, they also showed some points of convergence even if they did not belong to the same party. For example, the women elected from the Christian Democratic Party were affiliated to markedly different currents, some more conservative others more progressive. Among the members of the Communist Party there are very diverse experiences of life and political culture especially between the older and the younger generations. Among the younger women, there were considerable differences in their political careers: some were closer to the leaders—Nilde Iotti remained in Parliament for 53 years—and others quickly distanced themselves from the official party lines and were expelled—this was the case of Nilde Iotti's peer, Teresa Mattei.

[11] Moreover, they also engaged—as a group—in interesting discussions on the family (Art. 29) and the right to vote (Art. 48). See, between others: Addis Saba, De Leo, Taricone (1996).

> effective participation of all workers in the political, economic, and social organization of the country.

The underlined parts indicate the points on which the women Constituents intervened most effectively.

They held a united front on the need for equal rights for women and men in the public domain. This unitary action resulted in the achievement of an important objective. Lina Merlin proposed the addition of reference to sex discrimination: 'without distinction of sex'.[12]

Teresa Mattei proposed the addition of the expression 'in fact' to integrate the reference to economic and social obstacles that limit freedom and equality.[13]

In this way, in the first paragraph of Article 3, equality under law is thus enshrined and in the second, de facto equality is established (Carullo, 1959; Falzone et al., 1948).

Another aspect relating to equality is touched upon in Article 37 of the Constitution, included in the first part on the Rights and Duties of Citizens, in Title III devoted to economic relations. The subject of equal rights and equal pay in employment is addressed here.

It is reproduced in part here:

> The working woman has the same rights and, for equal work, the same wages as the male worker.
>
> Working conditions must permit the fulfillment of her essential family functions and ensure special, appropriate, protection for the mother and child.

In the first paragraph the women Constituents moved in unison.

The addition of the underlined phrase is due to the initiative of female Constituents. Their aim in this case was to promote women's work, while at the same time protecting the family and their maternal role.[14] We can say that in this case they were able to introduce a principle still capable of providing a guideline for equality,

---

[12] See her speech of 13 September 1946 in Assemblea Costituente – Commissione per la Costituzione (1946, pp. 33–34).

[13] The reasons given by Teresa Mattei for the addition of the clause were well expressed in her speech of 18 March 1947: "While recognising the constitutional declaration as a great achievement, this is not enough for us. Italian women want something more, something more explicit and concrete to help them take their first steps towards de facto equality, in every sphere, economic, political, social, and national life [...] That is why we demand that there be no ambiguity, in any article or in any word of the Constitution, that could be an easy foothold for those who still want to prevent and restrain women on this liberating path [...] Unfortunately, an underestimation of women is still ingrained in the current mentality, it is comprised of a bit of contempt and a bit of pity, which has hitherto greatly hindered or even forbidden the full contribution of women's energies and abilities in numerous domains of national life. This obstacle must be overcome. The article helps us, but it must be accompanied by a profound change in the current mentality, in every sphere, in every field of Italian life. [....] You will say that this [i.e. the insertion of the expression 'in fact'] is a pleonasm. We, however, believe that 'in fact' should be specified. [...] Help us all to truly and completely loosen all the bonds that still bind the hands of women, and you will have new arms, freely working for the reconstruction of Italy, for safely building the Italian Republic of workers" (Assemblea Costituente, 1947a, pp. 2267–2271).

[14] It is interesting to emphasise that jurists today tend to give a non-restrictive interpretation of Article 37, which seeks to combine the essential family function referred to in the article not only

taking into account certain specificities: work and family are not in conflict (as it should be, both for women and for men). This perspective renders attainable the expression 'essential family function', on which, moreover, there had already been many discussions at the time.[15]

A mention should be made to Article 51, on equal access to careers. Article 48 (then 51) of the Constitution Project begins with:

> All citizens of both sexes have equal access to public offices in accordance with their aptitudes, according to the rules established by law.

To grasp the significance of the debate on this article of the Constitution, it is important to briefly review the features of the prevailing norms during the fascist period, which sought to restrict the presence of women in the workforce and in professions considered crucial to the regime's policies. That period was characterised by a legislation defined as 'expulsive' (Ballestrero,, 1979, p. 73) in view of the many restrictions on the presence of women in public employment, emblematically in schools, the sector with the highest rate of female workers. For example, women were barred from teaching history, philosophy, and economics in classical and scientific high schools and technical institutes. They could only teach these subjects in schools that prepared primary school teachers, which were institutions attended almost exclusively by female pupils.[16]

There was also a cap of 10% to the number of administrative posts available to women through public competitions as well as a priori exclusion from certain jobs (Scarponi, 2019, p. 343).

In this context, the phrase 'in accordance with their aptitudes' as presented in the draft article, was perceived as particularly hurtful by the women Constituents since it limited women's involvement in public affairs to cases where women's abilities did not clash with their required responsibilities. The insertion of this phrase sparked protests from the female Assembly members, who stood united in their dissent. Maria Federici proposed a different wording without the phrase. During the discussion she pointed out that the inclusion of the aptitude clause was not only offensive, but it passed judgement on women's abilities without considering the possibility of evaluating them.

In her speech at the Assembly on 22 May 1947, Federici states:

---

with regard to women, but as an objective of equality for both sexes, so as to facilitate and increase parental leave for both parents. An evolutionary interpretation of the article thus emphasises the value of equality also with respect to the family, in order to encourage the participation of fathers in family management (Catelani, 2019, pp. 72–73).

[15] For the complete debate see: Assemblea Costituente, 1947b. Also important in this regard were the positions taken by Nilde Iotti in the discussion on this subject within the *Commissione dei 75* (Assemblea Costituente. Commissione per la Costituzione, 1946c). For a juridical historical perspective on this topic, see D'Amico (2019).

[16] See Royal Decree, RD 2480/1926. Previous, Royal Decrees (Royal Decree 1054/1923 and Royal Decree 899/1940) already prevented women from being heads of schools or institutions in secondary education. On the consideration of women in the fascist period see: De Grazia (1993).

> we women from all sections of the Assembly have picked up a particular intention in Article 48, namely that it is intended to restrict women's access to public office or elected positions [...] clearly there is an idea here to create a barrier against women. And yet what evidence is there to suggest that women are not capable of holding managerial positions? And that women cannot hold public or state office? It is a prejudice, a preconception. And indeed, the whole history of women's affirmations shows that preconceptions have always had to be overcome. We must therefore also overcome this barrier [...] Talking about requirements is quite different from talking about aptitudes.[17]

After the debate, the following wording was approved for Article 51:

> All citizens of either sex have equal access to public offices and elected positions, in accordance with the requirements established by law.[18]

5 Women in the Judiciary: The Case of Article 106

The emblematic case of Article 106 of the Italian Constitution is linked to Article 51, hence to the issue of women's access to (or exclusion from) professions. In article 106 the possibility is discussed for women to access the magistrate's career. In the Draft Constitution, it is specified that also women can be appointed as magistrates. This provision is subsequently omitted from the article approved by the Assembly.

The very first draft of the article, proposed by the jurist Piero Calamandrei, explicitly includes the possibility of admitting women to the judiciary.[19]

While the formulation of Article 98 of the Draft discussed in the *Commissione dei 75* states that 'Women may also be appointed in cases provided for by the judicial system', Article 106 of the Constitution completely omits any reference to women:

> Magistrate appointments take place by competitive exam.

[17] We should pay attention to Federici's subsequent statements, which reveal her political sensitivity, different from that of other Constituents, at least at this stage. Her speech balances the need for emancipation and the need to respect party and Church instructions. After stating that "it is strange that a woman, who pays taxes and bears all the burdens of social life, should not then be able to proceed in her career on an equal footing with men. I hope this is the last time a constitution has to mention women's rights in order to claim them", Federici adds: "we know and want that a woman, as queen of the home, must ask the Constitution and obtain the right to be in charge of bringing up her children, and of governing her own home. This is the crown of woman. But a woman must be free to make her choice, follow her spontaneous desire, guided by education or other elements of value, even spiritual ones, but never by reason of an injustice that offends her deeply" (Assemblea Costituente, 1947c, p. 4171).

[18] Constitutional Law n. 1 of 30 May 2003 amended the first paragraph of this Article by adding the sentence underlined: "All citizens of either sex may have access to public office and elected positions under conditions of equality, according to the requirements established by law. <u>To this end, the Republic shall promote equal opportunities between women and men by appropriate measures</u>".

[19] "Magistrates are appointed by Presidential decree upon the proposal of the Superior Council of the Judiciary, on the basis of competitive exam followed by a probationary period. The requirements for admission to the exam are established by the Law on Judicial Order; women are also eligible" (Assemblea Costituente. Commissione per la Costituzione, 1946a).

A veritable male wall was erected, creating a hostile environment for women seeking to enter the judiciary. However, the women Constituents, united on this issue, presented and achieved the ratification of an agenda formulated as follows:

> The Constituent Assembly, considering that Article 48 [then 51] guarantees all citizens of both sexes the right to access elective and public office, under conditions of equality, according to the requirements established by law, affirms that with regard to women's access to the Judiciary, Article 48 [51] contains the necessary guarantees for the enforcement of this right. (Assemblea Costituente, 1947e, p. 2517)

After having participated in that shameful debate, the women Constituents were fully aware that it would be difficult to convince men to vote in favour of an amendment that explicitly restores complete equality in access to the judiciary. Most women Constituents, therefore, preferred to eliminate any normative reference on that point, hoping to be able to achieve access with the provisions in Article 51.

It is evident that at this point the women Constituents were faced with a cultural obstacle: what has been established 'by law' may not become so 'in fact'. The women Constituents emphasised on several occasions the need to overcome gender prejudice and, even more, the already mentioned 'feminine mystique'.

Opposition to allowing women access to the magistracy cut across party lines and was characterised by often overlapping arguments that ranged from women having a highly emotional nature, to their lack of rationality, to their supposedly inadequate physiology, to the belief that they are more naturally suited for domestic occupations, which should not be compromised by diverting their attention elsewhere.

A florilegium of some expressions that emerge in the debate on Article 106 is useful to define the cultural climate within which women were immersed. Some men expressed the fear that women could 'invade the field of justice', or 'create a two-tier justice'. Other opponents pointed out that access to the judiciary for 'women do not seem very appropriate'; a 'woman is psychologically and intellectually different from a man'; 'this function, which is so serious, so complex, is not suited to the female spirit'; 'equilibrium is lacking in women even due to physiological reasons'. And others stated that 'it is good for women to leave this heavy and sometimes terrible responsibility to men', or that 'an excess of [female] sentimental contributions must be resisted and addressed' (Assemblea Costituente, 1947d).

Looking at the verbal expressions used in the debates at the Constituent Assembly cross-party affiliations, in my view provide an accurate account of the extent of the problem: the right of women to access the magistracy in fact became an emblematic node around which a debate developed that revealed the profoundly misogynist attitudes of many male Constituents. These attitudes would permeate the legislation and jurisprudence of subsequent years.

In reading the debate, the lack of vision of the 'Constituent Fathers' becomes painfully apparent. Many of the opinions expressed reveal how the principle of equality established in Article 3 fails to even scratch the surface of the prejudices that exist against women. In fact, the debate is a very short-sighted entrenched approach in favour of preserving the status quo. Sadly, the Constituent Assembly on this matter missed the crucial opportunity of translating the principles expressed in the first part of the constitutional dictate into an effective implementation in favour of women's rights.

The desire expressed by the Constituents, hoping that the approved agenda mentioned above could serve as a key to unlock women's access to the judiciary, did not align with the reality at the time. It was only through the ruling of Law No. 33 in 1960 that the Constitutional Court declared as unconstitutional the exclusion of women from various positions, including the judiciary. This legal decision marked a notable step towards ensuring gender equality in the judicial system. This pronouncement was followed in 1963 by Law No. 66, which allowed access to all public offices, professions and jobs, including the judiciary. It was not, however, until 1965 that the first female magistrate was appointed in Italy.[20]

6 A Less Predictable Arena: Trade Unions

The debate on Article 106 in the Constituent Assembly clearly showed the need for women to engage in a significant cultural battle. That battle started with this article but also spilled over to less expected arenas, such as Trade Unions.

This second example allows us to open a window on a further, much more complex issue: that of trade unions as a place of affirmation of women's rights.

Several of the women Constituents came from a strong trade union background, proving that the trade union was a fundamental environment for them to get training and gain experience. Therefore, it was logical for women with that type of background to believe that the trade union could serve as a platform to effectively promote and implement equality in treatment and wages, as advocated by the Constituent Assembly and partially incorporated during the women's militancy.

But this was not the case.

Some remarks may help to showcase how this aspect is essential for understanding both the roots of the women's proposals in the Constituent Assembly and the subsequent developments.

On the right to participate also with one's own work in the reconstruction of Italy, prior to the Constituent Assembly the most advanced positions were those of the UDI(Italian Women's Union)[21] who in 1944 published an article in the Association's

[20] In this regard, it may be interesting to note that women magistrates in Italy today account for 55% of the total (Consiglio superiore della Magistratura, 2022).

[21] In the UDI, which had grown out of the 'Women's Defence Groups' established in 1944 during the Resistance, trade union committees were set up to start drafting proposals on the difficult wage and contractual conditions of female workers. At the stage when the trade union did not yet have an independent structure, these committees were the main forum for drafting and advocating women's issues. It is also important to note that UDI submitted a set of requests to the female members of the Constituent Assembly on women's rights, asking them to do their utmost to have them included in the Constitution. These demands include legal equality, the right to enter all professions, and equal pay (UDI, 1944). On the role of UDI, see: Tola (2016).

magazine[22] 'Noi Donne' ('Us Women'). The article reports on a conference of Roman women workers promoted by the UDI in December 1944 that ended with a trade union plan for women (UDI, 1944). The main points of this plan concerned: the right for women to earn a wage equal to men for equal work; the enforcement of protective laws; and the possibility for women to participate in core trade union bodies so as to stimulate the union to address women's issues.

Although immediately after WWII the CGIL (Italian General Confederation of Labour), the unitary national Italian trade union, placed equal pay among its top issues to address,[23] a number of barriers came in the way of this goal.

The best-known version of what happened is that within the unitary CGIL, reconstituted with the Rome Pact of June 1944 that was to hold until July 1948, there were no homogeneous positions on women's work (Barbadoro, 1973; Betti, 2018; Carera & Coppola, 2014; Lunadeiet al., 1999).

The lack of a united front was mainly attributed to the Catholic component, which was against equating women's work with men's work, believing this to be a potential threat to the 'natural' function of women in the family unit. In addition, the presence of women in the labour force, during a time of dramatic unemployment, was possibly perceived as a threat even by those who did not fully share this view of the female role.

Another factor that complicates the notion of this 'right' is the matter of veterans who, upon returning from the war, found in various cases that their jobs are no longer available and that they had been replaced by women. Moreover, even in left-wing organisations the male model as the breadwinner-worker prevails and women's wages are seen at best as complementary to those of men's (Pescarolo, 2019). For reasons including the ones mentioned, the goal of equal salaries seemed, at least at this stage, unattainable or, rather premature. The issue of equal pay for women quickly slipped from being a priority to becoming postponable.

At the Naples Congress in 1945, Giuseppe Di Vittorio, the communist union leader, stated that neglecting women means neglecting 'an important part of the Italian working masses' (CGIL, 1977, p. 162). At the same congress, a special structure within the organisation was established to deal with women's labour issues. Although female trade unionists continued to insist on the inclusion of equal pay (Secco, 1945), in the Trade Union agreements of May and October 1946 the reference was omitted (Daviso, 1950; Pennacchi, 1976; Tobagi, 1976).

Among the strongest voices opposing the traditional cultural model were those of the Constituents Teresa Noce and Adele Bei. Noce, the general secretary from 1947 to 1955 of FIOT (the Italian Federation of Textile Workers), never tired of pointing to

[22] The magazine was published in Italy during the Resistance and emerged from clandestinity in Naples in July 1944. Constituent Nadia Gallico Spano was among the managers of the magazine. Rina Picolato was its first editor; she was a member of the Communist Party and a former member of the Consulta Nazionale - the National Council. Subsequently she became a Constituent Assembly candidate but was not elected. For a history of UDI, see: Gabrielli (2005), Rodano (2010).

[23] At the time, equal pay was also a declared goal of the International Labour Movement and the World Trade Union Federation officially stated that it was a means to improving the economic conditions for all workers and for the progress of society (Boris et al., 2018).

her male colleagues' lack of vision. Noce saw the undervaluation of women's work, including in terms of wages, as an intentional strategy promoted by entrepreneurs to generate competition between men and women in the labour market (Betti, 2020; Misiani et al.,1996.

Adele Bei criticised CGIL trade union leader Antonio Di Vittorio frontally on this point (Righi, 1999), and in an article in the communist newspaper *Unità* in November 1946 called for:

> solidarity of all workers to bring an end to a state of affairs that contradicts the spirit of the new era' and to ensure that 'the role of women is justly recognised and implemented promptly and concretely.

With respect to equal pay, she stated: 'everything stops at good intentions' (Bei, 1946).

By June 1947, things had changed completely. At the CGIL Unitary Congress in Florence, the National Women's Committee was created with a well-balanced political representation (CGIL, 1947a).

The objectives also changed. The National Women's Committee in its entirety focused on the issue of 'contingency parity' and 'where economic conditions allow, through collective bargaining agreements or local contracts, the implementation of economic measures aimed at reducing the existing gap in wages between men and women'. Special work was also devoted to providing rights to homemakers and maternity-related concerns (CGIL, 1947b).

Few traces remained, however, of the work on equality and of the progressive positions that matured during the Resistance.

In September 1947, the CGIL Union and Confindustria—the Confederation of the Italian manufacturing industry—reached an agreement on something that could no longer be postponed: dismissal criteria. The Agreement basically states that in addition to the purged, workers who could count on additional sources of income, and those hired after 30 June 1943 (excluding veterans, partisans, and those who were politically persecuted) would be sacrificed. These terms affected women harshly: many were fired since they fell into the two categories: being married—and having access to other sources of income in their family—or having been employed during the war (Pepe et al., 2000).

Even the enforcement of the Constitutional dictate on Article 37, the wording of which, as we saw, required significant effort on the part of the women Constituents, became ambiguous due to the lack of implementing regulations. Employers for a long time felt justified in not applying the constitutional principle—'The working woman has the same rights and, for equal work, the same wages as the male worker'—since they considered the value of the women's work inferior to the work of men in terms of productivity and professional qualifications.[24]

[24] This does not imply that Article 37 was an important point of reference for women, at least until the ratification of the International Labour Office Convention No. 100 in 1951, on equal pay for male and female labour for work of equal value—which came into force in May 1953. On the implementation of Convention No. 100 in Italy see: Betti (2020).

7 On a Long-Needed Cultural Battle

The first aspect that emerges from this analysis is that the question of equal rights to work and equal pay hardly finds a central role in the period considered.

The situation in Italy did not improve for a long time, not even after the ratification of the International Labour Office Convention No. 100 (Stolzi, 2019). Note the significant fact that not until July 1960 was an agreement reached between Confindustria and the Trade Unions on wage parity. Unfortunately, the same issue of the lack of a regulatory framework for its implementation affected this agreement and it was never truly translated into action. This problem was addressed with the 1977 Law (Law n. 903 of 9 December 1977), and the Equal Pay Law (Law n. 162 of 5 November 2021), which amend and supplement the Code on Equal Opportunities for men and women, specifically with reference to employment in order to remedy the gender pay gap estimated at 27.3% for managers and 18% for graduates (Istat, 2021) (Fig. 2).

To get a more solid grasp on the reasons for this lag, the scope of the current research must certainly be broadened, nonetheless, a few main points can be deduced.

The Liberation struggle was an important moment for the definition of women's political and social identity. The awareness that women derived from participation in the Resistance, created a close link between the Liberation struggle and their desire for equality.

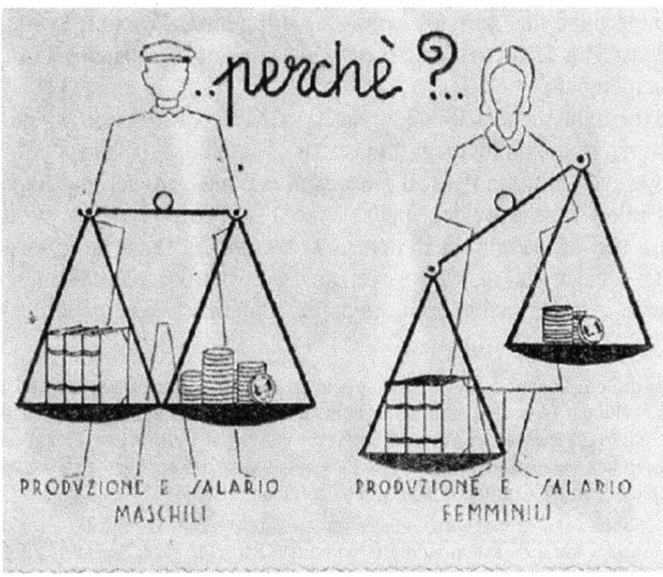

Fig. 2 Why? On the gender pay gap (1945): Male production and wage *versus* Female production and wage (*Source* "Noi donne", n. 4, April 1, 1945, p. 5)

After WWII egalitarian demands were intertwined with specific claims related to the role of women. This paved the way for a process of emancipation that was unfortunately almost immediately countered by 'familist ideology' (Ginsborg, 1998).

This mechanism existed in both the Constituent Assembly and within the trade union.

In the Constituent Assembly, the united action of women was effective in clarifying the provision in Article 3 on the equality of citizens; Article 37 on equal rights and equal pay in the workplace; and Article 51 on access to the professions. Certainly, these articles express moments of general unity in reaching a common goal.[25] Not so for article 106, on access to the judiciary: here an insurmountable barrier was erected revealing the granitic cultural resistance of the male component of the Assembly.

The action of women Constituents was nevertheless important insofar as they were able to surpass their differences to promote women's rights to work and equal pay. This winning alliance was nevertheless compromised by the Italian elections of 1948, won by the Christian Democrats. Subsequently, the conflict re-emerged between the working woman model and the traditional model of the woman as housewife and carer of the family, while previously in the Constituent Assembly there had been a united action to pursue the achievement of women's rights.

In the unitary CGIL, after a promising start with the 1944 UDI trade union plan, there is a progressive shift starting in 1947 away from advocating women's rights, despite the resilient attitude of the female members.[26]

In general, the Trade Union contains and limits its internal differences so as to form a united front of solidarity in opposition to the 'master'. Gender differences must not undermine this unity by proposing differentiated policies with respect to specific needs. This leads to the marked downsizing of the objectives of the female trade union members.

Beyond the immediate challenges related to the Reconstruction period—production reconversion, unemployment, the return of veterans—it is my view that what stands above everything is the resistance to accepting a model that implies a shift in societal roles. This is evident both in the discussion on certain articles of the Constitution and in the change in demands of CGiL.[27] There is no longer a clear reference to equal rights, equal pay, or equal access to careers. Women's emancipation is seen as postponable until the political and economic conditions are ripe.

---

[25] As already noted, attention must also be paid to the differences embraced by the women Constituents. While it is not possible to explore this aspect in depth, one can easily mention, for example, the right to work considered not as an individual right but as a right of the family unit. There is an interesting discussion among the women on Article 37 in the *Commissione dei 75* (Assemblea Costituente – Commissione per la Costituzione, 1946b).

[26] Some exceptions exist in categories where female employment is prevalent, for example for *tabacchine*, tobacco workers, and *mondine*, rice pickers (Bianchi, 2008; Borgato, 2008).

[27] While the conservative stance of the Catholic component of the union is well known and not surprising, there are also some eyewitness accounts on how even the left-wing culture also considered women immature for political and trade union leadership. See significant evidence reported in Lunadei , Motti, and Righi (1999). Also interesting in this regard is the short film *Giovanna* by director Gillo Pontecorvo, presented at the Venice Film Festival in 1956 (https://www.youtube.com/watch?v=T816yOHIvAQ, accessed January 2023).

The discussion is deflected to objectives considered more attainable; for example, reducing i.e., decreasing, not eliminating, the wage gap.

Several questions to why this occurred remain open: to what degree are these outcomes the result of necessity? What role, alongside necessity, does mentality play? What influence do these choices have on the autonomy of women as economic agents? What are the effects on development patterns?

From today's perspective, it is worth emphasising a positive aspect of the united actions of the female constituents. Although their achievements in the wording of the articles leave room for a degree of ambiguity—some concessions were required due to the mentality of the time—their united advocacy is an example in favour of the principle of equality, thanks to which provisions for further developing social consciousness were incorporated into the Constitution. This is by all means no small achievement.

Even the trade Unions postpone important goals apparently *sine die*; nonetheless a collective process of emphasising the 'non-emerging emancipation'[28] takes shape thanks to the constant and stubborn presence of women, even when they do not reach top positions.

In the historical phase examined here, which stops before the internal split within CGIL that led to the birth of CISL and UIL, no particularly significant achievements were made for women. Certainly, however, 'sowing' work is carried out in a politically new context, and attention is paid to what is happening in the rest of the world. This important work constitutes the pre-condition for the changes and achievements of working women in the following years, achievements also connected to the great economic transformations which were taking place.

Therefore, if the great change came later in various spheres—from consumption[29] to access to careers—it is nonetheless essential to look at the phase that preceded it in order to grasp the strength and motivation behind the energies expended by women in these years.

During this phase, small and large steps were taken that have helped shape the history of Italian women. The strides are important both for the gradual improvement of women's conditions at the time, but also for bolstering important battles, not only for women, today.

Bibliography

Addis Saba, M., De Leo, M., & Taricone, F. (1996). *Donne e Costituente: alle origini della Repubblica.* Dipartimento per l'informazione e l'editoria.

[28] This concept is well expressed by Chiara Valentini (1999, p. 12). It is Antonietta Catalano in an interview with Simona Lunadei who speaks of "non-emerging emancipation". See her biographical file in Lunadei, Motti, Righi (1999), pp. 471–476.

[29] On the change in consumption and how it affects development, see Asquer (2022).

Ambrosini, M. L. (1946). Nuovi orientamenti sul problema della disoccupazione. In Ministero per la Costituente. *Atti della Commissione per lo studio dei problemi del lavoro. Memorie su argomenti economici* (Vol. III, pp. 213–248). Stabilimento tipografico UESISA.
Asquer, E. (2022). Culture di consumo, vissuti e memorie delle donne. *Italia Contemporanea, 300*(3), 85–92.
Assemblea Costituente (1947a). *Seduta pomeridiana di martedì 18 marzo 1947*. Retrieved June 2023, from https://documenti.camera.it/_dati/Costituente/Lavori/Assemblea/sed068/sed068.pdf
Assemblea Costituente. (1947b). *Seduta antimeridiana del 10 maggio 1947*. Retrieved June 2023, from https://documenti.camera.it/_dati/Costituente/Lavori/Assemblea/sed119/sed119.pdf
Assemblea Costituente. (1947c). *Seduta di giovedì 22 maggio 1947*. Retrieved June 2023, from http://legislature.camera.it/_dati/costituente/lavori/Assemblea/sed129/sed129nc.pdf
Assemblea Costituente. (1947d). *Seduta di venerdì 7 novembre 1947*. Retrieved June 2023, from https://www.nascitacostituzione.it/05appendici/05p2generali/03/index.htm?004.htm&2
Assemblea Costituente. (1947e). *Seduta pomeridiana di mercoledì 26 novembre 1947*. Retrieved June 2023, from https://documenti.camera.it/_dati/Costituente/Lavori/Assemblea/sed307/sed307.pdf
Assemblea Costituente. Commissione per la Costituzione. (1946a). A*ppendici del Titolo IV della Parte seconda - Discussioni di carattere generale*. Retrieved December 2022 from https://www.nascitacostituzione.it/05appendici/06p2/04p2t4/01/index.htm?001.htm&2
Assemblea Costituente – Commissione per la Costituzione. (1946b). *Seduta della terza sottocommissione di venerdì 13 settembre 1946*. Retrieved June 2023, from http://legislature.camera.it/_dati/costituente/lavori/III_Sottocommissione/sed006/sed006nc.pdf
Assemblea Costituente. Commissione per la Costituzione (1946c). *Prima sottocommissione. Resoconto sommario della seduta di martedì 8 ottobre 1946*. Retrieved April 2023 from http://legislature.camera.it/_dati/costituente/lavori/I_Sottocommissione/sed020/sed020nc.pdf
Ballestrero, M.V. (1979). *Dalla tutela alla parità*. Il Mulino.
Barbadoro, I. (1973) *Storia del sindacalismo italiano*. La Nuova Italia.
Bei, A. (1946, November). Le lavoratrici e l'accordo salariale. *L'Unità, XXIII*(278), 27. Retrieved June 2023, from https://archive.org/details/unita_1946-11-27/mode/2up?view=theater
Bellassai, S. (2000). *La morale comunista. Pubblico e privato nella rappresentazione del Pci 1946–1957*. Carocci.
Betti, E. (2018). Unexpected alliances: Italian women's struggles for equal pay, 1940s–1960s. In E. Boris, S. Zimmermann, & D. Hoehtker (Eds.), *Women's ILO: Transnational networks, global labour standards and gender equity, 1919 to present* (pp. 276–299). Brill.
Betti, E. (2020). *Le alleanze delle donne italiane per la parità salariale: il contributo dell'Organizzazione Internazionale del Lavoro*. Organizzazione Internazionale del Lavoro. Ufficio OIL per l'Italia e San Marino.
Bianchi, O. (2008). Le lavoratrici del tabacco nella storia del sindacalismo italiano. In G. Chianese (Ed.), *Mondi femminili in cento anni di sindacato* (pp. 87–141). Ediesse.
Bizzarri, E. (1980). *L'organizzazione del movimento femminile cattolico dal 1943 al 1948. Quaderni della FIAP, 37.*
Borgato, R. (2008). Le mondine. In G. Chianese (Ed.), *Mondi femminili in cento anni di sindacato* (pp. 335–399). Ediesse.
Boris, E., Hoehtker, D., & Zimmermann, S. (Ed.). (2018). *Women's ILO: Transnational networks, global labour standards and gender equity, 1919 to Present*. Brill.
Bravo, A., & Bruzzone, A. (2000). *In guerra senza armi. Storie di donne (1940–1945*) (2nd ed.). Laterza.
Camera dei Deputati. (1948). *La Consulta Nazionale. 25 settembre 1945 – 1° giugno 1946*. Segretariato Generale Ufficio Studi Legislativi.
Camera dei Deputati. (1965). *Il voto alle donne. Le donne dall'elettorato alla partecipazione politica*. Tipografia della Camera dei Deputati.

Carera, A., & Coppola, A. (2014). *Ponti invisibili. Voci di donne. Storia della Cisl 1050–2012*. FNP Cisl.

Carullo, V. (1959). *La Costituzione della Repubblica italiana illustrata con i lavori preparatori*. Giuffré.

Casalini, M. (2005). *Le donne della sinistra (1944–1948)*. Carocci.

Casalini, M. (2007). Il dilemma delle comuniste. Politiche di genere della sinistra nel secondo Dopoguerra. In N. M. Filippini, & A. Scattigno (Eds.), *Una democrazia incompiuta: donne e politica in Italia dall'Ottocento ai nostri giorni* (pp. 131–153). Franco Angeli.

Catelani, E. (2019). La donna lavoratrice nella "sua essenziale funzione familiare" a settant'anni dall'approvazione dell'art. 37 Cost. *Federalismi.it. Rivista di diritto pubblico italiano, comparato, europeo* (5/2019), 25 ottobre, 67–87.

CGIL (1947a). Costituzione della Commissione Femminile. *Notiziario CGIL, 8*(I), 20 settembre, 16–17.

CGIL (1947b). Programma di lavoro della Commissione Femminile. *Notiziario CGIL, I*(11), 20 Ottobre, 8.

CGIL (1977). *I congressi della CGIL. I Congresso Nazionale unitario della CGIL, Firenze, 1–7 giugno 1947*. Editrice Sindacale Italiana.

Chianese, G. (Ed.). (2008). *Mondi femminili in cento anni di sindacato*. Ediesse.

Consiglio superiore della Magistratura. (2022). *Distribuzione per genere del personale della Magistratura*. Ufficio statistico CSM.

Corghi, C. (1979). *Donne nella Democrazia Cristiana nel ventennio 1944–1964. Vita sociale*, n. 45, luglio-ottobre.

D'Amico, C., & D'Amico N. (2020). *Le ventuno tessitrici della Costituzione*. Franco Angeli.

D'Amico, M. (2019). Gendergap e principi costituzionali. In *Lavoro Diritti Europa. Rivista Nuova Di Diritto Del Lavoro, 2*, 1–10.

Daviso, E. (1950). Il Lavoro della donna e la Costituzione italiana. *Notiziario CGIL, 20*, 20 luglio, 528–529.

Dau Novelli, C. (1995). (Ed.), *Donne del nostro tempo: il Centro italiano femminile, 1945–1995*. Studium.

De Gasperi, A. (1908). *L'adunanza femminile pro università (promossa dalla sezione femminile del Giovane Trentino) 9 dicembre 1908*. Retrieved January 2023, from https://alcidedigitale.fbk.eu/platform/

De Gasperi, A. (1949). *Discorso al Congresso delle donne cattoliche. Roma,23 luglio*. Retrieved January 2023, from https://alcidedigitale.fbk.eu/platform/

De Grazia, V. (1993). *Le donne nel regime fascista*. Marsilio.

Falzone, V., Palermo, F., & Cosentino, F. (Eds.) (1948). *La Costituzione della Repubblica italiana illustrata con i lavori preparatori*. Colombo.

Fiume, G. (2007). Le stagionali della politica: Donne all'assemblea regionale siciliana. In G. Fiume (Ed.), *Donne diritti democrazia* (pp. 213–271). XLedizioni.

Fondazione Pietro Nenni. (1995). *Il Ministero per la Costituente: l'elaborazione dei principi della carta costituzionale*. La Nuova Italia.

Gabrielli, P. (2005). *La pace e la mimosa. L'Unione donne italiane e la costruzione politica della memoria (1944–1955)*. Donzelli Editore.

Ginsborg, P. (1998). *Storia d'Italia (1943–1996) Famiglia, società e stato*. Einaudi.

Istat. (2011). *L'Italia in 150 anni. Sommario di statistiche storiche 1861–2010*. Istat.

Istat. (2021). *La struttura delle retribuzioni in Italia, Statistiche Report anno 2018*. Retrived April 2023, from https://www.istat.it/it/files/2021/03/REPORT_STRUTTURA_RETRIBUZIONI_2018.pdf

Lunadei, S., Motti, L., & Righi, M. L. (1999). *E' brava ma... donne nella Cgil 1944–1962*. Ediesse.

Mafai, M. (1979). *L'apprendistato della politica. le donne italiane nel dopoguerra*. Editori Riuniti.

Misiani, S., Neglie, P., Osti, A., & Vascellaro, D. (1996). *Il filo d'Arianna. Una federazione sindacale nella storia d'Italia: il tessile-abbigliamento nel Novecento*. Rubbettino.

Mori, G. (Ed.). (1980). L*a cultura economica nel periodo della ricostruzione*. il Mulino.

Pepe, A., Iuso, P., Misiani, S. (2000). *La CGIL e la costruzione della democrazia.* Collana Storia del sindacato in Italia (vol. III). Ediesse.
Orlandini, L. (2018). *La democrazia delle donne: I Gruppi di Difesa della Donna nella costruzione della Repubblica (1943–1945).* Bradypus Editore.
Pennacchi, L. (1976). La concezione del ruolo del sindacato nella CGIL dal Patto di
Roma alla rottura dell'unità. In A. Accornero (Ed.), *Problemi del movimento sindacale in Italia 1943–73* (pp. 257–286). Feltrinelli.
Pescarolo, A. (2019). *Il lavoro delle donne nell'Italia contemporanea.* Viella.
Pontecorvo, G. (1955). "Giovanna", short movie. Retrieved January 2023, from https://www.youtube.com/watch?v=T816yOHIvAQ
Pio, XII. (2003). Alle Associazioni femminili (21 ottobre 1945). In Pontificio Consiglio della Cultura (Ed.), *Antologia di testi del Magistero pontificio Da Leone XIII a Giovanni Paolo II* (pp. 216–222). Retrieved February 2023, from http://www.cultura.va/content/dam/cultura/docs/pdf/Antologia/Antologia.pdf
Pombeni, P. (2007). *Il primo De Gasperi. La formazione di un leader politico.* Il Mulino.
Righi, M. L. (1999). L'azione delle donne nella Cgil 1944–1962. In S. Lunadei, L. Motti, & M. L. Righi (Eds.), *E' brava ma... donne nella Cgil 1944–1962* (pp. 29–154). Ediesse.
Rodano, M. (2010). *Memorie di una che c'era. Una storia dell'Udi.* Il Saggiatore.
Rossi-Doria, A. (1994). Le donne sulla scena politica. In F. Barbagallo et al. (Eds.), *Storia dell'Italia repubblicana,* vol. I, *La costruzione della democrazia* (pp. 779–846). Einaudi.
Rossi-Doria, A. (1996). *Diventare cittadine. Il voto delle donne in Italia.* Giunti.
Rotondi, C. (2011). Progettare l'Italia nuova: Antonio Pesenti e il Ministero per la Costituente. *Il Pensiero Economico Italiano, 1*, 103–116.
Sarsini, D. (2021). L'azione delle donne nella Costituente. *Studi Sulla Formazione, 24*, 41–45.
Scarponi, S. (2019). L'art. 51 della Costituzione e l'accesso delle donne ai pubblici uffici e al lavoro nel settore pubblico. *Biblioteca '20 Maggio', 2*, 343–356.
Secco, M. (1945). Ad uguale lavoro, uguale salario! *Noi Donne, 4*(1945), 5.
Serantoni, L. (Ed.) (2009). *Il Genio femminile delle "Madri Costituenti". Il contributo delle donne all'Assemblea Costituente 1946.* Centro italiano femminile Emilia Romagna.
Stolzi, I. (2019). La parità ineguale. Il lavoro delle donne in Italia fra storia e diritto. *Studi storici, 60*(2), aprile-giugno, 253–287.
Tobagi, W. (1976). La fondazione della politica salariale della CGIL. In A. Accornero (Ed.), *Problemi del movimento sindacale in Italia 1943–73* (pp. 409–446). Feltrinelli.
Togliatti, P. (1973). Discorso alla conferenza delle donne comuniste, Roma 2 - 5 giugno 1945. In P. Togliatti (Ed.), *L'emancipazione femminile. Discorsi alle donne* (pp. 37–39). Editori Riuniti.
Tola, V. (2016). (Ed.) *Unione donne in Italia. Fare storia, custodire memoria, 1945–2015. I primi settant'anni dell'UDI.* Ediesse.
UDI. (1944). Nel loro primo convegno sindacale, le lavoratrici di Roma esaminano i loro più urgenti problemi. *Noi Donne, 1*(8), 6–7.
Valentini, C. (1999). Prefazione. In S. Lunadei, L. Motti, & M. L., Righi (Eds.). *E' brava ma... donne nella Cgil 1944–1962* (pp. 11–12). Ediesse.
Weber, M. (1977). *Il voto alle donne.* Editrice Biblioteca della libertà.

Sitography

Archivi della transizione Costituzionale / Archives of the Constitutional Transition. https://archivio.camera.it/patrimonio/archivi-della-transizione-costituzionale-1944-1948
Camera dei Deputati. Portale storico / Chamber of Deputies. Historical Portal. https://storia.camera.it/
Istat. Serie Storiche / Istat. Historical Series. http://www.seriestoriche.istat.it

Index

M. Mosca (ed.), *Women at Work in Italy (1750–1950)*, Springer Studies in the History of Economic Thought, https://doi.org/10.1007/978-3-031-64281-4

D

GPSR Compliance
The European Union's (EU) General Product Safety Regulation (GPSR) is a set of rules that requires consumer products to be safe and our obligations to ensure this.

If you have any concerns about our products, you can contact us on

ProductSafety@springernature.com

In case Publisher is established outside the EU, the EU authorized representative is:

Springer Nature Customer Service Center GmbH
Europaplatz 3
69115 Heidelberg, Germany

www.ingramcontent.com/pod-product-compliance
Lightning Source LLC
Chambersburg PA
CBHW071347300625
28900CB00033B/40
9783031642807